WPF 3d

Three-Dimensional Graphics with WPF and C#

Rod Stephens

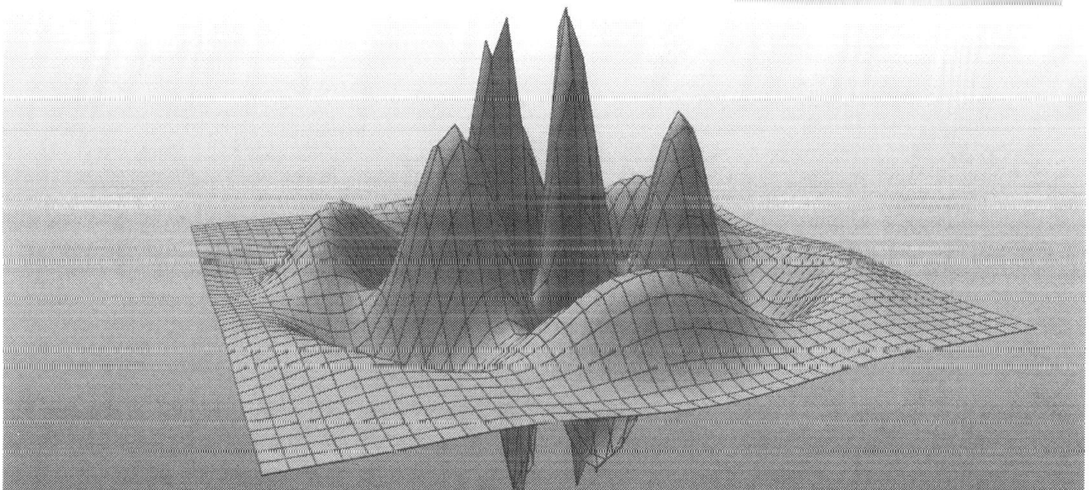

WPF 3d, Three-Dimensional Programming with WPF and C#

Published by Rod Stephens, RodStephens@CSharpHelper.com

ISBN–13: 978-1983905964

ISBN–10: 1983905968

Also by Rod Stephens

The C# Helper Top 100

Interview Puzzles Dissected

C# 24-Hour Trainer

Beginning Software Engineering

C# 5.0 Programmer's Reference

Essential Algorithms: A Practical Approach to Computer Algorithms

MCSD Certification Toolkit (Exam 70-483): Programming in C#

Start Here! Fundamentals of Microsoft .NET Programming

WPF Programmer's Reference

Beginning Database Design Solutions

Stephens' Visual Basic Programming 24-Hour Trainer

Learn more about these and Rod's other books at `www.csharphelper.com/books.html`.

About the Author

In a previous life, Rod Stephens studied mathematics, but during his stay at MIT he discovered the joys of computer algorithms and he hasn't looked back. Since then he's worked on an eclectic assortment of applications in such diverse fields as automated repair dispatching, billing, telephone switch programming, fuel tax collections, scientific visualization, wastewater treatment, concert ticket sales, cartography, optometry, and coaching tools for professional football players. His favorite topics remain algorithms and graphics.

Rod has been a Microsoft Most Valuable Professional (MVP) for more than 14 years. He consults (email him if you want help with an interesting application), maintains his web sites, and occasionally speaks at users' group meetings and conferences.

He has written more than 30 books, many of which have been translated into languages from all over the world. He's written more than 250 magazine articles and even created a few video training courses.

Rod's popular C# Helper website www.CSharpHelper.com contains thousands of example programs that demonstrate tips, tricks, and useful techniques for C# programmers. His VB Helper website www.vb-helper.com provides similar material for Visual Basic developers.

You can contact Rod (particularly if you want help on an interesting project) at `RodStephens@CSharpHelper.com`.

Contents

Introduction

A picture may be worth a thousand words, but only if it's the right picture. A photograph of a kitten sleeping in a snow boot may be adorable, but it's probably not the best way to visualize a proposed skyscraper or condominium development.

Three-dimensional images allow you to effectively visualize three-dimensional scenes. If you can control the scene, changing the viewing direction and zooming in and out as needed, you can get an even better feel for how the pieces of the scene fit together. For example, you can gain insights into how people might navigate a new real estate development and how different buildings will look next to each other in the real world.

There are many three-dimensional drawing programs available that let you build and study scenes ranging in price from free to several thousand dollars per year. Those tools provide many useful features and I recommend that you experiment with them. They can draw some amazing things and can even be a lot of fun.

But what if you want to integrate three-dimensional drawings into your C# programs? You can export drawings from some other tool and incorporate them into your program, but then they are static. They won't let you zoom and rotate to better understand the scene.

Or what if you want to use a C# program to generate the scene? If you have a data set that defines the objects in a scene, you might need to use the data to create objects by hand. Alternatively, you might need to learn a tool-specific scripting language to build the scene.

Another approach is to use Visual Studio and WPF to build and control three-dimensional scenes. With a little XAML code and some C# code behind, you can create remarkably sophisticated three-dimensional scenes that use different kinds of lighting, materials, and textures.

This book shows how you can create those kinds of three-dimensional graphics in WPF and C#. It explains the basic techniques you need to create three-dimensional drawings. It shows how to build simple objects that you may find useful in your scenes and that you can use as examples for building your own objects. It also explains some more advanced topics such as allowing the user to move objects and using skeletons to control figures such as people, animals, or vehicles.

Who This Book is For

This book is intended to help C# programmers who want to incorporate three-dimensional drawings in their programs. It explains everything you need to know to draw three-dimensional graphics with WPF and C#.

The book explains all of the geometric and mathematical concepts that you need to understand three-dimensional graphics, so you don't need to already understand those.

This book also does not assume that you're an expert C# developer. It does assume that you have at least some familiarity with C# basics. If you know how to declare and use variables, write methods, and create classes, then you should be able to follow the examples.

How This Book is Structured

This book is divided into three parts.

The first part of the book explains basic concepts that you need to understand to produce graphics. It describes the coordinate system that you use to define objects. It also explains the WPF classes that you can use to display three-dimensional scenes. Those classes include not only WPF geometry and viewport classes, but also classes that you need to make a scene seem realistic such as cameras, lights, and materials. This part of the book also explains transformations and the mathematics behind three-dimensional graphics.

The second part of the book presents a collection of C# extension methods that you can use to easily create basic three-dimensional shapes. Some of the shapes it explains include boxes, wireframes, cylinders, spheres, geodesic spheres, and fractal terrains.

The last part of the book covers more advanced topics such as more complex objects, hit testing, and skeletons.

I've tried to keep the chapters in this book reasonably short so you can read and absorb each one in a single sitting. You may want to spend some time modifying the examples presented in a chapter, but hopefully you'll be able to grasp the key concepts relatively quickly and easily.

How to Use This Book

I recommend that you read the chapters in the first part of the book in order. You need the material in the earlier chapters before you can understand the material in the later chapters.

You can read about the methods for drawing solids described in the second part of the book in any order. If you want to skip the chapter that explains how to draw pyramids and jump to spheres, that should be fine.

Similarly, you can read the chapters in the final part of the book in any order. If you need to display three-dimensional text on a scene, you can jump to that chapter.

In general, however, the chapters are designed to be read in order. The tools described in a chapter may be used in later chapters, so to catch every detail you may want to read the chapters in order.

After you've finished the book, you can use the methods described in the second and third parts of the book as a reference. If you later want to write a program that displays a wireframe, you can jump to that part of the book to see how to do it.

You should also download the book's source code. Experiment with the examples and create your own variations. You can also use the extension methods described in the second part of the book as a three-dimensional toolkit. By using those methods, you can create complicated three-dimensional scenes remarkably quickly.

Finally, engage with the book. Post comments on the book's web page and keep an eye out for other readers' comments. Sometimes another reader's comments may add a whole new dimension to an example that makes it even more interesting and useful. I expect readers of this book in particular to post additional extension methods for creating interesting scenes on the book's web site.

And if you create a particularly interesting scene, please post it for everyone to admire!

What You Need to Use This Book

To simply read the book, you don't need any special equipment (except possibly a decent lamp and a pair of reading glasses). Note that the book's text only describes each example's key features. *It does not explain every last little thing* that might be necessary to make a program run. That means you cannot always start a new project, type in the code that's shown in the book, and expect the program to work. You can read the text to get the main ideas, but there are often extra details that are too mundane to be worth describing in the text. In particular, later examples use the tools defined by earlier chapters and those tools are not explained every time they are used. To make a program run, you need to download it from the book's web site.

To get the most out of the book, however, you need to write some programs. This book's examples were written with Visual Studio Community 2017, which you can download for free at `tinyurl.com/julu7wl`.

Very few of the examples use any special features of that version of Visual Studio, however, so you can use their techniques in most of the recent Visual Studio versions. I've run most of the examples as far back as Visual Studio 2008 without major problems.

Unfortunately, Visual Studio is not forward compatible so you cannot load the examples in earlier versions of Visual Studio. If you want to run an example in Visual Studio 2008, you may need to rewrite or copy and paste a lot of code to make the example work.

Alternatively, you could just install Visual Studio 2017. I have several versions of Visual Studio running on my computer and they coexist peacefully for the most part.

A Note About Unity

Unity (`unity3d.com`) is a cross-platform game engine that lets you build three-dimensional scenes. It lets you drag and drop simple objects such as boxes, spheres, and cylinders into a scene and then attach scripts, written in either C# or JavaScript, to control those objects.

This book does not cover Unity, although the basic three-dimensional graphics principles covered in the first part of the book also apply to Unity and other three-dimensional design tools.

One big difference between Unity and three-dimensional models created in WPF is the "handedness" or chirality of their coordinate systems. Briefly, WPF uses a right-handed coordinate system but Unity uses a left-handed coordinate system. Figure 0-1 shows left-handed and right-handed coordinate systems.

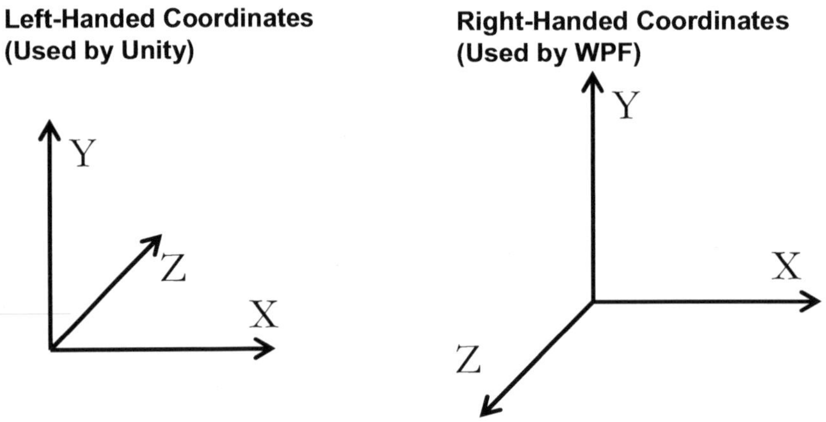

Figure 0-1: Left-handed and right-handed coordinate systems

I'll say more about right- and left-handed coordinate systems in Chapter 3.

Conventions

To help the text make the most sense, I've adopted a few conventions. I've used the following styles in the text.

- Important words are *italicized* when they are introduced.
- Keyboard strokes are shown as in Ctrl+A.
- Filenames, URLs, and code within the text are shown with a `monospaced font like this`.

- Blocks of code are shown as in the following.

```
for (int i = 0; i < 500; i++)
    Console.WriteLine("I will not throw paper airplanes in class.");
```

- Particularly important notes are highlighted with a box and a notepad icon.

> **NOTE:** This is something important or interesting and you should take special notice.

Finally, some of the URLs used by the book are long. Really, *really* long. In fact, some are so long that they can't fit on one line in the book. I don't think it would be fair to ask you to type in a 120 character URL in your browser, so to make reading and entering URLs in your browser easier, I've used TinyURL (`tinyurl.com`) to shorten most of the URLs used in this book. For instance, consider the following ungainly URL.

```
https://www.pluralsight.com/blog/film-games/key-rigging-terms-get-moving
```

To make it easier for you to type this into a browser, the book shortens this to the more economical URL `tinyurl.com/y95okt2e`. Simply type the shorter URL into your browser and you should be able to visit the original web page.

Note that URLs sometimes change so some of those shown in this book may stop working. If you find such a URL, post a comment on the book's web site and I'll try to find a replacement.

Important URLs

The following sections describe the most important URLs associated with this book.

Web Page

This book's main web page is `www.CSharpHelper.com/wpf3d.htm`. There you can find links to an overview, table of contents, discussions, errata, and the source code.

That page also includes links to some places where you can purchase the book. In addition to letting you buy the book, those pages provide reviews.

> **NOTE:** Please post a review when you have a chance!

This is a self-published book and self-published books live and die based on the reviews they receive, so please help me out and post a review. Your review can also help others decide whether they should buy the book.

Discussion

If there's some aspect of an example that you would like to discuss with others, please go to the book's web page, follow the discussion link, and post a comment. You can also post responses to previous comments in their own threads so others can follow the discussion.

Errata

I do my best to ensure that my books contain content of the highest possible quality, but mistakes do sneak through the editing process. Imagine trying to debug a 200,000+ word program without a compiler to help you find mistakes. For example, consider the following two sentences.

> Look out for man eating lions.
> Look out for man-eating lions.

Both of these are syntactically correct so grammar checkers won't flag them, but they have very different meanings. If you find an error or a case such as this where the book's meaning isn't clear, I would be grateful for your feedback. Posting errata may save other readers time and frustration, and will help me provide better information in the future.

To post errata, go to the book's web page and follow the errata link. First look to see if "your" error has already been reported and, if it has not, add it as a comment on that page. Please include your email address (which won't be posted publically) so I can contact you if I have questions. I'll review your comment and post a follow-up if necessary.

Email

If you have questions, comments, or suggestions while you're working through the book, please feel free to email me at `RodStephens@CSharpHelper.com`. I can't promise to solve all of your problems, but I'll do my best to point you in the right direction.

Summary

After reading this book, studying the examples, and working on some variations of your own, you should have a good understanding of three-dimensional graphics in general and particularly within WPF and C#. You'll have a toolkit of examples and methods that you can use to quickly assemble and manipulate new three-dimensional scenes. You'll also have a good knowledge of the basics of three-dimensional graphics that you can apply to other three-dimensional drawing platforms such as Unity.

Part I

Getting Started

The chapters in this part of the book explain basic concepts that you need to understand to work with three-dimensional graphics. Many of these concepts apply whether you're creating three-dimensional scenes in WPF, Unity, or some other drawing tool.

In order to get you started as quickly as possible, the first two chapters describe examples that display simple three-dimensional scenes. The first chapter shows how to make a scene entirely with XAML code. The second chapter shows how to build a similar scene using C# code behind. Understanding how to build objects with C# code is essential if you want to build anything other than the simplest of scenes.

The rest of the chapters in this part of the book provide more detail about the objects that you use to build and control a three-dimensional WPF application. They explain how to define an object's vertices and triangles. They also describe the cameras, lights, and materials that you use to determine an object's appearance.

After you finish reading this part of the book, you will be able to build simple scenes and give objects interesting and somewhat realistic appearances.

Chapter 1
XAML Example

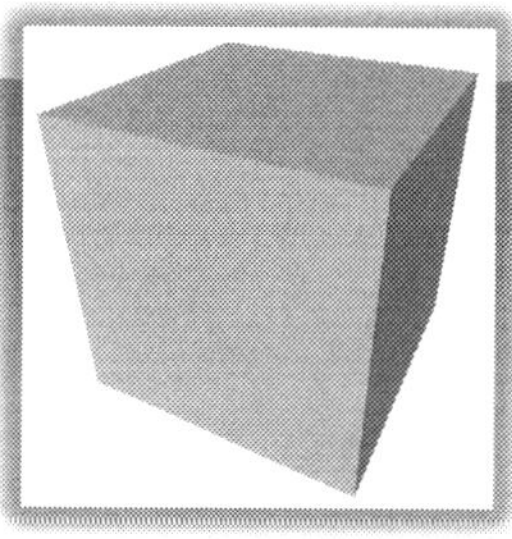

Even the simplest three-dimensional drawing in WPF requires a lot of objects. The following list describes the key objects that you may need to use to build and view a scene.

- `Viewport3D`—This object provides a viewport into the three-dimensional scene. You can think of it as a window looking out into the scene. The viewport also includes the camera.
- `ModelVisual3D`—This object contains three-dimensional models. It can contain child objects that contain other objects to create an object hierarchy. The children can include such things as lights, `Model3DGroup` objects, and other `ModelVisual3D` objects.
- `GeometryModel3D`—This object contains three-dimensional data and a material that defines the object's appearance. For example, it might include the triangles that make up a cube plus a material that makes the cube appear blue.
- `MeshGeometry3D`—This object contains points in the three-dimensional space and information about how they should be used to define triangles. (I'll say more about this later, but basically this is where a "physical" object is defined.)
- `Model3DGroup`—This is a collection of three-dimensional objects that you can treat as a group. For example, a `Model3DGroup` could include lights and `GeometryModel3D` objects.
- `Material`—This object determines the appearance of an object's surface. It defines the object's color, brightness, reflectiveness, and other surface properties.
- Lights—Lights determine the color and kind of light that falls on the scene's objects. Different kinds of lights include ambient, spot, and directional lights.
- Camera—The camera determines the part of the scene that the viewport should display. It determines the position and orientation of the view much as a real-world camera does in a physical scene.

To really understand how WPF produces three-dimensional scenes, you need to understand all of those objects. The chapters that follow cover the most important of them in detail.

For now, however, I want to show you a "Hello World" program as quickly as possible. The example doesn't actually say, "Hello World," (you'll learn different ways to do that in Chapters 7, 30, and 31), but it does display a minimal three-dimensional scene that you can modify and use for experiments.

The following sections describe a simple example that define a three-dimensional scene using only XAML code.

Code Overview

Figure 1-1 shows the Cube example program that's available for download on the book's web site. It uses only XAML code to draw a light blue cube. It's extremely basic and doesn't allow you to change the orientation of the cube, modify the viewing position, zoom in and out, or do anything else that might be interesting. It's not very functional, but then again, what "Hello World" program is?

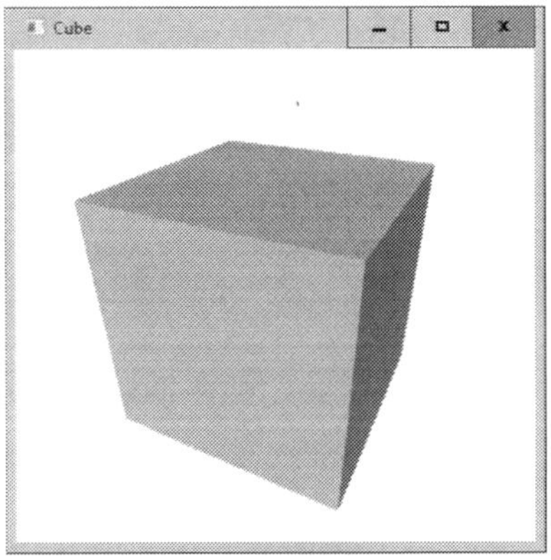

Figure 1-1: This program uses only XAML code to draw a cube.

I created the program by using Visual Studio's New ➢ Project command, expanding the New Project dialog's Installed ➢ Templates ➢ Visual C# ➢ Windows Classic Desktop branch, and then selecting WPF App (.NET Framework).

The template created the initial XAML code with a main `Window` that contained a `Grid` control. I then added a `Viewport3D` control to the `Grid`. The `Viewport3D` holds all of the lights, geometry, camera, and other WPF objects that make up the scene.

> **NOTE:** All of the example programs used in this book are available for download on the book's web site.

The following XAML code shows how the program defines the `Viewport3D` and its contents.

```
<Viewport3D>
    <Viewport3D.Camera>
        <PerspectiveCamera
          Position = "1.5, 2, 3"
          LookDirection = "-1.5, -2, -3"
          UpDirection = "0, 1, 0"
          FieldOfView = "60" />
    </Viewport3D.Camera>

    <ModelVisual3D>
        <ModelVisual3D.Content>
```

```
                <Model3DGroup>
                    <!-- Lights -->
                    <AmbientLight Color="Gray" />
                    <DirectionalLight Color="Gray" Direction="1,-2,-3" />

                    <GeometryModel3D>
                        <GeometryModel3D.Geometry>
                            <!-- Cube -->
                            <MeshGeometry3D
                                Positions="
                                  -1,-1,-1   1,-1,-1   1,-1, 1  -1,-1, 1
                                  -1,-1, 1   1,-1, 1   1, 1, 1  -1, 1, 1
                                   1,-1, 1   1,-1,-1   1, 1,-1   1, 1, 1
                                   1, 1, 1   1, 1,-1  -1, 1,-1  -1, 1, 1
                                  -1,-1, 1  -1, 1, 1  -1, 1,-1  -1,-1,-1
                                  -1,-1,-1  -1, 1,-1   1, 1,-1   1,-1,-1
                                  "
                                TriangleIndices="
                                   0  1  2     2  3  0
                                   4  5  6     6  7  4
                                   8  9 10    10 11  8
                                  12 13 14    14 15 12
                                  16 17 18    18 19 16
                                  20 21 22    22 23 20
                                  " />
                        </GeometryModel3D.Geometry>

                        <GeometryModel3D.Material>
                            <DiffuseMaterial Brush="LightBlue" />
                        </GeometryModel3D.Material>
                    </GeometryModel3D>
                </Model3DGroup>
            </ModelVisual3D.Content>
        </ModelVisual3D>
    </Viewport3D>
```

The code starts with a `Viewport3D` object. This is the main WPF object that contains all of the other three-dimensional objects. It contains two children: a camera and a `ModelVisual3D` object. The following sections describe those objects in some detail.

Camera

The Cube program uses the following code to define its camera.

```
<PerspectiveCamera
  Position = "1.5, 2, 3"
  LookDirection = "-1.5, -2, -3"
  UpDirection = "0, 1, 0"
  FieldOfView = "60" />
```

This example uses a `PerspectiveCamera`, so the resulting picture uses perspective. (You probably guessed that from its name.) Perspective means objects that are farther away from the camera appear smaller than those that are closer. That's the way your eyes work, so this produces a reasonably realistic result.

Figure 1-2 shows the scene using an orthographic camera. When you use this kind of camera, objects that are farther from the camera have the same size as those that are closer. Compare Figures 1-1 and 1-2 to see the difference. You'll learn more about cameras in Chapter 4.

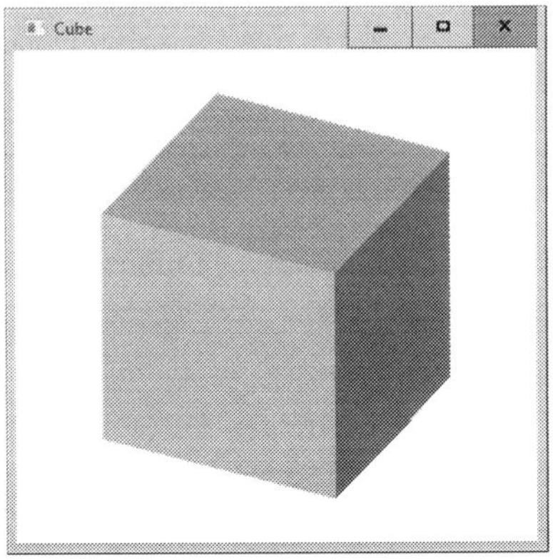

Figure 1-2: This picture uses an orthographic camera.

The camera's `Position` property indicates where the camera is positioned in the coordinates used by the model. The `LookDirection` property indicates the direction in which the camera is pointed. In this example, `LookDirection` <-1.5, -2, -3> is the opposite of `Position` (1.5, 2, 3), so the camera is pointing back toward the origin.

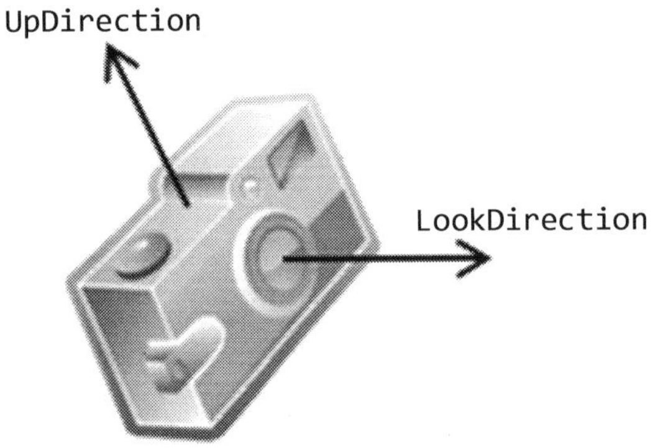

Figure 1-3: The `LookDirection` and `UpDirection` properties determine the camera's orientation.

The `UpDirection` property determines the camera's orientation. Usually programs orient the camera so it is more or less right-side up, but you can tilt it at an angle if you want to make the scene look crooked. (Like the villains' hideouts in the old *Batman* television series.) Figure 1-3 shows how the `LookDirection` and `UpDirection` properties determine the camera's orientation.

Finally, the `FieldOfView` property determines the width of the camera's horizontal field of view in degrees.

Lights

After it defines the camera, the XAML code adds a `ModelVisual3D` object that contains a `Model3DGroup`. The `Model3DGroup` contains the lights and the "physical" three-dimensional objects that make up the scene.

Next, the program uses the following code to define the scene's lights.

```
<AmbientLight Color="Gray" />
<DirectionalLight Color="Gray" Direction="1,-2,-3" />
```

If a scene has no lights, then the objects are not illuminated so they all appear black. In this example, you would see a black silhouette of the cube. (Give it a try. Download the example and remove the lights to see what happens.)

Ambient lights apply to all of the scene's objects equally. Normally you include ambient light so you can see every object at least a little.

However, the color of objects illuminated by ambient light depends only on the objects' materials and not on their orientations. That means if you include only ambient light, all of the surfaces with the same material have the same color. In this example, all of the cube's faces would have exactly the same color, so you couldn't tell where one side ended and the next began. The result would be a silhouette of the cube in the cube's color instead of black. (Download the example and remove the directional light to see the result.)

The ambient light's color is `Gray`, so it contains the same amounts of red, green, and blue light. Basically the ambient color is shining a dim white light on the scene. That gives the cube a dull version of its material's color. (You'll see later that it's light blue.)

Directional lights shine from a particular direction and produce a result that depends on the angle at which the light hits a surface. In this example, the directional light hits the cube's faces at different angles, so the faces have different apparent colors.

Often you need to use several lights to make a scene look good from every angle. Chapter 6 says more about lights.

Geometry

After it defines the lights, the program uses the following code to define a `GeometryModel3D` object. This object defines the "physical" cube and the material that makes it blue.

```
<GeometryModel3D>
    <GeometryModel3D.Geometry>
        <!-- Cube -->
        <MeshGeometry3D
            Positions="
              -1,-1,-1   1,-1,-1   1,-1, 1  -1,-1, 1
              -1,-1, 1   1,-1, 1   1, 1, 1  -1, 1, 1
               1,-1, 1   1,-1,-1   1, 1,-1   1, 1, 1
               1, 1, 1   1, 1,-1  -1, 1,-1  -1, 1, 1
              -1,-1, 1  -1, 1, 1  -1, 1,-1  -1,-1,-1
              -1,-1,-1  -1, 1,-1   1, 1,-1   1,-1,-1
              "
            TriangleIndices="
               0  1  2     2  3  0
               4  5  6     6  7  4
               8  9 10    10 11  8
              12 13 14    14 15 12
              16 17 18    18 19 16
              20 21 22    22 23 20
              " />
    </GeometryModel3D.Geometry>

    <GeometryModel3D.Material>
        <DiffuseMaterial Brush="LightBlue" />
```

```
        </GeometryModel3D.Material>
    </GeometryModel3D>
```

The `MeshGeometry3D` object's `Positions` property is a collection containing the three-dimensional points that define the cube's vertices. For example, the first entry in this program is the point (-1, -1, -1) in three-dimensional space.

The object's `TriangleIndices` property lists the point indices that define the triangles that make up the cube. For example, its first three entries are 0, 1, and 2. That means the first triangle consists of the vertices with indices 0, 1, and 2 in the `Positions` collection. If you look again at the `Positions` collection, you'll see that those positions correspond to the points (-1, -1, -1), (1, -1, -1), and (1, -1, 1).

All three-dimensional objects are defined as triangles. (Unless you play Minecraft. In that case everything is made up of cubes, although the cubes are probably triangles behind the scenes.)

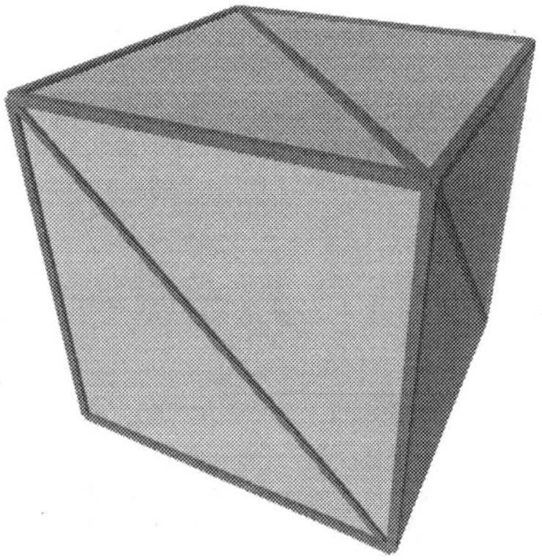

Figure 1-4: All solids are made up of triangles.

Even something that seems to be made up of rectangles or other polygons, such as the cube shown in Figure 1-1, is actually made up of triangles. Figure 1-4 shows the same cube with its triangles outlined.

In Figure 1-1, you can't see the edges between the triangles that make up each of the cube's faces because they lie in the same plane. The directional lights used by this example make those kinds of coplanar triangles the same color, so you can't see where one ends and the next begins.

After defining the `GeometryModel3D` object's geometry, the XAML code defines the object's material. This example uses a simple light blue diffuse material to produce a pretty normal-looking cube.

If you think this is a lot of work to display a simple cube, you're absolutely right! However, this example does demonstrate all of the basic tools you need to display more complicated scenes. It shows how to use a camera, lights, and geometry to define a scene. It's rather verbose because that's the way XAML code is, but at least it works.

Summary

This chapter explained the basic WPF objects that you use to display a three-dimensional scene. Unfortunately, the arrangement of objects is fairly complicated, and the verbose nature of XAML doesn't make the code any less confusing.

Fortunately, you can use the same arrangement of objects in any three-dimensional program. You can copy and paste much of the XAML code and then modify the camera, lights, `Positions`, and `TriangleIndices` to define a new scene.

The following XAML code shows the basic arrangement of WPF objects. You just need to replace the highlighted comments with the objects that you want to use for your new program.

```
<Viewport3D>
    <Viewport3D.Camera>
        <!-- Camera -->
    </Viewport3D.Camera>

    <ModelVisual3D>
        <ModelVisual3D.Content>
            <Model3DGroup>
                <!-- Lights -->

                <GeometryModel3D>
                    <GeometryModel3D.Geometry>
                        <!-- MeshGeometry3D -->
                    </GeometryModel3D.Geometry>

                    <GeometryModel3D.Material>
                        <!-- Material -->
                    </GeometryModel3D.Material>
                </GeometryModel3D>
            </Model3DGroup>
        </ModelVisual3D.Content>
    </ModelVisual3D>
</Viewport3D>
```

You can use the Cube example program as a template for simple programs that define their scenes in XAML code.

You can also experiment with the example. Download the program from the book's web site and make a few changes. See what happens if you change the lights, move the camera, change some of the cube's point coordinates, or change the material's color. If you're feeling really adventurous, see if you can modify the example to display a tetrahedron or some other shape.

The Cube program works well enough if all you want to do is display a single cube. If you want to display a more complicated scene, however, creating everything in XAML code would be difficult and tedious. In many cases, it would be better to use C# code to generate the data used to create the scene.

Fortunately, anything that you can do in XAML code you can also do in C# code. The next chapter explains how you can make a modified version of the Cube program so it creates its cube in C# code.

Chapter 2
C# Example

Chapter 1 showed how you could use XAML code to display a cube. If you want to display a more complicated scene, however, creating everything in XAML code would be difficult and tedious. For example, you could use XAML code to display the mathematical surface shown in Figure 2-1. That would be a huge amount of work, however, because that surface contains 2,400 triangles.

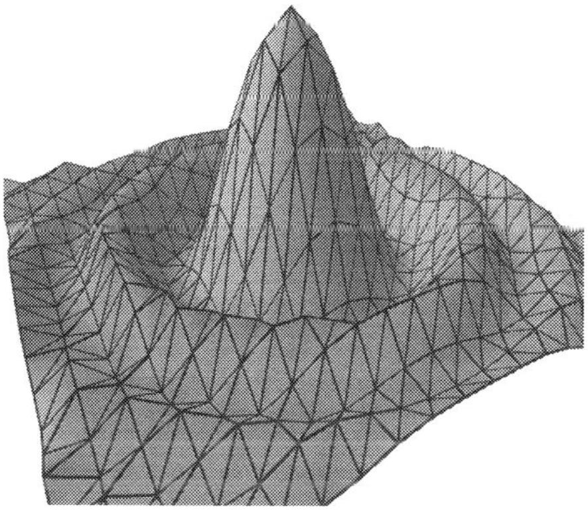

Figure 2-1: Creating this scene in XAML code would be difficult.

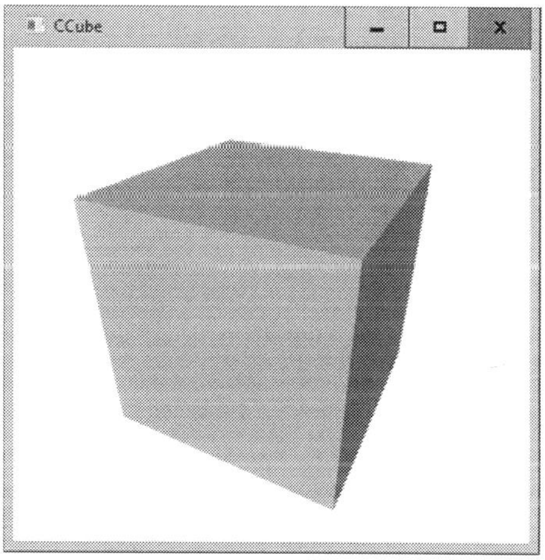

Figure 2-2: This program uses C# code to draw a cube.

In fact, that scene actually includes long skinny triangles that draw the dark wireframe outlining the surface's triangles. If you include those, then the scene contains almost 90,000 triangles. In theory you could define all of those triangles in XAML code, but it would be extremely painful.

Fortunately, anything you can do in XAML code you can also do in C# code. The CCube example program produces the same result as the Cube program, but it uses C# code to define its scene. This program, which is shown in Figure 2-2, produces the same result as the Cube program described in Chapter 1. (Except for the different title.)

The following sections explain how the CCube program uses C# code to draw its scene.

XAML Code

The CCube program does most of its work in C# code, but it is a WPF program so it needs a little XAML code to get started. The following code shows the program's XAML.

```
<Window x:Class="CCube.MainWindow"
        xmlns="http://schemas.microsoft.com/winfx/2006/xaml/presentation"
        xmlns:x="http://schemas.microsoft.com/winfx/2006/xaml"
        xmlns:d="http://schemas.microsoft.com/expression/blend/2008"
        xmlns:mc="http://schemas.openxmlformats.org/markup-compatibility/2006"
        xmlns:local="clr-namespace:CCube"
        mc:Ignorable="d"
        Title="CCube"
        Height="400" Width="400"
        Loaded="Window_Loaded">
    <Grid>
        <Viewport3D Name="mainViewport" />
    </Grid>
</Window>
```

This code defines a `Window` that has a `Loaded` event handler named `Window_Loaded`. That event handler contains all of the C# code that builds the three-dimensional objects.

The `Window` contains a `Grid` that holds a `Viewport3D` object named `mainViewport`. The program's C# code adds all of the other objects to this viewport.

Window_Loaded

The structures and other items needed to work with three-dimensional objects are defined in the `System.Windows.Media.Media3D` namespace, so the program includes the following `using` directive.

```
using System.Windows.Media.Media3D;
```

The following C# code shows the `Window_Loaded` event handler.

```
private void Window_Loaded(object sender, RoutedEventArgs e)
{
    // Define WPF objects.
    ModelVisual3D visual3d = new ModelVisual3D();
    Model3DGroup group3d = new Model3DGroup();
    visual3d.Content = group3d;
    mainViewport.Children.Add(visual3d);

    // Define the camera, lights, and model.
    DefineCamera(mainViewport);
    DefineLights(group3d);
    DefineModel(group3d);
}
```

This code creates a `ModelVisual3D` object and a `Model3DGroup`. It sets the visual's content to the group and adds the group to the `Viewport3D` object's `Children` collection. So far this simply builds the same object hierarchy defined by the Cube program's XAML code.

Next, the event handler calls the `DefineCamera`, `DefineLights`, and `DefineModel` methods described in the following sections to define the three-dimensional scene.

DefineCamera

The following code shows the `DefineCamera` method.

```
// Define the camera.
private void DefineCamera(Viewport3D viewport)
{
    Point3D position = new Point3D(1.5, 2, 3);
    Vector3D lookDirection = new Vector3D(
        -position.X, -position.Y, -position.Z);
    Vector3D upDirection = new Vector3D(0, 1, 0);
    double fieldOfView = 60;
    PerspectiveCamera camera =
        new PerspectiveCamera(position, lookDirection, upDirection, fieldOfView);

    viewport.Camera = camera;
}
```

This method creates a `Point3D` object to represent the camera's position. It then defines a `Vector3D` structure to represent the camera's "look" direction. You could explicitly enter components for the "look" vector, but this program sets them to the negatives of the `position` point's coordinates. That makes the "look" vector point from the camera's position back toward the origin. If you change the camera's position in the first statement, the code will still make the camera point toward the origin.

NOTE: The `Point3D` structure represents a point in three-dimensional space. It simply holds X, Y, and Z coordinates to define the point's position. Points are usually written with their coordinates enclosed in parentheses as in (1, 3, 5).

The `Vector3D` structure represents a *direction* in three-dimensional space. It holds X, Y, and Z values that define a direction. Vectors are usually written with their components enclosed in pointy brackets as in <7, 11, 13>.

The difference between a point and a vector can be somewhat confusing. A point represents a location and a vector represents a direction without a position. For example, the vector <10, 20, 30> represents the direction moving 10 units in the X direction, 20 units in the Y direction, and 30 units in the Z direction.

Chapter 8 has more to say about points, vectors, and their relationships.

Next, the code defines the camera's "up" vector. (If you don't remember how the "look" and "up" vectors work, see Figure 1-3 in Chapter 1.)

The code also defines a variable to hold the camera's field of view value 60 degrees. The `position`, `lookDirection`, `upDirection`, and `fieldOfView` values match the ones used by the Cube program's XAML code.

The `DefineCamera` method then uses the position, "look" and "up" directions, and field of view to create a new `PerspectiveCamera` object.

Finally, the method sets the `Viewport3D` object's `Camera` property to the new camera.

If you look back at the Cube program's XAML code, you'll see that it does basically the same things using XAML code.

DefineLights

The following code shows the `DefineLights` method.

```
// Define the lights.
private void DefineLights(Model3DGroup group)
{
    group.Children.Add(new AmbientLight(Colors.Gray));

    Vector3D direction = new Vector3D(1, -2, -3);
    group.Children.Add(new DirectionalLight(Colors.Gray, direction));
}
```

This method creates an `AmbientLight` object and adds it to the `Model3DGroup` object's `Children` collection.

Next, the code creates a `Vector3D` structure to represent a direction. It uses that direction to define a `DirectionalLight` and then adds it to the `Model3DGroup` object's `Children` collection.

Again, if you look back at the Cube program's XAML code, you'll find that it does the same thing as this method.

DefineModel

The `DefineModel` method shown in the following code creates the scene's three-dimensional cube and its material. This is the most interesting part of most three-dimensional applications.

```
// Define the model.
private void DefineModel(Model3DGroup group)
{
    // Create the geometry.
    MeshGeometry3D mesh = new MeshGeometry3D();

    // Define the positions.
```

```
        Point3D[] points =
        {
            new Point3D(-1, -1, -1), new Point3D(1, -1, -1),
            new Point3D(1, -1, 1), new Point3D(-1, -1, 1),
            ...
            new Point3D(1, 1, -1), new Point3D(1, -1, -1),
        };
        foreach (Point3D point in points) mesh.Positions.Add(point);

        // Define the triangles.
        Tuple<int, int, int>[] triangles =
        {
                new Tuple<int, int, int>(0, 1, 2),
                new Tuple<int, int, int>(2, 3, 0),
                ...
                new Tuple<int, int, int>(22, 23, 20),
        };
        foreach (Tuple<int, int, int> tuple in triangles)
        {
            mesh.TriangleIndices.Add(tuple.Item1);
            mesh.TriangleIndices.Add(tuple.Item2);
            mesh.TriangleIndices.Add(tuple.Item3);
        }

        // Define the object's material.
        DiffuseMaterial material = new DiffuseMaterial(Brushes.LightBlue);

        // Create the model, which includes the geometry and material.
        GeometryModel3D model = new GeometryModel3D(mesh, material);

        // Add the model to the grometry group.
        group.Children.Add(model);
    }
```

This method first creates a `MeshGeometry3D` object to define the cube's geometry.

Next, the code creates an array of `Point3D` objects to define the cube's points. To save space, I've omitted most of the points from the preceding code. The method then loops through those points and adds them to the mesh's `Positions` collection.

> **NOTE:** You could simply add each point to the mesh's `Positions` collection directly without creating an array of points and looping through it. In this example, I decided that the array made the code a bit easier to write and read.

The method then uses a similar approach to define the mesh's triangle indices. It creates an array of tuples holding the indices that make up each of the triangles. It then loops through the array and adds the indices for each triangle to the mesh's `TriangleIndices` collection.

> **NOTE:** Again you could add the indices to the mesh directly. I used the array of tuples to make writing and reading the code easier. In particular, the tuples make it more obvious which sets of three points make up each of the triangles.

Next, the method creates a light blue `DiffuseMaterial`. It uses the mesh and the material to create a `GeometryModel3D` for the cube.

> **NOTE:** The `GeometryModel3D` object includes the cube's geometry (defined by the mesh) and its material in a single package. It is the object that represents the cube. If the scene contained several three-dimensional objects, each would have its own `GeometryModel3D` object.

Finally, the method adds the model to the program's `Model3DGroup` object's `Children` collection.

This program defines a single three-dimensional object (the cube), so it uses a single `DefineModel` method. If this were a more complicated program that used several different objects, the `DefineModel` method could contain all of the object-creation code, or it could call other methods to create those objects separately. Use whichever technique makes the most sense to you.

Take a few minutes to download the CCube example program and experiment with it. Try changing the C# code to modify the lights, camera, and mesh properties. The examples described in later chapters all use this same basic structure, so it's important that you understand how it works now when it's relatively simple.

Summary

This chapter explained how you can use C# code to display three-dimensional scenes. The program still requires the same WPF objects used by the XAML version of the program, but at least the objects are defined in more manageable pieces. This example also sets the stage for much more complicated examples that are described in the chapters that follow.

To use this program as a template for future projects, start with the following XAML code.

```
<Window ... Loaded="Window_Loaded">
    <Grid>
        <Viewport3D Name="mainViewport" />
    </Grid>
</Window>
```

This is the key XAML code that creates the `Viewport3D` object named `mainViewport`. The C# code adds the rest of the program's objects to that one.

Next, add the following `Window_Loaded` event handler.

```
private void Window_Loaded(object sender, RoutedEventArgs e)
{
    // Define WPF objects.
    ModelVisual3D visual3d = new ModelVisual3D();
    Model3DGroup group3d = new Model3DGroup();
    visual3d.Content = group3d;
    mainViewport.Children.Add(visual3d);

    // Define the camera, lights, and model.
    DefineCamera(mainViewport);
    DefineLights(group3d);
    DefineModel(group3d);
}
```

Finally, create the `DefineCamera`, `DefineLights`, and `DefineModel` methods to define your scene.

All of the examples described later in this book use this same basic strategy.

Later chapters explain how to draw some much more complicated scenes. Before you read those chapters, however, you should learn more about the pieces that you use to display any three-dimensional scene. The new few chapters provide more detail about the WPF coordinate system, cameras, lights, and materials.

> Graphics programmers usually just say "right-handed" or "left-handed," but "chirality" is a cool word that you should know to impress people at parties.

Axis orientation is important for two reasons. First, there's no way you can rotate a right-handed system so it lines up with a left-handed one. That means if you draw something in one system, it won't be the same thing you get if you draw it in the other system. If you use the wrong system, you'll get the mirror image of what you wanted to draw.

The second reason why the axis orientation is so important is that three-dimensional drawing systems use the orientation of the triangles that make up objects to decide whether those triangles need to be drawn.

The following sections explain some methods that you can use to easily remember which direction the Z axis points in a right-handed coordinate system. The section after that explains how drawing systems use a triangle's orientation to decide whether to draw it.

Right-Hand Rule

I know of four ways to remember which way the Z axis points in a right-handed coordinate system. The following sections describe those methods.

Remember It

If you look again at Figure 3-1, you'll see that the X and Y axes are aligned horizontally and vertically. If you ignore the Z axis for a moment, that's the normal orientation that you would use if you were drawing a two dimensional graph.

When the X and Y axes have that arrangement, you can just remember that the Z axis points toward you out of the computer's screen.

This method isn't too hard to use, but it only works well if the X and Y axes are arranged normally. When you're sketching the objects that you want to draw, you can use this technique. It's a lot harder to use this method if you need to rotate the scene so the axes don't have their normal orientations. (This method is also tricky when you're trying to determine whether a triangle is outwardly oriented. More on that shortly.)

Right-Hand Rule, Version 1

To use the right-hand rule, align your right hand so your fingers point along the X axis. Then curl your fingers toward the Y axis. (If you can't curl your fingers in that direction, then you probably need to flip your hand over.) When you do that, your thumb points toward the Z axis.

Chapter 3
Coordinates

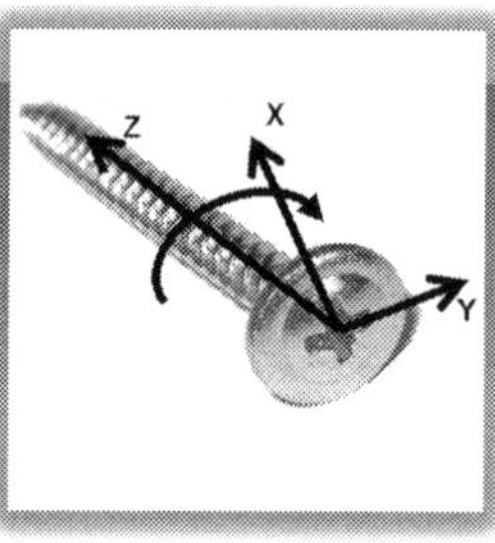

WPF (or pretty much any three-dimensional drawing system) uses Cartesian coordinates where you use X, Y, and Z coordinates to specify a point's location. If you remember even a little of the graphing you did in elementary school, you should be able to easily pick up three-dimensional coordinates. You simply specify the point's X, Y, and Z coordinates inside parentheses. For example, Figure 3-1 shows the point (4, 2, 3).

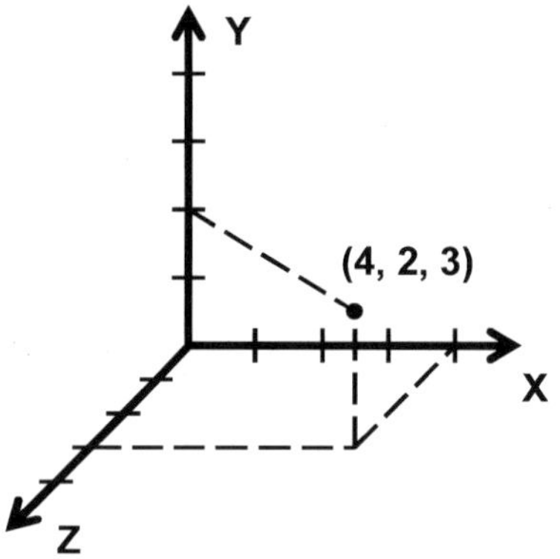

Figure 3-1: Points are specified in Cartesian coordinates.

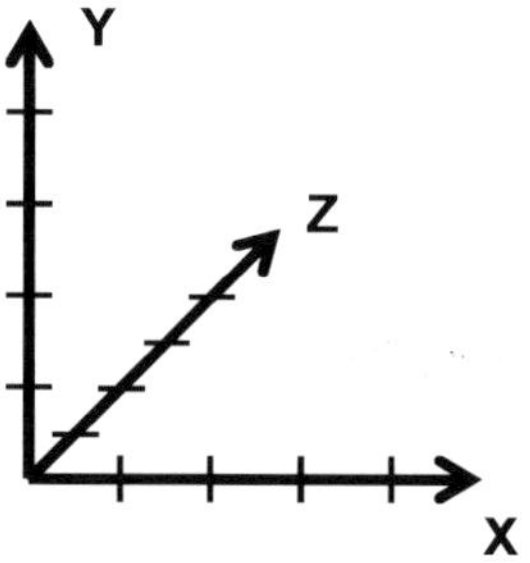

Figure 3-2: This is a left-handed coordinate system.

That would be the end of the story (and this would be an extremely short chapter) if it weren't for one very important detail: axis orientation.

WPF uses a "right-handed" axis orientation similar to the one shown in Figure 3-1. In contrast, about half of the three-dimensional drawing programs out there use a left-handed orientation like the one shown in Figure 3-2. For example, the Unity game engine uses a left-handed coordinate system.

> **NOTE:** The axis orientation is also known as its *handedness* or *chirality* (pronounced kahy-ral-i-tee). Your left and right hands have different chiralities because you can't rotate and translate one so it looks like the other.

Figure 3-3 shows this version of the right-hand rule. Figure 3-4 shows the same rule with the axes rotated into a different position. In both cases, the right-hand rule shows you where the Z axis should point.

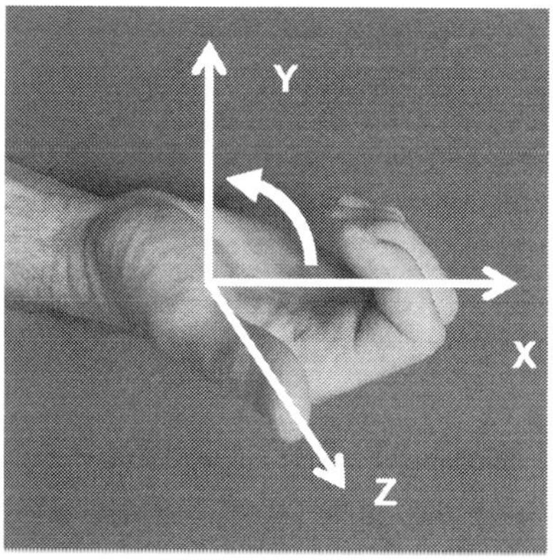

Figure 3-3: In the right-hand rule, curl your fingers from the X axis toward the Y axis.

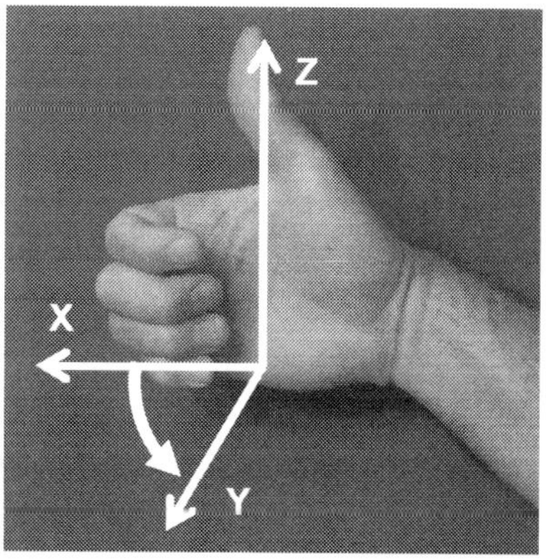

Figure 3-4: The right-hand rule works in different orientations.

It should be obvious from the name of the rule, but just to be unambiguous let me write it out explicitly: *Do not to use your left hand when applying the right-hand rule!* If you do, then you'll find out where the Z axis belongs in a left-handed coordinate system but not where it should be for WPF.

Right-Hand Rule, Version 2

Figures 3-5 and 3-6 show another version of the right-hand rule that uses individual fingers instead of curled fingers.

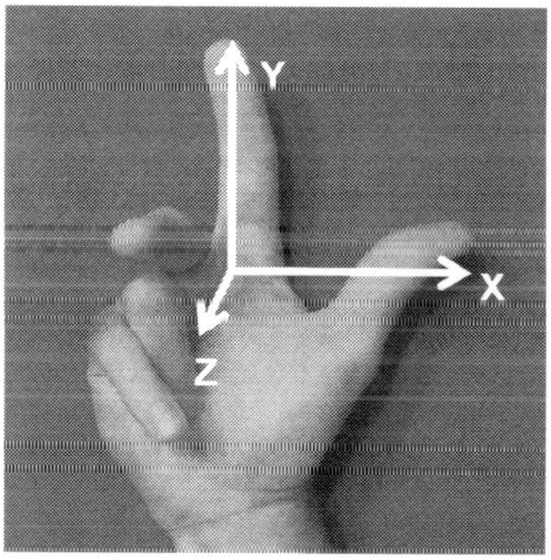

Figure 3-5: In this version, your thumb, index finger, and middle finger point along the axes.

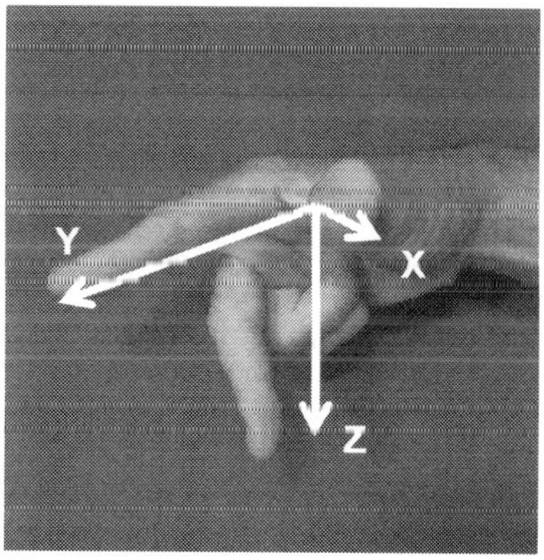

Figure 3-6: This version also works in different orientations.

In this version, point your thumb along the X axis and your index finger along the Y axis. Then bend your middle finger downward to make a 90° angle with the other two fingers. That's the direction of the Z axis.

I prefer the first version, both because it's easier on my fingers and because it makes more sense to me when testing outward orientation, which is covered a bit later in this chapter.

Screwdriver Rule

This technique only works if you frequently use a screwdriver so you remember which way to turn it to move screws in or out. Imagine that you have a normal screw pointed perpendicular to the X and Y axes. You know that the it lies along the Z axis, but you don't know which direction the Z axis should point. Now if you imagine that you turn the screw from the X axis toward the Y axis, the direction the screw moves is the direction of the Z axis.

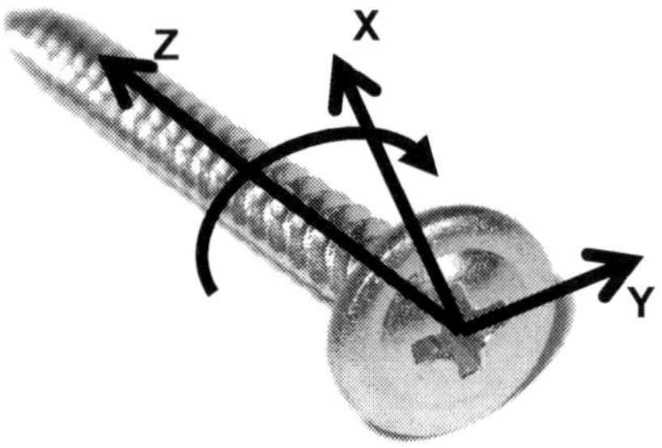

Figure 3-7: When you turn the screwdriver from the X axis to the Y axis, the screw moves along the Z axis.

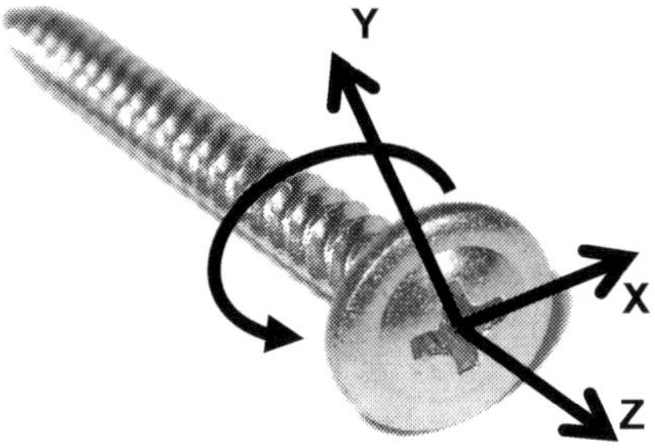

Figure 3-8: If the X and Y axes are switched, the screw moves out along the Z axis.

If the screw is pointed in the same direction as the Z axis, as shown in Figure 3-7, then the screw moves "into the wood" along the axis.

Now imagine that the X and Y axes are switched as in Figure 3-8. Basically you're looking at the picture from the other side. Now when you turn from the X axis to the Y axis, the screw moves "out of the wood," again in the direction of the Z axis.

> **NOTE:** I suppose you could use the right-hand rule to remember which way to turn a screw to make it go in or out, but most people use the mnemonic, "Righty-tighty, left-loosey." (Turn right to tighten, left to loosen.)

Magnetic Fields

You can also use the various versions of the right-hand rule to understand the interaction between flowing current and magnetic fields.

You can use the first version of the right-hand rule to determine the direction of the magnetic field created by a current flowing through a wire. If you point your thumb in the current's direction, then your fingers curl in the direction of the magnetic field.

You can use the second version of the right-hand rule to determine the direction of the force that's applied by an external magnetic field to a wire that has current flowing through it. Point your thumb in the direction of the current and your index finger in the direction of the magnetic field. Then if you point your middle finger perpendicular to those two directions, it points in the direction of the force.

For more on this, see the Khan Academy page at `tinyurl.com/yb7dl6ot`.

Cross Products

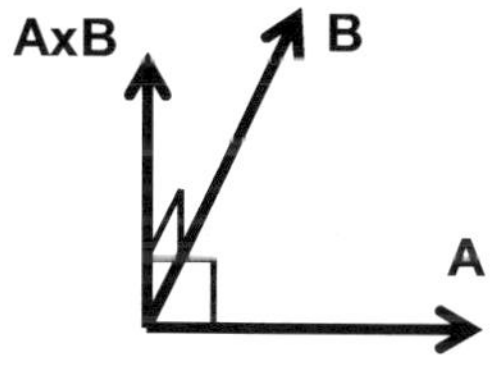

Figure 3-9: The right-hand rule gives the direction of the cross product.

The *cross product* of two non-parallel vectors is a third vector perpendicular to the first two. If A and B are two vectors, then their cross product is written A×B. Figure 3-9 shows two vectors A and B and their cross product.

Note that the vectors A and B do not need to be perpendicular; they just need to be nonparallel.

Chapter 8 says more about cross products, such as how you calculate them. The reason they're mentioned here is that you can use the right-hand rule to determine the direction that A×B points.

There are two directions that are perpendicular to both A and B. In Figure 3-9, the vector A×B points upward. A vector pointing downward in the direction opposite A×B is also perpendicular to A and B. The question is, "Does the cross product give you the up or down direction?"

The right-hand rule tells you which one to pick when you perform the cross product. If you treat vector A as the X axis and vector B as the Y axis, then the Z axis as determined by the right-hand rule gives you the direction of the cross product.

Note that this means A×B is not the same as B×A. If you take a moment to use your hand on Figure 3-9, you'll see that A×B points upward and B×A points downward.

Outward Orientation

The right-hand and screwdriver rules are useful for figuring out the arrangement of the coordinate axes, but often you get to pick where the axes are, so you can arrange the axes so they seem natural to you. For example, if you want to make a sketch of a scene that you're building, you can simply decide that the X axis points right, the Y axis points up, and the Z axis points out. A more important use for these rules is to determine a triangle's *outward orientation*.

A triangle ΔABC in a solid shape is *outwardly oriented* if its vertices are arranged so that the cross product of the vectors AB and AC points out away from the solid.

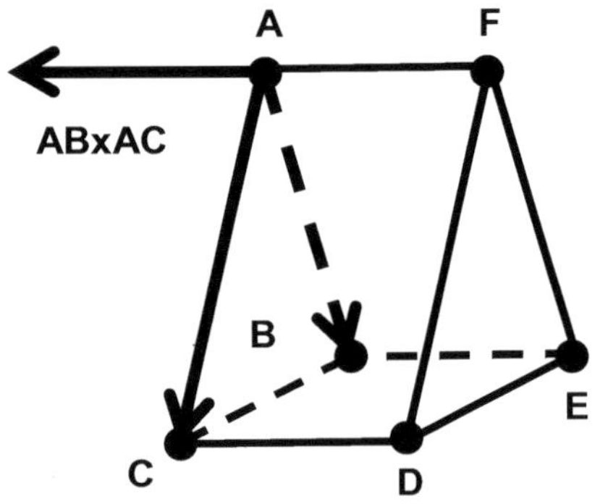

Figure 3-10: Triangle ΔABC is outwardly oriented.

For example, consider the prism shown in Figure 3-10. The triangle ΔABC is outwardly oriented because AB×AC points out of the prism.

If you change the ordering of the triangle's vertices, then the triangle is no longer outwardly oriented. For example, triangle ΔACB is not outwardly oriented because AC×AB points into the prism. (You should take a few moments to verify that by holding your hand on front of Figure 3-10 and curling your fingers in various directions. If someone walking by doesn't think you look silly twisting your arm and curling your fingers into strange positions, then you're not doing three-dimensional drawing right.)

The whole point of outward orientation is that it lets the graphics system quickly discard or "cull" triangles that it doesn't need to draw. To do that, it uses a cross product to find a vector perpendicular to a triangle's surface. (AB×AC in Figure 3-10.) If the vector points more or less away from the camera, then it is a *backface* on the far side of the solid so you can't see it and therefore the drawing system doesn't need to draw it.

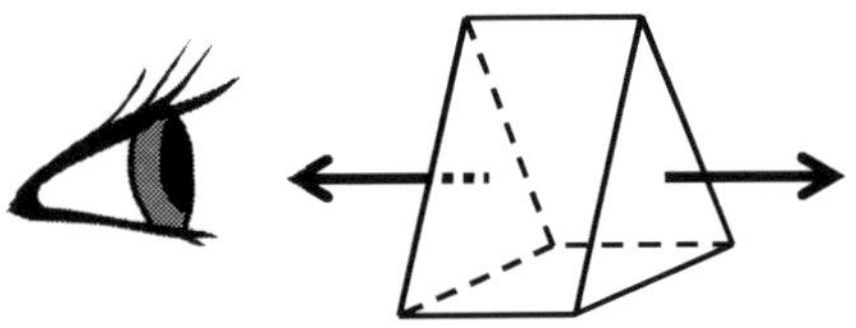

Figure 3-11: Outward orientation lets a program quickly cull triangles.

Figure 3-11 shows the perpendicular vectors for two of the prism's triangles. Because the triangles are outwardly oriented, the vectors show that the triangle on the left is visible from the viewing position but the triangle on the right is a backface so it doesn't need to be drawn.

NOTE: I prefer the first "curl your fingers" version of the right-hand rule for testing outward orientation. If you curl your fingers in the direction of a triangle's vertices, as in A-B-C in Figure 3-10, then your thumb shows the triangle's orientation.

If you accidentally give a triangle the wrong orientation, the result usually looks like the solid is missing a piece. Figure 3-11 shows a cube with one triangle oriented incorrectly. The white area on the top of the cube is where the triangle should be, but the drawing system culled it thinking it was a backface.

Figure 3-12: Incorrect orientation makes holes in the solid.

You can prevent the drawing system from culling the triangles in a mesh if by setting the mesh's `BackMaterial` property. That property tells the drawing system how to draw a triangle that is a backface. This is useful for meshes that are not solids such as planes and surfaces if you want to let the user view them from both sides.

Giving a mesh a `BackMaterial` makes drawing slower, however, so you should only do it if you need to view the mesh from both sides.

Summary

WPF uses a right-handed coordinate system. Take a few minutes to get to know the right-hand rule and be sure you can use it to orient the coordinate axes and to outwardly orient the triangles that define a solid. For practice, copy the Cube program from Chapter 1 or the CCube program from Chapter 2. Then modify the cube's `TriangleIndices` values to see what happens when you break a triangle's outward orientation.

This chapter only explains how to define objects in a three-dimensional coordinate system. If you want to actually *see* the objects on your computer, at some point you're going to need to transform those points onto a two-dimensional screen. (Unless you have a holographic screen. Now that would be cool!) Chapter 4 describes the objects that WPF provides to make that transformation from three dimensions to two.

NOTE: This is the only chapter in the book that has no example programs, so don't bother looking for them on the book's web site.

Chapter 4 Projections

This chapter describes the camera classes that WPF provides to let you view three-dimensional objects. The position and orientation of the camera determines which items are shown on the viewport and their orientation.

When you draw a three-dimensional scene on a computer, you need to convert the three-dimensional data into a two-dimensional format that can fit on your screen. You need to map each point's three-dimensional coordinates (x, y, z) to a new two-dimensional point (x', y') on your screen. The process of making that conversion is called *projection.*

> **NOTE:** Three-dimensional graphics uses several different coordinate systems. The three-dimensional coordinates that you use to model a scene are called *world coordinates*. A projection maps world coordinates into *viewport coordinates*, which give a two-dimensional representation of the scene. The viewport coordinates are then mapped onto the computer's screen as *screen coordinates* or *device coordinates.*
>
> In WPF you generally only work with world coordinates. Camera objects and the drawing system deal with viewport and device coordinates.

WPF provides two main kinds of camera classes that perform projection: perspective and orthographic. The following sections describe those kinds of projection and the cameras that provide them.

Orthographic Projection

In an orthographic projection, the program uses parallel rays to map the points in the three-dimensional scene onto a perpendicular viewing surface. One result of this kind of projection is that objects that are the same size and orientation appear to still have the same size after projection no matter how far they are away from the plane of projection.

Figure 4-1 shows the orthographic projection of two rectangles. Because the rectangles have the same size and orientation, they produce similar results in the projection.

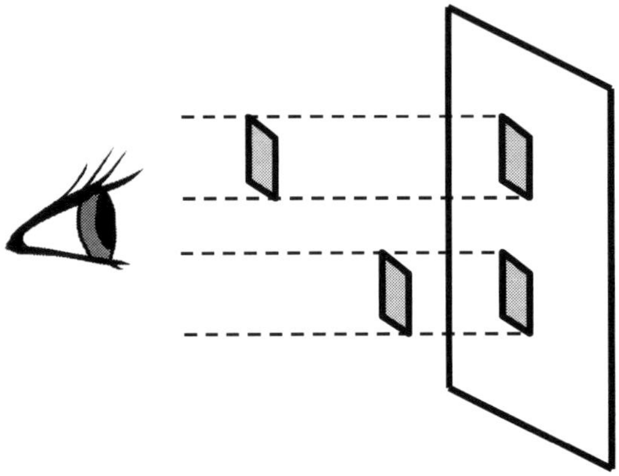

Figure 4-1: Orthographic projections use parallel rays.

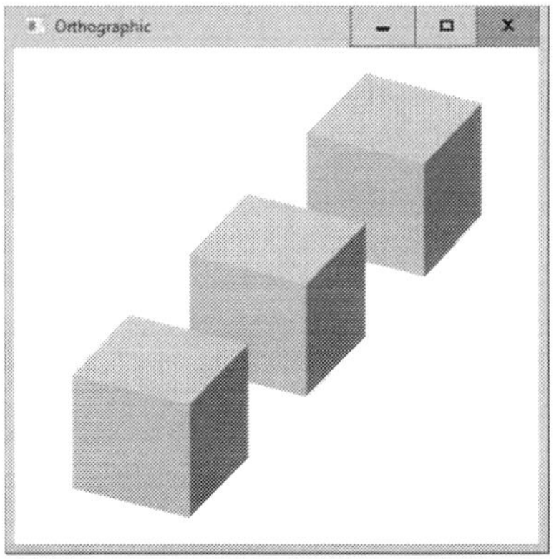

Figure 4-2: The Orthographic program draws three cubes.

The Orthographic example program, which is shown in Figure 4-2, displays an orthographic projection of three cubes that have the same size in world coordinates. You can see in the figure that they also have the same size in the projection.

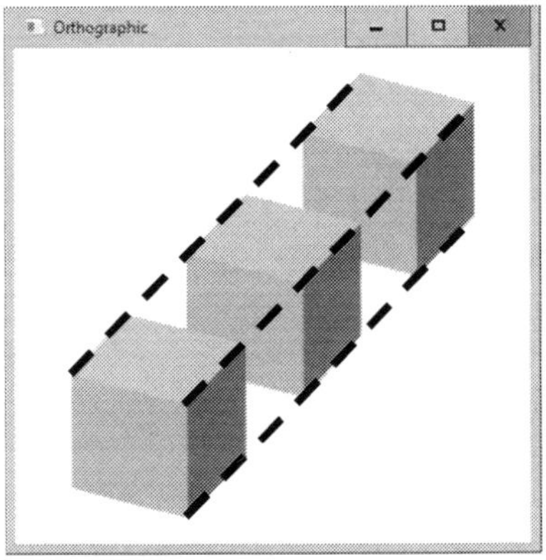

Figure 4-3: In an orthographic projection, parallel lines remain parallel.

An interesting feature of orthographic projections is that parallel lines remain parallel after projection. For example, the cube edges that are parallel to the Z axis in world coordinates are still parallel in the projection shown in Figure 4-2. Figure 4-3 shows the same projection with dashed lines along the edges that are parallel to the Z axis.

The same is true for the cubes' other parallel edges. Edges that are parallel to the X axis in world coordinates are parallel in the projection, and edges parallel to the Y axis in world coordinates are parallel in the projection.

A WPF program uses the `OrthographicCamera` class to perform an orthographic projection. The following code shows how the Orthographic example program shown in Figures 4-2 and 4-3 defines its camera.

```
// Define the camera.
private void DefineCamera(Viewport3D viewport)
{
    Point3D position = new Point3D(1.5, 2, 3);
    Vector3D lookDirection = new Vector3D(
        -position.X, -position.Y, -position.Z);
    Vector3D upDirection = new Vector3D(0, 1, 0);
    double width = 4;
    OrthographicCamera camera =
        new OrthographicCamera(position, lookDirection, upDirection, width);
    viewport.Camera = camera;
}
```

This code passes the camera's constructor the camera's location, the direction it should point (back toward the origin), and an "up" vector to determine the camera's orientation. The final parameter, `width`, indicates how wide the camera's view box should be in world coordinates. The camera scales the result to map that width onto the width of the viewport.

Two other camera properties determine which objects are actually visible: the front and back clipping planes.

Any object that is closer to the camera than the front clipping plane is clipped. If part of the object lies beyond the clipping plane, that part is still visible, but any pieces that are between the camera and the front clipping plane are invisible.

Similarly, any object that lies farther from the camera than the back clipping plane is clipped.

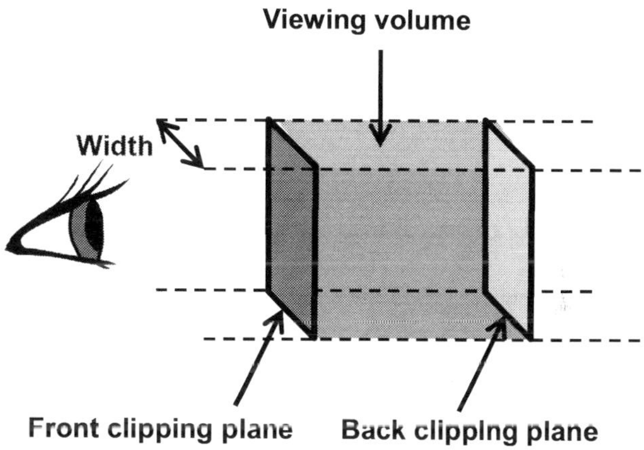

Figure 4-4: The front and back clipping planes, plus the width, define the viewing volume.

The `OrthographicCamera` class's `NearPlaneDistance` and `FarPlaneDistance` properties determine how far the clipping planes are from the camera in world coordinates. Together, the clipping planes and the camera's width define a box-shaped *view box* or *viewing volume*. Figure 4-4 shows how those values define the viewing volume.

Perspective Projection

In a perspective projection, the program uses rays that originate from a single point (the camera's viewing position) to map the points in the three-dimensional scene onto the viewing surface. One result of this kind of projection is that objects that are farther from the viewing position appear smaller than those that are closer. That's the way your eyes work in the real world, so this kind of projection produces a relatively realistic result.

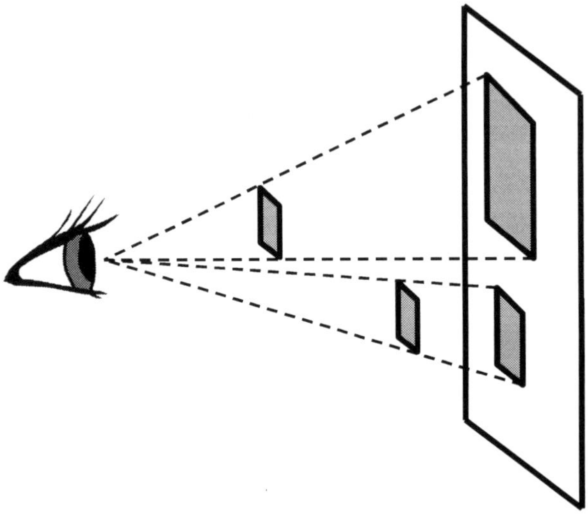

Figure 4-5: In perspective projection, objects closer to the viewing position appear larger.

Figure 4-5 shows the perspective projection of two rectangles with the same size. The one that is closer to the viewing position appears larger in the projection.

Because of the way perspective projection works, parallel lines in world coordinates do not necessarily end up parallel in the projection. Two lines' projections will be parallel if they are perpendicular to the viewing direction in world coordinates. For example, in Figure 4-5 the rectangles' top and bottom edges are perpendicular to the viewing direction so their projections are parallel.

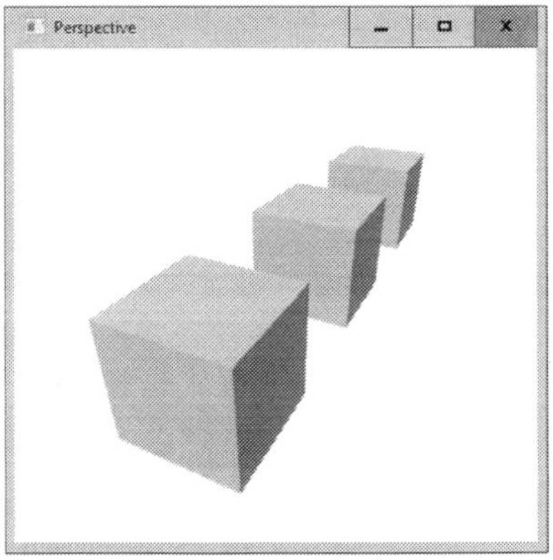

Figure 4-6: The Perspective program draws three cubes.

In general, however, parallel lines are not necessarily parallel in the projection. For example, the Perspective program shown in Figure 4-6 draws three cubes of the same size. Because none of the cubes' edges are perpendicular to the viewing direction, none of them are parallel in the projection.

Even the edges of a single cube are not parallel in Figure 4-6. For example, the closest cube's edges are not parallel.

A WPF program uses the `PerspectiveCamera` class to perform a perspective projection. The following code shows how the Perspective example program shown in Figure 4-6 defines its camera.

```
// Define the camera.
private void DefineCamera(Viewport3D viewport)
{
    Point3D position = new Point3D(1.5, 2, 3);
    Vector3D lookDirection = new Vector3D(
        -position.X, -position.Y, -position.Z);
    Vector3D upDirection = new Vector3D(0, 1, 0);
    double fieldOfView = 60;
    PerspectiveCamera camera =
        new PerspectiveCamera(position, lookDirection, upDirection, fieldOfView);

    viewport.Camera = camera;
}
```

This code is similar to the version that the Orthographic example program uses. It passes the camera's constructor the camera's location, the direction it should be pointed (back toward the origin), and an "up" vector to determine the camera's orientation.

This time the final parameter, `fieldOfView`, indicates how wide the camera's view should be in degrees.

Like an `OrthographicCamera`, the `PerspectiveCamera` class uses `NearPlaneDistance` and `FarPlaneDistance` properties to define front and back clipping planes. Together the clipping planes and field of view define a *viewing frustum* as shown in Figure 4-7.

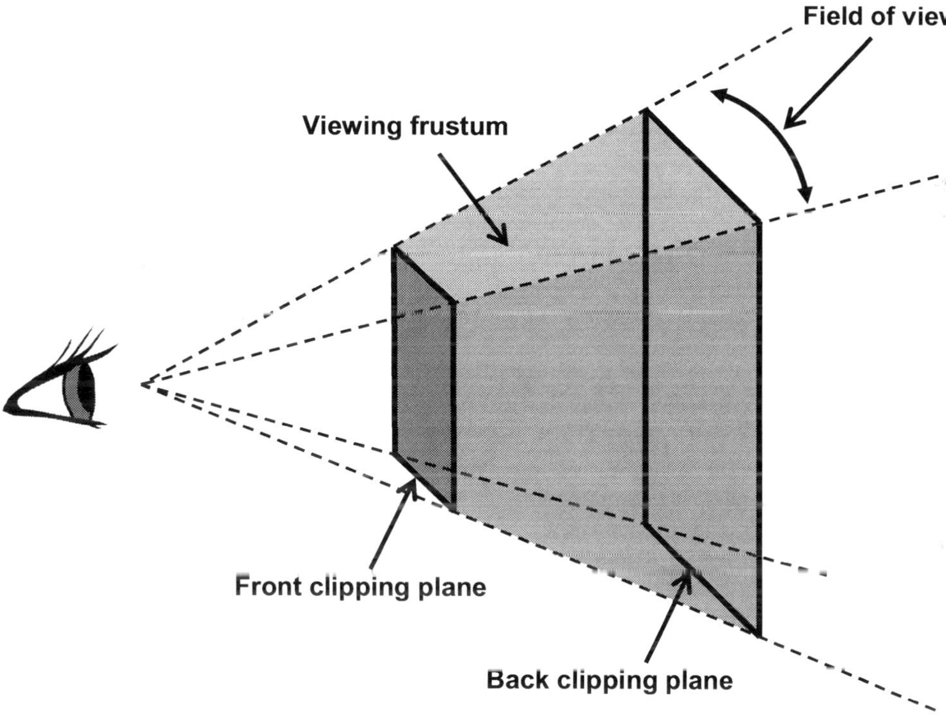

Figure 4-7: The front and back clipping planes, plus the field of view, define the viewing frustum.

> **NOTE:** "Frustum" is just a fancy term for a truncated cone or pyramid. (Another good word to use at parties after you've introduced everyone to the word "chirality.") For consistency, some people call an orthographic viewing volume a viewing frustum, even though it's really a box and not a frustum.

Other Parallel Projections

WPF only provides two kinds of projection, orthographic and perspective, but there are several other kinds of projection that you might want to use in a three-dimensional application. WPF doesn't provide direct support for those other kinds of projections, but can use them with some extra work. They are are occasionally useful, particularly in architectural and mechanical drawings, so they deserve some mention. (Besides, they'll make good follow-on topics to impress your friends after you show off your use of the words "chirality" and "frustum.")

A *parallel projection* is any projection that uses parallel rays to project three-dimensional objects onto a two-dimensional viewing plane. You can divide parallel projections into two categories: orthographic projections and oblique projections.

Orthographic Projections

In an orthographic projection such as those described earlier in this chapter, the viewing plane is perpendicular to the projecting rays. You can divide orthographic projections into two main sub-categories: primary projections and axonometric projections.

Primary Projections

A *primary projection* is an orthographic projection parallel to a coordinate axis. There are six possible primary projections along the positive and negative X, Y, and Z axes.

The top-down view along the Y axis is called the *plan view*. A side view along the X or Z axis is called an *elevation view*.

A multiview projection isn't really a projection, it's a group of several primary projections. For example, an architectural drawing showing top, front, and side views contains three primary projections.

NOTE: None of the example programs for this chapter use primary projections. The primary projection of a cube aligned with the axes is just a square, and that's boring.

To perform a primary projection in WPF, simply use an `OrthographicCamera` pointing along one of the coordinate axes. For example, to create a front view, you could position the camera at (0, 0, 10) looking in direction <0, 0, -10>.

You can make similar cameras for other primary views. For extra credit, you can make several `Viewport3D` objects display different primary projections to make a single program display a multiview projection.

Axonometric Projections

An *axonometric projection* is an orthographic projection where you can view all three coordinate dimensions in the same picture. Basically that means the direction of projection is not parallel to any of the XY, XZ, or YZ planes.

You can further divide axonometric projections into three categories depending on how measurements in the X, Y, and Z directions are scaled.

In a *trimetric projection*, distances along the axes are all scaled by different amounts. To make a trimetric projection in WPF, use a camera where the viewing direction makes different angles with each of the coordinate axes. For example, you could use the viewing direction <-1.5, -2, -3>.

In a *bimetric projection*, distances along two of the axes are scaled by the same amount and distances along the third axis are scaled by a different amount. To make a bimetric projection in WPF, use a camera with a viewing direction that has two components the same. For example, you could use the viewing direction <-1.5, -1.5, -3>.

In an *isometric projection*, distances along all three axes are scaled by the same amount. To make a trimetric projection in WPF, use a camera with a viewing direction that has the same X, Y, and Z components such as <-1.5, -1.5, -1.5>.

The Axonometric example program shown in Figure 4-8 displays trimetric, dimetric, and isometric projections of cube. The dark line segments show the sides of the cubes that have the same lengths in the projections.

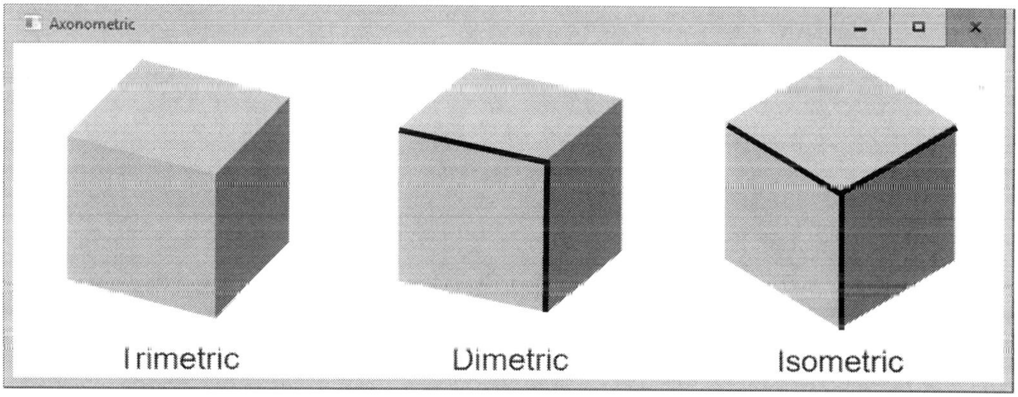

Figure 4-8: The Axonometric example program demonstrates trimetric, dimetric, and isometric projections.

Oblique Projections

In an *oblique projection*, the projecting rays are still parallel, but they are not perpendicular to the viewing plane. Figure 4-9 shows an oblique projection of a cube.

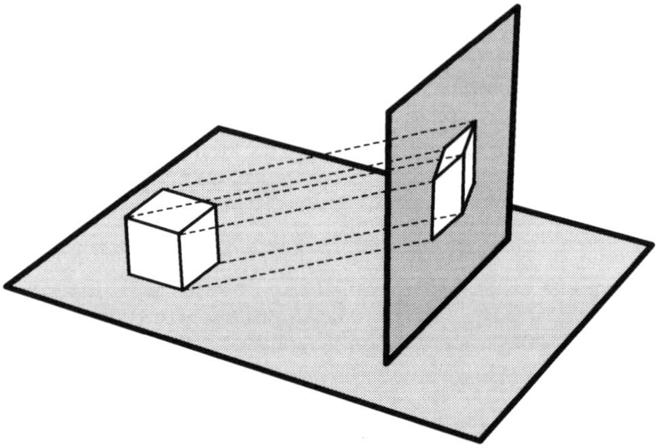

Figure 4-9: In an oblique projection, the viewing plane is not perpendicular to the projecting rays.

Oblique projections are usually used to preserve the information in some dimensions while distorting information in other dimensions. For example, in a cabinet projection (described shortly), the viewing plane is parallel to the XY plane so features that are parallel to that plane are not distorted. Z coordinates are distorted to give an impression of distance in that direction.

The following sections describe three subcategories of oblique projections: cavalier, cabinet, and military.

Cavalier Projections

In a *cavalier projection*, the plane of projection is parallel to the XY plane. Features in the Z direction are pulled back at an arbitrary angle, which is often chosen to be 30° or 45 °, to make the result look nice and give the appearance of a sort of faux perspective.

Distances in all three directions are scaled by the same amount, so you can compare measurements on the result in the X, Y, and Z directions.

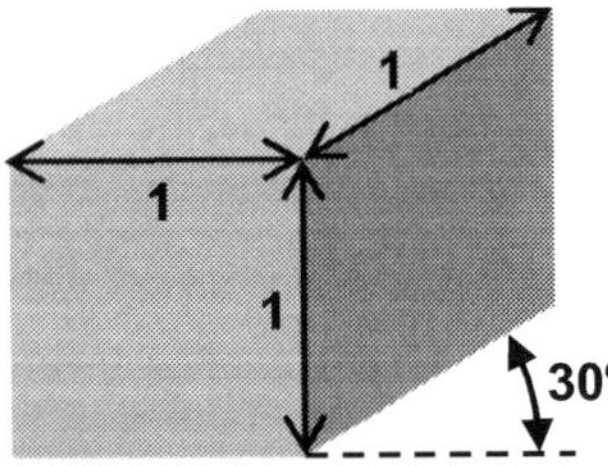

Figure 4-10: In a cavalier projection, all three dimensions are scaled by the same amount.

Figure 4-10 shows a 30° cavalier projection of a cube. Measurements in the X, Y, and Z directions are all scaled by the same amount, so the cube's sides all have the same length in the projection.

Note that the projection's distortion means you cannot compare distances that do not lie parallel to the coordinate axes. For example, the diagonals of the cube's top face do not have the same lengths.

Because the plane of projection is parallel to the XY plane, measurements of surfaces parallel to that plane are preserved. For example, the diagonals of the cube's front face *do* have the same length.

> **NOTE:** Cavalier projections were originally used to make drawings of medieval fortifications. Some say the name comes from the way a cavalier (horseback rider) looks down on an object from above. Others say it comes from a hill or tower called a *cavalier* that was raised inside a fortification so you could see (and shoot at) the enemy outside.

You can create orthographic projections in WPF by orienting an `OrthographicCamera` properly. That won't work with oblique projections because the orthographic camera always projects onto a plane that is perpendicular to the direction of projection. Fortunately, it's not hard to manipulate the model to produce the same result as an oblique projection.

For a cavalier projection, aim the camera perpendicular to the XY plane. Then loop through the model's points and adjust their X and Y coordinates to reflect their Z values.

For example, consider the point (0, 0, -z). Because it lies z units behind the XY plane, its projection should be shifted a distance z diagonally. If you want the Z axis to make angle θ with the X axis, then you need to add z cos(θ) to the point's X coordinate and z sin(θ) to the point's Y coordinate, as shown in Figure 4-11.

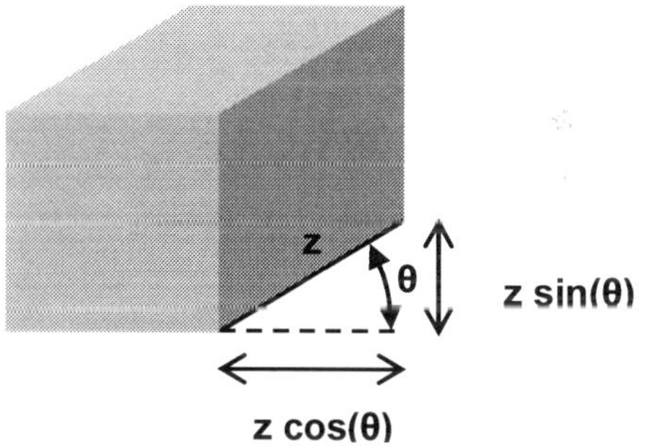

Figure 4-11: X and Y coordinates are shifted depending on the Z value.

After you shift all of the points, the model has been warped out of shape. A cube is no longer a cube, but some sort of squashed prism. When you perform the projection, however, the result looks like a cavalier projection.

The following `MakeOblique` method transforms the points in a `MeshGeometry3D` object to prepare it for a cavalier projection.

```
// Transform the points for a cavalier or cabinet projection.
private void MakeOblique(MeshGeometry3D mesh, double angle, double scale)
{
    angle *= Math.PI / 180;
    double sin = Math.Sin(angle) * scale;
    double cos = Math.Cos(angle) * scale;

    for (int i = 0; i < mesh.Positions.Count; i++)
    {
        double x = mesh.Positions[i].X;
        double y = mesh.Positions[i].Y;
        double z = mesh.Positions[i].Z;
        mesh.Positions[i] =
            new Point3D(x - cos * z, y - sin * z, z);
    }
}
```

The parameter `angle` gives the angle between the Z and X axes. (The angle θ in Figure 4-11.) The `scale` value indicates a scale factor that should be applied to Z distances. For a cavalier projection, this value should be one.

The method first converts the angle from degrees (which are intuitive for most people) into radians (which is what the `Math.Sin` and `Math.Cos` methods use). It then calculates the scale times the sine and cosine of the angle θ.

Next, the code loops through the mesh's points and adjusts each point's X and Y coordinates according to Figure 4-11. The code subtracts from the X and Y coordinates because it assumes the projection is along the negative Z axis so points with more negative Z values should be moved in the positive X and Y directions.

Cabinet Projections

A *cabinet projection* is similar to a cavalier projection except dimensions along the Z axis are scaled by a factor of 1/2, as shown in Figure 4-12. As is the case with a cavalier projection, the angle θ between the X and Z axes is arbitrary and chosen to produce a nice result.

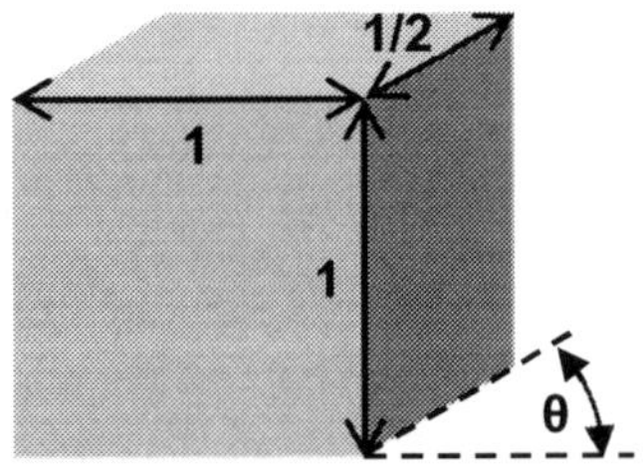

Figure 4-12: A cabinet projection is similar to a cavalier projection with Z dimensions scaled by 1/2.

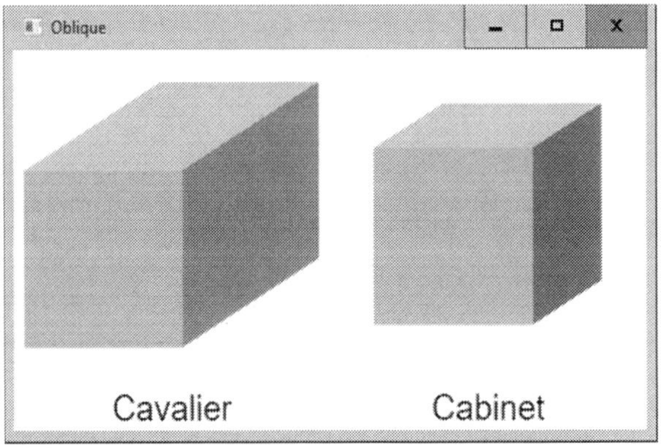

Figure 4-13: The Oblique example program displays cavalier and cabinet projections.

The Oblique example program shown in Figure 4-13, displays a cavalier projection on the left and a cabinet projection on the right.

Scaling the Z dimensions by 1/2 gives a more natural appearance, although it makes it harder to measure directly on the result. You can still take measurements; you just need to remember to double measurements in the Z direction.

In WPF you can use the `MakeOblique` method code described in the preceding section to create a cabinet projection by simply setting the `scale` parameter to 0.5.

> **NOTE:** Cabinet projections get their name from their popularity in the furniture industry. You may have made cabinet drawings in your middle school woodshop class, although your teacher may not have used that term and probably didn't ask you to use sines and cosines.
>
> Both cavalier and cabinet projections are useful because they let you take direct measurements from the resulting drawing. They are also a lot easier to draw by hand than a true perspective projection.

Military Projections

In a *military projection*, the plane of projection is parallel to the XZ plane. That means distances in the X and Z directions are scaled by the same amount. The result is then rotated 45°, and points are shifted down by some multiple of their Y values. The final result looks sort of like a top-down drawing but with points shifted down by some scale factor to give you a sense of height.

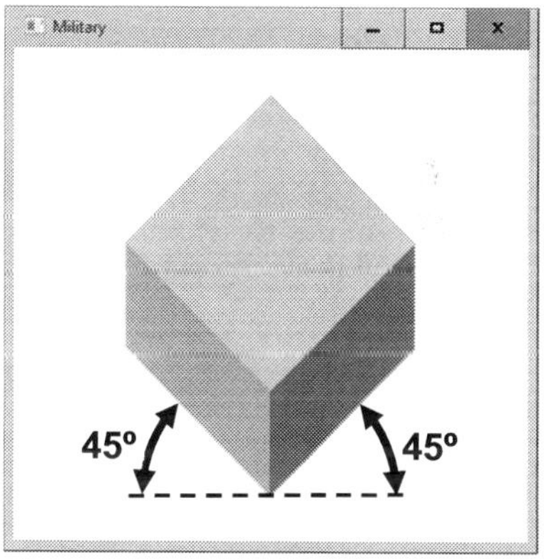

Figure 4-14: A military projection scales distances in the X and Z directions equally.

The Military example program shown in Figure 4-14 draws a military projection.

To make a military projection in WPF, you can use techniques similar to those that you use to make cavalier or cabinet projections. The main difference is that you need to rotate the final result by 45°.

To make the projection, place the camera on the Y axis looking straight down at the scene from above. Set the "up" direction to <-1, 0, -1>. That effectively rotates the result by 45° and puts the top of the camera in the negative X and Z quadrant.

The following code shows how the Military example program defines its camera.

```
// Define the camera.
private void DefineCamera(Viewport3D viewport)
{
    Point3D position = new Point3D(0, 3, 0);
    Vector3D lookDirection = new Vector3D(
        -position.X, -position.Y, -position.Z);
    Vector3D upDirection = new Vector3D(-1, 0, -1);
    double width = 5;
    OrthographicCamera camera =
        new OrthographicCamera(position, lookDirection, upDirection, width);

    viewport.Camera = camera;
}
```

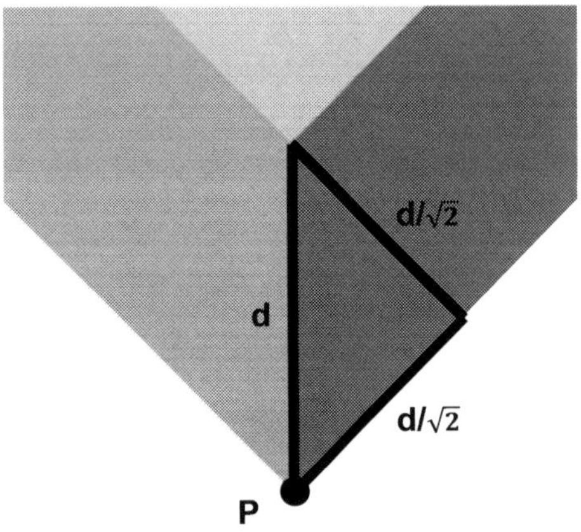

Figure 4-15: A military projection scales X and Z directions equally.

This method places the camera at (0, 3, 0) looking downward and sets the "up" vector to <-1, 0, -1> as specified in the previous instructions.

Next, loop through the model's points and translate them downward according to their Y coordinates. Figure 4-15 shows a close-up of the bottom corner of the cube shown in Figure 4-14. Suppose you want to move the point P down distance d. Because the triangle drawn in thick lines is a 45-45-90 triangle, the lengths of its shorter sides are $d/\sqrt{2}$ as shown in the figure. That means you need to add $d/\sqrt{2}$ to the point's X and Z coordinates. That effectively pulls the point distance d away from its original location in the direction of <1, 0, 1>, and that gives it the desired offset in the projection.

The Military example program uses the following `MakeMilitary` method to adjust a mesh's coordinates for a military projection.

```
// Transform points for a military projection.
private void MakeMilitary(MeshGeometry3D mesh, double scale)
{
    double xscale = scale / Math.Sqrt(2);
    for (int i = 0; i < mesh.Positions.Count; i++)
    {
        double x = mesh.Positions[i].X;
        double y = mesh.Positions[i].Y;
        double z = mesh.Positions[i].Z;
        mesh.Positions[i] = new Point3D(
            x - xscale * y,
            y,
            z - xscale * y);
    }
}
```

This code first divides the scale by which it should multiply each point's Y value by $\sqrt{2}$. It then loops through the mesh's points and adjusts their X and Z coordinates accordingly.

NOTE: As you can probably guess, military projections get their name from their use in military drawings.

Example Code

The example programs shown in this chapter's figures draw multiple cubes. You could draw each cube individually, but those programs use the following `MakeCubeMesh` method to make drawing cubes easier.

```
// Make a mesh containing a cube centered at this point.
private MeshGeometry3D MakeCubeMesh(double x, double y, double z, double width)
{
    // Create the geometry.
    MeshGeometry3D mesh = new MeshGeometry3D();

    // Define the positions.
    width /= 2;
    Point3D[] points =
    {
        new Point3D(x - width, y - width, z - width),
        new Point3D(x + width, y - width, z - width),
        new Point3D(x + width, y - width, z + width),
        new Point3D(x - width, y - width, z + width),
        new Point3D(x - width, y - width, z + width),
        new Point3D(x + width, y - width, z + width),
        new Point3D(x + width, y + width, z + width),
        new Point3D(x - width, y + width, z + width),
        new Point3D(x + width, y - width, z + width),
        new Point3D(x + width, y - width, z - width),
        new Point3D(x + width, y + width, z - width),
        new Point3D(x + width, y + width, z + width),
        new Point3D(x + width, y + width, z + width),
        new Point3D(x + width, y + width, z - width),
        new Point3D(x - width, y + width, z - width),
        new Point3D(x - width, y + width, z + width),
        new Point3D(x - width, y - width, z + width),
        new Point3D(x - width, y + width, z + width),
        new Point3D(x - width, y + width, z - width),
        new Point3D(x - width, y - width, z - width),
        new Point3D(x - width, y - width, z - width),
        new Point3D(x - width, y + width, z - width),
        new Point3D(x + width, y + width, z - width),
        new Point3D(x + width, y - width, z - width),
    };
    foreach (Point3D point in points) mesh.Positions.Add(point);

    // Define the triangles.
    Tuple<int, int, int>[] triangles =
    {
            new Tuple<int, int, int>(0, 1, 2),
            new Tuple<int, int, int>(2, 3, 0),
            new Tuple<int, int, int>(4, 5, 6),
            new Tuple<int, int, int>(6, 7, 4),
            new Tuple<int, int, int>(8, 9, 10),
            new Tuple<int, int, int>(10, 11, 8),
            new Tuple<int, int, int>(12, 13, 14),
            new Tuple<int, int, int>(14, 15, 12),
            new Tuple<int, int, int>(16, 17, 18),
            new Tuple<int, int, int>(18, 19, 16),
            new Tuple<int, int, int>(20, 21, 22),
```

```
                new Tuple<int, int, int>(22, 23, 20),
            };
            foreach (Tuple<int, int, int> tuple in triangles)
            {
                mesh.TriangleIndices.Add(tuple.Item1);
                mesh.TriangleIndices.Add(tuple.Item2);
                mesh.TriangleIndices.Add(tuple.Item3);
            }

            return mesh;
        }
```

This method takes as parameters the coordinates where the cube should be centered and the cube's width. It starts by creating a `MeshGeometry3D` object, which it will eventually return.

Next, the method creates an array of `Point3D` structures to hold the cube's vertices. It loops through those points and adds them to the new `MeshGeometry3D`.

The code then defines an array of tuples holding the indices of the points needed to make up the cube's triangles. It loops through the tuples and uses them to define the mesh's `TriangleIndices`. This is all similar to the way the CCube example program described in Chapter 2 builds its cube except this code is in a handy method for easy reuse.

The method then returns the mesh.

The following code shows how the Orthographic example program uses this method to define its cubes.

```
// Define the model.
private void DefineModel(Model3DGroup group)
{
    // Make three cubes.
    for (int i = 0; i < 3; i++)
    {
        double z = -2 + i * 2;
        MeshGeometry3D mesh = MakeCubeMesh(0, 0, z, 1);
        DiffuseMaterial material = new DiffuseMaterial(Brushes.LightBlue);
        GeometryModel3D model = new GeometryModel3D(mesh, material);
        group.Children.Add(model);
    }
}
```

This code loops three times and calls `MakeCubeMesh` to create cubes centered at positions (0, 0, -2), (0, 0, 0), and (0, 0, 2). It gives each mesh a light blue material and adds each to the main `Model3DGroup`.

The `MakeCubeMesh` method demonstrates a useful technique: it builds a higher-level object than the triangles that make up a `MeshGeometry3D` object. Chapters later in this book use this technique a lot. They use methods to build all sorts of solids such as tetrahedrons, spheres, and tori. They even show better methods for building cubes. However, this version is simple and good enough for the next few chapters.

Summary

The following table summarizes the kinds of projections described in this chapter.

Projection	Meaning
Parallel	Projecting rays are parallel
Orthographic	Rays are perpendicular to the plane of projection
Primary	Rays are parallel to a coordinate axis
Axonometric	Rays are not parallel to an axis, so all three dimensions are visible
Trimetric	All dimensions are scaled by different amounts
Dimetric	Two dimensions are scaled by the same amount
Isometric	All dimensions are scaled by the same amount
Oblique	Projecting rays are not perpendicular to the plane of projection
Cavalier	All dimensions are scaled by the same amount, the plane of projection is parallel to the XY plane, and Z dimensions are drawn at an angle up and to the right
Cabinet	Similar to cavalier except Z dimensions are scaled by 1/2
Military	X and Z dimensions are scaled equally, the result is rotated 45°, and points are moved down to show height
Perspective	Projecting rays are not parallel and originate at a common viewing position

Different kinds of projections emphasize different aspects of the model so they may be useful for different purposes. Several kinds of projections scale distances along the coordinate axes either by the same amount or by known factors so you can measure directly on the resulting picture. For example, a cabinet projection lets you measure distances in the X and Y directions directly, and in the Z direction scaled by a factor of 1/2. That can be handy if you want to verify a measurement before you start cutting wood to make a filing cabinet, bookcase, or credenza.

Perspective transformations produce the most realistic result, however, so they are used most often and most of the programs in this book use perspective transformations.

All of the example programs shown so far have used a fixed camera position. For example, the Military example program used a specific position and orientation to produce a military projection. The next chapter explains different ways that you can allow the user to control the camera's position and orientation.

Chapter 5
Camera Control

Three-dimensional graphics can be useful for allowing the user to visualize complicated scenes or data. Often it's even more useful if you let the user view the scene from different directions.

This chapter explains several different that ways that you can allow the user to move the camera's viewing position and orientation. Different methods may be appropriate under different circumstances. For example, a spherical coordinate system is quite useful for viewing a single object, but a hovering style system might be better for a more complicated scene.

Spherical Coordinates

In this system, the scene is centered at the origin with the camera orbiting around it. The user can use the mouse or arrow keys to change the camera's position and distance, but the camera always faces the origin.

The following section explains how spherical coordinates work. The section after that explains how the SphericalCoordinates example program uses them to let you change the camera's position.

Spherical Mathematics

Cartesian coordinates let you determine a point's location with x, y, and z values. In *spherical coordinates*, you indicate a location by using the values r, θ (theta), and φ (phi).

Figure 5-1 shows the relationship between Cartesian and spherical coordinates for the point P. The value r is the distance from the origin O to point P, θ is the angle that the projection of P onto the XZ plane makes with the Z axis, and φ is the angle that the segment OP makes with the Y axis.

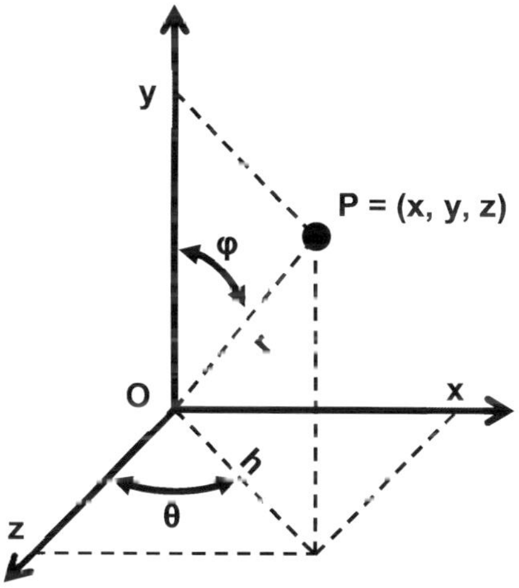

Figure 5-1: This picture shows how to convert between spherical and Cartesian coordinates.

The values r, θ, and φ are sometimes called the *radial distance*, *azimuth angle*, and *polar angle*, respectively.

Spherical coordinates are a natural way to keep track of the camera's position in this kind of program. Click and drag or use the arrow keys to change the camera's θ and φ values. Use the + and - keys or the mouse wheel to zoom in and out.

> **NOTE:** Figure 5-1 isn't exactly the way you'll see spherical coordinates described in other contexts. The relevant posts on Wikipedia (`tinyurl.com/c6qccu3`) and Wolfram MathWorld (`tinyurl.com/73xbm`) orient their axes so Z is up, Y is to the right, and X points out of the screen. (They still obey the right-hand rule.) Wikipedia also says that the roles of θ and φ are often switched in physics discussions.
>
> Some sources also switch the order of the values when they are inside parentheses. For example, some may use (r, θ, φ) and others may use the ordering (r, φ θ).
>
> I used the system shown in Figure 5-1 because it makes sense for the WPF coordinate system. The math is the same in all of the versions, just with some values trading roles.

You can use Figure 5-1 to convert between the two coordinate systems. First, suppose you know point P's Cartesian coordinates (x, y, z). The distance formula lets you calculate r.

$$r = \sqrt{x^2 + y^2 + z^2}$$

The distance formula in two dimensions also lets you calculate the distance h.

$$h = \sqrt{x^2 + z^2}$$

Now trigonometry lets you find θ and φ.

$$\theta = \operatorname{atan}\left(\frac{x}{z}\right)$$

$$\varphi = \operatorname{atan}\left(\frac{h}{y}\right)$$

The following C# method uses those equations to convert from Cartesian to spherical coordinates.

```
// Convert from Cartesian to spherical coordinates.
private void CartesianToSpherical(double x, double y, double z,
```

```
    out double r, out double theta, out double phi)
{
    r = Math.Sqrt(x * x + y * y + z * z);
    double h = Math.Sqrt(x * x + z * z);
    theta = Math.Atan2(x, z);
    phi = Math.Atan2(h, y);
}
```

To convert from spherical to Cartesian to coordinates, suppose you know point P's spherical coordinates (r, θ, φ). Trigonometry gives you the point's Y coordinate.

$$y = r \cdot \cos(\varphi)$$

Trigonometry also lets you calculate h.

$$h = r \cdot \sin(\varphi)$$

Once you know h, it's easy to calculate x and z.

$$x = h \cdot \sin(\theta)$$

$$z = h \cdot \cos(\theta)$$

The following C# method uses those equations to convert from spherical to Cartesian coordinates.

```
// Convert from spherical to Cartesian coordinates.
private void SphericalToCartesian(double r, double theta, double phi,
    out double x, out double y, out double z)
{
    y = r * Math.Cos(phi);
    double h = r * Math.Sin(phi);
    x = h * Math.Sin(theta);
    z = h * Math.Cos(theta);
}
```

Camera Controller

The SphericalCoordinates example program shown in Figure 5-2 uses the previous methods to manage the camera's position and orientation. Click and drag or use the arrow keys to change the camera's θ and φ values. Use the + and - keys or the mouse wheel to zoom in and out.

Figure 5-2: This program uses spherical coordinates to track camera position.

The key to this example is a class named `SphericalCameraController` that encapsulates the mathematics of the preceding section. The following sections describe the class's main pieces.

Camera Position

The `SphericalCameraController` class uses the following variables to keep track of the camera's position.

```
// The camera.
public PerspectiveCamera TheCamera = null;

// The controls that provide events.
private UIElement KeyboardControl = null;
private UIElement WheelControl = null;
private UIElement MouseControl = null;

// Adjustment values.
public double CameraDR = 0.1;
public double CameraDTheta = Math.PI / 30;
public double CameraDPhi = Math.PI / 15;

// The current position.
private double CameraR = 8.0;
private double CameraTheta = Math.PI / 3.0;
private double CameraPhi = Math.PI / 3.0;
```

The variable `TheCamera` is the camera that this object will control. The next three `UIElement` variables hold references to the user interface elements that will provide the controller with keyboard, mouse wheel, and mouse events.

The next three variables hold the amounts by which the camera's spherical coordinates will be modified when the user presses various movement keys. For example, if you press the left arrow, the program increases θ by `CameraDTheta`. This makes the camera move to the right and makes it look like the scene is rotating to the left.

The last three variables store the camera's current position in spherical coordinates.

The class provides property procedures to let the main program get and set the camera's position in either spherical or Cartesian coordinates. They use the `CartesianToSpherical` and `CartesianToSpherical` methods described in the preceding section, but they are otherwise not very interesting, so I won't described them here. Download the example if you want to see the details.

The following code shows the class's constructor.

```
// Constructor.
public SphericalCameraController(PerspectiveCamera camera, Viewport3D viewport,
    UIElement keyboardControl, UIElement wheelControl, UIElement mouseControl)
{
    TheCamera = camera;
    viewport.Camera = TheCamera;

    KeyboardControl = keyboardControl;
    KeyboardControl.PreviewKeyDown += KeyboardControl_KeyDown;

    WheelControl = wheelControl;
    WheelControl.PreviewMouseWheel += WheelControl_PreviewMouseWheel;
```

```
        MouseControl = mouseControl;
        MouseControl.MouseDown += MouseControl_MouseDown;

        PositionCamera();
    }
```

This code saves a reference to the camera and sets the viewport's `Camera` property. It then saves references to the `UIElements` that will provide the controller with events and registers event handlers for them. It finishes by calling the following `PositionCamera` method to set the camera's initial position.

```
    // Use the current values of CameraR, CameraTheta,
    // and CameraPhi to position the camera.
    private void PositionCamera()
    {
        // Calculate the camera's position in Cartesian coordinates.
        double x, y, z;
        SphericalToCartesian(CameraR, CameraTheta, CameraPhi,
            out x, out y, out z);
        TheCamera.Position = new Point3D(x, y, z);

        // Look toward the origin.
        TheCamera.LookDirection = new Vector3D(-x, -y, -z);

        // Set the Up direction.
        TheCamera.UpDirection = new Vector3D(0, 1, 0);
    }
```

This method converts the camera's desired position from spherical to Cartesian coordinates and uses the results to update the camera's position. It makes the camera look back toward the origin and sets its "up" direction to the vector <0, 1, 0>.

Keyboard

When the user presses a key, the `SphericalCameraController` class executes the following event handler.

```
    // Adjust the camera's position.
    private void KeyboardControl_KeyDown(object sender, KeyEventArgs e)
    {
        switch (e.Key)
        {
            case Key.Up:
                IncreasePhi();
                break;
            case Key.Down:
                DecreasePhi();
                break;
            case Key.Left:
                IncreaseTheta();
                break;
            case Key.Right:
                DecreaseTheta();
                break;
            case Key.Add:
```

```
            case Key.OemPlus:
                IncreaseR();
                break;
            case Key.Subtract:
            case Key.OemMinus:
                DecreaseR();
                break;
        }

        // Update the camera's position.
        PositionCamera();
    }
```

This code checks the key pressed and calls a method to update the camera's spherical coordinates appropriately. It then calls `PositionCamera` to move the camera into its new position.

The methods that update the camera's position are straightforward. For example, the following code shows the `IncreasePhi` and `DecreasePhi` methods.

```
public void IncreasePhi()
{
    IncreasePhi(CameraDPhi);
}
public void DecreasePhi(double amount)
{
    IncreasePhi(-amount);
}
```

NOTE: Keyboard events are sometimes hard to capture. If a text box or other control that handles keypresses has the focus, that control may process and discard the event before this event handler can see it. If your program has those kinds of controls, you may prefer to not bother with keyboard events and just let the user change the camera position with the mouse.

Scroll Wheel

When the user rolls the mouse wheel, the `SphericalCameraController` class executes the following event handler.

```
// Zoom in or out.
private void WheelControl_PreviewMouseWheel(object sender, MouseWheelEventArgs e)
{
    DecreaseR(Math.Sign(e.Delta) * CameraDR);
    PositionCamera();
}
```

The `e.Delta` parameter indicates the amount by which the scroll wheel was adjusted. The event handler uses the sign of that amount (-1 or +1) and ignores its value. It multiples the sign by `CameraDR` and passes the result to `DecreaseR`.

The method finishes by calling `PositionCamera` to move the camera to its new location.

> **NOTE:** If you have a touchpad or touchscreen, you can place two fingers on the pad or screen and move them farther apart to zoom in. Similarly you can move your fingers closer together to zoom out. The system handles those gestures through the mouse scroll wheel so you don't need to write any extra code to handle them.

Click and Drag

The example program lets the user click and drag to change the camera's position. When the user presses the mouse down, the `SphericalCameraController` class executes the following event handler.

```
// Use the mouse to change the camera's position.
private Point LastPoint;
private void MouseControl_MouseDown(object sender, MouseButtonEventArgs e)
{
    MouseControl.CaptureMouse();
    MouseControl.MouseMove += new MouseEventHandler(MouseControl_MouseMove);
    MouseControl.MouseUp += new MouseButtonEventHandler(MouseControl_MouseUp);
    LastPoint = e.GetPosition(MouseControl);
}
```

The `LastPoint` variable tracks the mouse's last recorded position.

The event handler starts by capturing the mouse so future mouse events go to the `MouseControl UIElement`. (If you don't do this and you click and drag the mouse off of the program, the `MouseControl` doesn't raise its `MouseUp` event to tell the program that the drag is over.)

The code then installs `MouseMove` and `MouseUp` event handlers, and saves the mouse's current location in `LastPoint`.

The following code shows the `MouseMove` event handler.

```
private void MouseControl_MouseMove(object sender, MouseEventArgs e)
{
    const double xscale = 0.1;
    const double yscale = 0.1;

    Point newPoint = e.GetPosition(MouseControl);
    double dx = newPoint.X - LastPoint.X;
    double dy = newPoint.Y - LastPoint.Y;

    CameraTheta -= dx * CameraDTheta * xscale;
    CameraPhi -= dy * CameraDPhi * yscale;

    LastPoint = newPoint;
    PositionCamera();
}
```

This code uses constants `xscale` and `yscale` to reduce the program's sensitivity to the mouse. If you don't use them, the program is extremely sensitive to the mouse's movement, so it's hard to move the camera in a controlled manner. You may want to decrease these scale factors even more if you want to move the camera very precisely.

After defining `xscale` and `yscale`, the event handler gets the mouse's position within the `MouseControl` and determines how much it has moved since the last time its position was recorded. It scales that value, multiples by `CameraDTheta` horizontally and `CameraDPhi` vertically, and updates the camera's θ and φ values. The code finishes by recording the mouse's current position and moving the camera to its new location.

When you finish dragging and release the mouse, the following `MouseUp` event handler executes.

```
private void MouseControl_MouseUp(object sender, MouseButtonEventArgs e)
{
    MouseControl.ReleaseMouseCapture();
    MouseControl.MouseMove -= new MouseEventHandler(MouseControl_MouseMove);
    MouseControl.MouseUp -= new MouseButtonEventHandler(MouseControl_MouseUp);
}
```

This code simply releases the earlier mouse capture and removes the `MouseMove` and `MouseUp` event handlers.

Main Program

The `SphericalCameraController` class is moderately complicated (download the example to see the rest of its details), but using it is relatively simple. The main example program uses the following code to declare a `SphericalCameraController`.

```
// The camera controller.
private SphericalCameraController CameraController = null;
```

The following code initializes the camera and controller.

```
// Define the camera.
private void DefineCamera(Viewport3D viewport)
{
    TheCamera = new PerspectiveCamera();
    TheCamera.FieldOfView = 60;
    CameraController = new SphericalCameraController
        (TheCamera, viewport, this, mainGrid, mainGrid);
}
```

This method creates a new `PerspectiveCamera` and sets its `FieldOfView` property. It then creates the camera controller, passing its constructor the camera and viewport. The program's window (`this`) raises keyboard events, and the program's main `Grid` control (`mainGrid`) raises mouse wheel and mouse movement events.

That's all there is to it! The controller automatically handles the necessary events and moves the camera appropriately. The main program doesn't need to worry about the details.

> **NOTE:** You might want to catch the `Viewport3D` control's mouse events instead of using the `Grid` control. Unfortunately, the `Viewport3D` class doesn't raise its `MouseDown` event unless you click on an object in the scene. If you click on the background, nothing happens.
>
> To work around this problem, the program handles the mouse events raised by its `Grid` control.

Download the SphericalCoordinates example program and give it a try. The events are set up so the mouse and arrow keys seem to manipulate the objects in the scene rather than the camera. You can change the way the event handlers work if you want to change that behavior. Either way, the program is very easy to use and moving the camera around is simple and intuitive.

All in all, this is an extremely easy way to view objects placed at the origin. If the scene is larger and the user needs to move around to view different parts of the scene, you'll need to use a different control method such as those described in the following sections.

Automobile

In this control method, the camera behaves sort of like an automobile. You can use the keyboard to move around in the scene, but the camera always remains on a single plane and always looks forward.

The Up and Down arrow keys move the camera forward and backward. The Left and Right keys rotate the camera to the left and right. You can also use the WASD keys instead of the arrow keys.

Additionally, the Q and E keys allow you to move left or right without rotating the camera. It's as if you're stepping left or right while facing straight ahead.

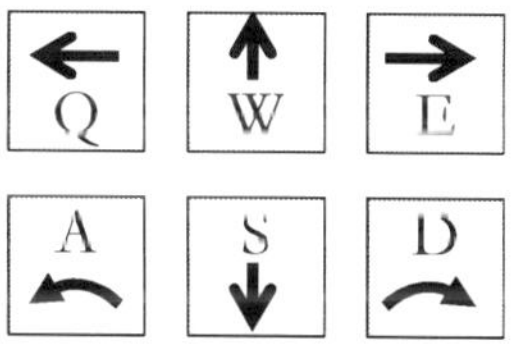

Figure 5-3: Use the arrow keys or the QWEASD keys to move.

Figure 5-3 shows the directions that the QWEASD keys move the camera.

The Automobile example program shown in Figure 5-4 demonstrates this camera control technique.

The `AutomobileCameraController` class acts as a controller for this example. The following code shows how the controller tracks the camera's position and orientation.

```
// The camera.
public PerspectiveCamera TheCamera = null;

// The controls that provide events.
private UIElement KeyboardControl = null;

// Adjustment values.
public double CameraDR = 0.1;
public double CameraDTheta = Math.PI / 30;

// The current position and orientation.
public Point3D CameraPosition { get; set; } = new
Point3D(4, 0.5, 5);
public double CameraTheta = Math.PI * 1.3;
```

Figure 5-4: In this program, the camera points horizontally.

This code is somewhat similar to the previous controller's code. The difference is that this version stores the camera's location in Cartesian coordinates in the variable `CameraPosition`. It also holds the camera's current viewing direction in the variable `CameraTheta`. The camera always points horizontally so this controller doesn't need a `CameraPhi` value.

The following code shows the controller's constructor.

```
// Constructor.
public AutomobileCameraController(PerspectiveCamera camera, Viewport3D viewport,
    UIElement keyboardControl)
{
    TheCamera = camera;
    viewport.Camera = TheCamera;

    KeyboardControl = keyboardControl;
    KeyboardControl.PreviewKeyDown += KeyboardControl_KeyDown;

    PositionCamera();
}
```

This is a bit simpler than the previous controller's constructor because this controller doesn't handle mouse events.

When the user presses a key, the following `KeyboardControl_KeyDown` event handler executes.

```
// Adjust the camera's position.
private void KeyboardControl_KeyDown(object sender, KeyEventArgs e)
{
    switch (e.Key)
    {
        case Key.Left:
```

```
            case Key.A:
                TurnLeft();
                break;
            case Key.Right:
            case Key.D:
                TurnRight();
                break;
            case Key.W:
                MoveForward();
                break;
            case Key.Up:
                TurnUp();
                break;
            case Key.S:
                MoveBackward();
                break;
            case Key.Down:
                TurnDown();
                break;
            case Key.Q:
                MoveLeft();
                break;
            case Key.E:
                MoveRight();
                break;
            case Key.LeftShift:
            case Key.RightShift:
                DoShift();
                break;
            case Key.Space:
                DoSpace();
                break;
        }

        // Update the camera's position.
        PositionCamera();
    }
```

This method checks the key pressed and then calls an appropriate method to update the camera's position and orientation.

The `TurnLeft` and `TurnRight` methods are straightforward. They simply increase or decrease the value `CameraTheta`.

The methods that change the camera's position are a bit more complicated because they depend on the camera's orientation. For example, the following `MoveForward` and `MoveBackward` methods move the camera in whatever direction it is currently facing.

```
    // Update the camera's position.
    protected void MoveForward()
    {
        CameraPosition += AngleToVector(CameraTheta, CameraDTheta);
    }
    protected void MoveBackward()
    {
        CameraPosition += AngleToVector(CameraTheta, -CameraDTheta);
    }
```

These methods use the `AngleToVector` method to get a vector pointing in the direction that the camera is facing. They then simply add or subtract the vector to the camera's position.

The following code shows the `AngleToVector` method.

```
// Convert the angle into a vector.
protected Vector3D AngleToVector(double angle, double length)
{
    return new Vector3D(
        length * Math.Cos(angle), 0, length * Math.Sin(angle));
}
```

This method uses some simple trigonometry to create a vector parallel to the XZ plane that is pointed in the direction that the camera is facing. Figure 5-5 shows how the method performs the calculation.

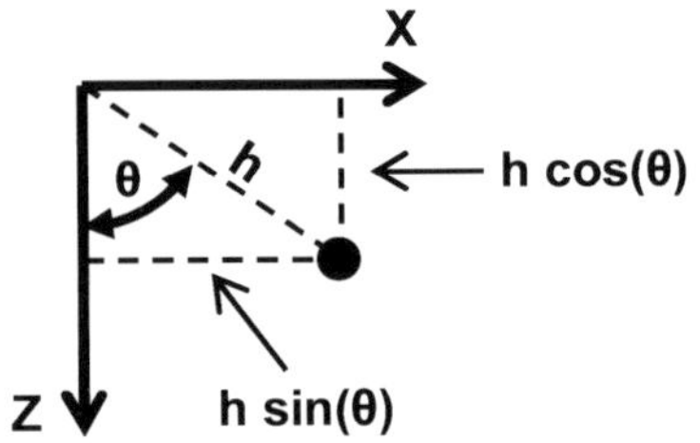

Figure 5-5: The AngleToVector method finds a vector pointing in the camera's direction.

If a point is h units away from the Y axis (which points up out of the page in Figure 5-5), then the point's X coordinate is h sin(θ) and its Z coordinate is h cos(θ). In other words, in two dimensions the vector from the origin to the point is < h sin(θ), h sin(θ)>. The `AngleToVector` method calculates that vector, setting its Y component to 0. It multiplies the vector by its `length` parameter to make the camera move by the desired distance forward or backward.

The following code shows the `MoveLeft` and `MoveRight` methods.

```
protected void MoveLeft()
{
    Vector3D v = AngleToVector(CameraTheta, CameraDR);
    CameraPosition += new Vector3D(v.Z, 0, -v.X);
}
protected void MoveRight()
{
    Vector3D v = AngleToVector(CameraTheta, CameraDR);
    CameraPosition += new Vector3D(-v.Z, 0, +v.X);
}
```

These methods use `AngleToVector` to get a vector pointing in the camera's direction. They then swap the vector's X and Z components and negate one of the components to create a vector perpendicular to the original vector.

NOTE: This is a handy technique for finding perpendicular vectors in two dimensions. To find a perpendicular vector, swap the coordinates and negate one. Figure 5-6 shows the vector <2, 1> and the two perpendicular vectors <1, -2> and <-1, 2>.

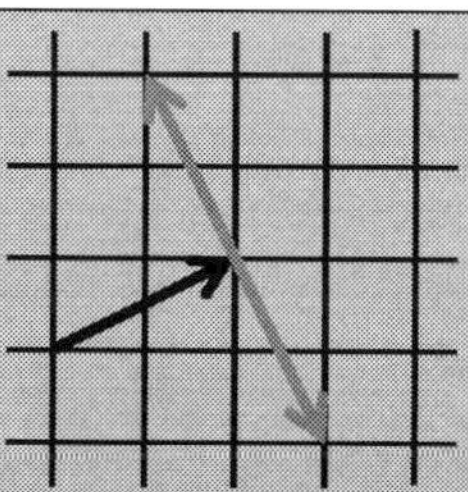

Figure 5-6: To find a perpendicular vector in two dimensions, swap the coordinates and negate one.

Next, the methods add the perpendicular vector to the camera's position to move the camera left or right without changing its orientation.

In this example, the `TurnUp` and `TurnDown` methods, which execute when the user presses the Up or Down arrow keys, simply call the `MoveForward` and `MoveBackward` methods. The controller uses separate methods for these so they can be overridden by a derived controller class later.

Similarly, when the user presses the Shift and Space keys, the program executes the `DoShift` and `DoSpace` methods. In this example, those methods don't do anything. They will be overridden by a later controller class.

The most interesting remaining piece of code used by this controller is the following `PositionCamera` method.

```
// Use the current values of CameraR, CameraTheta,
// and CameraPhi to position the camera.
protected virtual void PositionCamera()
{
    TheCamera.Position = CameraPosition;
    TheCamera.LookDirection = AngleToVector(CameraTheta, 1);
    TheCamera.UpDirection = new Vector3D(0, 1, 0);
}
```

This method sets the camera's position to the location stored in the `CameraPosition` variable. It then uses `AngleToVector` to get a vector pointing in the camera's direction and sets the camera's "look" direction to that vector. It finishes by setting the camera's "up" direction to the vector <0, 1, 0> so the camera is right-side up.

That's all there is to this example. Download it and give it a try.

Mouse

This controller makes the camera behave somewhat like a mouse; the little rodent, not the thing attached to your computer. It's the same as the automobile controller except the camera is also allowed to look upward or downward.

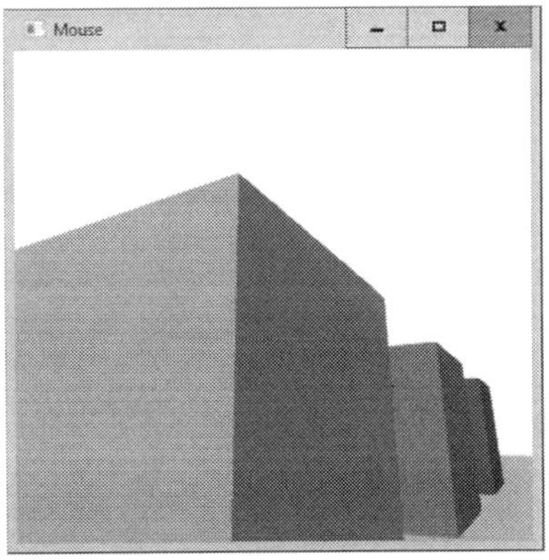

Figure 5-6: The Mouse program lets you look up and down.

You can use the automobile-style code to control the camera's position. The only question is, "How do you control the camera's upward or downward direction?"

The Mouse example program shown in Figure 5-6 uses a new variable `CameraPhi` to keep track of the camera's angle with respect to the Y axis much as the SphericalCoordinates example did.

When you press the Up or Down arrow, the program's `KeyDown` event handler adds or subtracts an appropriate amount to `CameraPhi`.

The following code shows the `MouseCameraController` class that provides this style of camera control.

```
public class MouseCameraController : AutomobileCameraController
{
    // New properties.
    public double CameraPhi = Math.PI / 2;
    public const double CameraDPhi = Math.PI / 30;
    public const double CameraPhiMin = 0.25 * Math.PI;
    public const double CameraPhiMax = 0.75 * Math.PI;

    // Constructor.
    public MouseCameraController(PerspectiveCamera camera, Viewport3D viewport,
        UIElement keyboardControl)
        : base(camera, viewport, keyboardControl)
    {
    }

    // Update the camera's position and orientation.
    protected override void TurnUp()
    {
        CameraPhi -= CameraDPhi;
        if (CameraPhi < CameraPhiMin) CameraPhi = CameraPhiMin;
    }
    protected override void TurnDown()
    {
        CameraPhi += CameraDPhi;
        if (CameraPhi > CameraPhiMax) CameraPhi = CameraPhiMax;
    }

    // Use the current values of CameraX, CameraY, CameraZ,
    // CameraTheta, and CameraPhi to position the camera.
    protected override void PositionCamera()
    {
        TheCamera.Position = CameraPosition;

        Vector3D v = AngleToVector(CameraTheta, 1);
        double y = Math.Cos(CameraPhi);
        TheCamera.LookDirection = new Vector3D(v.X, y, v.Z);
        TheCamera.UpDirection = new Vector3D(0, 1, 0);
    }
}
```

The class is derived from the AutomobileCameraController class so it inherits that class's behavior. It defines new variables to track the CameraPhi value. Its constructor simply invokes the base class constructor.

The class then overrides the AutomobileCameraController class's TurnUp and TurnDown methods. The new versions increase or decrease CameraPhi, checking that it remains within the bounds CameraPhiMin ≤ CameraPhi ≤ CameraPhiMax.

This controller also overrides the previous version of the PositionCamera method. The new version is mostly the same. The only difference is that it adds a Y component to the camera's "look" vector so the camera can look upward or downward.

That's all there is to the Mouse example. There are many other ways you could let the user adjust the value CameraPhi. For example, you could let the mouse change CameraPhi and possibly CameraTheta, as well. Download the example and experiment if you want to try that approach.

Hover

The HoverCameraController class is derived from the MouseCameraController class so it inherits that class's basic abilities. It then adds the ability for the camera to move vertically (in the Y direction). The following code shows the new class.

```
public class HoverCameraController : MouseCameraController
{
    // New properties.
    public const double CameraDY = 0.5;

    // Constructor.
    public HoverCameraController(PerspectiveCamera camera, Viewport3D viewport,
        UIElement keyboardControl)
        : base(camera, viewport, keyboardControl)
    {
    }

    // Update the camera's position and orientation.
    protected override void DoShift()
    {
        CameraPosition = new Point3D(
            CameraPosition.X, CameraPosition.Y - CameraDY, CameraPosition.Z);
    }
    protected override void DoSpace()
    {
        CameraPosition = new Point3D(
            CameraPosition.X, CameraPosition.Y + CameraDY, CameraPosition.Z);
    }
}
```

The class defines a new CameraDY value to indicate the amount by which the camera's Y position should change when the user presses the Shift or Space key. Its constructor simply invokes the base class constructor.

The class then overrides the `DoShift` and `DoSpace` methods so they update the camera's Y position when the user presses Shift or Space.

Those are the only changes needed by this controller. The `PositionCamera` method used by the `MouseCameraController` class still works because both classes store the mouse's position in the variable `CameraPosition`. The new class updates the position in that variable and the `PositionCamera` method uses it as before.

Figure 5-7 shows the Hover example program demonstrating this controller. That program lets you view the scene from any position and from most angles. Its main restriction is that it always orients the camera more or less vertically.

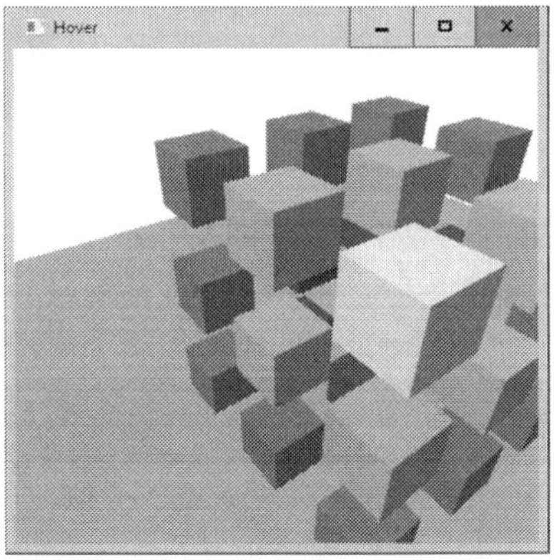

Figure 5-7: The Hover program lets you move the camera up and down.

Summary

The examples described in this chapter demonstrate several ways that you can let the user control the program's camera. The spherical coordinate technique used by the first controller is fairly useful and extremely easy to use, so it's the approach taken by most of the examples described in this book.

The method used by the Hover example is more flexible, allowing you to view the scene from more positions and angles, but it's also a bit harder to use.

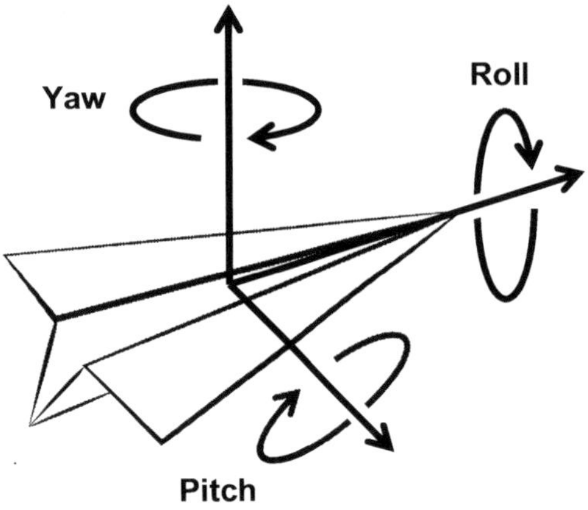

Figure 5-8: A plane's orientation is determined by roll, pitch, and yaw.

Download the examples and see how they work. (And see what they look like in color.) Use the keyboard and mouse to move around and get a feel for the different control methods.

Note that these aren't the only possible control methods. For example, you could emulate an airplane, giving the camera roll, pitch, and yaw settings as shown in Figure 5-8. Or you could emulate a tank where the body moves in one direction while the turret can point in another.

All of these techniques let the user view the scene from different positions. The user won't see anything, however, unless the scene is illuminated. The next chapter explains the light classes that you use to illuminate a scene and make objects visible.

Chapter 6
Lights

At this point, you should be able to define objects and cameras to view them, but without lights you won't see very much. Figure 6-1 shows a scene containing one big cube and three small cubes but no lights. Without any lights, all of the scene's objects are black.

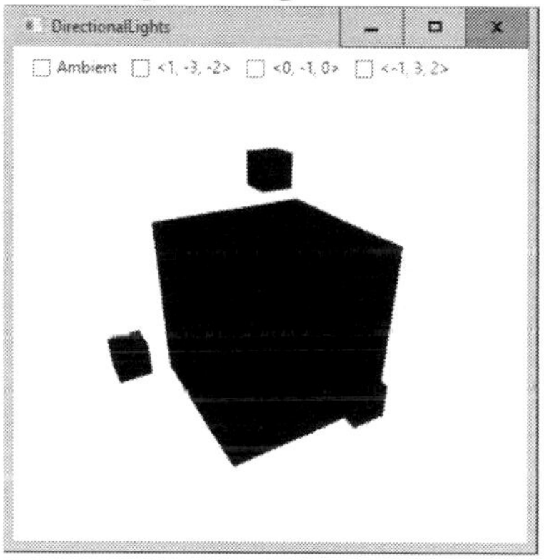

Figure 6-1: You can't see much without lights.

WPF provides four kinds of lights: ambient, directional, point, and spot. The sections in this chapter describe WPF's four light classes and explain how to use them. But first, a word about color.

Color

Three factors determine the final color of an object: the light color, the object's color, and the direction of the light.

Light Color

Lights have a color that consists of red, green, and blue color components. The components can have values between 0 and 255 where 0 means the component isn't present and 255 means the component is as bright as possible.

You can represent a color by giving its red, green, and blue components. For example, the color (255, 0, 0) is red, (0, 0, 0) is black, and (255, 255, 255) is white.

> **NOTE:** The `Color` class that you use to specify colors also includes an *alpha* component, which determines the color's opacity. The value 0 means the color is completely transparent and 255 means it is completely opaque. The alpha component is ignored by lights.

Often scenes use neutral-colored lights so they don't change the objects' basic hues. If you want to use neutral lights, set their red, green, and blue components to the same value. Alternatively, when you specify a light's color, you can use a predefined neutral color such as `Colors.Gray`, `Colors.LightGray`, `Colors.DarkGray`, or `Colors.White`.

You can use any or all of the different kinds of lights in a scene. You can even use multiple instances of the same kind of light. For example, you could use several directional lights that point in different directions.

All of the lights in a scene add up on the surfaces they affect. For example, if you shine two gray lights on the same surface, the result will be brighter than it would be with just one light.

Object Color

A light's color indicates the amounts of red, green, and blue that are available to illuminate objects, but that doesn't mean the objects will use those amounts. For example, a blue cube reflects blue light and absorbs red and green light. That's what makes it blue. If a white light shines on the cube, the cube appears blue.

However, if you shine a red light on the cube, the light doesn't contain any blue light to reflect. The cube absorbs the red light and appears black.

This is why neutral lights (whites and grays) are so useful. They let every object display its underlying hue.

Light Direction

When light strikes a surface, the amount of light that is reflected depends on the angle at which the light hits the surface. If the light hits the surface squarely, the surface it relatively bright. If the light strikes the surface at a shallow angle, the surface appears darker.

> **NOTE:** You can actually test this. Hold a sheet of white paper so it faces a light. Then rotate the paper and watch how its brightness changes. (A good party trick for when you run out of interesting vocabulary words.)

As you'll see shortly, ambient light is directionless, so this doesn't apply to ambient light.

Directional lights do not apply to backfaces as seen from the light. For example, suppose you have a directional light shining on the top of a cube. The cube's bottom is a backface as seen from the light, so the light doesn't affect it.

> **NOTE:** Just because a face is a backface *as seen from the light*, doesn't mean it's a backface *as seen from the camera*. It just means directional light won't affect its color.

To determine the color of a triangle, the graphics system adds up all of the lights hitting that triangle. For each light, it uses the light's direction and the triangle's normal to determine the amount of light present.

> **NOTE:** A *normal* is a vector perpendicular to a surface. Sometimes it is assumed that the normal has length one.

A triangle is flat, so usually it has a single normal that applies across its entire surface. That means the entire triangle is drawn with a single color. This can sometimes cause unexpected results for point and spot lights. (I'll say more about that when I discuss those kinds of lights later in this chapter.)

If you explicitly set normal vectors for the triangle's corners, or if the corners share position entries with other triangles in the mesh, then the triangle's corners make have different normals. In that case, the graphics system uses interpolation to determine the color at points inside the triangle and the triangle may not have a uniform color.

Ambient Light

Ambient light is a directionless light that shines evenly on all of the objects in the scene. In the real world, it's the light that lets you see under your desk even though no light is shining directly under there.

The following code shows how a program can create an ambient light.

```
AmbientLight light = new AmbientLight(Colors.LightGray);
MainGroup.Children.Add(light);
```

The first statement creates the light object and the second adds it to the scene's `Model3DGroup`.

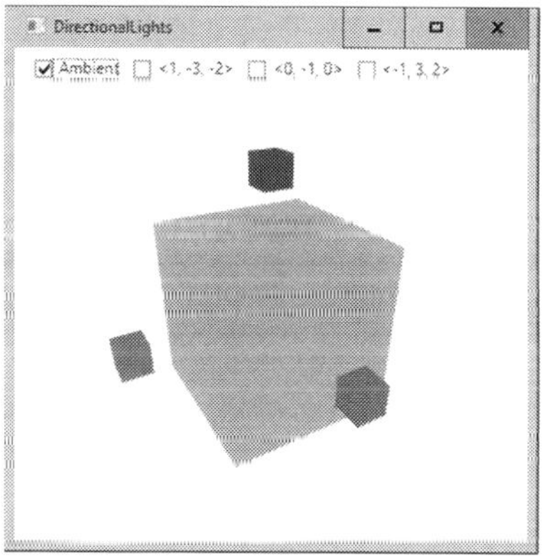

Figure 6-2: Ambient light lets you see the difference between objects with different colors.

You can use ambient light to give objects their basic hues. Figure 6-2 shows the same cubes shown in Figure 6-1, this time illuminated by ambient light. Because the four cubes have different colors, you can see them easily.

Because ambient light is directionless, however, it strikes all of a cube's faces at the same angle so it gives all of the faces the same color. For example, all of the large cube's faces are drawn with the same light blue so you can't see where one face ends and another begins.

You could use different materials or textures

(described in Chapter 7) to give each of the cube's faces a different appearance. In that case, you might need only ambient light.

Alternatively, for scenes such as the one shown in Figure 6-2, you can differentiate the faces by adding some directional light.

Directional Light

A directional light points in a single direction. It's as if it were a light source infinitely far away, much as the sun is for most practical purposes.

The following code shows how a program can create a directional light.

```
DirectionalLight light = new DirectionalLight(Colors.Gray, new Vector3D(-1, -2, -3));
MainGroup.Children.Add(light);
```

The first statement creates the light object pointing in the direction <-1, -2, -3>. The second statement adds it to the scene's `Model3DGroup`.

Because the light shines in a particular direction, surfaces that make different angles with that direction are affected differently. The adjacent faces of a cube point in different directions, so a directional light that shines on them will brighten them by different amounts, and you'll be able to see the edges between them.

Figure 6-3 shows the scene in Figure 6-2 but this time with an ambient light and a directional light. Now you can clearly see the edges between the cubes' sides.

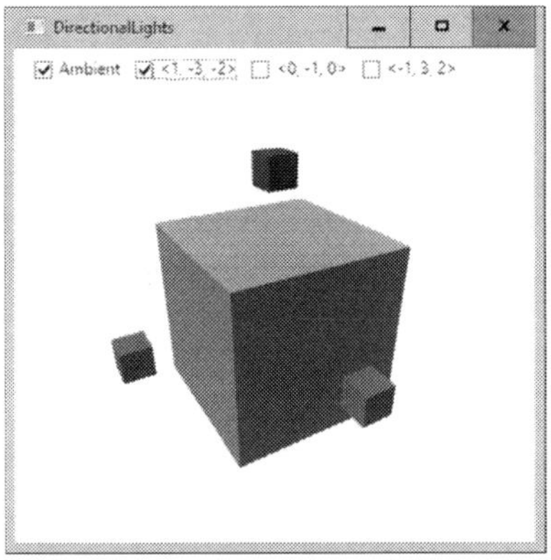

Figure 6-3: Directional lights affect the sides of a cube differently.

There are still some cases where a directional light might not make a cube's faces distinguishable. In particular, if a light strikes multiple faces at the same angle, then it will brighten them by the same amount.

For example, suppose a cube's faces are aligned parallel to the XY, YZ, and XZ coordinate planes. If the light's direction vector has two or three identical components, then it will strike some of the cube's faces at the same angle so, if they have the same material, they will have the same color.

For another example, suppose a scene includes multiple cubes with parallel faces. Then directional lights will strike corresponding faces at the same angle so they will have the same color. (Again assuming the cubes have the same material. Chapter 7 covers materials.) If the cubes overlap as seen from the camera's position, then their faces may blend together.

Figure 6-4 shows both situations. It contains two cubes with faces parallel to the coordinate axes and a light shining in the direction <1, 0, 1>. The light strikes the cube's bold faces at a 45° angle so all of those faces have the same color.

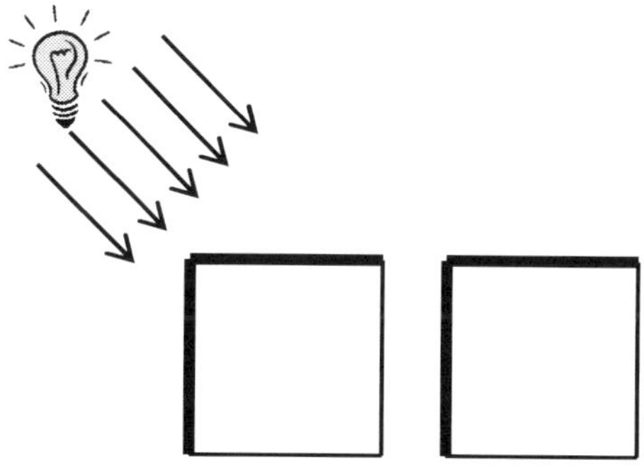

Figure 6-4: This directional light strikes some faces at the same angle.

In this example, you can avoid this problem by giving the light's direction vector different X, Y, and Z components. The light used in Figure 6-3 points in direction <1, -3, -2> so it doesn't have this problem.

Even if the light strikes each face at a different angle, some faces may end up with the same color. Recall that directional lights do not affect backfaces. Figure 6-5 shows the same scene as Figure 6-3 and with the same lights, but viewed from behind. Because directional lights do not affect backfaces, the adjacent cube faces shown in this figure have the same colors.

Figure 6-5: Directional lights do not affect backfaces.

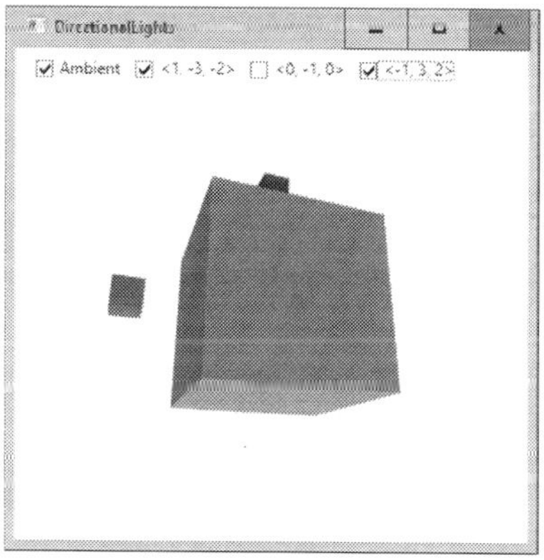

Figure 6-6: A second directional light fills in backfaces.

To avoid this problem, you can use other lights pointing in different directions to illuminate the scene's other faces. Figure 6-6 shows the same view as Figure 6-5 but with an additional directional light.

Often programs use even more lights to highlight surfaces facing in other directions.

If you include too many lights in a scene, you may saturate the objects' colors. For example, suppose you have a red cube and a bright white ambient light. In that case the ambient light provides so much illumination that the cube will be pure red even if there are no other lights in the scene. Adding more lights can't make the cube's sides any brighter, so they will all merge together in a red mass.

Similarly if you have too many directional lights, they will saturate the objects' colors and their faces will blend together.

To avoid this problem, start with less intense lights and gradually add others if you need them.

> **NOTE:** All of the figures in this chapter so far except Figure 6-4 show the DirectionalLights example program. That program lets you selectively turn ambient and directional lights on and off to see the result. You might want to download the example and experiment with it before you move on to learn about other kinds of lights.

Point Light

A point light acts as if it were shining in all directions from a single point. It's as if it were a candle. (Or an arc welder, depending on how bright it is.) The light illuminates nearby surfaces, but it doesn't appear itself, so you don't see a bright spot at the light's position. (More like an invisible candle or arc welder, if that makes any sense.)

The following code shows how a program can create a point light.

```
PointLight light = new PointLight(Colors.White, new Point3D(0, 0, 0));
MainGroup.Children.Add(light);
```

The first statement creates a point light positioned at the origin. The second statement adds it to the scene's `Model3DGroup`.

The PointLights example program shown in Figure 6-7 displays four cubes surrounding the origin and illuminated by ambient light and two directional lights. Figure 6-8 shows the same scene with a point light added at the origin.

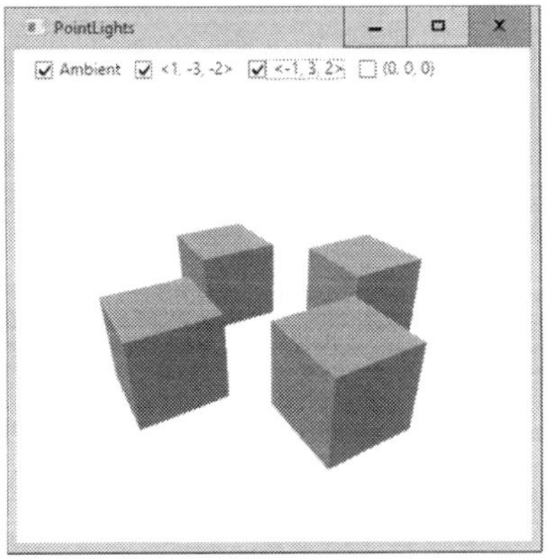

Figure 6-7: This scene has ambient and directional light.

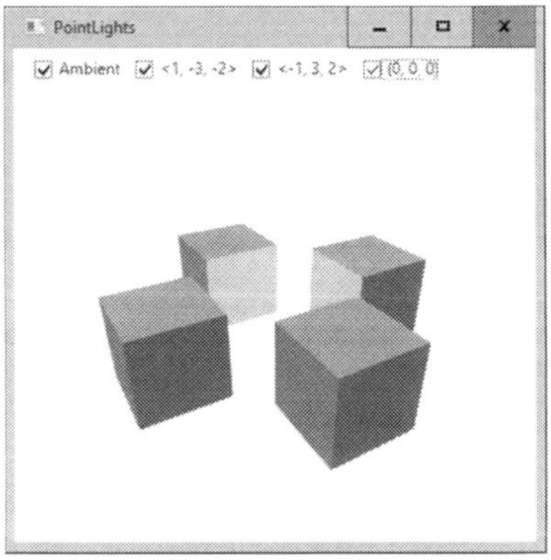

Figure 6-8: Here a point light shines at the origin like a campfire.

The intensity of a point light drops off as you move away from the light. For example, Figure 6-9 shows a rectangle in the XZ plane with $-5 \le \{x, z\} \le 5$ and illuminated by a point light at position (0, 1, 0). The light's illumination decreases as you move away from the light.

The rate at which the light falls off is called its *attenuation*. You can control the attenuation by adjusting the `PointLight` class's `ConstantAttenuation`, `LinearAttenuation`, and `QuadraticAttenuation` properties. The illumination delivered by the light at distance d is divided by the following value.

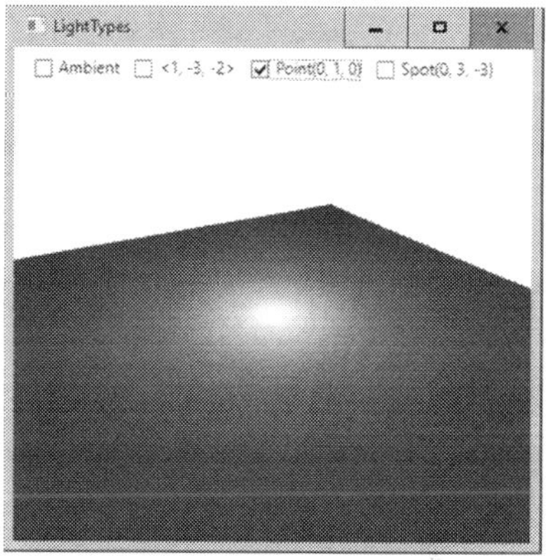

Figure 6-9: A point light's illumination drops off as you move away from it.

$$C + L \cdot d + Q \cdot d^2$$

Here:

- C = `ConstantAttenuation`
- L = `LinearAttenuation`
- Q = `QuadraticAttenuation`

In the real world, light drops off with the square of the distance, which corresponds to the values C = 0, L = 0, and Q = 1.

By default, however, the `PointLight` class sets `ConstantAttenuation` = 1, `LinearAttenuation` = 0, and `QuadraticAttenuation` = 0. The program shown in Figure 6-9 uses those values and it produces a reasonable result. You can tweak the values for your scenes if you like.

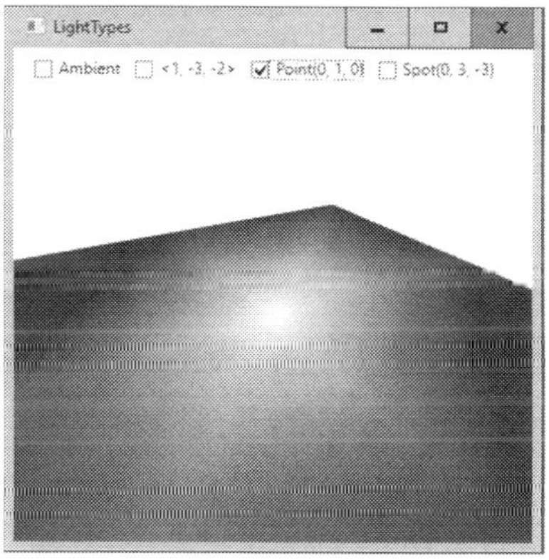

Figure 6-10: Objects near point lights should be made up of small triangles.

The class's `Range` property also affects the light's illumination. The light is completely ignored beyond its `Range`. By default, `Range` is infinity.

Earlier in this chapter, I explained that the graphics system normally calculates a single color for each triangle. This is particularly important for point and spot lights because adjacent triangles may have noticeably different illumination if the triangles are large.

Figure 6-9 shows a smooth dropoff because the rectangle is made up of more than 61,000 tiny triangles. Figure 6-10 shows the same scene built with eight big triangles. If you look closely, you can make out the six triangles that receive the most illumination. You can even make out the edges between the triangles as slightly brighter places. If you use even larger triangles, you might see a single area of uniform brightness, and the result won't look like you're using a point light source at all.

The moral of the story is, if you use point lights (or the spot lights described next), the objects near them must be made up of many small triangles or you won't get the result you expect.

Spot Light

A spot light acts like a real-world spotlight or flashlight. (Or torch if you're British.) Its light expands outward in a cone from a single point.

The following code shows how a program can create a point light.

```
SpotLight light = new SpotLight(Colors.White,
    new Point3D(2, 2, 2), new Vector3D(-2, -2, -2),
    45, 30);
MainGroup.Children.Add(light);
```

The first statement creates a point light positioned at the point (2, 2, 2) and pointing in the direction <-2, -2, -2>. The arguments 45 and 30 set the light's outer and inner cone angles, respectively. I'll say more about them shortly.

The `SpotLight` class is a subclass of the `PointLight` class, so it has many of the same properties including `ConstantAttenuation`, `LinearAttenuation`, `QuadraticAttenuation`, and `Range`.

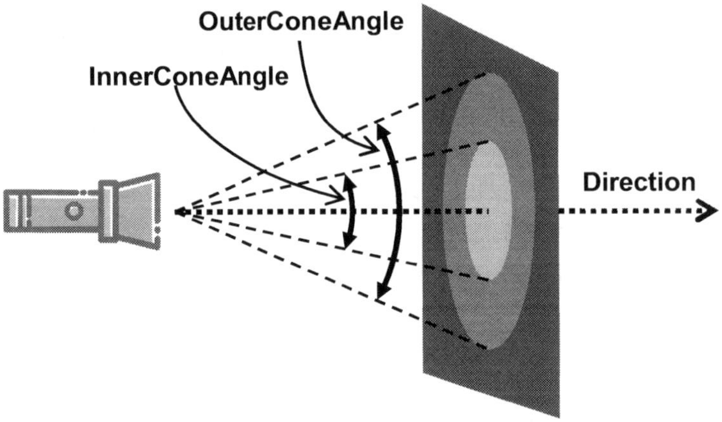

Figure 6-11: `Direction`, `InnerConeAngle`, and `OuterConeAngle` determine where a `SpotLight` shines.

It also has three new properties that define the light's cone of illumination: `Direction`, `InnerConeAngle` and `OuterConeAngle`. The `Direction` property defines the cone's central axis. `InnerConeAngle` determines the angle within which the light has its full intensity. Any points that lie outside of the `OuterConeAngle` receive no light. Figure 6-11 shows how those properties define the light's cone.

The light's inherited attenuation and range properties determine how the light falls off with distance from the light's position.

The `SpotLight` class has two constructors. The first takes no parameters and creates a default light with `InnerConeAngle` = 180 and `OuterConeAngle` = 90. That produces a very bright light with an abrupt cutoff at 90º.

The second constructor takes as parameters a color, position, direction, outer cone angle, and inner cone angle as shown in the earlier code snippet.

The LightTypes example program, which I'll describe in more detail later, creates several kinds of lights including a spot light. The following code shows how it creates its spot light.

```
SpotLight light = new SpotLight(Colors.White,
    new Point3D(0, 3, -3), new Vector3D(0, -3, 3),
    45, 30);
MainGroup.Children.Add(light);
```

The first statement creates a light at position (0, 3, -1) and shining in direction <0, -3, 3>, with outer cone angle 45º and inner cone angle 30º. The second statement adds the light to the scene's `Model3DGroup`.

Figure 6-12 shows this light shining on a rectangle in the XZ plane. In this example, the direction does not point squarely at the surface so the result is an ellipse not a circle.

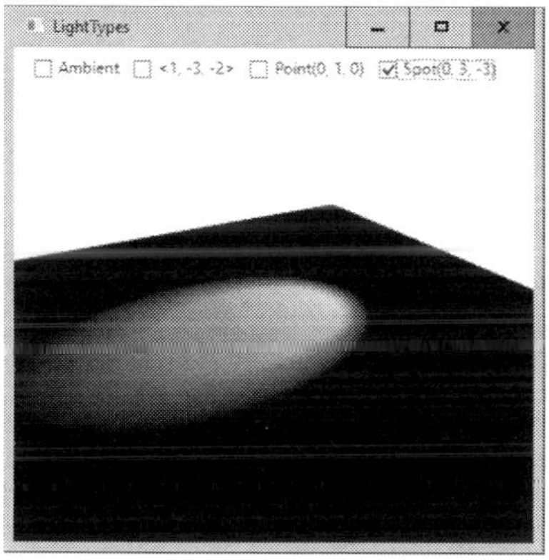

Figure 6-12: A spot light shining at an angle illuminates an ellipse.

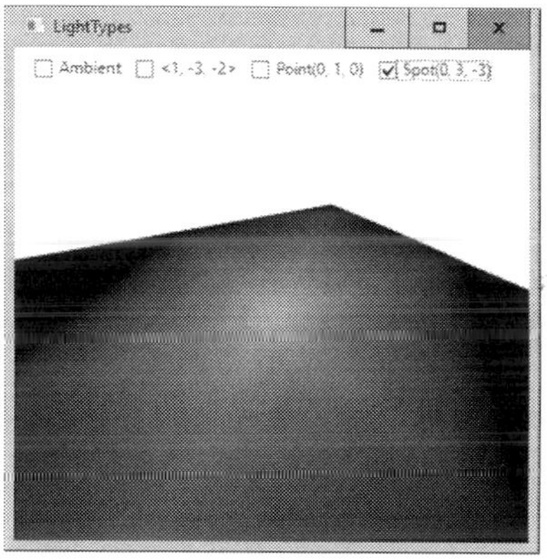

Figure 6-13: Objects near spot lights must be made up of small triangles.

If you look closely at Figure 6-12, you can see the inner cone area that receives full illumination, the outer cone area where illumination drops off, and the areas outside of the outer cone that receive no illumination at all.

As is the case with point lights, the size of the triangles near a spot light makes a difference. The surface shown in Figure 6-12 uses many tiny triangles. In contrast, Figure 6-13 shows the same scene built with only eight triangles. Because the triangles are large, the result doesn't show the normal dropoff that you would expect from a spot light. As with point lights, you should use many small triangles near a spot light.

Figures 6-9, 6-10, 6-12, and 6-13 all show the LightTypes example program. That program lets you enable or disable ambient, directional, point, and spot lights so you can see their effects.

Example Program Techniques

The example programs used in this chapter use a couple of handy techniques. The following section explains how the LightTypes example program builds its rectangle. The section after that describes the way that all three of the examples used in this chapter allow the user to turn lights on and off at runtime.

Building a Rectangle

The LightTypes program shown in Figures 6-9, 6-10, 6-12, and 6-13 uses the following code to draw a rectangle in the XZ plane.

```
// Define the model.
private void DefineModel(Model3DGroup group)
{
    // Make a floor containing a bunch of rectangles.
    MeshGeometry3D mesh = new MeshGeometry3D();
    double dx = 0.1;
    double dz = 0.1;
    for (double x = -5; x < 5; x += dx)
    {
        for (double z = -5; z < 5; z += dz)
        {
            Point3D p1 = new Point3D(x, 0, z);
            Point3D p2 = new Point3D(x, 0, z + dz);
            Point3D p3 = new Point3D(x + dx, 0, z + dz);
            Point3D p4 = new Point3D(x + dx, 0, z);
            AddRectangle(mesh, p1, p2, p3, p4);
        }
    }
    DiffuseMaterial material = new DiffuseMaterial(Brushes.White);
    GeometryModel3D model = new GeometryModel3D(mesh, material);
    group.Children.Add(model);
}
```

This code loops variables `x` and `z` through values between -5 and 5. For each `x/z` pair, the code defines four points with Y coordinate 0 and calls the `AddRectangle` method described next to create a rectangle using those points as corners.

You can change the `dx` and `dz` values to make the program create more or fewer triangles.

After it creates all of the rectangles, the code gives the mesh a material and adds it to the program's `Model3DGroup`.

The following code shows the `AddRectangle` method.

```
// Add a rectangle to the mesh.
private void AddRectangle(MeshGeometry3D mesh,
    Point3D p1, Point3D p2, Point3D p3, Point3D p4)
{
    int index = mesh.Positions.Count;
    mesh.Positions.Add(p1);
    mesh.Positions.Add(p2);
    mesh.Positions.Add(p3);
    mesh.Positions.Add(p4);

    mesh.TriangleIndices.Add(index);
    mesh.TriangleIndices.Add(index + 1);
    mesh.TriangleIndices.Add(index + 2);

    mesh.TriangleIndices.Add(index);
    mesh.TriangleIndices.Add(index + 2);
    mesh.TriangleIndices.Add(index + 3);
}
```

This method records the index that the mesh's next `Positions` entry will have. It then adds the four points to the mesh's `Positions` list.

The code finishes by adding entries to the mesh's `TriangleIndices` list to define the new rectangle's two triangles.

Note that the method assumes that the points actually define a rectangle. If they are not coplanar, then the result is two triangles that define a bent rectangle or a sort of potato chip shape.

Turning Lights On and Off

All three of the examples used by this chapter (the DirectionalLights, LightTypes, and PointLights programs) allow the user to turn lights on and off at runtime.

First the programs' XAML code adds room for the `CheckBox` controls that will control the lights. The following XAML code shows how the `LightTypes` program defines its user interface.

```
<Window x:Class="LightTypes.MainWindow"
        ...
        Title="LightTypes"
        Height="400" Width="400"
        Loaded="Window_Loaded"
        PreviewKeyDown="Window_KeyDown"
        PreviewMouseWheel="Window_PreviewMouseWheel"
    >
    <Grid>
        <Grid.RowDefinitions>
            <RowDefinition Height="30"/>
            <RowDefinition/>
        </Grid.RowDefinitions>
        <Grid.Resources>
            <Style TargetType="CheckBox">
                <Setter Property="Margin" Value="10,0,0,0"/>
            </Style>
```

```
        </Grid.Resources>

        <StackPanel Grid.Row="0" Name="lightStackPanel"
            Orientation="Horizontal" Margin="4" VerticalAlignment="Center">
        </StackPanel>

        <Border Name="MainBorder" Grid.Row="1" Background="White"
            MouseDown="MainBorder_MouseDown">
            <Viewport3D Name="mainViewport"/>
        </Border>
    </Grid>
</Window>
```

This code gives the program's main `Grid` control two rows. The first contains a `StackPanel` named `lightStackPanel` that holds the `CheckBox` controls. The second row contains the `Viewport3D` object that will display the three-dimensional scene.

When the program starts, the following method creates the lights.

```
// Define the lights.
private void DefineLights(Model3DGroup group)
{
    // Make the lights.
    MakeAmbientLight(Colors.Gray);
    MakeDirectionalLight(Colors.Gray, 1, -3, -2);
    MakePointLight(Colors.White, 0, 1, 0);
    MakeSpotLight(Colors.White,
        0, 3, -3,
        0, -3, 3,
        45, 30);
}
```

This method simply calls the `MakeAmbientLight`, `MakeDirectionalLight`, `MakePointLight`, and `MakeSpotLight` methods to do all of the real work. The following code shows the `MakeDirectionalLight` method. The other methods that create lights are similar.

```
// Make a new directional light and give it a CheckBox.
private void MakeDirectionalLight(Color color, double x, double y, double z)
{
    MakeLightCheckbox(
        new DirectionalLight(color, new Vector3D(x, y, z)),
        $"<{x}, {y}, {z}>");
}
```

This method uses its parameters to create a new `DirectionalLight` and passes it to the following `MakeLightCheckbox` method.

```
// Make a CheckBox for a light.
private void MakeLightCheckbox(Light light, string caption)
{
    CheckBox chk = new CheckBox();
    chk.Tag = light;
    chk.Content = caption;
    chk.Click += DisplayLights;

    lightStackPanel.Children.Add(chk);
```

```
    }
```

This method creates a new CheckBox control and saves the newly created light in its Tag property. It sets the control's caption and registers the DisplayLights method described shortly to handle its Click event. The method finishes by adding the new CheckBox to the StackPanel that was created by the program's XAML code.

When the user clicks one of the CheckBox controls, the following DisplayLights method executes.

```
    // Display the selected the lights.
    private void DisplayLights(object sender, RoutedEventArgs e)
    {
        // Display the selected lights.
        foreach (CheckBox chk in lightStackPanel.Children)
        {
            ShowOrHideLight(chk.Tag as Light, chk.IsChecked.Value);
        }
    }
```

This method simply loops through the CheckBox controls inside the program's StackPanel. It gets each control's light from its Tag property and passes the light plus an indication of whether the light should be displayed into the following ShowOrHideLight method.

```
    // Show or hide this light.
    private void ShowOrHideLight(Light light, bool show)
    {
        if (show)
        {
            // Show it if necessary.
            if (!MainGroup.Children.Contains(light))
                MainGroup.Children.Add(light);
        }
        else
        {
            // Hide it if necessary.
            if (MainGroup.Children.Contains(light))
                MainGroup.Children.Remove(light);
        }
    }
```

This method checks the show parameter to see whether the light should be used. If the light should be used, the code checks whether the main Model3DGroup contains the light. If the light isn't in the group, the code adds it.

If the light should not be used, the code checks whether the main Model3DGroup contains the light. If the light is in the group, the code removes it.

Download the example programs to see additional details. You may also want to spend some time experimenting with the examples. Add some more cubes, rectangles, or lights. Try adding some point and spot lights near large and small triangles. You could also experiment with colors. For example, see what happens if three spot lights with different colors shine so their illumination cones overlap.

Efficiency

There's one more topic that I want to cover in this chapter: efficiency.

First, note that there's no real reason to add more than one ambient light to a scene. Because ambient light affects all surfaces equally, adding multiple ambient lights is equivalent to adding one brighter light. Instead of using several lights, use a single light that has their combined color components.

Black lights are also unnecessary. In the real world, black lights may make fluorescent objects glow, but in WPF a light with no color doesn't contribute to the scene. It does require extra computation, however, so leave it out.

When you use the other kinds of lights (directional, point, or spot), a triangle's illumination depends on the angle at which the light strikes the triangle. That means the graphics system needs to perform calculations for every pair of light and triangle. If you have one light and 100 triangles, that's 100 sets of calculations. If you add a second light, that adds another 100 sets of calculations.

WPF's drawing system is pretty fast and can sometimes take advantage of hardware acceleration, so you don't need to be too stingy with lights, but the more lights you use the longer it takes to render a scene.

> **NOTE:** The Microsoft article "Maximize WPF 3D Performance" at `tinyurl.com/yaf7kkdq` says you shouldn't exceed 110 directional lights, 70 point lights, or 40 spot lights or you'll pay an extra penalty in performance due to software emulation.

Finally, different kinds of lights have different efficiencies. Ambient light is the most efficient because it applies no matter how the triangles are oriented. Directional light is the next most efficient because it's light strikes all of the parts of a triangle at the same angle.

Point lights require more calculation and spot lights require even more. Those kinds of lights also require you to use lots of relatively small triangles to produce a nice result, and that may make your scene even slower.

Usually you can use a fair number of lights with assorted types, but try not to go completely crazy.

> **NOTE:** I worked on a Unity project that used a beautiful science-fictiony space station. It was assembled out of smaller components such as walls, floors, doors, control panels, and other pieces.
>
> Unfortunately, the person who built the pieces had included point and spot lights inside the pieces to make them look good. When the pieces were added to the bigger model, they each included their own lights and the resulting scene contained thousands of lights. The final model was huge, slow to load, and slow to run.
>
> Fortunately, the point and spot lights had only slight local effects, so removing them didn't make much difference to the final result.

Summary

Most scenes use an ambient light and two or more directional lights. Lights pointed in the directions <1, -3, -2> and <-1, 3, 2> often produce a reasonable result, at least for objects that are more or less oriented parallel to the XY, YZ, and XZ planes.

Download this chapter's example programs and give them a try. See what happens if you add or remove lights from the scenes. Also make other changes and see what happens.

Lights play an important role an object's final color, but the object's material is also key. A green light will never make a blue object appear green.

The next chapter explains how you can use materials to change an object's appearance. Materials let you change an object's color, brightness, shininess, and texture.

Chapter 7
Materials

As Chapter 6 explained, an object's final appearance depends on both the lights illuminating it and on its material. The examples so far have used relatively simple diffuse materials, but WPF provides three different material classes: `DiffuseMaterial`, `SpecularMaterial`, `EmissiveMaterial`.

Each of those types of materials can also be used with different kinds of brushes. WPF defines six brush types (`SolidColorBrush`, `LinearGradientBrush`, `RadialGradientBrush`, `ImageBrush`, `DrawingBrush`, and `VisualBrush`), so there are 18 possible combinations of materials and brushes.

This chapter describes the different material types and explains how you can use them to change the appearance of objects in your three-dimensional scenes.

Drawing Surfaces

The Materials example program used in this chapter displays the parabolic surface shown in Figure 7-1. The following equation defines the surface mathematically.

$$y = 2 - \frac{x^2 + z^2}{5}$$

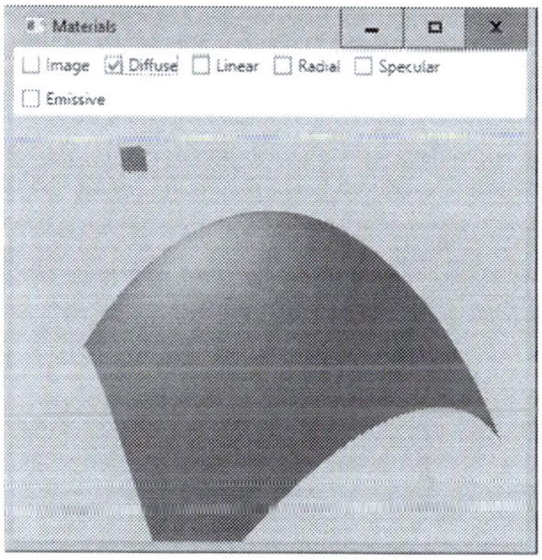

Figure 7-1: This example displays a parabolic surface.

Before I describe the different kinds of materials, I want to explain how the example program works. You've seen many of the details before, but two features are worth covering. The following section explain how the program lets the user select materials. The section after that explains how the program creates its surface.

Selecting Materials

You can use the program's checkboxes to determine which materials apply to the surface.

The program manages its checkboxes by using a technique similar to the one used by the example programs in Chapter 6 to let you select lights. In this example, the program's XAML code defines a `WrapPanel` control named `materialWrapPanel`.

When the it starts, the program creates various materials and adds checkboxes to the WrapPanel to represent them. The following AddMaterial method takes as parameters a material and its caption, and uses them to create a checkbox.

```
// Add a material and its CheckBox.
private void AddMaterial(Material material, string caption)
{
    CheckBox rad = new CheckBox();
    rad.Tag = material;
    rad.Content = caption;
    rad.Click += UseMaterials;

    materialWrapPanel.Children.Add(rad);
}
```

The method first creates a new CheckBox control and saves the material in the control's Tag property. It sets the checkbox's caption and registers the UseMaterials method to handle the control's Click event. It then adds the CheckBox to the materialWrapPanel control.

When you check or uncheck one of the checkboxes, the following UseMaterials event handler executes.

```
// Use the selected materials.
private void UseMaterials(object sender, RoutedEventArgs e)
{
    // Remove the existing model.
    MainGroup.Children.Remove(SurfaceModel);

    // Make a new MaterialGroup holding the selected materials.
    MaterialGroup group = new MaterialGroup();
    foreach (CheckBox chk in materialWrapPanel.Children)
    {
        if (chk.IsChecked.Value)
            group.Children.Add(chk.Tag as Material);
    }

    // Add a new model using the new material.
    SurfaceModel = new GeometryModel3D(SurfaceMesh, group);
    MainGroup.Children.Add(SurfaceModel);
}
```

This method removes the GeometryModel3D that holds the surface from the main Model3DGroup. It then creates a new MaterialGroup to hold all of the materials that are checked.

It is important that the code uses a group instead of a single material in this step. You could add a single material to the model, but the specular and emissive material types described later don't work very well by themselves. Usually you combine them with a diffuse material. The MaterialGroup class allows you to combine several materials.

After it creates the MaterialGroup, the code loops through the checkboxes in the materialWrapPanel and adds the selected materials to the MaterialGroup.

The code then uses the `MaterialGroup` to create a new `GeometryModel3D` for the surface and adds it to the main `Model3DGroup`.

Drawing the Surface

The following method creates triangles to represent a surface defined by a mathematical function.

```
// Add a surface to the mesh.
private void AddSurface(MeshGeometry3D mesh,
    double xmin, double zmin, double xmax, double zmax,
    int numx, int numz, Func<double, double, double> F)
{
    double dx = (xmax - xmin) / numx;
    double dz = (zmax - zmin) / numz;

    // Make the points.
    double x = xmin;
    for (int i = 0; i <= numx; i++)
    {
        double z = zmin;
        for (int j = 0; j <= numz; j++)
        {
            double y = F(x, z);
            mesh.Positions.Add(new Point3D(x, y, z));
            mesh.TextureCoordinates.Add(
                new Point(x / (xmax - xmin), z / (zmax - zmin)));
            z += dz;
        }
        x += dx;
    }

    // Make the triangles.
    for (int i = 0; i < numx; i++)
    {
        for (int j = 0; j < numz; j++)
        {
            int i1 = i * (numz + 1) + j;
            int i2 = i1 + 1;
            int i3 = i2 + (numz + 1);
            int i4 = i3 - 1;
            mesh.TriangleIndices.Add(i1);
            mesh.TriangleIndices.Add(i2);
            mesh.TriangleIndices.Add(i3);

            mesh.TriangleIndices.Add(i1);
            mesh.TriangleIndices.Add(i3);
            mesh.TriangleIndices.Add(i4);
        }
    }
}
```

This method takes as parameters the mesh that should contain the surface, the X and Z bounds for the surface, the number of divisions the method should use in the X and Z directions, and the function `F` that defines the surface. This example uses the following function to implement the equation shown earlier.

```
// Return a function F(x, z);
private double F(double x, double z)
{
    return 2 - (x * x + z * z) / 5;
}
```

The `AddSurface` method first calculates values `dx` and `dz` to divide the indicated area into the desired number of pieces. The code then loops over the X and Z values, creating the points that will define the surface's triangles.

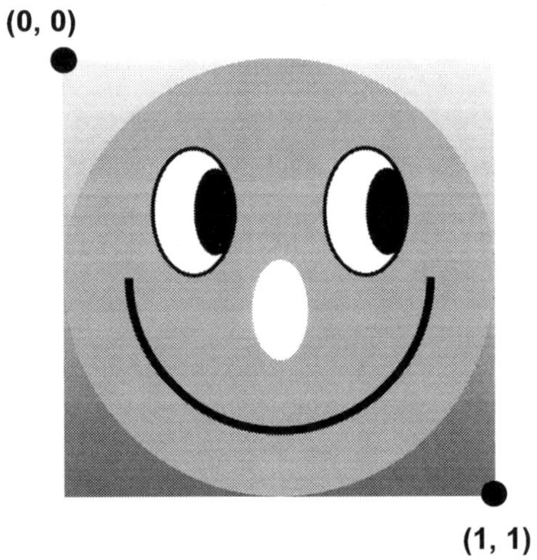

Figure 7-2: Texture coordinates range from (0, 0) in the upper left to (1, 1) in the lower right.

The code also adds *texture coordinates* for each of the points. These indicate the part of the material where the points should be mapped, if the material has some sort of texture or non-uniform brush.

If the material has a single, simple color, such as blue, then every point on the surface will be blue. However, if the material includes an image, color gradient, or pattern, then the texture coordinates indicate the part of that pattern that should be mapped to each point.

Texture coordinates start with the point (0, 0) in the upper left and end with (1, 1) in the lower right as shown in Figure 7-2.

The `AddSurface` method defines texture coordinates to space the points on the surface evenly across the range (0, 0) to (1, 1).

NOTE: Usually texture coordinates are considered to be U and V values instead of X and Y values, probably to avoid confusion when orienting objects in XYZ-space.

After it defines the points and their texture coordinates, the `AddSurface` method sets `TriangleIndices` values to define the surface's triangles.

NOTE: Calculating the points' indices is nothing more than careful counting and a little math, but it's still kind of tricky. In Part II od the book, I'll describe a method that makes this a lot easier, albeit a bit less efficient.

Diffuse Materials

In *diffuse reflection*, light is scattered in all directions and the brightness of the light depends on the angle at which the light strikes the object. If the light strikes the object squarely, the result is fairly bright. If the light strikes the object at a shallow angle, the result is relatively dim.

A diffuse material models diffuse reflection. It's what gives an object most of its color.

The Materials example program lets you create diffuse materials that use several different kinds of brushes. The following sections explain how it uses each type of brush.

Solid Brush

The following code snippet shows how a C# program can apply a solid diffuse material to a mesh.

```
DiffuseMaterial material = new DiffuseMaterial(Brushes.White);
GeometryModel3D model = new GeometryModel3D(mesh, material);
group.Children.Add(model);
```

The first statement makes a `DiffuseMaterial` object, passing a white brush into its constructor. If you want the object to have a single color, use a solid brush, as in this example.

The next statement creates a new `GeometryModel3D` object, passing its constructor the mesh and the material. The final statement adds the new model to the program's main `Model3DGroup`.

Figure 7-3 shows the Materials example program displaying its surface with a solid-colored diffuse material. (It's light blue when you see it in color.)

The program uses a medium gray ambient light and a gray point light. The small cube in the upper left (which is yellow when you run the program) marks the position of the point light. In Figure 7-3, you can see a bright spot on the surface below the point light.

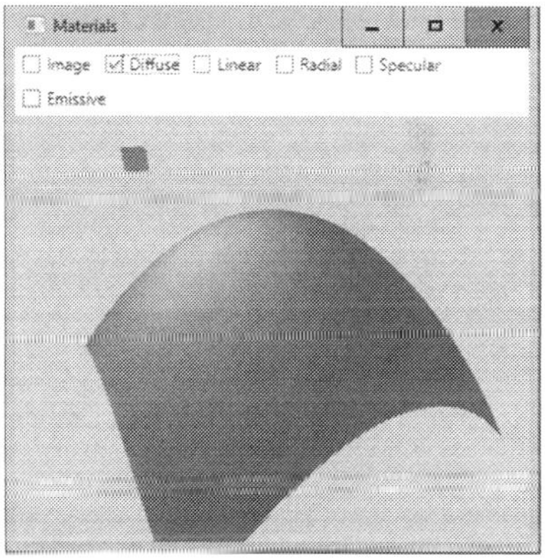

Figure 7-3: Check Diffuse to use a `SolidColorBrush`.

Image Brush

Figure 7-4 shows the Materials program using an `ImageBrush`. The following code adds the `ImageBrush` to the program's checkboxes.

```
ImageBrush smileyBrush = new ImageBrush();
smileyBrush.ImageSource = new BitmapImage(new Uri("Smiley.png", UriKind.Relative));
```

```
AddMaterial(new DiffuseMaterial(smileyBrush), "Image");
```

The first statement creates a new `ImageBrush` object.

Assigning images to brushes in WPF is a bit awkward. The second statement creates a `Uri` (Universal Resource Identifier) to indicate the location of the file `Smiley.png`. To ensure that this file is located where the executable program is running, I added it to the project at design time by selecting Project ➤ Add Existing Item, selecting the file, and clicking Add. Then I selected the file in Project Explorer, set its Build Action property to Content, and set its Copy to Output Directory property to Copy if Newer. Now when I run the program from within Visual Studio, Visual Studio copies `Smiley.png` into the executable directory before running the program so the file is where it needs to be at run time.

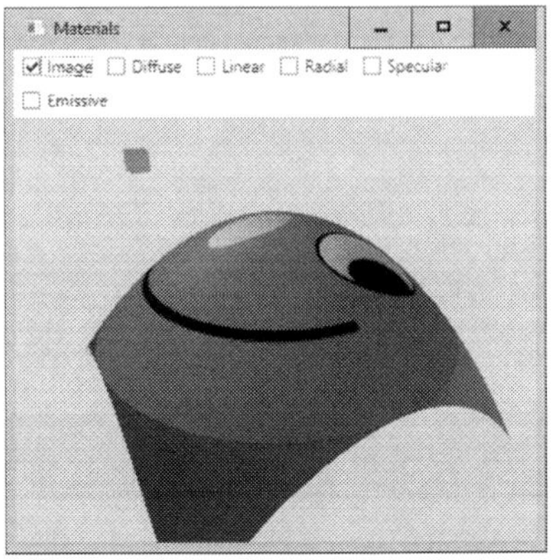

Figure 7-4: Check Image to use an `ImageBrush`.

The second line in the preceding code sets the brush's `ImageSource` property to the URI so it knows what image to use.

The third line of code creates a new `DiffuseMaterial`, passing its constructor the `ImageBrush`. It passes the material to the `AddMaterial` method described earlier to create the appropriate checkbox.

Linear Gradient Brush

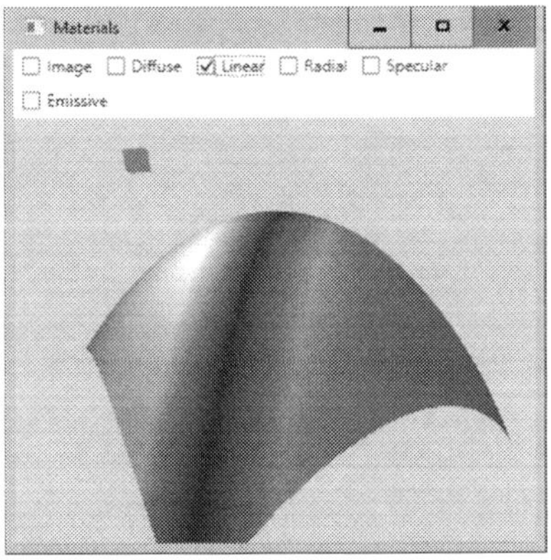

Figure 7-5: Check Linear to use a `LinearGradientBrush`.

Figure 7-5 shows the Materials program using a `LinearGradientBrush`. The following code snippet shows how the program creates this material.

```
LinearGradientBrush linear =
    new LinearGradientBrush();
linear.GradientStops.Add(new GradientStop(Colors.Blue, 0.0));
linear.GradientStops.Add(new GradientStop(Colors.White, 0.4));
linear.GradientStops.Add(new GradientStop(Colors.Green, 0.5));
linear.GradientStops.Add(new GradientStop(Colors.White, 0.6));
linear.GradientStops.Add(new GradientStop(Colors.Red, 1.0));
linear.StartPoint = new Point(1, 0);
linear.EndPoint = new Point(0, 1);
AddMaterial(new DiffuseMaterial(linear), "Linear");
```

This code creates a new `LinearGradientBrush`. It then defines gradient stops to make the gradient shade through the colors blue, white, green, white, and red.

Next, the code indicates the points in texture coordinates where the gradient should start and end. Normally this should match up with the values assigned to the points' `TextureCoordinates`. If the values don't match up, then either the material won't use the entire gradient or points assigned beyond the edges of the gradient will use the gradient's edge values. For example, a point with `TextureCoordinates` beyond the blue edge of the gradient would be blue.

The code then creates a new `DiffuseMaterial`, passing its constructor the gradient brush. It finishes by calling the `AddMaterial` method to create the material's checkbox.

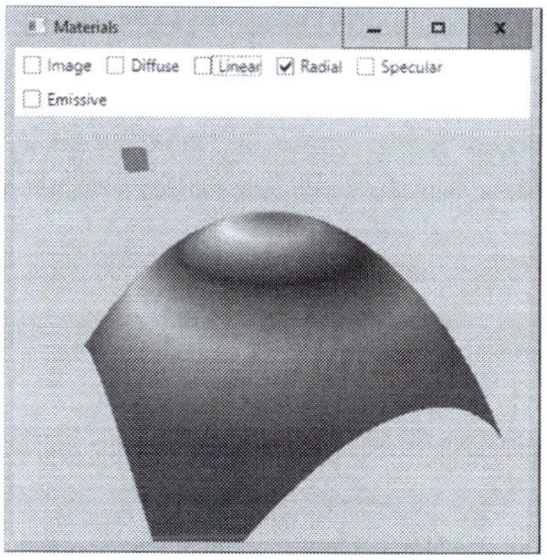

Figure 7-6: Check Radial to use a RadialGradientBrush

Radial Gradient Brush

Figure 7-6 shows the Materials program using a `RadialGradientBrush`. The following code snippet shows how the program creates this material.

```
RadialGradientBrush radial = new RadialGradientBrush();
radial.GradientStops.Add(new GradientStop(Colors.Blue, 0.0));
radial.GradientStops.Add(new GradientStop(Colors.White, 0.25));
radial.GradientStops.Add(new GradientStop(Colors.Green, 0.5));
radial.GradientStops.Add(new GradientStop(Colors.White, 0.75));
radial.GradientStops.Add(new GradientStop(Colors.Red, 1.0));
AddMaterial(new DiffuseMaterial(radial), "Radial");
```

This code creates a new `RadialGradientBrush` and makes it shade radially through the colors blue, white, green, white, and red.

A `RadialGradientBrush` object's `Center` property determines the center of the gradient. The program leaves this at its default value (0.5, 0.5).

The brush's `Radius` property determines how wide the gradient is. The program leaves this at its default value 0.5, so the gradient covers the area (0, 0) to (1, 1).

Next, the code creates a `DiffuseMaterial`, passing its constructor the gradient brush. It finishes by calling the `AddMaterial` method to create the material's checkbox.

Most of an object's appearance comes from diffuse materials, but specular and emissive materials can add a bit of extra refinement when used in conjunction with diffuse materials. The following sections describe those kinds of materials.

Specular Material

In *specular reflection*, a shiny object reflects light mostly in the surface's mirror direction. The *mirror direction* is the direction in which light would be reflected by a perfectly reflective mirror.

Figure 7-7 shows light striking point A on an object. The light strikes the surface making *incident angle* θ_i with the object's *normal* (the dashed line perpendicular to the object) at that point. If the object were a perfect mirror, then the light would reflect in the direction of the *angle of reflection* θ_r.

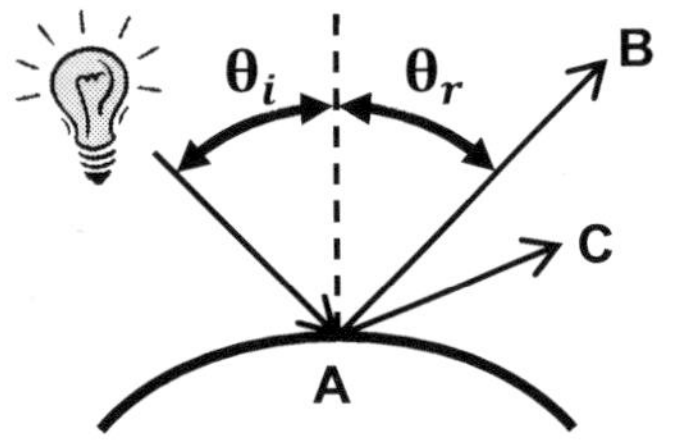

Figure 7-7: Specular reflection is greatest along the mirror angle.

The law of reflection states that, for a perfect mirror, the angle of reflection is the same as the angle of incidence. (That's why the angle of reflection is sometimes called the *mirror angle*.)

With specular reflection, most of the light is reflected along the mirror angle. The farther from the mirror angle a viewing position is, the less light it receives from that point on the object.

For example, in Figure 7-7 point B lies along the mirror angle so it receives a lot of reflected light. Point C lies farther from the mirror angle so it receives less reflected light.

Exactly how tightly the light is reflected along the mirror angle depends on the object's shininess. A highly polished apple might reflect the light mostly along the mirror angle, making a small but bright highlight. A well-worn baseball might reflect light over a wide area so it would create little if any bright spot.

To use specular reflection in WPF, create a material group and add a diffuse material to it. Then create a specular material and add it to the group.

> **NOTE:** The order in which you add materials to the group is important because WPF's drawing system uses the materials in order. If you add the specular material first, then the later diffuse material will cover it up so you won't see it.

The following code shows how the Materials example program creates its specular material.

```
AddMaterial(new SpecularMaterial(Brushes.LightBlue, 100), "Specular");
```

This code creates a `SpecularMaterial` object, passing its constructor a light blue solid brush. The value 100 is the *specular exponent* or *Phong exponent*, which determines how tightly focused the specular highlight is. A larger value makes the object shinier, so the highlight is relatively small and bright. A smaller value makes the object less shiny and the highlight is spread over a wider area.

> **NOTE:** To understand exactly how the specular exponent works requires some pretty involved mathematics, so I'm not going to cover it here. If you want to see the details, read the Wikipedia article "Specular highlight" at `tinyurl.com/ybhdum6c`.

After it creates the material, the code calls `AddMaterial` to create its checkbox.

Figure 7-8 shows the Materials example program displaying a diffuse material made with a solid brush combined with a specular material. If you compare this to Figure 7-3, you'll see that the specular material added a bright highlight.

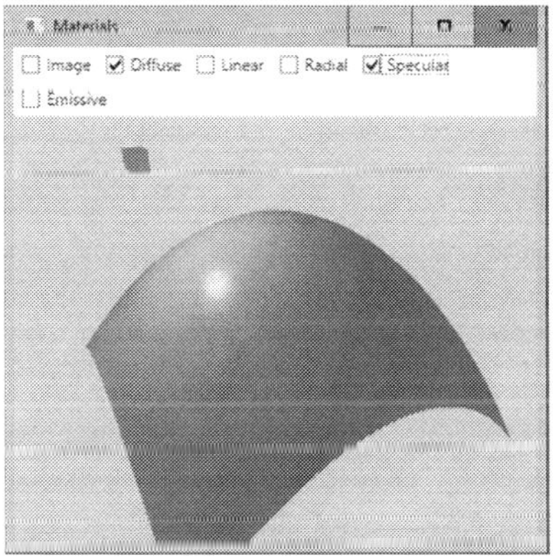

Figure 7-8: This scene uses a solid-colored diffuse material plus a specular material.

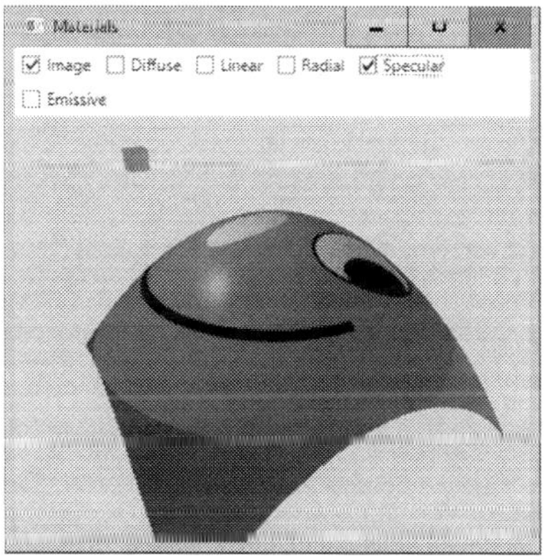

Figure 7-9: This scene uses a diffuse material containing an image plus a specular material.

You can also use specular materials with other kinds of diffuse materials. For example, in Figure 7-9 the Materials program is using a diffuse material containing an `ImageBrush`. A specular material adds a bright highlight between the smiley face's nose and smile.

> **NOTE:** The drawing system calculates specular highlights for every directional, point, or spot light in the scene. If the scene includes four lights of those types, then each object could have up to four specular highlights (depending on the geometry).

Specular highlights only appear when the viewing direction is close to the mirror angle at a particular point on the object. For that reason, they look nice and make sense when the object is relatively smooth and made up of lots of small triangles, as in the Materials example program.

However, suppose the object is made up of large triangles. Often the viewing position will not be near the mirror direction for any of the triangles, so no highlight appears.

When the viewing position is near a triangle's mirror direction, that triangle will appear very bright. Because the triangles are large, it usually looks odd to have a bunch of relatively dull triangles surrounding one big bright triangle.

For that reason, specular materials are most useful with objects made up of many small triangles.

> **NOTE:** However, the result can be striking if you place the viewing position in the right spot and then animate the object. For example, imagine a rotating icosahedron where the faces periodically flash brightly as their mirrow angles sweep across the viewing position. Sort of like a spinning crystal.

Emissive Material

An emissive material adds its own light to an object. "Emissive" is a bit of a misnomer here because the material doesn't actually emit any light. In particular, it does not add light to the objects around it. All it does is modify the colors of the object that uses the material.

Note that this is different from the way ambient colors work. Suppose an object uses a blue material and you illuminate it with a red ambient light. The light provides only red color but the blue object doesn't reflect red, so the object appears black.

In contrast, suppose you have the same blue object illuminated by a white light so it appears blue. Now if you add a red emissive material to the object, it gains red coloring so it becomes magenta.

The following code shows how the Materials example program creates its emissive material.

```
AddMaterial(new EmissiveMaterial(Brushes.DarkBlue), "Emissive");
```

This code creates a new `EmissiveMaterial` object, passing its constructor the brush that it should use to brighten objects. In this example, the material adds dark blue to its objects. The code then passes the new material to the `AddMaterial` method to create its checkbox.

Figure 7-10 shows two pictures of the Materials example program. On the left, the program is using only a diffuse material with a solid brush. On the right, it adds an emissive material.

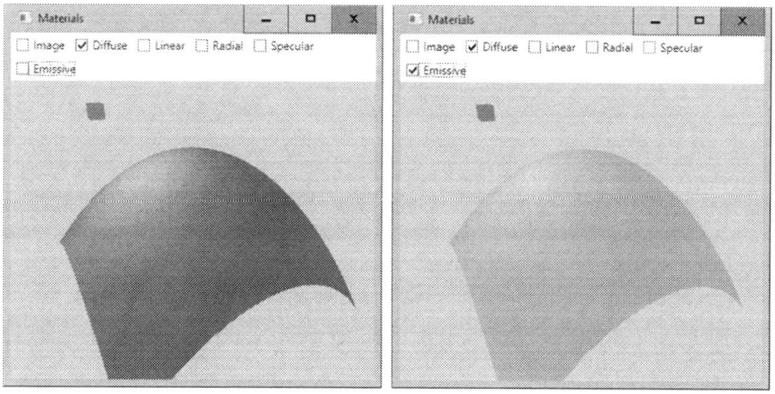

Figure 7-10: An emissive material adds color to an object, generally making it brighter.

You can't really tell in the book, but on the left the object looks sort of grayish-blue. On the right the object looks bright blue.

As is the case with specular materials, you can also combine emissive materials with diffuse materials that have non solid brushes. For example, Figure 7-11 shows the Materials example program using a diffuse material made with an `ImageBrush` with and without an emissive material.

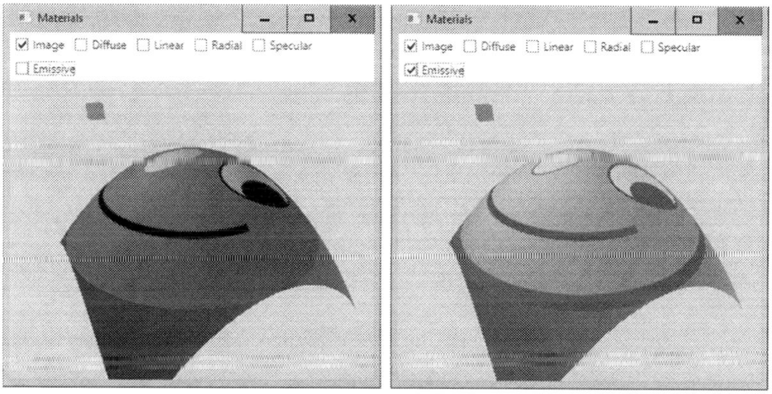

Figure 7-11: You can combine emissive materials with diffuse materials that use non-solid brushes.

Because the emissive material's brush is dark blue, the material not only brightens the image but it also makes its colors bluer. In this example, the difference is fairly small. The smiley's white areas look pale blue, the green areas look greenish-blue, and the other colors generally look a bit lighter and more washed out.

If the colors were brighter, you might see more noticeable results. For example, if the emissive material were bright blue, red areas might turn purple and green areas might turn cyan.

Other Brushes

I mentioned earlier that the order in which you add materials to a material group is important. If you add a specular material before you add a red diffuse material, the red material will cover the specular material so you won't see it.

Actually the situation is a bit more complicated than that if you use translucent colors. For example, suppose you add a specular material and then the diffuse material created by the following code.

```
DiffuseMaterial material =
    new DiffuseMaterial(new SolidColorBrush(Color.FromArgb(128, 0, 255, 0)));
```

This material's color has alpha (opacity) component 128, which makes it halfway transparent. In this case, you will see the specular highlight shining through the translucent green material.

The examples described in this chapter also use solid brushes for specular and emissive materials, but you can use other brushes if you like. For example, you could give an emissive material a linear gradient brush. Then the colors that it adds to its object would vary across the brush's defined area.

Similarly, you could use an image brush or a gradient brush for a specular material. In that case, the color of the specular highlight would depend on the part of the object that was displaying the highlight. As you moved the viewing position around, the highlight's color would change.

Textures

A *texture* is all of the things that go into an object's surface appearance. It includes the object's color, image detail, shininess, bumpiness, and other factors.

Texture mapping is the process of mapping the characteristics of a texture onto an object. For example, you might map colors onto the sides of a cube, or you might map an image of a globe onto a sphere.

Often when people talk about an object's texture, however, they just mean an image that is mapped onto the object.

Textures let you make scenes much more realistic. They let you make a table look like it's made from wood, a stairway look like it's made of metal, and the ground look like it's covered in grass. They're a big part of the difference between the movies *Tron* (1982) and *Tron: Legacy* (2010).

In a WPF program, a diffuse material that uses an image brush can provide textures. The Garden example program shown in Figure 7-12 uses that kind of brush to draw rectangles covered with grass, rocks, water, bricks, metal, and wood. It even displays some clouds as a sort of background. (Download the example if you want to see what the other sides of the cube are displaying.)

Figure 7-12: The Garden example program demonstrates textures.

The result isn't realistic enough to fool anyone into thinking this is a photograph. After all, the ground is infinitely thin and you can see the seams in the sky. With some work, however, you can use these techniques to build a scene that is realistic enough to help the user suspend disbelief and get in the spirit of the program. You could display the interior or exterior of a new building, design a golf course, or draw a realistic-looking space station. You could also create an environment similar to those used by one of the myriad three-dimensional games that are available today such as Halo, Assassin's Creed, or World of Warcraft.

The Garden example program only adds one new piece of code to previous examples: an `AddRectangle` method that builds a rectangle. It also adds `TextureCoordinates` values so the rectangle can display a material that uses an image brush. Download the Garden example program to see the details.

Texture Scaling

The way an image is mapped onto a surface depends on four things: the image, the brush's viewbox, the brush's viewport, and the surface's texture coordinates.

The image determines what picture is available for drawing. That much is easy to understand.

The *viewbox* determines what part of the image is used to build the brush's tile. The *tile* is the picture that is used to build the graphic that will eventually be mapped onto the surface. For example, you can use the viewbox to select only part of the image to be placed on the tile.

The *viewport* determines how the tile is mapped onto the graphic. For example, you can make the viewport stretch the tile, repeat the tile to fill the area, or just stop after drawing the tile once.

Finally, the texture coordinates determine which parts of the graphic are drawn on a part of the surface.

Figure 7-13 shows the steps in the mapping process. The viewbox selects the area in the image that will be used for the tile. The viewport determines how the tile is mapped to a graphic. Texture coordinates determine how the graphic is mapped to the parts of the mesh.

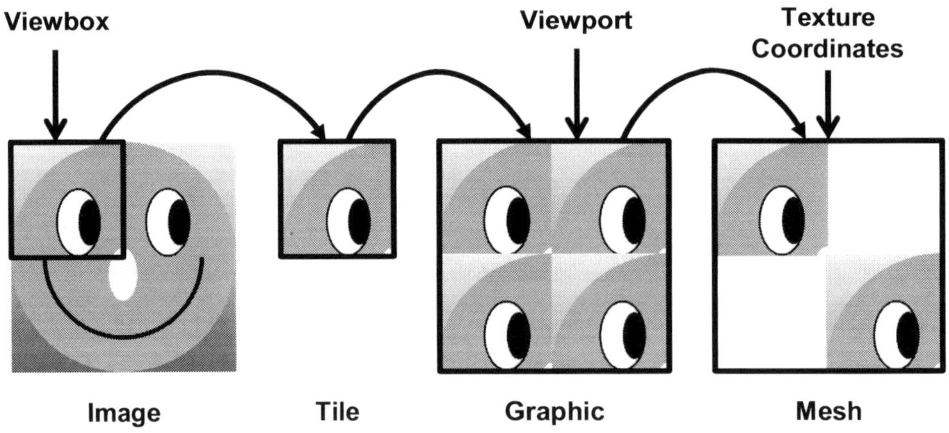

Figure 7-13: A brush's viewbox and viewport determine how the image is mapped to a mesh.

The ImageScaling example program shown in Figure 7-14 demonstrates several mapping scenarios. The following sections describe the images drawn in Figure 7-14.

Upper Left

In the simplest scenario, which is shown in the upper left in Figure 7-14, you want to map a picture onto a mesh that has texture coordinates spanning the whole UV coordinate range (0, 0) to (1, 1). In that case, you can simply create an `ImageBrush` holding the picture and use it to make the mesh's material without worrying about viewboxes and viewports.

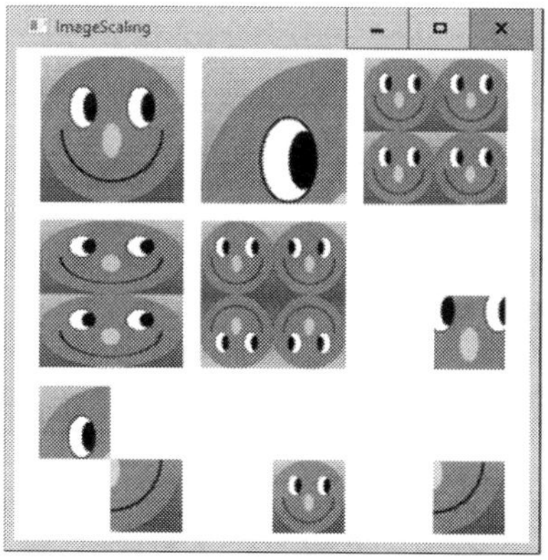

Figure 7-14: The ImageScaling example program demonstrates viewboxes and viewports.

The following code snippet shows how the ImageScaling example program assigns the brush for the image in the upper left in Figure 7-14. I've omitted the code that creates the mesh because it's straightforward and fairly long. Download the example program to see the details.

```
ImageBrush brush1 = new ImageBrush(
    new BitmapImage(new Uri("Smiley.png", UriKind.Relative)));
GeometryModel3D model1 = new GeometryModel3D(mesh1, new DiffuseMaterial(brush1));
group.Children.Add(model1);
```

This code simply creates the brush and uses it to create a `DiffuseMaterial`. It then uses the material to create the mesh's model and adds the model to the program's `Model3DGroup`.

Upper Middle

To draw the upper middle picture in Figure 7-14, the program uses the following code to create a viewbox that only includes the image's upper left corner.

```
brush2.Viewbox = new Rect(0, 0, 0.5, 0.5);
```

The viewbox selects the upper left quarter of the image. The viewport then maps that piece to the entire graphic area as before, and the graphic area is mapped onto the mesh.

Upper Right

The program uses the following code to tile the mesh in the upper right corner of Figure 7-14 with four copies of the entire image.

```
brush3.Viewport = new Rect(0, 0, 0.5, 0.5);
brush3.TileMode = TileMode.Tile;
```

The code doesn't specify the viewbox, so it defaults to selecting the entire image.

The viewport specifies only the upper left corner of the graphic area, so that's where the image is mapped. If that were the end of this code, only the upper left corner of the mesh would be colored and the rest would remain undrawn. The `TileMode` statement, however, makes the viewport repeat the graphic as much as necessary to cover the mesh.

> **NOTE:** An undrawn part of the surface is *not* drawn in white or the background color or something. It's just not drawn at all, as if you hadn't created those triangles. Objects that lie behind will show thorough.

Center Left

To display the two stretched copies of the image in the center left part of Figure 7-14, the program uses the following code.

```
brush4.Viewport = new Rect(0, 0, 1, 0.5);
brush4.Stretch = Stretch.Fill;
brush4.TileMode = TileMode.Tile;
```

The code doesn't specify the viewbox, so it defaults to selecting the entire image. The viewport selects the upper half of the graphic area. The `Stretch` property indicates that the tile (which holds the entire image) should be stretched to cover the graphics area (which is the upper half of the possible area).

The `TileMode` property indicates that the graphics area should be repeated as much as necessary to cover the mesh.

Center Middle

To create the center middle picture in Figure 7-14, the program uses the following code to tile the mesh with reflected versions of the image.

```
brush5.Viewport = new Rect(0, 0, 0.5, 0.5);
brush5.TileMode = TileMode.FlipXY;
```

As in the previous few examples, this code doesn't specify the viewbox, so it defaults to selecting the entire image. The viewport selects the upper left corner of the graphic area, so the image is mapped there.

The `Stretch` value `FlipXY` means the image should be tiled. Each time a tile moves to the right, the image is reflected horizontally. Each time a tile moves down, the image is reflected vertically.

Center Right

To build the mesh on the center right in Figure 7-14, the program uses the following code to draw part of the image on part of the mesh.

```
brush6.Viewbox = new Rect(0.25, 0.25, 0.5, 0.5);
```

```
brush6.Viewport = new Rect(0.5, 0.5, 0.5, 0.5);
```

This time the viewbox selects the center of the image and the viewport selects the lower right corner of the graphics area. That makes the brush map the image's center to the mesh's lower right corner.

Note that the brush would still tile the graphic across the entire mesh if the code set the `Tile` property to `Tile`. The fact that the viewport selects the lower right corner of the graphic area doesn't mean a tile cannot move "backward" to the left and up from there.

Lower Left

To make the mesh in the lower left of Figure 7-14, the program creates two rectangles with texture coordinates ranging over (0, 0) to (0.5, 0.5) and (0.5, 0.5) to (1, 1).

The code doesn't set either the viewbox or viewport, so the brush maps the entire image to the graphic area. The texture coordinates then place the appropriate pieces of the graphic on the appropriate rectangles.

Lower Middle

The lower middle part of Figure 7-14 shows some rather non-intuitive default behavior by the brush. The program creates a mesh containing a single rectangle with texture coordinates (0.5, 0.5) to (1, 1). It then creates a brush without specifying any viewbox or viewport properties.

You might think that the texture coordinates would make the rectangle display only the lower right corner of the image. As you can see from the figure, that isn't the case. The brush draws the entire image over this rectangle even though its texture coordinates don't span the full range $0 \leq \{u, v\} \leq 1$.

To see why this happens, go back to Figure 7-13. The viewbox selects the whole image by default, so the tile contains the entire image. The viewport then maps the whole image onto the graphic that is used to draw the rectangle.

Next, the graphic is mapped onto the mesh's rectangles. By default, the viewport's coordinate system is relative to the mesh's texture coordinates. Because those coordinate only include the range $0.5 \leq \{u, v\} \leq 1$, that is the area where the graphic is mapped. The result is that the whole image in the graphic is mapped to just the texture coordinates that are actually used so it fills the rectangle.

There are situations where this might be useful. For instance, the Materials example program described earlier in this chapter looped over X and Z values to create points on a surface. It calculated texture coordinates so the area covered had U and V values between 0 and 1.

That wasn't too hard in this example, but it turns out that it was unnecessary. If the program simply used the points' X and Z values for U and V, then the viewport would map the graphic onto the surface's triangles anyway.

The TexturedSurface example program shown in Figure 7-15 demonstrates that approach. It builds its surface much as the Materials program does except it sets each points' texture coordinates to its X and Z coordinates. In this example, that means the texture coordinates range over $-3 \leq \{u, v\} \leq 3$.

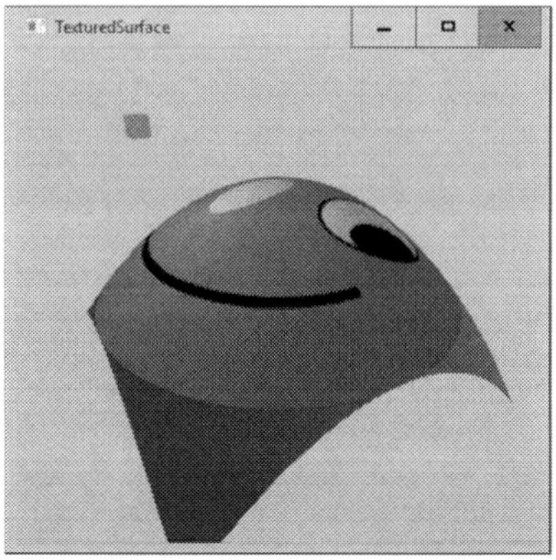

Figure 7-15: In the TexturedSurface example program, texture coordinates range over $-3 \leq \{u, v\} \leq 3$.

Lower Right

You might be able to imagine a situation where the result in the lower middle of Figure 7-14 makes sense, but to me it seems like an odd default behavior. If texture coordinates are supposed to range from 0 to 1, I would expect the result shown on the lower right of that figure. The ImageScaling example program uses the following code to create that result.

```
brush9.ViewportUnits = BrushMappingMode.Absolute;
```

The `ViewportUnits` property can take the values `Absolute` and `RelativeToBoundingBox`. If the value is `Absolute`, the viewport maps the graphic into the range of texture coordinates $0 \leq \{u, v\} \leq 1$, and that produces the result shown in the lower right corner of Figure 7-14.

If the value is `RelativeToBoundingBox`, which is the default, then the viewport maps the graphic onto the entire range of texture coordinates used by the mesh's triangles. That gives the less intuitive result shown in the lower middle of Figure 7-14.

Viewbox and Viewport Summary

If you want to display the entire image on the entire mesh, you can ignore the viewbox and viewport and you'll probably get the right result. If you want to display only part of the image or display it on only part of the mesh's triangles, then you can use the viewbox and viewport to make that happen.

Most of the examples in the rest of this book use texture coordinates between 0 and 1, so they set `ViewportUnits` to `Absolute`.

Shadows and Reflections

Unfortunately, WPF does not support shadows or reflections. Its lighting model allows a light to illuminate front faces and not backfaces, but it cannot tell when one object blocks the light going to another object.

The mathematics behind shadows and reflections is actually similar to the mathematics of the camera's projection. A reflection is basically what you see if you place a camera on the other side of a mirror looking out at you. At least for a flat surface like a normal mirror. Reflection on curved surfaces (such as spheres) or moving surfaces (such as water) is much more complicated.

If you place a camera at a point or spot light's position, then the parts of the scene that it can "see" should be illuminated and the other parts of the scene should be in shadow. For directional lights, you can use a orthographic camera pointed in the light's direction.

At some point, I suspect that graphics hardware will handle shadows and reflections. At that point, if we're lucky, WPF will start supporting them, too.

In the meantime, there is something that you can do to create shadows, although it can be tedious. If your scene's lights and objects don't move, then the shadows won't move, either. For example, suppose a light shines on a table. Then the shadows of the table's legs stay in the same position on the floor even if you move the camera's viewing position around. In theory, you could figure out where the shadows belong and then add them to the texture used to draw the floor.

> **NOTE:** Sometimes this process is called *texture baking* or *render baking*.
>
> More generally, *baking* is the process of pre-computing something so you can work with it more quickly later.
>
> Texture baking can make rendering much faster, although it can take a long time to bake a complicated scene with many objects and lights.

For a simple scene with just the right geometry, you might be able to calculate exactly where the shadows should lie. For a complicated scene with several lights and many objects, this would be impractical to do by hand.

You still may be able to make some improvements, however. For example, you could give objects under a table or beneath a staircase darker textures. You may not be able to produce accurate shadows, but you can give the user some visual cues to make the scene easier to understand.

Summary

Often you can use simple diffuse materials with solid colors to give objects their own colors in a scene. Other kinds of brushes can add more realism. For example, specular materials can make highlights appear on shiny surfaces. A diffuse material that uses an image brush can provide texture. For example, it can make an object look like it's made of metal, wood, or grass.

Download this chapter's examples and experiment with them. You should be able to use the techniques they demonstrate to build your own scenes, at least if they consist only of surfaces, cubes, and rectangles.

The next part of the book describes methods for creating shapes other than simple triangles and cubes. It explains how you can create shapes such as spheres, pyramids, cones, and surfaces of transformation. It also explains how you can use transformations to change the shapes of existing meshes.

Part II
Building Shapes

Most of the chapters in this part of the book explain how to build different kinds of three-dimensional shapes. Before that, however, Chapters 8 and 9 explain some useful techniques that make building shapes easier.

Chapter 8 provides a primer on point and vector arithmetic. Several of the later chapters use techniques that involve combining points and vectors, and Chapter 8 gives you the background you need to understand those techniques.

Chapter 9 explains transformations, which add extra flexibility to the shapes that you build. For example, building a sphere centered at the origin is relatively simple. Building a sphere that is squashed, rotated, and then moved to some other location would be harder. Transformations allow you to convert the standard, origin centered sphere into one that is squashed, rotated, and translated wherever you want it to be.

The rest of the chapters in this part of the book explain how you can build specific shapes such as cubes, spheres, and cones.

Chapter 8

Vector Arithmetic

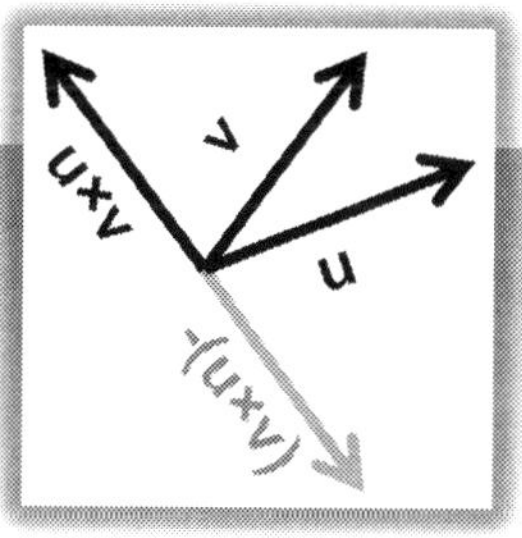

Some of the following chapters use vectors to build three-dimensional shapes. Those chapters will be easier to understand if you know a bit about vector arithmetic. Vector arithmetic may also help you understand how some three-dimensional drawing operations work because WPF uses vectors to indicate such things as normals and a camera's "look" and "up" directions.

Vector and point arithmetic is quite intuitive and follows the normal rules of algebra, so you'll probably find this material easy.

Vectors

As I mentioned way back in Chapter 2, a vector represents a direction and a distance. In three dimensions, a vector has X, Y, and Z components to indicate how far you would move in the X, Y, and Z directions to follow the vector.

Usually a vector is written in pointy brackets. For example, the vector $<1, -2, 3>$ means move 1 unit parallel to the X axis, -2 units parallel to the Y axis, and 3 units parallel to the Z axis.

It's important to keep in mind that a vector only represents a direction and a distance, and not a starting location.

Vectors Plus Point

Because a vector represents a direction, you can add a vector to a point to get a new point. The new point is where you would end up if you went to the first point and then moved in the direction of the vector.

Figure 8-1 shows the process of adding vector v to point A to get point B. In equations, A+v=B.

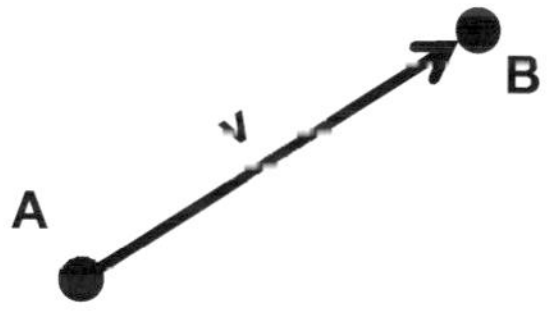

Figure 8-1: A point plus a vector gives you a new point.

Mathematically it's easy to add a vector to a point. Simply add the vector's components to the point's corresponding coordinates. For example, suppose you have the point $A=(a_1, a_2, a_3)$ and the vector $v=<v_1, v_2, v_3>$. Then $B=(a_1+v_1, a_2+v_2, a_3+v_3)$.

Point Minus Point

You can find a vector between two points by subtracting one point from the other. For example, consider again the points A and B in Figure 8-1. Subtracting B from A gives the equation B-A=v.

This should make some sense mathematically because we know that A+v=B. These two equations are related by simple algebra that should look familiar. (Just subtract A from both sides of A+v=B to get v=B-A.)

Mathematically you can perform this operation by subtracting the points' corresponding coordinates. If $A=(a_1, a_2, a_3)$ and $B=(b_1, b_2, b_3)$, then $v=<b_1-a_1, b_2-a_2, b_3-a_3>$.

Note that the order of subtraction is important. The vector A-B is the opposite of B-A. The two have the same lengths but point in opposite directions. You must subtract the vector's start point from its end point.

Vector Plus Vector

When you add two vectors, the result is the vector you would get if you travelled along the first vector and then along the second. Figure 8-2 shows this operation graphically. The equation is w=u+v.

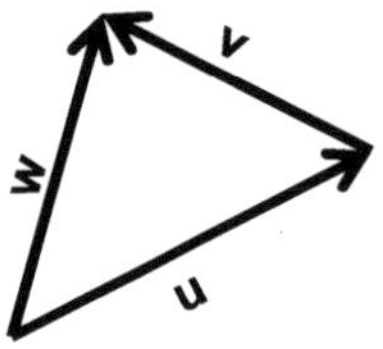

Figure 8-2: A vector plus a vector gives another vector.

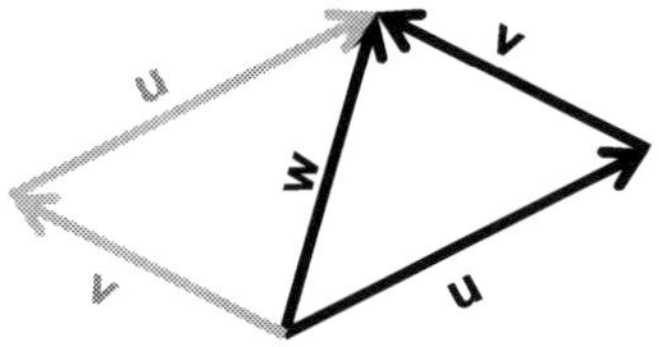

Figure 8-3: Addition order doesn't matter.

Note that the order of operation doesn't matter in vector addition so u+v=v+u. For example, Figure 8-3 shows u+v and v+u in gray.

Vector Length

The length of vector v is written |v| or ||v||. You can use the distance formula to calculate a vector's length. For example, the vector $<v_1, v_2, v_3>$ has the following length.

$$|v| = \sqrt{v_1{}^2 + v_2{}^2 + v_3{}^2}$$

Scaling Vectors

If you multiply a vector by a number n, you get a new vector pointing in the same direction and having length equal to n times the original vector's length. This should make some sense, at least for integer values n, because in that case you can replace multiplication with vector addition. For example, if v is a vector, then $3 \times v = v + v + v$. Figure 8-4 shows that calculation.

To multiply a vector by a number arithmetically, simply multiply each of the vector's components by the number. For example, the vector $<v_1, v_2, v_3>$ multiplied by n is $<n \times v_1, n \times v_2, n \times v_3>$.

Note that n can be an integer, a non-integer, or negative. In particular, a vector times -1 gives you a vector with the same length as the original but pointing in the opposite direction.

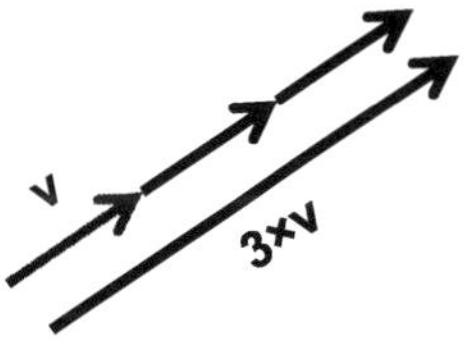

Figure 8-4: A vector times a number is scaled by that number.

Normalizing Vectors

To *normalize* a vector, you make a new vector pointing in the same direction but with length one.

> **NOTE:** This is not quite the same as a "normal vector" when you're talking about a three-dimensional object. In that context, a normal vector is a vector that is perpendicular to the object's surface at a particular point. For example, a normal vector for a sphere points away from the center of the sphere.
>
> A *unit normal* is a normal vector that is normalized. In other words, it is perpendicular to the object and has length one.

Mathematically, you can use the scaling described in the preceding section to normalize a vector. Simply divide the vector by its length. For example, if v is a vector, then the normalized version of v, which is sometimes written v_n, is given by $v_n = v / |v|$.

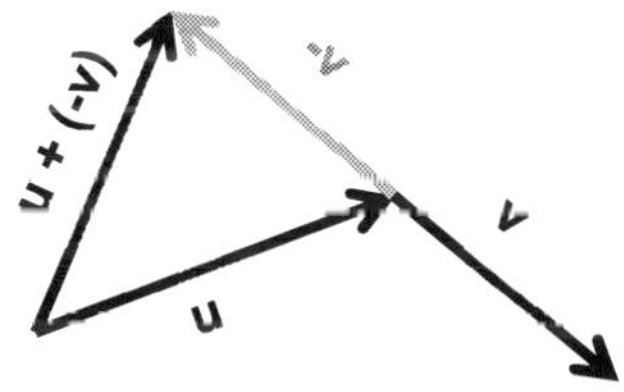

Figure 8-5: To subtract a vector, add its negative.

Subtracting Vectors

To subtract one vector from another, multiply the vector by -1 and then add the result. Figure 8-5 shows this operation graphically.

Mathematically you can simply subtract the vectors' corresponding components. For example, $<u_1, u_2, u_3>-<v_1, v_2, v_3>=<u_1-v_1, u_2-v_2, u_3-v_3>$.

> **NOTE:** If you scale, add, or subtract two vectors, the result is always in the same plane as the two original vectors.

Dot Products

The *dot product* of two vectors u and v, which is written $u \cdot v$, is given by the sums of the products of the vectors' corresponding components. In three dimensions, $u \cdot v$ is given by the following equation.

$$u \cdot v = u_1 v_1 + u_2 v_2 + u_3 v_3$$

The result is a number, not another vector or a point.

The dot product has another meaning that makes it more useful. If u and v are vectors, then the following equation is also true.

$$u \cdot v = |u||v| \cos \theta$$

Here $|u|$ and $|v|$ are the vectors' lengths, and θ is angle between the two vectors.

This gives you a way to calculate the angle between any two vectors. Calculate their dot product, divide by their lengths, and then take the inverse cosine of the result.

$$\theta = \cos^{-1} \frac{u \cdot v}{|u||v|}$$

Dot products also let you calculate a couple of other useful values relatively easily. For example, $\cos(90^\circ)=0$. Any non-null vector has a length greater than zero, so if the dot product of two non-null vectors is zero, then they must meet at a 90° angle.

> **NOTE:** As you probably know, when two vectors meet at a 90° angle they are said to be *perpendicular*. Sometimes objects that meet at 90° angles are also said to be *orthogonal*, particularly if you're working in three or more dimensions.

If $0^\circ \le \theta < 90^\circ$, then $\cos(\theta) > 0$. Again because the lengths of the vectors are greater than zero, that means if the dot product of two vectors is positive, you know that $0^\circ \le \theta < 90^\circ$.

Conversely, if the dot product of two vectors is negative, then $90^\circ < \theta \le 180^\circ$.

Finally, if θ=0° or θ=180°, then cos(θ) =1 and the dot product equals the products of the vectors' lengths. That means if the dot product equals the products of the lengths, the two vectors are parallel.

NOTE: In real applications, rounding errors often make values slightly different from what they should be. For example, the dot product of two perpendicular vectors might not be exactly 0, it might be 0.000001. Similarly the dot product of two vectors that are parallel might not be exactly the same as the product of the vectors' lengths.

To handle these sorts of issues, you may need to subtract the two values that should be the same, take the absolute value, and then see if the result is close to zero.

Cross Products

Cross products are a bit less intuitive than dot products, but they are also very useful. If u and v are non-parallel three-dimensional vectors, then their cross product written u×v is a new vector perpendicular to both u and v and having length given by the following formula.

$$|u \times v| = |u||v| \sin \theta$$

If you think about the situation in three dimensions, you'll realize that there are two vectors pointing in opposite directions that are perpendicular to u and v. The vector given by the cross product is the one defined by the right-hand rule described in Chapter 3. (If you don't remember it, look at the section "Right-Hand Rule" in Chapter 3. It's pretty important and you'll use it a lot!)

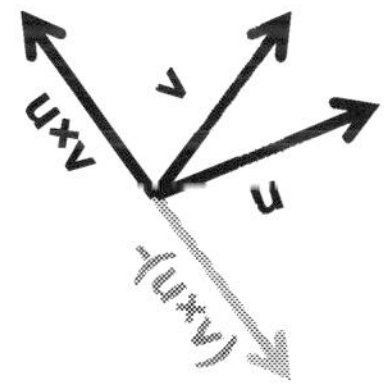

Figure 8-6: The direction of the cross product is given by the right-hand rule.

Figure 8-6 shows vectors u and v, and their cross product. The gray vector shows the other vector perpendicular to u and v and pointing opposite the cross product.

Calculating the cross product mathematically is straightforward although a bit long. The following equation shows how to calculate u × v.

$$u \times v = \langle w_1, w_2, w_3 \rangle$$

Where:

$$w_1 = u_2 v_3 - u_3 v_2$$

$$w_2 = u_3 v_1 - u_1 v_3$$

$$w_3 = u_1 v_2 - u_2 v_1$$

You can use the cross product to study the angle between two vectors much as you can use the dot product. The dot product is easier to calculate, however, so it's often more useful.

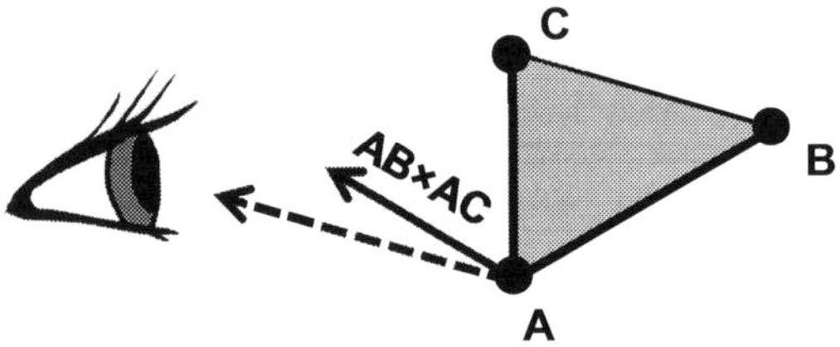

Figure 8-7: The cross product helps with backface removal.

However, the cross product is *really* useful for calculating normal vectors for three-dimensional objects. For example, consider the shaded triangle shown in Figure 8-7 with vertices A, B, and C and assume that the triangle is part of a solid object. If the triangle's vertices are outwardly oriented, then AB×BC gives a vector pointing away from the solid. If you then calculate a vector from point A to the viewing position (the dashed arrow in Figure 8-7), then you can use the dot product to examine the angle between that vector and the cross product. If the angle is less than 90°, then the cross product and the viewing vector point in more or less the same direction, so the triangle should be visible from the viewing position. If the angle is greater than 90°, then the triangle is a backface and doesn't need to be drawn.

Perpendicular Two-Dimensional Vectors

The cross product finds a vector perpendicular to two vectors in three dimensions. Sometimes it's useful to find a perpendicular vector in two dimensions. For example, some of the camera controllers described in Chapter 7 need to find vectors perpendicular to the direction that the controller is facing.

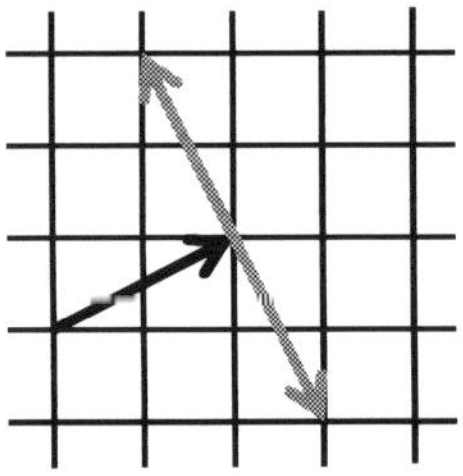

Figure 8-8: To find a perpendicular vector in two dimensions, swap the coordinates and negate one.

As I mentioned in Chapter 5, finding this kind of vector is easy. Simply switch the vector's components and change the sign of one of them. If v=<x, y>, then the two perpendicular vectors are <y, -x> and <-y, x>. Figure 8-8 shows a vector and two perpendicular vectors created by this method.

The two new vectors have the same length as the original, but you can scale the new vectors if you like. For example, you can divide them by their lengths to normalize them.

Vector Code

Some of the calculations described in this chapter may seem daunting, particularly the cross product calculation. Fortunately, the .NET Framework's `Vector3D` and `Point3D` structures know how to perform these calculations for you. For example, they know how to add and subtract vectors, scale vectors, add vectors to points, and calculate dot and cross products. They even know how to calculate the angle between two vectors.

The VectorArithmetic example program uses the following code to demonstrate `Point3D` and `Vector3D` methods.

```
using System.Windows.Media.Media3D;
...
static void Main(string[] args)
{
    Vector3D u = new Vector3D(0, 3, 4);
    Vector3D v = new Vector3D(0, 4, -3);
    Point3D a = new Point3D(10, 12, 15);
    Point3D b = a + u;      // Point + Vector = Point
    Vector3D w = b - a;     // Point - Point = Vector
    Vector3D t = u + v;     // Vector + Vector = Vector

    double angle = Vector3D.AngleBetween(u, v);
    Vector3D cross = Vector3D.CrossProduct(u, v);
    double dot = Vector3D.DotProduct(u, v);

    Vector3D normal = cross;
    normal.Normalize();
    Vector3D scaled = normal * 10;

    Console.WriteLine("u:\t" + u.ToString());
    Console.WriteLine("v:\t" + v.ToString());
    Console.WriteLine("w:\t" + w.ToString());
    Console.WriteLine("a:\t" + a.ToString());
    Console.WriteLine("b:\t" + b.ToString());
    Console.WriteLine("angle:\t" + angle.ToString());
    Console.WriteLine("cross:\t" + cross.ToString());
    Console.WriteLine("dot:\t" + dot.ToString());
    Console.WriteLine("normal:\t" + normal.ToString());
    Console.WriteLine("scaled:\t" + scaled.ToString());
    Console.ReadLine();
}
```

The `Point3D` and `Vector3D` structures are defined in the `System.Windows.Media.Media3D` namespace, so the program begins with a `using` directive to include that namespace. This namespace is defined in the `PresentationCore` library, so I added a reference to that library at design time. Normally that reference is added automatically when you create a WPF application, but it's initially missing from this example because this program is a console application.

The program's `Main` method performs a series of calculations to demonstrate `Point3D` and `Vector3D` operations. It displays the results and then waits for you to press the Enter key before closing.

Summary

Point and vector algebra let you combine points and vectors to generate new points and vectors. These operations are relatively straightforward, with the possible exception of dot and cross products.

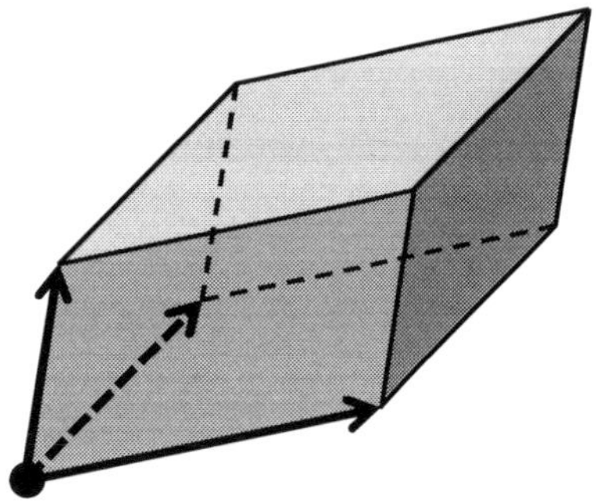

Figure 8-9: A point and three noncoplanar vectors define a prism.

Later chapters will use these operations to specify and generate shapes. For example, Figure 8-9 shows how you can use a point and three noncoplanar vectors to define a prism.

The next chapter describes some other ways that you can manipulate points and vectors. The chapters after that one explain how to use the techniques described in this chapter and the next one to create a variety of solids such as boxes, octahedrons, tori (donuts), and spheres.

Chapter 9 Transformations

A *transformation* is an operation that maps points to new points. For example, when you scale an object, you map the points that define the object to new points that define a scaled version of the object.

This chapter describes the transformations that are most useful in three-dimensional graphics. It also explains how you can use matrices to represent those transformations and how to perform transformations in C#.

> **NOTE:** Some of the sections that follow are fairly mathy. If you don't want to read about *how* the transformations work, you can skim those sections and start reading more carefully at the section "Transformation Order."

Affine Transformations

Normally, three-dimensional graphics applications use affine transformations. An *affine transformation* is one that preserves lines and parallel lines. Preserving lines means if three points lie along a line before the transformation, then their transformed points also lie along a line. Preserving parallel lines means if two lines are parallel, then the transformed lines are also parallel.

Affine transformations also preserve ratios, so if a point lies halfway between two other points, then the transformed point lies halfway between the other transformed points. Figure 9-1 shows examples of affine transformations.

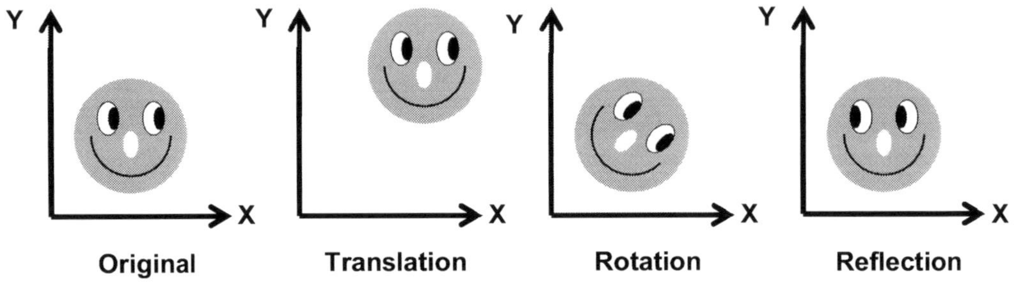

Figure 9-1: Translation, rotation, and reflection are affine transformations.

It's less obvious, but scaling is also an affine transformation, whether you scale horizontally, vertically, or both. Figure 9-2 shows those three kinds of scaling.

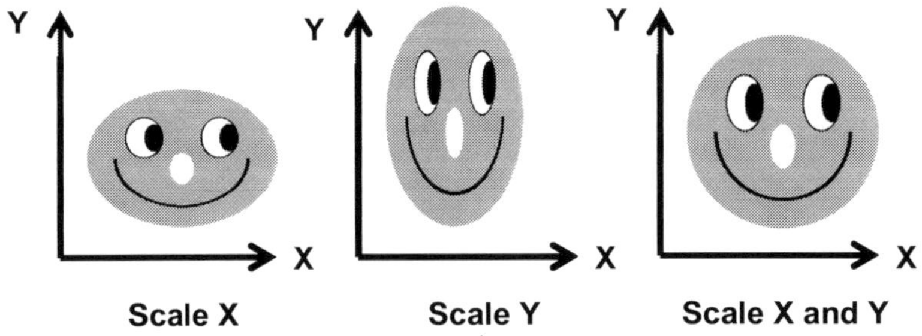

Figure 9-2: Scaling is an affine transformation.

It's harder to visualize, but *skewing* (also called *shearing*) an image is also an affine transformation. In general, warping transformations are not affine but skewing is. Figure 9-3 shows a skew transformation and two warping transformations.

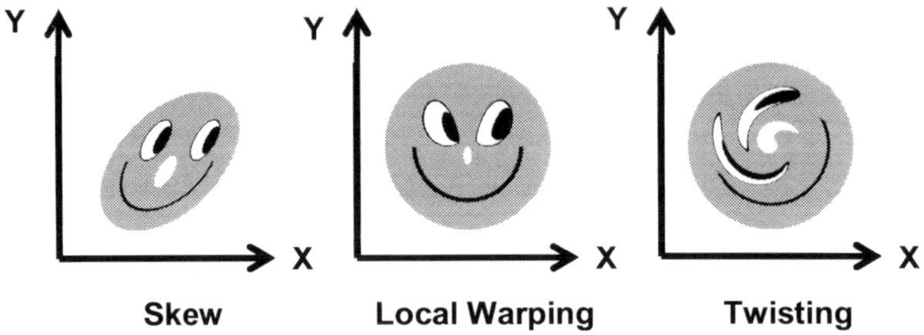

Figure 9-3: Skewing is affine but warping and twisting are not.

Figures 9-1 through 9-3 show two-dimensional transformations, but translation, rotation, reflection, and scaling are also affine transformations in three dimensions; they're just a bit harder to visualize.

Orthographic projection is also affine, although perspective projection is not. (See Chapter 4 if you need a refresher on projections.)

Usually translation, scaling, and rotation are the most useful transformations in three-dimensional graphics, so those are the ones described in the rest of this chapter.

Homogeneous Coordinates

It turns out that you can represent translation, scaling, and rotation transformations as four-by-four matrices. If you do that, then you can multiply a point's coordinates by a matrix to get the new transformed point. That makes it easy to apply transformations to many points in a uniform (homogeneous) way. It also allows you to combine transformations in a nice way. I'll say more about that later in this chapter.

Unfortunately, you cannot multiply a four-by-four matrix by a three-dimensional point. To make the math work out, we convert points into *homogeneous coordinates* by adding a fourth component to the point.

> **NOTE:** To differentiate this kind of homogeneous point from a regular geometric point, people usually place the components in square brackets. For example, the value [2, 3, 5, 1] in homogeneous coordinates represents the point (2, 3, 5).

Any multiple of a homogeneous value is considered to represent the same point. For example, the values [2, 3, 5, 1] and [6, 9, 15, 3] both represent the point (2, 3, 5).

Normally a point's fourth homogeneous component is set to 1. When that value is not 1, you can consider it a scale factor and you can divide the vector's components by the scale factor to find the point that the vector represents. For example, the vector [16, 20, 8, 4] is equivalent to the vector [16/4, 20/4, 8/4, 4/4]=[4, 5, 2, 1], which represents the point (4, 5, 2).

Matrix Multiplication

To multiply a vector by a matrix, you multiply the entries in corresponding rows and columns. For example, consider Figure 9-4. To get the first component of the result, you multiply the vector's values by the corresponding values in the matrix's first column.

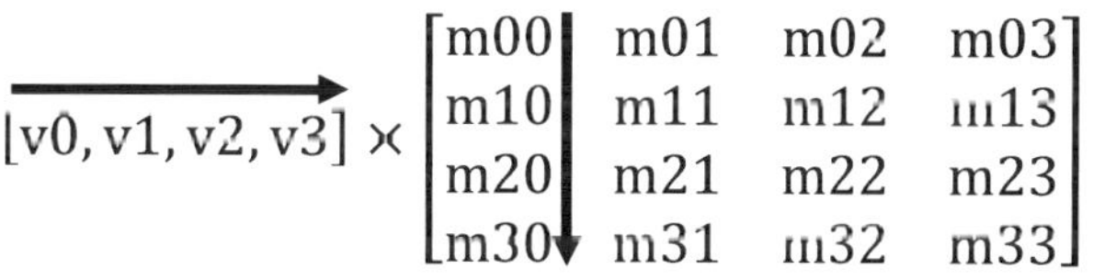

Figure 9-4: To multiply a vector by a matrix, multiply corresponding entries by rows and columns.

In this example, that means the result's first component is:

$$r0 = v0 \times m00 + v1 \times m10 + v2 \times m20 + v3 \times m30$$

To find the result's second component, you multiply the vector's values by the corresponding values in the matrix's second column.

$$r1 = v0 \times m01 + v1 \times m11 + v2 \times m21 + v3 \times m31$$

Similarly:

$$r2 = v0 \times m02 + v1 \times m12 + v2 \times m22 + v3 \times m32$$

Finally:

$$r3 = v0 \times m03 + v1 \times m13 + v2 \times m23 + v3 \times m33$$

The following sections explain exactly how matrices can represent translation, scaling, and rotation. To do that, they multiply an arbitrary point [x, y, z, 1] by a matrix and show that the result does what it should.

For example, consider the following equation.

$$[x, y, z, 1] \times \begin{bmatrix} 1 & 0 & 0 & 0 \\ 0 & 1 & 0 & 0 \\ 0 & 0 & 1 & 0 \\ 0 & 0 & 0 & 1 \end{bmatrix}$$

If you evaluate this expression (which might be good practice if you haven't worked with matrices lately), you'll find that the result is [x, y, z, 1]. That means this matrix represents the identity transformation; what you put in is what you get out.

Translation

The following matrix represents a translation by the distances dx, dy, and dz in the X, Y, and Z directions respectively.

$$\begin{bmatrix} 1 & 0 & 0 & 0 \\ 0 & 1 & 0 & 0 \\ 0 & 0 & 1 & 0 \\ dx & dy & dz & 1 \end{bmatrix}$$

You can verify that this works by evaluating the following expression.

$$[x, y, z, 1] \times \begin{bmatrix} 1 & 0 & 0 & 0 \\ 0 & 1 & 0 & 0 \\ 0 & 0 & 1 & 0 \\ dx & dy & dz & 1 \end{bmatrix}$$

If you perform the calculations, you'll get the result [x+dx, y+dy, z+dz, 1], which represents the point translated by the distance <dx, dy, dz>.

Scaling

In general, you could scale objects so they grow or shrink with respect to a particular point in space. For example, you could scale a cube centered at the point (5, 20, 3) so it remained centered at that point. Unfortunately, that's somewhat tricky. If you simply multiply the coordinates of the object's points by a scale factor, the points move. For example, if you multiply the point (5, 20, 3) by 2, you get the point (10, 40, 6). That means if you scale a cube centered at (5, 20, 3) by 2, it is no longer centered at that point.

Although scaling around an arbitrary point is hard, scaling with respect to the origin is simple. The following matrix represents scaling with respect to the origin by the amounts sx, sy, and sz in the X, Y, and Z directions respectively.

$$\begin{bmatrix} sx & 0 & 0 & 0 \\ 0 & sy & 0 & 0 \\ 0 & 0 & sz & 0 \\ 0 & 0 & 0 & 1 \end{bmatrix}$$

You can verify that this works by evaluating the following expression.

$$[x, y, z, 1] \times \begin{bmatrix} sx & 0 & 0 & 0 \\ 0 & sy & 0 & 0 \\ 0 & 0 & sz & 0 \\ 0 & 0 & 0 & 1 \end{bmatrix}$$

If you perform the calculations, you'll get the result [x×sx, y×sy, z×sz, 1], which represents the point scaled by the appropriate amounts.

The section "Combining Transformations" later in this chapter explains how to scale with respect to other points.

Reflection

In two dimensions, you reflect a point across a line. In three dimensions, you reflect a point across a plane.

It's not obvious how to find a matrix to reflect across a general three-dimensional plane, but it's easy to reflect across the coordinate planes. For example, reflecting across the YZ plane is the same as scaling X coordinates by a factor of -1. The following matrix performs that reflection.

$$\begin{bmatrix} -1 & 0 & 0 & 0 \\ 0 & 1 & 0 & 0 \\ 0 & 0 & 1 & 0 \\ 0 & 0 & 0 & 1 \end{bmatrix}$$

If you multiply the point [x, y, z, 1] by this matrix, you get [-x, y, z, 1] as desired.

Similarly the following matrix reflects across the XZ plane.

$$\begin{bmatrix} 1 & 0 & 0 & 0 \\ 0 & -1 & 0 & 0 \\ 0 & 0 & 1 & 0 \\ 0 & 0 & 0 & 1 \end{bmatrix}$$

Finally, the following matrix reflects across the XY plane.

$$\begin{bmatrix} 1 & 0 & 0 & 0 \\ 0 & 1 & 0 & 0 \\ 0 & 0 & -1 & 0 \\ 0 & 0 & 0 & 1 \end{bmatrix}$$

The section "Combining Transformations" later in this chapter explains how to reflect across other, non-coordinate planes.

Rotation

In two dimensions, you rotate a point around another point. In three dimensions, you rotate a point around a line.

As is the case with general scaling and reflection, it's not obvious how to find a matrix to rotate arbitrarily, but you can find a matrix for some special cases. For rotation, the special cases are rotation around the coordinate axes.

For example, suppose you want to rotate around the Z axis and consider Figure 9-5 where the Z axis is pointing straight out of the page. The goal is to rotate point P by the angle θ to get point P'.

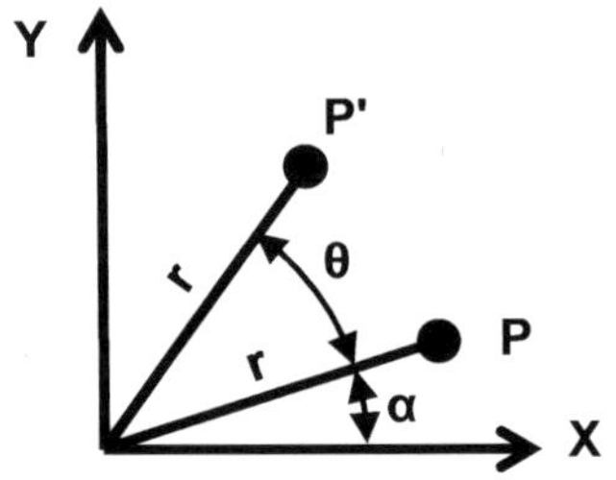

Figure 9-5: Rotation around the Z axis is easier than arbitrary rotation.

The value r is the distance from point P to the origin.

The original point P has coordinates x=r cos(α) and y=r sin(α).

The final point P' has coordinates x'=r cos(α+θ) and y'=r sin(α+θ).

To take the next step, you need to know the following trigonometry identities.

$$\cos(\alpha + \theta) = \cos\alpha\ \cos\theta - \sin\alpha\ \sin\theta$$

$$\sin(\alpha + \theta) = \sin\alpha\ \cos\theta + \cos\alpha\ \sin\theta$$

Using these in the previous equations for x' and y' gives the following.

$$x' = r\cos(\alpha + \theta) = r\,(\cos\alpha\ \cos\theta - \sin\alpha\ \sin\theta) = r\cos\alpha\ \cos\theta - r\sin\alpha\ \sin\theta$$

$$y' = r\sin(\alpha + \theta) = r\,(\sin\alpha\ \cos\theta + \cos\alpha\ \sin\theta) = r\sin\alpha\ \cos\theta + r\cos\alpha\ \sin\theta$$

Now we can replace x = r cos(α) and y= r sin(α) and rearrange the y' equation a bit to get the following.

$$x' = x\ \cos\theta - y\ \sin\theta$$

$$y' = x\ \sin\theta + y\ \cos\theta$$

The expressions on the right side of the equals signs involve linear combinations of x and y, so we can write this as the following matrix.

$$\begin{bmatrix} \cos\theta & \sin\theta & 0 & 0 \\ -\sin\theta & \cos\theta & 0 & 0 \\ 0 & 0 & 1 & 0 \\ 0 & 0 & 0 & 1 \end{bmatrix}$$

If you multiply this by the point [x, y, z, 1], you'll get the following point as desired.

$$[x\ \cos\theta - y\ \sin\theta, x\ \sin\theta + y\ \cos\theta, z, 1]$$

You can perform similar to calculations to find the matrices for rotation around the X and Z axes. The matrix for rotation around the X axis is the following.

$$\begin{bmatrix} 1 & 0 & 0 & 0 \\ 0 & \cos\theta & \sin\theta & 0 \\ 0 & -\sin\theta & \cos\theta & 0 \\ 0 & 0 & 0 & 1 \end{bmatrix}$$

Finally, the following shows the matrix for rotation around the Y axis.

$$\begin{bmatrix} \cos\theta & 0 & -\sin\theta & 0 \\ 0 & 1 & 0 & 0 \\ \sin\theta & 0 & \cos\theta & 0 \\ 0 & 0 & 0 & 1 \end{bmatrix}$$

You can verify this for special cases easily enough. For example, suppose you want to rotate the point [1, 0, 0, 1] around the Z axis by the angle 90°. If you plug the values sin(90°)=1 and cos(90°)=0 into the correct matrix, you get the following.

$$\begin{bmatrix} 0 & 1 & 0 & 0 \\ 1 & 0 & 0 & 0 \\ 0 & 0 & 1 & 0 \\ 0 & 0 & 0 & 1 \end{bmatrix}$$

Multiplying by [1, 0, 0, 1] gives the following.

$$[1,0,0,1] \begin{bmatrix} 0 & 1 & 0 & 0 \\ 1 & 0 & 1 & 0 \\ 0 & 0 & 0 & 1 \end{bmatrix} = [0,1,0,1]$$

Figure 9-6 shows this rotation graphically.

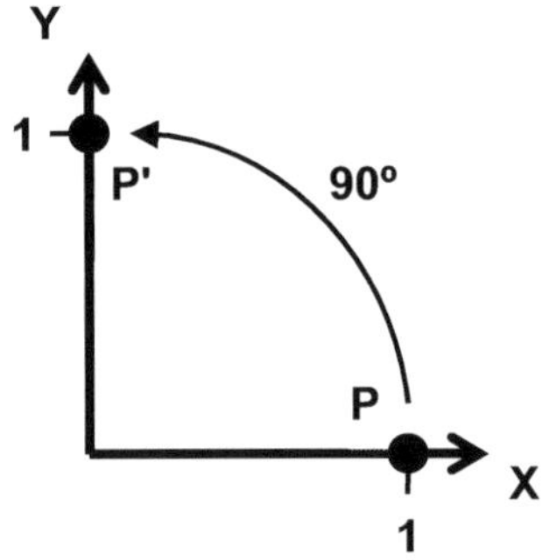

Figure 9-6: Rotating the point (1, 0, 0) by 90° around the Z axis gives the point (0, 1, 0).

Combining Transformations

Homogeneous coordinates are an elegant solution that allows you to treat translation, scaling, and rotation in a uniform way, but they do something even better. They let you combine transformations by combining their matrices.

For example, suppose you want to perform a rotation represented by matrix R. After that, you want to perform a translation represented by matrix T. If you multiply R and T, then the resulting matrix represents the rotation followed by the translation.

In fact, you can multiply as many transformation matrices as you like together and then use the resulting single matrix to represent them all. That means you can transform a set of points by multiplying them only once instead of applying each transformation one at a time.

> **NOTE:** You can multiply two matrices A and B much as you multiply a vector and a matrix. First you multiply A's first row by B's first column to get the entry in the result's first row and column. This value goes in the upper left entry of the result matrix.

$$r00 = a00 \times b00 + a01 \times b10 + a02 \times b20 + a03 \times b30$$

Figure 9-7 shows the entries that you multiply for this first result entry.

$$\begin{bmatrix} a00 & a01 & a02 & a03 \\ a10 & a11 & a12 & a13 \\ a20 & a21 & a22 & a23 \\ a30 & a31 & a32 & a33 \end{bmatrix} \times \begin{bmatrix} b00 & b01 & b02 & b03 \\ b10 & b11 & b12 & b13 \\ b20 & b21 & b22 & b23 \\ b30 & b31 & b32 & b33 \end{bmatrix}$$

Figure 9-7: To multiply two matrices, multiply corresponding entries in rows and columns.

To get the result's second entry in the first column. You multiply A's second row by B's first column.

$$r10 = a10 \times b00 + a11 \times b10 + a12 \times b20 + a13 \times b30$$

You continue multiplying A's rows by B's first column until you have filled in the result's first column.

After you finish filling in the result matrix's first column, you generate the second result column by multiplying A's rows by B's second column.

Continue this process until you've filled in all of the result matrix's entries.

Matrices also let you perform more general transformations than some of those described earlier. For example, the section "Scaling" only explained how to scale with respect to the origin, but what if you want to scale with respect to some other point P?

Now you can build a combined transformation to do that out of simpler pieces. First, translate to move point P to the origin. Then scale with respect to the origin. Finally, translate to move point P back to its original position.

If you combine the matrices representing the translation, scaling, and reverse translation, the resulting matrix represents the more general scaling with respect to point P.

Similarly, you can build matrices to represent rotation around a general line. For example, you could combine matrices representing the following transformations.

1. Translate so the line intersects the origin.
2. Rotate around the Y axis so the line lies in the YZ plane.
3. Rotate around the X axis so the line lies along the Y axis.
4. Rotate by the desired amount around the Y axis.

5. Reverse the rotation in step 3.
6. Reverse the rotation in step 2.
7. Reverse the translation in step 1.

Often you use a similar technique to build a complex transformation out of a sequence of simpler operations.

Transformation Order

Note that, in general, the order in which you apply transformations is important. If you perform the same operations in a different order, you will usually get a different result.

For example, the top of Figure 9-8 shows a shape being rotated around the origin and then translated. The bottom of the figure shows the same shape being translated and then rotated around the origin. The results are somewhat similar but not identical.

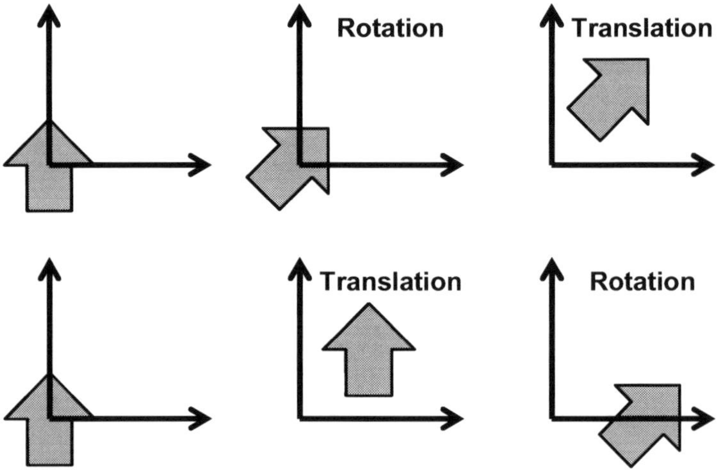

Figure 9-8: In general, the order of transformations makes a difference.

Inverse Transformations

Another handy property of transformation matrices is that the inverse of a transformation matrix represents the inverse of the transformation. For example, if matrix R represents a rotation, then the inverse matrix R^{-1} represents the reverse of the rotation.

For simple operations, it's easy enough to just build an inverse transformation matrix directly. For example, the inverse of a translation by the vector <dx, dy, dz> is simply a transformation by the vector <-dx, -dy, -dz>. Similarly, the inverse of scaling with respect to the origin by values sx, sy, and sz is scaling by values 1/sx, 1/sy, and 1/sz. Finally, the inverse of a rotation around a coordinate axis by angle θ is a rotation around the same axis by the angle -θ.

For more complex operations, it may sometimes be easier to invert a matrix rather than building an inverse matrix from scratch.

.NET Framework Classes

If your eyes glazed over during the preceding discussion of how the different kinds of transformation matrices work, don't despair. The .NET Framework provides classes that can do most of the math for you. There are two main ways that you can work with transformation matrices: the `Matrix3D` structure and transformation classes. The following sections describe those two approaches.

Matrix3D

The `Matrix3D` structure represents a four-by-four transformation matrix. Like the `Vector3D` and `Point3D` data types described in Chapter 8, the `Matrix3D` class knows how to perform basic arithmetic. For example, it knows how to multiply two matrices to get a third. It also knows how to multiply a point by a matrix to get another point.

The `Matrix3D` structure has two constructors. The first takes no parameters and creates an identity matrix with 1s on the diagonal and 0s everywhere else. The second lets you specify every entry in the matrix.

You can use the second constructor to build translation, scaling, and rotation matrices by filling in the matrix's components explicitly, but usually it's easier to use .NET tools to build transformations.

The following table summarizes `Matrix3D` methods that add transformations to an existing matrix.

Method	Purpose
`Rotate`	Specifies a rotation using a quaternion. (I'm not going to describe quaternions because they're confusing and hard to use. The `RotateTransform3D` class described in the following section lets you rotate without using quaternions.)
`RotateAt`	Specifies a rotation using a quaternion.
`Scale`	Scales with respect to the origin.
`ScaleAt`	Scales with respect to an arbitrary point.
`Translate`	Translates by a given amount.

For example, the following code makes a `Matrix3D` representing scaling at the origin.

```
Matrix3D transform = new Matrix3D();
transform.Scale(new Vector3D(4, 4, 4));
```

Those methods assume that you are appending the new transformation to the end of the matrix. The `Matrix3D` structure also includes versions of the methods that prepend the new transformation. Those methods are called RotatePrepend, RotateAtPrepend, ScalePrepend, ScaleAtPrepend, and TranslatePrepend.

After you create a Matrix3D object, you can use its Transform method to transform a point, vector, array of points, or array of vectors.

Transformation Classes

In addition to the Matrix3D class, which represents a matrix, WPF also provides classes that represent transformations in a more abstract way. The TranslateTransform3D, ScaleTransform3D, and RotateTransform3D classes provide basic transformations.

The TranslateTransform3D class has three constructors that take no parameters, three double values giving the translation offsets, or a Vector3D that gives the translation offsets.

The ScaleTransform3D class provides constructors that let you specify either scale parameters, or scale parameters and a center point around which to scale.

The RotateTransform3D class is a bit more complicated. It has several constructors, onw of which lets you rotate around a line passing through a specific point. That constructor takes as parameters a Rotation3D object that describes the rotation and the point.

The Rotation3D class is an abstract base class for two concrete subclasses: AxisAngleRotation3D and QuaternionRotation3D. I'm not going to cover the second one because, as I mentioned earlier, quaternions are confusing.

Fortunately, the AxisAngleRotation3D class is relatively straightforward. One of its constructors takes as parameters a vector defining the direction of the axis of rotation and the angle through which to rotate.

To summarize, to rotate around an arbitrary axis, you follow these steps.

1. Create a vector giving the direction of the axis of rotation.
2. Use the vector and the desired angle to create an AxisAngleRotation3D object representing the rotation.
3. Use the AxisAngleRotation3D object and the point through which the axis should pass to create the RotateTransform3D object.

To make this a little easier, I created the following D3 class.

```
public static class D3
{
    // Make a transformation for rotation around an arbitrary axis.
    public static RotateTransform3D Rotate(Vector3D axis, Point3D center, double angle)
    {
        Rotation3D rotation = new AxisAngleRotation3D(axis, angle);
        return new RotateTransform3D(rotation, center);
    }
}
```

This class's static `Rotate` method creates an `AxisAngleRotation3D` object that rotates around an arbitrary axis. It creates a `Rotation3D` object representing the rotation, and then uses it to create the `RotateTransform3D` object.

The `TranslateTransform3D`, `ScaleTransform3D`, and `RotateTransform3D` classes derive from the abstract `AffineTransform3D` class, which derives from `Transform3D`. That class defines a `Value` property that returns the transformation's matrix. That means, for example, that you could make a `ScaleTransform3D` object and the use its `Value` property to get a `Matrix3D` structure representing the transformation matrix.

The `Transform3D` class also defines `Transform` methods that let you transform points, vectors, arrays of points, and arrays of vectors.

Transformation Groups

The basic transformation classes (`TranslateTransform3D`, `ScaleTransform3D`, and `RotateTransform3D`) only work for single transformations. Sometimes you may need to combine several transformations to get the result that you want. To handle that situation, WPF defines the `Transform3DGroup` class to let you group transformations.

The `Transform3DGroup` class is also derived from `Transform3D`, so you can add basic transformations to a group and then use the group to transform an object.

For example, you could make a `Transform3DGroup` and add translation, scaling, and rotation transformations to it. You could then use the group's `Value` method to get a `Matrix3D` representing the combined transformation, or you could use its `Transform` method to apply the combined transformation to points or vectors.

Applying Transformations

As the preceding sections mention, you can use the `Transform` method of the `Matrix3D` or transformation classes to transform points or vectors. When you build three-dimensional graphics programs, it's often useful to apply transformations to a `MeshGeometry3D` object.

For example, you could build a sphere centered at the origin and then use transformations to move it to a different position, possibly scaled by different amounts in the X, Y, and Z directions to turn the sphere into an ellipsoid.

To make that kind of operation a bit easier, I created the following `MeshExtensions` class.

```
public static class MeshExtensions
{
    public static void ApplyTransformation(this MeshGeometry3D mesh,
        Matrix3D transformation)
    {
        Point3D[] points = mesh.Positions.ToArray();
        transformation.Transform(points);
```

```
            mesh.Positions = new Point3DCollection(points);
        }

        public static void ApplyTransformation(this MeshGeometry3D mesh,
            Transform3D transformation)
        {
            Point3D[] points = mesh.Positions.ToArray();
            transformation.Transform(points);
            mesh.Positions = new Point3DCollection(points);
        }
    }
```

The first iteration of this class defines two versions of the `ApplyTransformation` extension method. They apply either a `Matrix3D` or a `Transform3D` to a mesh. The methods convert the mesh's points into an array, apply the transformation to the array, and then store the results back in the mesh's `Positions` collection. These methods make it relatively easy to transform even complicated meshes.

Example Programs

This chapter's downloads include three programs that demonstrate transformation groups, the `ApplyTransformation` mesh extension method, and the `D3` class's `Rotate` method. The following sections describe the examples.

Axes

The Axes example program shown in Figure 9-9 uses transformations to display the coordinate axes and a cube at the origin. The axes are cubes that have been stretched so they are long and skinny.

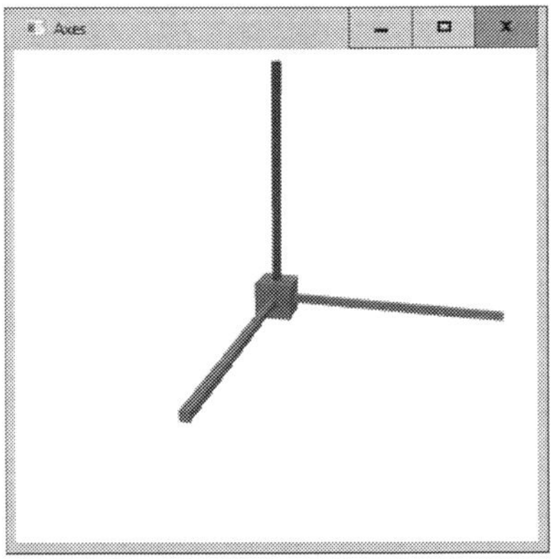

Figure 9-9: The Axes example program demonstrates the `ApplyTransformation` method.

The following code shows how the program builds its three-dimensional objects.

```
// Define the model.
private void DefineModel(Model3DGroup group)
{
    // Origin cube.
    MeshGeometry3D mesh = MakeCubeMesh(0, 0, 0, 0.5);
    Material material = new DiffuseMaterial(Brushes.Yellow);
    GeometryModel3D model = new GeometryModel3D(mesh, material);
    group.Children.Add(model);

    const double thickness = 0.1;
    const double length = 3;

    // X axis.
    MeshGeometry3D xmesh = MakeCubeMesh(0, 0, 0, 1);
    xmesh.ApplyTransformation(new ScaleTransform3D(length, thickness, thickness));
```

```
        xmesh.ApplyTransformation(new TranslateTransform3D(length / 2, 0, 0));
        Material xmaterial = new DiffuseMaterial(Brushes.Red);
        GeometryModel3D xmodel = new GeometryModel3D(xmesh, xmaterial);
        group.Children.Add(xmodel);

        // Y axis cube.
        MeshGeometry3D ymesh = MakeCubeMesh(0, 0, 0, 1);
        ymesh.ApplyTransformation(new ScaleTransform3D(thickness, length, thickness));
        ymesh.ApplyTransformation(new TranslateTransform3D(0, length / 2, 0));
        Material ymaterial = new DiffuseMaterial(Brushes.Green);
        GeometryModel3D ymodel = new GeometryModel3D(ymesh, ymaterial);
        group.Children.Add(ymodel);

        // Z axis cube.
        MeshGeometry3D zmesh = MakeCubeMesh(0, 0, 0, 1);
        Transform3DGroup zgroup = new Transform3DGroup();
        zgroup.Children.Add(new ScaleTransform3D(thickness, thickness, length));
        zgroup.Children.Add(new TranslateTransform3D(0, 0, length / 2));
        zmesh.ApplyTransformation(zgroup);
        Material zmaterial = new DiffuseMaterial(Brushes.Blue);
        GeometryModel3D zmodel = new GeometryModel3D(zmesh, zmaterial);
        group.Children.Add(zmodel);
    }
```

The code first uses the `MakeCubeMesh` method to create a cube centered at the origin. The `MakeCubeMesh` method is straightforward so I won't describe it here. Download the example if you want to see how it works. (I'll describe a better method for building cubes in a later chapter anyway.) The code gives this cube a yellow material.

Next, the program uses `MakeCubeMesh` again to create another cube. It uses the `ApplyTransformation` extension method to make the cube long and skinny but still centered at the origin. It then uses `ApplyTransformation` again to move the stretched cube so one end is at the origin.

The code repeats those steps to build the cube that represents Y axis.

The method takes a different approach to build the Z axis. It makes a cube as before. Then it creates a `Transform3DGroup` to hold multiple transformations. It adds scale and translation transformations to the group to stretch and position the cube. It then uses the `ApplyTransformation` extension method to apply the group's combined transformation to the Z axis cube.

Download the example to see additional details.

RotatedCube

The RotatedCube example program shown in Figure 9 10 uses the following code to rotate a cube to place one of its vertices on the Y axis.

```
// Make a cube.
MeshGeometry3D mesh = MakeCubeMesh(0, 0, 0, 2);
Material material = new DiffuseMaterial(Brushes.LightBlue);
```

```
GeometryModel3D model = new GeometryModel3D(mesh, material);
group.Children.Add(model);

// Rotate around the Y axis.
mesh.ApplyTransformation(
    D3.Rotate(new Vector3D(0, 1, 0), new Point3D(0, 0, 0), 45));

// Rotate around the X axis.
double angle = Math.Atan2(Math.Sqrt(2), 1);
angle = angle * 180 / Math.PI;
mesh.ApplyTransformation(
    D3.Rotate(new Vector3D(1, 0, 0), new Point3D(0, 0, 0), angle));
```

This code creates a cube, rotates it around the Y axis so its vertices lie above the X and Z axes, and then rotates it around the X axis to move one of its vertices onto the Y axis.

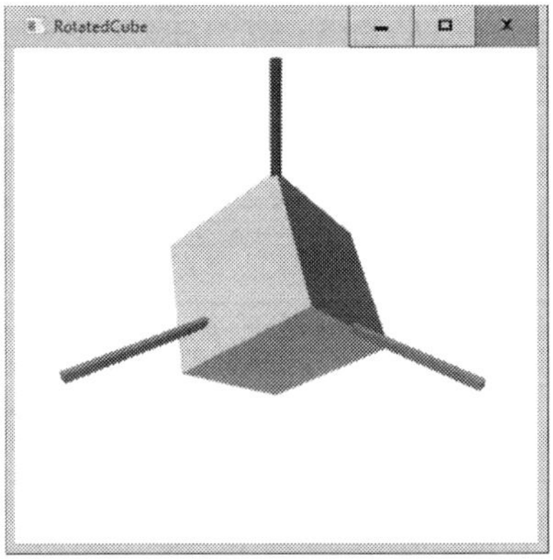

Figure 9-10: The RotatedCube example program rotates a cube so a vertex lies on the Y axis.

Spinner

The Spinner example program creates a cube similar to the one used by the RotatedCube program. It then rotates the cube five degrees per second around the Y axis.

The program uses the following code to keep track of the cube's mesh and the rotation transformation.

```
// The cube's mesh and rotation transformation.
private MeshGeometry3D CubeMesh = null;
private RotateTransform3D CubeRotator = null;
```

The following code snippet shows the key pieces of the `DefineModel` method, which defines the program's scene.

```
// Define the model.
private void DefineModel(Model3DGroup group)
{
    // Make a cube.
    ...

    // Make a transformation to rotate the cube
    // 5 degrees around the Y axis.
    CubeRotator = D3.Rotate(
        new Vector3D(0, 1, 0), new Point3D(0, 0, 0), 5);
    ...
}
```

This method defines its cube the same way the RotatedCube example does. It then uses the `D3.Rotate` method to create a transformation to represent rotating five degrees around the Y axis. It saves the transformation in the `CubeRotator` variable.

After it calls `DefineModel`, the window's `Loaded` event handler uses the following code to create a timer to rotate the cube.

```
// Make a timer to rotate the cube.
DispatcherTimer timer = new DispatcherTimer();
timer.Tick += timer_Tick;
timer.Interval = new TimeSpan(0, 0, 0, 0, 50);
timer.Start();
```

This code creates a new `DispatcherTimer`. (That class is defined in the `System.Windows.Threading` namespace, so the program includes an appropriate `using` directive.) It sets the timer's `Tick` event handler, makes the timer fire every 50 milliseconds (20 times per second), and starts the timer.

The following code shows the timer's `Tick` event handler.

```
// Rotate the cube.
private void timer_Tick(object sender, EventArgs e)
{
    CubeMesh.ApplyTransformation(CubeRotator);
}
```

This method uses the `ApplyTransformation` mesh extension method to apply the `CubeRotator` transformation to the cube's mesh. That rotates the cube five degrees from its previous position.

Download the example to see additional details and to see it in action.

Summary

Homogeneous coordinates let you represent three-dimensional transformations as four-by four matrices. The .NET Framework lets you represent those matrices either by using the `Matrix3D` structure or by using transformation classes.

If you use `Matrix3D` structures, then you can multiply them together to create complex transformations. If you use transformation classes, then you can add them to a `Transform3DGroup` object to create complex transformations.

Either way, you can apply transformations to points and vectors. The `ApplyTransformation` mesh extension methods make transforming `MeshGeometry3D` objects easy.

Download the Axes, RotatedCube, and Spinner examples and experiment with them. You can use them as the starting point for all sorts of programs that display cubes and rectangular prisms that are translated and rotated into any position you like. You can even use timers to animate mesh's by applying transformations to them.

At this point, you have all of the tools that you need to build complicated three-dimensional scenes. However, the book has so far mostly worked with simple triangles, rectangles, and cubes. It's much less obvious how to build more complex shapes such as icosahedrons, geodesic spheres, and tori (donuts). The following chapters explain how to build those shapes and more.

Chapter 10
Polygons

Earlier chapters built rectangles in a fairly ad-hoc fashion. This chapter explains a more systematic approach that you can use to create rectangles and other polygons quickly and easily. It also explains some helper methods that make turning meshes into models easier.

Sharing Points

Earlier I mentioned that triangles can share vertices. For example, if you want two triangles to share point number 100 in a mesh's `Positions` list, simply use 100 in both triangles' `TriangleIndices` entries.

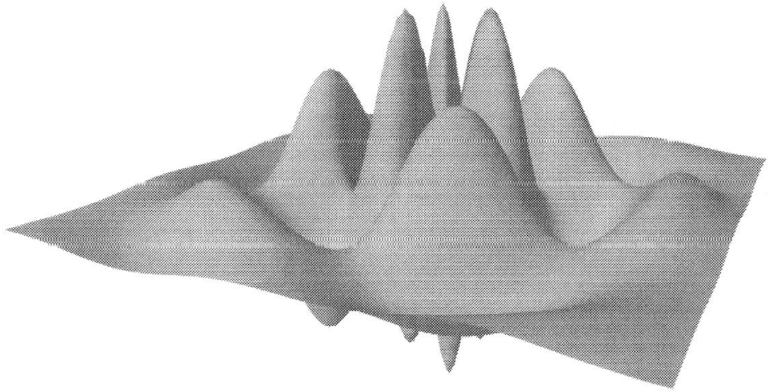

Figure 10-1: If triangles share vertices, the surface is smoother.

If two triangles share a vertex, then the drawing system uses an average of their normals for the normal at that point. This produces a smoother result, and the two triangles blend together.

This is useful for smooth shapes such as the surface shown in Figure 10-1. It's not useful along edges that should be sharp, such as the edges of a cube. That means you should share points when you're drawing a smooth surface but you shouldn't share points along the edges of a cube.

There are several ways that you can figure out which triangles should share vertices. First, you can keep careful track of where every vertex is and how it should be used. This method works is and efficient, but it can be tricky. Keeping track of which vertices should make up which triangles can be hard for complex shapes such as a sphere, cone, or torus.

That method also isn't very general. The system you use to keep track of the vertices that make up a sphere probably won't work for a torus or cylinder.

Another approach is to look in the mesh's `Positions` collection every time you need a vertex. If the vertex is already present, you can reuse it. If it isn't in the `Positions` collection yet, you can add it.

This method works and is easy to apply to surfaces, spheres, cylinders, or any other smooth shape. Unfortunately, it can be slow. As a mesh grows larger, the number of vertices it holds also grows, so searching the `Positions` collection takes longer and longer. This isn't a big deal for small objects such as cubes, but it can take a while if the mesh contains several thousand vertices.

A third approach, and the one that I use routinely, uses a dictionary to store vertex information. When you need to use a vertex, you check the dictionary to see if it is already present. You then reuse the existing vertex if it exists or create a new vertex if it hasn't been added to the dictionary yet.

The `MeshExtensions` class contains the following code to perform the lookup.

```
// If the point is already in the dictionary, return its index in the mesh.
// If the point isn't in the dictionary, create it in the mesh and add its
// index to the dictionary.
private static int PointIndex(this MeshGeometry3D mesh,
    Point3D point, Dictionary<Point3D, int> pointDict = null)
{
    // See if the point already exists.
    if ((pointDict != null) && (pointDict.ContainsKey(point)))
    {
        // The point is already in the dictionary. Return its index.
        return pointDict[point];
    }

    // Create the point.
    int index = mesh.Positions.Count;
    mesh.Positions.Add(point);

    // Add the point's index to the dictionary.
    if (pointDict != null) pointDict.Add(point, index);

    // Return the index.
    return index;
}
```

This is an extension method for the `MeshGeometry3D` class. The `point` parameter is the vertex that the program needs to use to build a triangle. The `pointDict` parameter is an optional dictionary of vertex information.

The dictionary uses `Point3D` objects as keys. The corresponding values are the points' indices in the mesh's `Positions` collection. You use the dictionary to look up a point and find its vertex.

The method first checks the dictionary to see if the vertex is present. If the point is in the dictionary, the method gets the point's index and returns it.

If the point isn't in the dictionary, the method adds it to the mesh's `Positions` collection and to the dictionary. It finishes by returning the new point's index.

The following code shows an overloaded version of the method that also takes a texture coordinate point as a parameter.

```
// If the point is already in the dictionary, return its index in the mesh.
// If the point isn't in the dictionary, create it and its texture coordinates
// in the mesh and add its index to the dictionary.
private static int PointIndex(this MeshGeometry3D mesh,
    Point3D point, Point textureCoord,
    Dictionary<Point3D, int> pointDict = null)
{
    // See if the point already exists.
    if ((pointDict != null) && (pointDict.ContainsKey(point)))
    {
        // The point is already in the dictionary. Return its index.
        return pointDict[point];
    }

    // Create the point.
    int index = mesh.Positions.Count;
    mesh.Positions.Add(point);

    // Add the point's texture coordinates.
    mesh.TextureCoordinates.Add(textureCoord);

    // Add the point's index to the dictionary.
    if (pointDict != null) pointDict.Add(point, index);

    // Return the index.
    return index;
}
```

This version works just like the previous version does except it also saves the vertex's texture coordinates when it creates a new vertex.

Adding Polygons

The reason this chapter cares about the issue of sharing vertices is that the pieces of a polygon should share vertices. For example, consider the cube shown in Figure 10-2. Triangles A and B form one side of the cube. Because they are part of a square, they should share vertices so they blend smoothly together at their common edge.

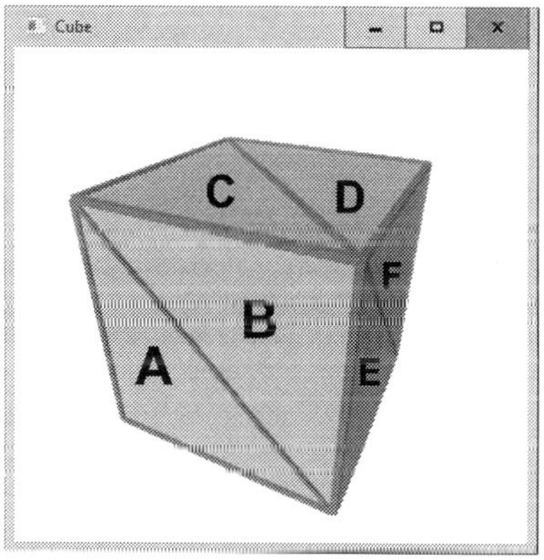

Figure 10-2: The triangles on a face should share vertices.

Similarly the pairs of triangles C/D and E/F should share vertices.

In contrast, triangles B and C lie on different cube faces so they should not share vertices so their common edge is sharp.

The following `AddPolygon` extension method adds a polygon to a mesh, making the polygon's triangles share vertices.

```
// Add a polygon with points stored in an array.
// Texture coordinates are optional.
public static void AddPolygon(this MeshGeometry3D mesh,
    Point3D[] points, Point[] textureCoords = null)
{
    // Make a point dictionary.
    Dictionary<Point3D, int> pointDict = new Dictionary<Point3D, int>();

    // Get the first two point indices.
    int indexA, indexB, indexC;

    if (textureCoords == null)
        indexA = mesh.PointIndex(points[0].Round(), pointDict);
    else
        indexA = mesh.PointIndex(points[0].Round(), textureCoords[0], pointDict);

    if (textureCoords == null)
        indexC = mesh.PointIndex(points[1].Round(), pointDict);
    else
        indexC = mesh.PointIndex(points[1].Round(), textureCoords[1], pointDict);

    // Make triangles.
    for (int i = 2; i < points.Length; i++)
    {
        indexB = indexC;

        if (textureCoords == null)
            indexC = mesh.PointIndex(points[i].Round(), pointDict);
        else
            indexC = mesh.PointIndex(points[i].Round(), textureCoords[i], pointDict);

        if ((indexA != indexB) &&
            (indexB != indexC) &&
            (indexC != indexA))
        {
            mesh.TriangleIndices.Add(indexA);
            mesh.TriangleIndices.Add(indexB);
            mesh.TriangleIndices.Add(indexC);
        }
    }
}
```

This method makes a dictionary to hold vertex information. It then loops through the points that make up the polygon to build its triangles.

Each time it considers a triangle, point A is the polygon's first point. Points B and C are two adjacent points along the polygon as shown in Figure 10-3.

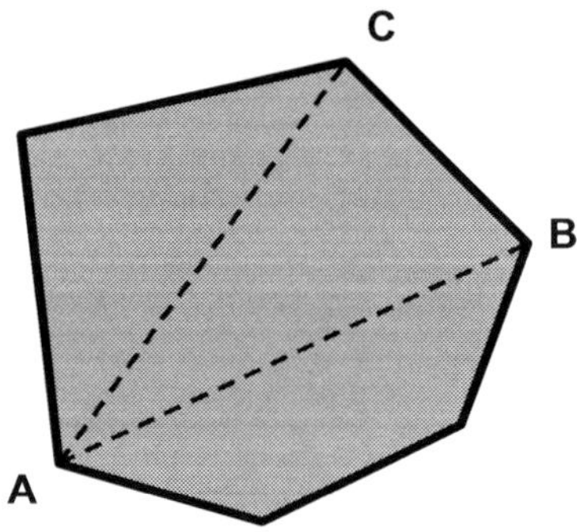

Figure 10-3: A polygon's triangles should share vertices.

The drawing system does a bad job handling odd situations such as triangles with two identical points. If the program creates this kind of zero-width triangle, it may hide or truncate some other triangles unexpectedly, and the affected triangles may change if you modify the camera's position. Those kinds of bugs can be very hard to track down because they are caused by a triangle that isn't even visible.

To avoid that kind of error, the `AddPolygon` method doesn't make any triangles of this kind. For each group of points A, B, and C, the method checks whether any of the three points is the same. If two of the points are the same, the method skips building that triangle.

If the triangle's points are all distinct, the `AddPolygon` method adds triangle ΔABC to the mesh.

Note that the triangle's three points have the same orientation as the original polygon. If the polygon is outwardly oriented, then so is triangle ΔABC.

When it finds the indices for the points it is using, the method uses the appropriate version of `PointIndex` and that method saves the texture coordinates for the vertices if necessary.

NOTE: The method assumes that the polygon can be represented by the "fan" of triangles generated by the code. It will work for convex polygons, but may not work for nonconvex polygons like the one shown in Figure 10-4.

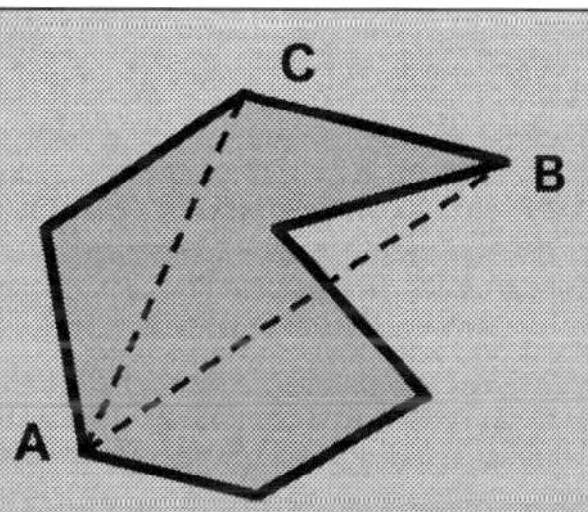

Figure 10-4: This polygon cannot be represented by a simple "fan" of triangles.

If you look at the code, you'll notice that it calls each point's `Round` method before passing it into `PointIndex`.

The `Round` method is an extension method defined in the following `Point3DExtensions` class.

```
public static class Point3DExtensions
{
    // Return a rounded Point3D so close points match.
    public static Point3D Round(this Point3D point, int decimals = 3)
    {
        double x = Math.Round(point.X, decimals);
        double y = Math.Round(point.Y, decimals);
        double z = Math.Round(point.Z, decimals);
        return new Point3D(x, y, z);
```

```
        }
    }
```

This method uses `Math.Round` to round the coordinates of a point to some number of digits after the decimal point. If you leave out that number, it defaults to three. That means each point is rounded to the nearest 0.001 or thousandth of a unit.

The reason I do this is to merge points that are very close together. Sometimes when a program performs calculations, rounding errors make two points different when they should be identical. Rounding them makes them match exactly so there are no small holes in the model.

There is still a chance that two points will not match exactly even though they should. That happens if one point's coordinate rounds up while the other rounds down. This method makes that less likely, however.

The following code shows an overloaded version of the `AddPolygon` method.

```
// Add a polygon with a variable argument list of points
// and no texture coordinates.
public static void AddPolygon(this MeshGeometry3D mesh,
    params Point3D[] points)
{
    Dictionary<Point3D, int> pointDict = new Dictionary<Point3D, int>();
    mesh.AddPolygon(points, null);
}
```

This method doesn't take texture coordinates as a parameter. Instead it ends with an array of `Point3D` values. Because that parameter is declared with the `params` keyword, you can invoke the method passing it any number of points. For example, the following code passes this method four points to create a rectangle.

```
Mesh.AddPolygon(
    new Point3D(-1, 0, -1),
    new Point3D(-1, 0,  1),
    new Point3D( 1, 0,  1),
    new Point3D( 1, 0, -1));
```

This version of `AddPolygon` simply invokes the previous version, passing it `null` for its texture coordinates parameter.

Adding Regular Polygons

In a regular polygon, every side has the same length and the angles between adjacent sides are the same. The following `AddRegularPolygon` extension method creates a regular polygon.

```
// Add a regular polygon with optional texture coordinates.
public static void AddRegularPolygon(this MeshGeometry3D mesh,
    int numSides, Point3D center, Vector3D vx, Vector3D vy,
    Point[] textureCoords = null)
{
```

```
        // Generate the points.
        Point3D[] points = G3.MakePolygonPoints(numSides, center, vx, vy);

        // Make the polygon.
        mesh.AddPolygon(points, textureCoords);
    }
```

This method takes as parameters the number of sides the polygon should have, the polygon's center, two vectors `vx` and `vy`, and an optional array of texture coordinates. The code starts by calling the `MakePolygonPoints` method described shortly to generate the polygon's vertices. It then passes those points into the `AddPolygon` method to create the polygon.

> **NOTE:** I created a separate `MakePolygonPoints` method so it would be easier to reuse later. I put the method in a new static class named `G3` (which stands for "three-dimensional geometry"). I'll add more to this class in later chapters.

The following code shows the `MakePolygonPoints` method.

```
    // Make points to define a regular polygon.
    public static Point3D[] MakePolygonPoints(int numSides,
        Point3D center, Vector3D vx, Vector3D vy)
    {
        // Generate the points.
        Point3D[] points = new Point3D[numSides];
        double dtheta = 2 * Math.PI / numSides;
        double theta = Math.PI / 2;
        for (int i = 0; i < numSides; i++)
        {
            points[i] = center + vx * Math.Cos(theta) + vy * Math.Sin(theta);
            theta += dtheta;
        }
        return points;
    }
```

The vectors `vx` and `vy` determine the plane that should contain the polygon and the polygon's radii in the directions of the vectors. If the vectors have the same length, then the result will be a regular polygon. If the vectors have different lengths, then the polygon will be stretched in one direction more than the other.

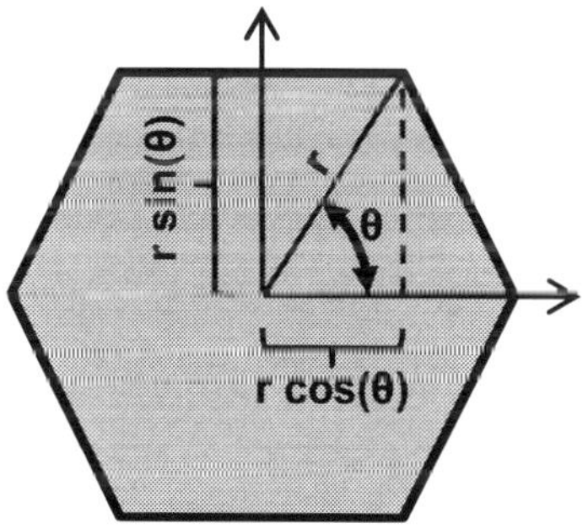

Figure 10-5: You can use trigonometry to find a regular polygon's points.

For example, to make a polygon with radius 4 in the XY plane, you would use the vectors <4, 0, 0> and <0, 4, 0>. To make a polygon with radius 5 in the XZ plane, you would use the vectors <5, 0, 0> and <0, 0, 5>.

The method loops through the desired number of sides to

find each vertex. If this were a two-dimensional polygon in the XY plane, then you would multiply the radius by the sine and cosine of the point's angle to find its coordinates as shown in Figure 10-5. In three-dimensional space, you multiply the sine and cosine by the vectors `vx` and `vy`. (I named them `vx` and `vy` so they would be analogous to the X and Y directions in the two-dimensional version.)

After multiplying the vectors by the angle's sine and cosine, the code adds the results to the center point to position the point relative to the polygon's center.

After it finishes building the `points` array, the method passes it to the `AddPolygon` method described earlier to add the polygon to the mesh.

Helper Methods

Chapter 9 introduced the static `D3` class. It defined the helper method `Rotate` to create a `RotateTransform3D` object representing rotation around an arbitrary axis.

Now it's time to add some more helper variables and methods to the `D3` class. The new version of the class defines the following variables.

```
// Return the origin.
public static Point3D Origin = new Point3D();

// Return vectors along the coordinate axes.
public static Vector3D XUnit = new Vector3D(1, 0, 0);
public static Vector3D YUnit = new Vector3D(0, 1, 0);
public static Vector3D ZUnit = new Vector3D(0, 0, 1);
public static Vector3D XVector(double length = 1)
{
    return new Vector3D(length, 0, 0);
}
public static Vector3D YVector(double length = 1)
{
    return new Vector3D(0, length, 0);
}
public static Vector3D ZVector(double length = 1)
{
    return new Vector3D(0, 0, length);
}
```

This code defines an `Origin` value that represents the point (0, 0, 0).

It then defines unit vectors pointing in the directions of the X, Y, and Z axes. The `XVector`, `YVector`, and `ZVector` methods return scaled vectors along the axes.

The `D3` class also defines the following method to generate texture coordinates for a regular polygon.

```
// Make texture coordinates for a polygon.
// The first point is at the top.
public static Point[] MakePolygonTextureCoords(int numSides)
{
    double dtheta = 2 * Math.PI / numSides;
```

```
        double theta = Math.PI / 2;
        Point[] coords = new Point[numSides];
        for (int i = 0; i < numSides; i++)
        {
            coords[i] = new Point(
                0.5 + Math.Cos(theta) / 2,
                0.5 - Math.Sin(theta) / 2);
            theta += dtheta;
        }
        return coords;
    }
```

This method uses trigonometry to find the points of a regular polygon centered in the two-dimensional area $0 \leq \{u, v\} \leq 1$.

Making Models

After you make a mesh, you need to create a material for it and then convert the mesh and material into a model. The following code shows how you might create a red rectangle.

```
MeshGeometry3D mesh = new MeshGeometry3D();
mesh.AddPolygon(
    new Point3D(-2, -2, -2),
    new Point3D( 2, -2, -2),
    new Point3D( 2,  2, -2),
    new Point3D(-2,  2, -2)
);
Material material = new DiffuseMaterial(Brushes.Red);
Model3D model = new GeometryModel3D(mesh, material);
group.Children.Add(model);
```

This code creates a `MeshGeometry3D` object and then uses the new `AddPolygon` method to add a rectangle to it. It creates a material that uses a solid red brush, uses the mesh and material to create a model, and then adds the model to the `Model3DGroup` named `group`.

To make this a bit easier, the `MeshExtensions` class defines the following two versions of the `MakeModel` method.

```
// Make a model with a diffuse brush.
public static GeometryModel3D MakeModel(this MeshGeometry3D mesh, Brush brush)
{
    Material material = new DiffuseMaterial(brush);
    return new GeometryModel3D(mesh, material);
}

// Make a model with a texture brush.
public static GeometryModel3D MakeModel(this MeshGeometry3D mesh, string uri)
{
    ImageBrush brush = new ImageBrush();
    brush.ImageSource = new BitmapImage(new Uri(uri, UriKind.Relative));
    return mesh.MakeModel(brush);
}
```

The first version takes a brush as a parameter. It uses the brush to make a material, uses the mesh and material to make a `GeometryModel3D`, and returns the result.

The second version does the same thing with a texture brush. It takes as a parameter the name of the image file that it should use to make the brush. It creates a `Uri` object to identify the file, uses that to create a `TextureBrush`, and then passes the brush to the first version of `MakeModel`.

Now instead of using separate statements to make a material and a model, the program can simply call the mesh's `MakeModel` method and add the result to the `GeometryModel3D` as shown in the following statement.

```
group.Children.Add(mesh.MakeModel(Brushes.Red));
```

Example Program

The Polygons example program demonstrates the `AddPolygon` method and various helper methods. It uses the following code to define its model.

```
private void DefineModel(Model3DGroup group)
{
    // Make a textured pentagon in the XZ plane.
    MeshGeometry3D mesh1 = new MeshGeometry3D();
    mesh1.AddRegularPolygon(5, D3.Origin,
        D3.XVector(2), D3.ZVector(-2),
        D3.MakePolygonTextureCoords(5));
    group.Children.Add(mesh1.MakeModel("Smiley.png"));

    // Clone and move down 2 units.
    MeshGeometry3D mesh2 = mesh1.Clone();
    mesh2.ApplyTransformation(new TranslateTransform3D(0, -2, 0));
    group.Children.Add(mesh2.MakeModel(Brushes.LightBlue));

    // Make a triangle with X = -2.
    MeshGeometry3D mesh3 = new MeshGeometry3D();
    mesh3.AddPolygon(
        new Point3D(-2, -2, -2),
        new Point3D(-2, +2,  0),
        new Point3D(-2, -2, +2)
    );
    group.Children.Add(mesh3.MakeModel(Brushes.Pink));

    // Make a rectangle with Z = -2.
    MeshGeometry3D mesh4 = new MeshGeometry3D();
    mesh4.AddPolygon(
        new Point3D(-2, -2, -2),
        new Point3D(+2, -2, -2),
        new Point3D(+2, +2, -2),
        new Point3D(-2, +2, -2)
    );
    group.Children.Add(mesh4.MakeModel(Brushes.LightGreen));
}
```

The method first uses the AddRegularPolygon method to make a pentagon centered at the origin. The parameters D3.XVector(2) and D3.ZVector(-2) create vectors with length two pointed in the X and -Z directions.

The method call uses D3.MakePolygonTextureCoords to make texture coordinates for a pentagon and passes those coordinates into the AddRegularPolygon method.

After calling AddRegularPolygon, the method calls the mesh's MakeModel method, passing it the file name "Smiley.png." (I added that file to the project at design time and set its Copy to Output Directory property to Copy if Newer as described in the section "Image Brush" in Chapter 7.) It then adds the new model to the Model3DGroup.

Next, the code calls the mesh's Clone method to make a copy of the mesh. It uses the ApplyTransform extension method to move the clone down two units. It calls the clone's MakeModel method, passing it a light blue brush, and adds the result to the Model3DGroup.

The method creates a third mesh and calls AddPolygon to make a triangle. It uses the mesh to build a pink model and adds it to the Model3DGroup.

Finally, the method repeats those steps to make a light green rectangle.

Figure 10-6 shows the final result.

Figure 10-6: The Polygons example program makes several kinds of polygons.

Summary

This chapter described the AddPolygon and AddRegularPolygon methods. It also described some helper routines, the most important of which is the PointIndex method that looks up an existing point or creates a new one if the point doesn't yet exist.

Be sure you understand how those methods work because they are used by the chapters that follow. For example, the next chapter explains how to use the AddPolygon method to make parallelograms in three dimensions.

Chapter 11

Parallelograms

People usually think in rectangles, but three-dimensional drawing programs work in triangles. To make working with rectangles easier, it would make sense to create one or more extension methods to create rectangles.

A rectangle is a particular kind of parallelogram. (A *parallelogram* is a four-sided polygon where the opposite sides are parallel.) It takes about the same amount of work to build a parallelogram as it does to build a rectangle, so I decided to create an `AddParallelogram` method and use it to create rectangles.

The following section explains the `AddParallelogram` method. The section after that describes the Parallelograms example program that demonstrates the method.

Adding Parallelograms

The following code shows the `AddParallelogram` method.

```
// Add a parallelogram defined by a corner point and two edge vectors.
// Texture coordinates and the point dictionary are optional.
public static void AddParallelogram(this MeshGeometry3D mesh,
    Point3D corner, Vector3D v1, Vector3D v2,
    Point[] textureCoords = null)
{
    // Find the parallelogram's corners.
    Point3D[] points =
    {
        corner,
        corner + v1,
        corner + v1 + v2,
        corner + v2,
    };

    // Make it.
    mesh.AddPolygon(points, textureCoords);
}
```

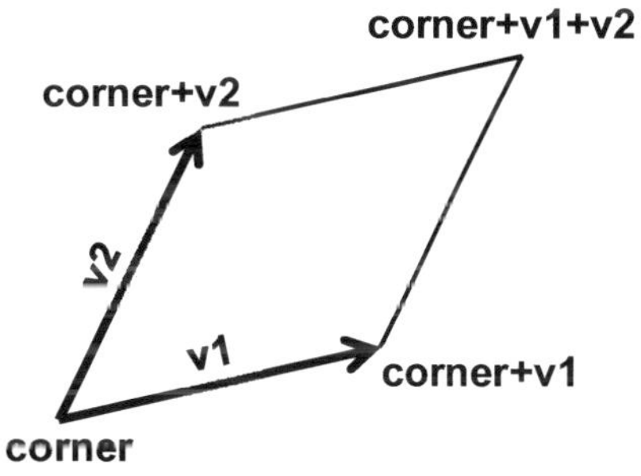

Figure 11-1: A point and two vectors define a parallelogram.

This method takes as parameters a corner point and two vectors `v1` and `v2` that define the edges of the parallelogram as shown in Figure 11-1.

The method uses vector arithmetic to find the parallelogram's four corners. It then passes the corners and any texture coordinates that it has into the `AddPolygon` extension method described in Chapter 10.

To make a rectangle, simply ensure that vectors `v1` and `v2` are perpendicular. To make a square, also ensure that they have the same length.

> **NOTE:** The `AddParallelogram` method, like the `AddPolygon` method described earlier and other shape-building methods described later, is an extension method defined in the `MeshExtensions` class. The basic approach for building a scene is to create a mesh and then use its extension methods to add objects to it.

Example Program

The Parallelograms example program demonstrates the `AddParallelogram` method. The following code defines the program's model.

```
private void DefineModel(Model3DGroup group)
{
    // Make some parallelograms.
    MeshGeometry3D mesh1 = new MeshGeometry3D();
    Point[] textureCoords =
    {
        new Point(0, 1),
        new Point(1, 1),
        new Point(1, 0),
        new Point(0, 0),
    };
    mesh1.AddParallelogram(new Point3D(-2, -2, -2),
        new Vector3D(4, 0, 0), new Vector3D(4, 4, 0), textureCoords);
    group.Children.Add(mesh1.MakeModel("Smiley.png"));

    MeshGeometry3D mesh2 = new MeshGeometry3D();
    mesh2.AddParallelogram(new Point3D(-2, -2, 2),
        new Vector3D(0, 0, -4), new Vector3D(0, 4, 0));
    group.Children.Add(mesh2.MakeModel(Brushes.Pink));

    MeshGeometry3D mesh3 = new MeshGeometry3D();
    mesh3.AddParallelogram(new Point3D(-2, -2, 0),
        new Vector3D(2, 0, 2), new Vector3D(2, 0, -2));
    group.Children.Add(mesh3.MakeModel(Brushes.LightBlue));
}
```

This method creates a mesh, builds an array of texture coordinates, and calls `AddParallelogram` to make a parallelogram. The two vectors it uses have Y component 0, so the resulting parallelogram is parallel to the XZ plane. The vectors are not parallel, so the result is not a rectangle.

After creating the parallelogram, the program calls the mesh's `MakeModel` method to give it a texture and turn it into a model. It then adds the model to the model group.

Next, the code makes a second mesh and calls `AddParallelogram` again. The two vectors have X component 0, so this parallelogram is parallel to the YZ plane. This time the vectors are perpendicular and have the same length, so the result is a square. The code converts the mesh into a pink model and adds the model to the model group.

The code then repeats the steps again to create a third parallelogram. This time the vectors' Y components are 0 so the result is parallel to the XZ plane. The vectors are perpendicular and have the same length, so this is another square.

Figure 11-2 shows the Parallelograms example program in action.

Figure 11-2: The Parallelograms example program displays three parallelograms.

Summary

The `AddParallelogram` method performs some simple vector arithmetic to find the parallelogram's vertices and then calls `AddPolygon` to do most of the work. This is typical of the methods described in the following chapters; they use previously built extension methods to create more and more elaborate objects. For example, Chapter 12 uses the `AddParallelogram` method to build boxes.

Chapter 12

Boxes

If people usually think in rectangles, they also think in cubes and rectangular boxes. Minecraft takes that idea to the extreme and makes everything out of cubes.

Just as a rectangle is a kind of parallelogram, a rectangular box is a kind of solid called a parallelepiped.

> **NOTE:** A *parallelepiped* is a three-dimensional shape that has six parallelograms for sides and opposite sides are parallel to each other.
>
> ("Parallelepiped" is another good word to pull out at a party when people are tired of Pictionary and Klingon Boggle and you've already used up the words "chirality" and "frustum.")

It takes roughly the same amount of work to build a parallelepiped as it does to build a rectangular box, so I decided to create an `AddBox` method that creates parallelepipeds. (I figured "`AddBox`" would be easier to type than "`AddParallelepiped`.") You can then use the `AddBox` method to make cubes and other rectangular boxes.

The following section explains how different versions of the `AddBox` method work. The sections after that describe some special uses of the method and an example program.

Adding Boxes

Just as you can use a corner and two vectors to define a parallelogram, you can use a corner and three vectors to define a parallelepiped as shown in Figure 12-1.

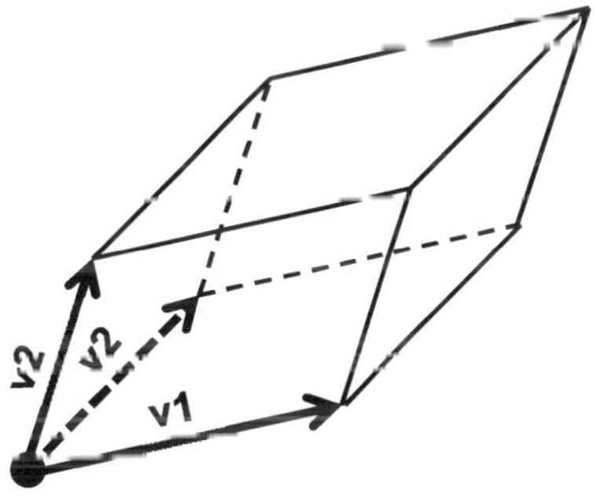

Figure 12-1: A point and three vectors define a parallelepiped.

The following `AddBox` extension method uses a corner point, three vectors, and six arrays containing texture coordinates (one for each face) to create a box.

```
// Add a parallelepiped with different texture coordinates for each face.
public static void AddBox(this MeshGeometry3D mesh,
    Point3D corner, Vector3D vx, Vector3D vy, Vector3D vz,
    Point[] frontCoords, Point[] leftCoords, Point[] rightCoords,
```

```
    Point[] backCoords, Point[] topCoords, Point[] bottomCoords)
{
    mesh.AddParallelogram(corner + vz, vx, vy, frontCoords);        // Front
    mesh.AddParallelogram(corner, vz, vy, leftCoords);              // Left
    mesh.AddParallelogram(corner + vx + vz, -vz, vy, rightCoords);  // Right
    mesh.AddParallelogram(corner + vx, -vx, vy, backCoords);        // Back
    mesh.AddParallelogram(corner + vy + vz, vx, -vz, topCoords);    // Top
    mesh.AddParallelogram(corner, vx, vz, bottomCoords);            // Bottom
}
```

The method uses vector arithmetic to calculate the vertices for the box's faces. It then passes those vertices and the appropriate texture coordinates into the `AddParallelogram` method described in Chapter 11.

This version of the method assumes that you will give a different texture to each of the box's faces. If you want to use a single texture for all of the faces, or if you don't want to use texture coordinates, then you can use the following version of the method.

```
public static void AddBox(this MeshGeometry3D mesh,
    Point3D corner, Vector3D vx, Vector3D vy, Vector3D vz,
    Point[] textureCoords = null)
{
    mesh.AddBox(corner, vx, vy, vz,
        textureCoords, textureCoords, textureCoords,
        textureCoords, textureCoords, textureCoords);
}
```

This method simply invokes the previous version, passing it the same texture coordinates for each of the box's faces. If you omit the `textureCoords` parameter, it defaults to `null`.

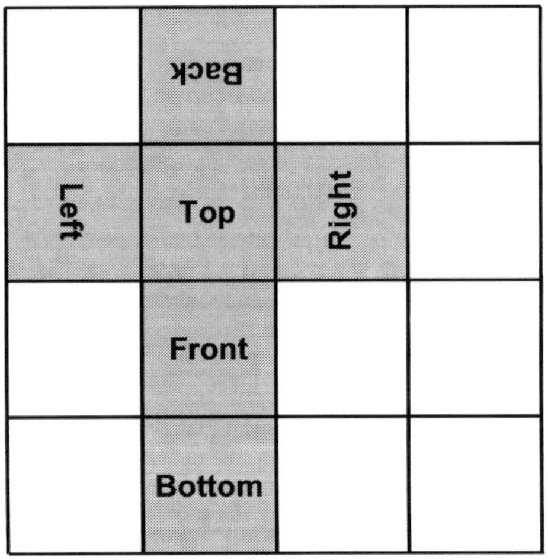

Figure 12-2: The AddBoxWrapped method wraps a box with the indicated part of a texture.

I created one more version of the method, although I named it `AddBoxWrapped` because it wraps the faces of the box as if it were using wrapping paper. Figure 12-2 shows the texture used as the wrapping paper. The shaded areas are mapped onto the box.

In fact, if you were to print out Figure 12-2 and cut out the shaded area, you could fold it into a cube.

If the box is not a cube, then the regions on the texture are mapped accordingly. For example, if the box is rectangular but not a cube, then some of the regions will be squashed or stretched to fit. If the box is not rectangular, then the regions will be skewed to fit the box's parallelogram sides.

The following code shows the `AddBoxWrapped` method.

```
// Add a parallelepiped with wrapped texture coordinates.
public static void AddBoxWrapped(this MeshGeometry3D mesh,
    Point3D corner, Vector3D vx, Vector3D vy, Vector3D vz)
```

```
{
    // Get texture coordinates for the pieces.
    Point[] frontCoords =
    {
        new Point(0.25, 0.75), new Point(0.50, 0.75),
        new Point(0.50, 0.50), new Point(0.25, 0.50),
    };
    Point[] leftCoords =
    {
        new Point(0.00, 0.25), new Point(0.00, 0.50),
        new Point(0.25, 0.50), new Point(0.25, 0.25),
    };
    Point[] rightCoords =
    {
        new Point(0.75, 0.50), new Point(0.75, 0.25),
        new Point(0.50, 0.25), new Point(0.50, 0.50),
    };
    Point[] backCoords =
    {
        new Point(0.50, 0.00), new Point(0.25, 0.00),
        new Point(0.25, 0.25), new Point(0.50, 0.25),
    };
    Point[] topCoords =
    {
        new Point(0.25, 0.50), new Point(0.50, 0.50),
        new Point(0.50, 0.25), new Point(0.25, 0.25),
    };
    Point[] bottomCoords =
    {
        new Point(0.25, 1.00), new Point(0.50, 1.00),
        new Point(0.50, 0.75), new Point(0.25, 0.75),
    };

    // Add a point to use all texture coordinates in the area (0, 0) - (1, 1).
    mesh.Positions.Add(new Point3D());
    mesh.TextureCoordinates.Add(new Point(1, 1));

    // Add the box.
    mesh.AddBox(corner, vx, vy, vz,
        frontCoords, leftCoords, rightCoords,
        backCoords, topCoords, bottomCoords);
}
```

This method creates arrays to hold the appropriate parts of the texture coordinates for each of the box's faces. It then calls the first version of `AddBox` to create the box with those texture coordinates.

Adding Axes

Often it's useful in a three-dimensional program to display the coordinate axes so you can get an idea of the position and orientation of the objects in the scene. The following `AddXAxis` extension method creates a model to represent the X axis.

```
public static void AddXAxis(Model3DGroup group,
    double length = 4, double thickness = 0.1)
```

```
{
    MeshGeometry3D mesh = new MeshGeometry3D();
    Point3D origin = D3.Origin -
        D3.XVector(thickness / 2) -
        D3.YVector(thickness / 2) -
        D3.ZVector(thickness / 2);
    mesh.AddBox(origin,
        D3.XVector(length), D3.YVector(thickness), D3.ZVector(thickness));
    group.Children.Add(mesh.MakeModel(Brushes.Red));
}
```

This method creates a box with a given length and thickness. It starts by creating a mesh object. It then calculates a point shifted one half of the `thickness` value in the negative X, Y, and Z directions. Using that point as the box's initial corner will center the box around the X axis.

Next, the code calls the `AddBox` method. The box is `length` units long in the X direction, and `thickness` units wide in the Y and Z directions. (The code uses the `D3` class's `XVector`, `YVector`, and `ZVector` methods to make vectors of the appropriate lengths parallel to the coordinate axes.)

The method finishes by calling the mesh's `MakeModel` method to turn the mesh into a red model and adding the model to the `Model3DGroup` object passed in as a parameter.

In addition to the `AddXAxis` method, the `MeshExtensions` class defines similar `AddYAxis` and `AddZAxis` methods that create a green box along the Y axis and a blue box along the Z axis respectively.

If a program uses all three of these methods, the result is three boxes that overlap at the origin. Because they have coplanar faces that overlap, they are subject to something called *z-fighting.*

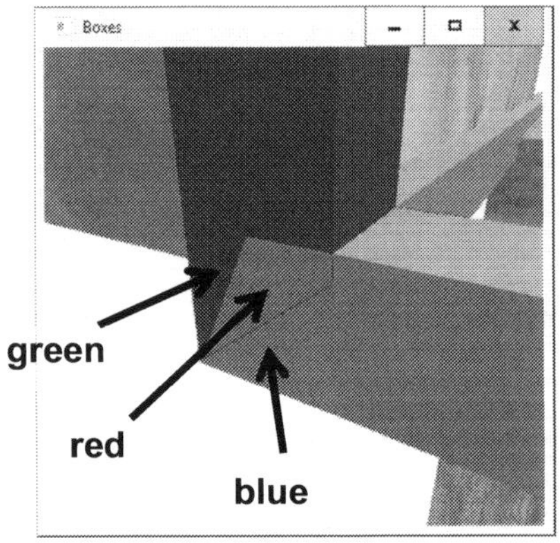

Figure 12-3: If coplanar faces overlap, they may cause z-fighting.

When the drawing system tries to render the scene, the boxes' faces all have equal claim to the pixels where they overlap. The drawing system can't easily break the tie, so the faces win random pieces of the contested area. In Figure 12-3, all three of the coordinate axis boxes have claimed parts of the area where they overlap. You can't tell in the book, but this area shows red, green, and blue areas.

To make matters worse, z-fighting doesn't give a consistent result. If you change the camera's viewing position or orientation slightly, different parts of the disputed area may be given to each of the faces. In the example shown in Figure 12-3, that means this area flickers red, green, and blue as you navigate the scene.

One solution to this problem is to ensure that the faces are not coplanar. For example, if the X, Y, and Z boxes have slightly different thicknesses, perhaps differing by as little as 0.02 units, then their faces won't be coplanar so the drawing system will assign a consistent winner.

Another solution is to cover the contested area with another shape. Figure 12-4 shows this approach. Here the origin is hidden by a small black box created by the following `AddOrigin` method.

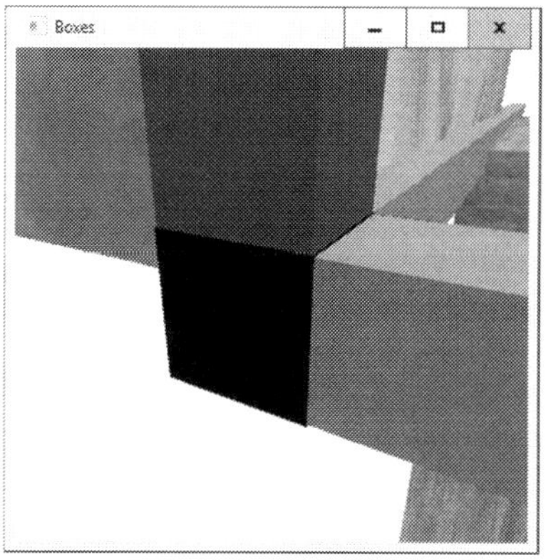

Figure 12-4: The `AddOrigin` method hides the origin with a small box.

```
// Make a cube at the origin.
public static void AddOrigin(Model3DGroup group,
    double cubeThickness = 0.102)
{
    MeshGeometry3D mesh = new MeshGeometry3D();
    Point3D origin = D3.Origin -
        D3.XVector(cubeThickness / 2) -
        D3.YVector(cubeThickness / 2) -
        D3.ZVector(cubeThickness / 2);
    mesh.AddBox(origin,
        D3.XVector(cubeThickness),
        D3.YVector(cubeThickness),
        D3.ZVector(cubeThickness));
    group.Children.Add(mesh.MakeModel(Brushes.Black));
}
```

This method creates a small cube at the origin. It is slightly bigger than the axis boxes, so it covers the problem area.

After it makes the box, the method converts it into a black model and adds it to the `Model3DGroup` object.

Z-fighting can also occur in unusual situations such as when objects are too close to the camera. You can avoid that by increasing the camera's `NearPlaneDistance` property.

> **NOTE:** Sometimes if a triangle has two identical vertices, random triangles may disappear or be truncated unexpectedly. That effect is often misdiagnosed as z-fighting.

The `MeshExtensions` class defines one more method to make it easier to display the coordinate axes. The following `AddAxes` method creates all three axis boxes plus the origin cube.

```
// Make X, Y, and Z axes, and the origin cube.
public static void AddAxes(Model3DGroup group,
    double length = 4, double thickness = 0.1,
    double cubeThickness = 0.102)
{
    AddXAxis(group, length, thickness);
    AddYAxis(group, length, thickness);
```

```
        AddZAxis(group, length, thickness);
        AddOrigin(group, length, cubeThickness);
    }
```

This method simply invokes the methods described earlier.

Example Program

The Boxes example program uses the following code to create its scene.

```
private void DefineModel(Model3DGroup group)
{
    // Make a box.
    MeshGeometry3D mesh1 = new MeshGeometry3D();
    mesh1.AddBox(new Point3D(1, -1, 0),
        D3.XVector(2), D3.YVector(2), D3.ZVector(2),
        D3.UnitTextures);
    group.Children.Add(mesh1.MakeModel("wood.jpg"));

    // Make a cube with every face different.
    MeshGeometry3D mesh2 = new MeshGeometry3D();
    Point[][] textureCoords = D3.SectionTextureCoords(2, 3);
    mesh2.AddBox(new Point3D(0, 1, -2),
        D3.XVector(2), D3.YVector(2), D3.ZVector(2),
        textureCoords[0], textureCoords[1], textureCoords[2],
        textureCoords[3], textureCoords[4], textureCoords[5]);
    group.Children.Add(mesh2.MakeModel("all.jpg"));

    // Make a green parallelepiped.
    MeshGeometry3D mesh3 = new MeshGeometry3D();
    mesh3.AddBox(new Point3D(-4, -1, -3),
        new Vector3D(2, 0.5, -0.5),
        new Vector3D(0, 2, -0.5),
        new Vector3D(-0.5, 0, 2));
    group.Children.Add(mesh3.MakeModel(Brushes.LightGreen));

    // Make a wrapped box.
    MeshGeometry3D mesh4 = new MeshGeometry3D();
    mesh4.AddBoxWrapped(new Point3D(-3, -1, 0),
        D3.XVector(2), D3.YVector(2), D3.ZVector(2));
    group.Children.Add(mesh4.MakeModel("wrapper.png"));

    // Show the axes.
    MeshExtensions.AddAxes(group);
}
```

The method starts by making a mesh and using the `AddBox` method to add a cube to it. It uses the mesh's `MakeModel` method to texture the mesh with the image file `wood.jpg`. It then adds the result to the program's `Model3DGroup`.

Next, the method creates a second mesh. It calls `D3.SectionTextureCoords` to create texture coordinates for a texture divided into two rows and three columns. I'll describe that method shortly.

The method then calls AddBox to create another cube, passing it the texture coordinates calculated by SectionTextureCoords. It turns the mesh into a model using the texture file all.jpg and adds the result to the program's Model3DGroup.

The SectionTextureCoords method divides a texture area into rows and columns and creates an array holding arrays of texture coordinates for each of the sections. Figure 12-5 shows the all.jpg texture file used by the example program. You can see that the file is divided into two rows and three columns.

Figure 12-5: The SectionTextureCoords method divides a texture into rows and columns.

The following code shows the SectionTextureCoords method.

```
// Divide the unit texture coordinates into even sections.
public static Point[][] SectionTextureCoords(int numRows, int numCols)
{
    int numTotal = numRows * numCols;
    Point[][] result = new Point[numTotal][];

    double dr = 1.0 / numRows;
    double dc = 1.0 / numCols;
    for (int r = 0; r < numRows; r++)
    {
        for (int c = 0; c < numCols; c++)
        {
            int i = r * numCols + c;
            result[i] = new Point[4];
            result[i][0] = new Point(c * dc, (r + 1) * dr);
            result[i][1] = new Point((c + 1) * dc, (r + 1) * dr);
            result[i][2] = new Point((c + 1) * dc, r * dr);
            result[i][3] = new Point(c * dc, r * dr);
        }
    }
    return result;
}
```

This method divides the unit area $0 \le \{u, v\} \le 1$ into rows and columns. It first creates an array to hold an array for each of the rows and columns. It then calculates the row heights and column widths.

The code then uses two loops to set each of the result array's entries. Each entry contains texture coordinates for the lower left, lower right, upper right, and upper left corners of an area in the unit texture.

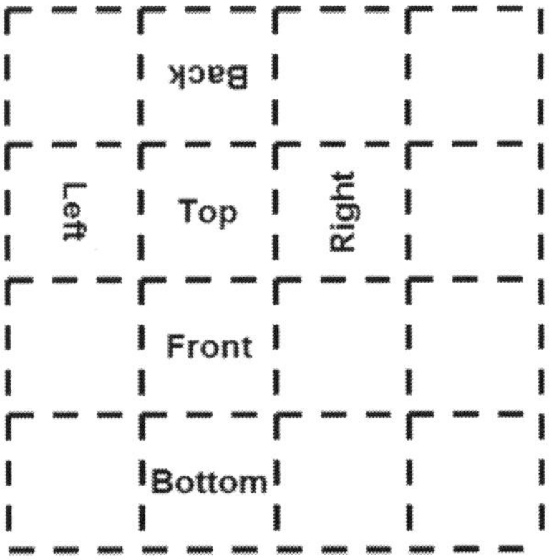

Figure 12-6: The Boxes example program wraps a box with this texture.

Now to return to the program's `DefineModel` method. After it creates the box that uses the `all.jpg` texture, the program uses `AddBox` to create a green parallelepiped.

Next, `DefineModel` creates a box wrapped by the texture file `wrapper.png` shown in Figure 12-6. The words and dashed lines are part of the texture so they appear in the final scene.

Finally, the method uses the `AddAxes` extension method to display the coordinate axes and origin cube. Figure 12-7 shows the running Boxes program. If you look closely, you can see the cube covered in wood in front, the cube with different sides above it, the wrapped cube on the left, the green parallelepiped in the back, and the coordinate axes.

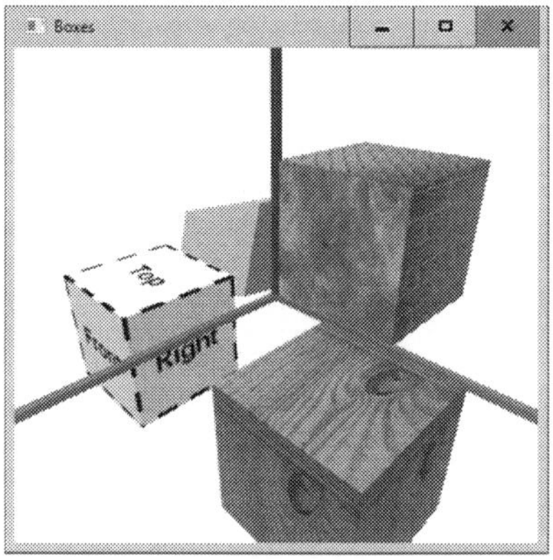

Figure 12-7: The Boxes example program draws several boxes.

Summary

The `AddBox` and `AddBoxWrapped` methods use the `AddParallelogram` method described in the preceding chapter to create cubes, rectangular boxes, and skewed parallelepipeds with or without textures. In a similar fashion, Chapter 13 explains methods that use the `AddPolygon` method described in Chapter 10 to create pyramids and frustums.

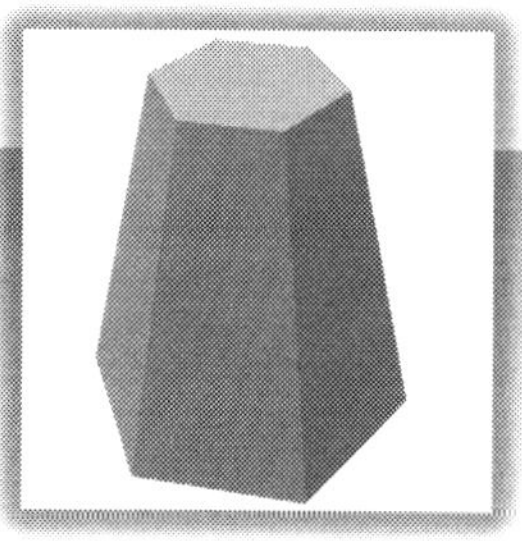

Chapter 13
Pyramids

This chapter explains how to build pyramids and frustums (truncated pyramids).

> **NOTE:** Actually a frustum can also be a truncated cone. I'll cover those in a later chapter.
>
> (Also if you're saving up words to impress your friends, note that the plural of "frustum" is either "frustums" or "frusta.")

Most people usually think of pyramids as those big limestone things in Egypt that are haunted by mummies. In geometry, a pyramid is a shape that has a polygon for its base and triangular sides that share a common vertex at its apex. The polygon doesn't have to be a square and the apex doesn't need to be centered over the base.

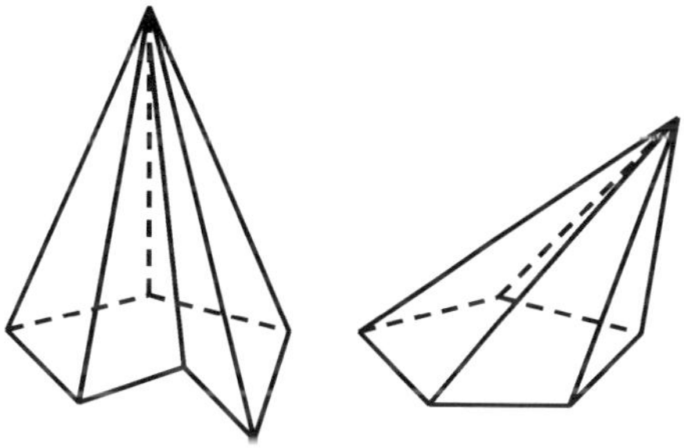

Figure 13-1: A pyramid can have a nonconvex base and the apex need not be over the base.

Figure 13-1 shows two pyramids, one with a non-convex base and one with its apex off to the side.

The following section explains how to draw pyramids in WPF. The section after that shows how to draw frustums.

Adding Pyramids

The following `AddPyramid` method adds a pyramid to a mesh.

```
// Add a pyramid defined by a center point, a polygon, and an axis vector.
// The polygon should be oriented toward its axis.
public static void AddPyramid(this MeshGeometry3D mesh,
    Point3D center, Point3D[] polygon, Vector3D axis)
{
    // Find the apex.
    Point3D apex = center + axis;

    // Make the sides.
    int numPoints = polygon.Length;
    for (int i = 0; i < polygon.Length; i++)
    {
```

```
            int i1 = (i + 1) % numPoints;
            mesh.AddPolygon(polygon[i], polygon[i1], apex);
        }

        // Make the bottom.
        Point3D[] bottom = new Point3D[numPoints];
        Array.Copy(polygon, bottom, numPoints);
        Array.Reverse(bottom);
        mesh.AddPolygon(bottom);
    }
```

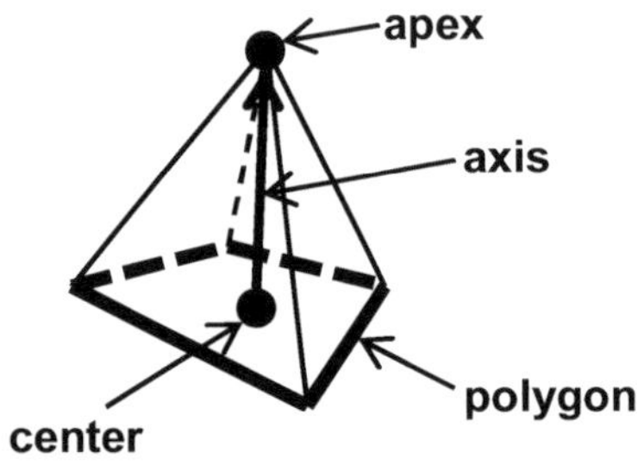

Figure 13-2: A center point, polygon, and axis define a pyramid.

This method takes as parameters a point to use as the center for the pyramid's base, an array of `Point3D` values representing the base polygon, and an axis vector that indicates how to get from the center to the apex. The polygon must be upward oriented according to the right-hand rule so its normal points toward the apex. Figure 13-2 shows a pyramid's parts.

The `AddPyramid` method adds the axis vector to the center point to find the pyramid's apex. It then loops through the base polygon's points. The method passes each adjacent pair of points and the apex to the `AddPolygon` method to make one of the pyramid's triangular sides. Figure 13-4 shows two adjacent points and the triangle they define.

After it finishes making the pyramid's sides, the method creates the base. The method assumes that the base polygon is upward-oriented so it can make the pyramid's sides correctly. Because the base is upward-oriented, the method needs to reverse its points to orient the polygon downward. That makes that polygon outward-oriented so you can see it when you look at the bottom of the pyramid.

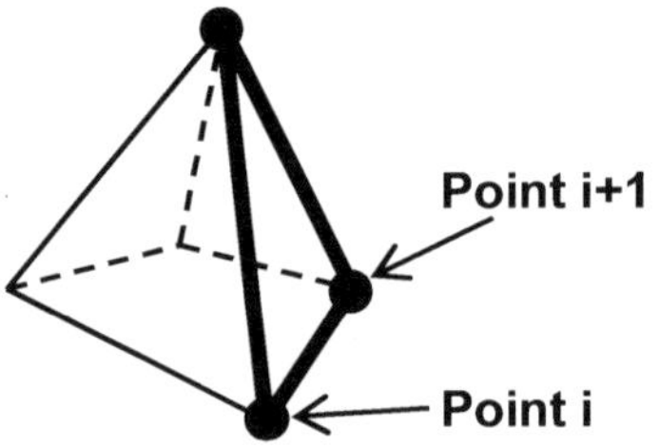

Figure 13-4: The `AddPyramid` method loops over the base polygon's points.

To reverse the polygon's points, the code uses `Array.Copy` to copy the points into a new array. It then uses `Array.Reverse` to reverse the points and finishes by calling the `AddPolygon` method to make the base polygon.

> **NOTE:** You may recall from Chapter 10 that the `AddPolygon` method assumes that the polygon can be built out of a "fan" of triangles. That works if the base polygon is convex, but it may not work if the polygon is non-convex. That means the `AddPyramid` method may not work for pyramids with non-convex bases.

Adding Frustums

The following `AddFrustum` method adds a frustum to a mesh.

```
// Add a frustum.
// Length is the length measured along the axis.
public static void AddFrustum(this MeshGeometry3D mesh,
    Point3D center, Point3D[] polygon, Vector3D axis, double length)
{
    // Find the length ratio.
    double ratio = length / axis.Length;

    // See where the apex would be.
    Point3D apex = center + axis;

    // Make the top.
    int numPoints = polygon.Length;
    Point3D[] top = new Point3D[numPoints];
    for (int i = 0; i < polygon.Length; i++)
    {
        Vector3D vector = apex - polygon[i];
        vector *= ratio;
        top[i] = polygon[i] + vector;
    }
    mesh.AddPolygon(top);

    // Make the sides.
    for (int i = 0; i < polygon.Length; i++)
    {
        int i1 = (i + 1) % numPoints;
        mesh.AddPolygon(polygon[i], polygon[i1], top[i1], top[i]);
    }

    // Make the bottom.
    Point3D[] bottom = new Point3D[numPoints];
    Array.Copy(polygon, bottom, numPoints);
    Array.Reverse(bottom);
    mesh.AddPolygon(bottom);
}
```

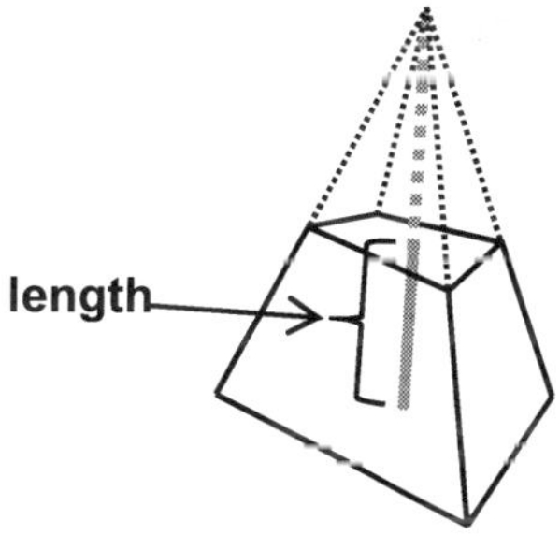

Figure 13-5: The `length` parameter determines how much of the axis is used.

This method's parameters are similar to those used by the `AddPyramid` method, but this method takes an additional `length` parameter. Figure 13-5 shows how that parameter determines where the pyramid is truncated.

The ratio of the axis's used to unused length is the same as the ratio of each edge's used to unused lengths. For example, if the frustum uses 0.75 of its axis, then uses 0.75 of its sides, too.

The `AddFrustum` method first calculates the ratio of the axis's used to unused length. It then finds where the solid's apex would be if this were a pyramid instead of a frustum.

Next, the code uses the used/unused ratio to find the points that will make up the frustum's top. For each base polygon vertex, the code subtracts the vertex from the apex point (more vector arithmetic) to find the edge that would be used from that vertex if this were a pyramid. The code multiplies the vector by the used/unused ratio to truncate the edge at the frustum's top. It adds the truncated vector to the vertex to find the corresponding point on the top and saves it in the `top` array.

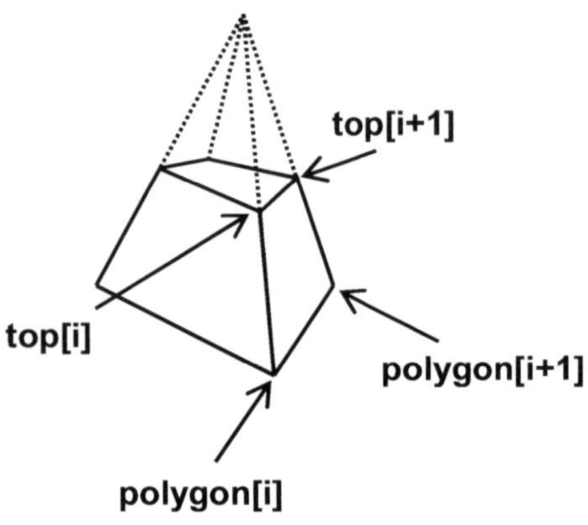

Figure 13-6: The top and bottom points define the frustum's sides.

After it finishes finding the points that define the frustum's top, the code passes the `top` array to the `AddPolygon` method to make the top polygon.

Next, the method loops through the top and bottom polygon points and uses them to make the frustum's sides. Figure 13-6 shows the points that are used to make one of the sides.

The method makes the frustum's bottom the same way the `AddPyramid` method did.

Adding More General Frustums

The `AddFrustum` method described in the preceding section assumes that the pyramid is truncated by a plane that is parallel to the base polygon. More generally, you can make a frustum by cutting a pyramid with any plane, even one that isn't parallel to the base polygon. Figure 13-7 shows that kid of frustum.

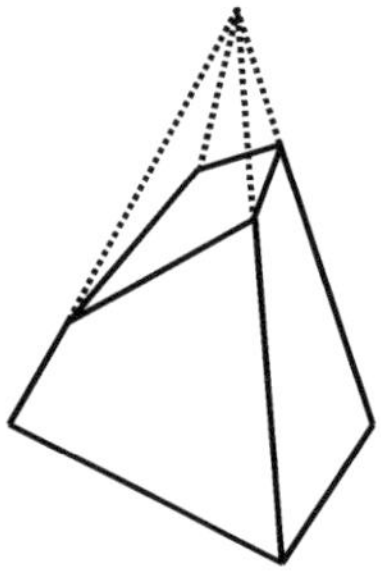

Figure 13-7: A pyramid can be truncated by a plane that isn't parallel to the base polygon.

Building this kind of frustum isn't too hard. The basic idea is to loop through the polygon's points and look at the segment connecting them to the apex, much as the `AddFrustum` method did in the preceding section. This time, instead of giving each edge the same fraction of that segment's length, we calculate where the segment intersects the top cutting plane.

The following code shows a method that finds the point where a line intersects a plane.

```
// Find the intersection of a plane and a line.
// The line is given by point linePt and vector v.
// The plane is given by point planePt and normal vector n.
private static Point3D IntersectPlaneLine (Point3D linePt, Vector3D v,
    Point3D planePt, Vector3D n)
{
    // Get the equation for the plane.
    // For information on getting the plane equation, see:
```

```
        // http://www.songho.ca/math/plane/plane.html
        double A = n.X;
        double B = n.Y;
        double C = n.Z;
        double D = -(A * planePt.X + B * planePt.Y + C * planePt.Z);

        // Find the intersection parameter t.
        // For information on finding the intersection, see:
        // http://www.ambrsoft.com/TrigoCalc/Plan3D/PlaneLineIntersection_.htm
        double t = -(A * linePt.X + B * linePt.Y + C * linePt.Z + D) /
            (A * v.X + B * v.Y + C * v.Z);

        // Find the point of intersection.
        return linePt + t * v;
    }
```

The line is specified by a point named `linePt` on the line and a vector named `v` that gives the line's direction. The plane is specified by a point named `planePt` on the plane and a vector named `n` that is normal (perpendicular) to the plane.

The method starts by finding the values A, B, C, and D to define the plane's equation in the following format.

$$A \times X + B \times Y + C \times Z + D = 0$$

Finding those values isn't too difficult, but explaining how to find them seems like more work that it's worth because it's kind of complicated. For information on how those values are calculated, see the post at the URL shown in the code or at `tinyurl.com/yawj2okk`.

Next, you can view the line as being defined by the parametric equation `linePt+t×v`. As the value `t` ranges over the real numbers ∞ to -∞, this vector equation generates points along the line.

The goal now is to find the value of `t` that generates a point that satisfies the equation for the plane. Again, explaining how this works seems like more trouble than it's worth. For an explanation, see the second URL shown in the code or `tinyurl.com/yb6dtoxs`.

Having found the desired value for `t`, the code simply plugs it into the parametric equation for the line to find the point of intersection and returns the result.

The following version of `AddFrustum` uses the `IntersectPlaneLine` method to create a frustum where the top is defined by a plane of intersection.

```
// Add a frustum where the top is determined by a plane of intersection.
// The plane is determined by the point planePt and the normal vector n.
public static void AddFrustum(this MeshGeometry3D mesh,
    Point3D center, Point3D[] polygon, Vector3D axis,
    Point3D planePt, Vector3D n)
{
    // See where the apex would be.
    Point3D apex = center + axis;
```

```
        // Make the top.
        int numPoints = polygon.Length;
        Point3D[] top = new Point3D[numPoints];
        for (int i = 0; i < polygon.Length; i++)
        {
            // Get the vector from the point to the apex.
            Vector3D vector = apex - polygon[i];

            // See where this vector intersects the plane.
            top[i] = IntersectPlaneLine(polygon[i], vector, planePt, n);
        }
        mesh.AddPolygon(top);

        // Make the sides.
        for (int i = 0; i < polygon.Length; i++)
        {
            int i1 = (i + 1) % numPoints;
            mesh.AddPolygon(polygon[i], polygon[i1], top[i1], top[i]);
        }

        // Make the bottom.
        Point3D[] bottom = new Point3D[numPoints];
        Array.Copy(polygon, bottom, numPoints);
        Array.Reverse(bottom);
        mesh.AddPolygon(bottom);
    }
```

This method is the same as the previous version except it uses the cutting plane to define the top points. It first finds the apex where the pyramid would end if this weren't a frustum. It then loops through the base polygon's points.

For each point, the method finds the segment connecting the point to the apex, uses the `IntersectPlaneLine` method to see where that segment intersects the cutting plane, and adds the point of intersection to the `top` array.

The rest of the method is the same as before.

> **NOTE:** This method assumes that the cutting plane intersects the pyramid between its apex and its base. If the plane doesn't intersect the pyramid or intersects the base polygon, you'll get some weird results.

Example Program

The Pyramids example program uses the following code to create its scene.

```
    private void DefineModel(Model3DGroup group)
    {
        // Define a polygon in the XZ plane.
        Point3D center = new Point3D(0, 0, 4.5);
        Point3D[] polygon = G3.MakePolygonPoints(6, center,
            new Vector3D(1, 0, 0), new Vector3D(0, 0, -1));
```

```
        // Make a transform to move the polygon in the -Z direction.
        TranslateTransform3D translate = new TranslateTransform3D(0, 0, -3);

        // Make a right pyramid.
        MeshGeometry3D mesh1 = new MeshGeometry3D();
        mesh1.AddPyramid(center, polygon, new Vector3D(0, 3, 0));
        group.Children.Add(mesh1.MakeModel(Brushes.Pink));

        // Make a skewed pyramid.
        translate.Transform(polygon);
        center = translate.Transform(center);
        MeshGeometry3D mesh2 = new MeshGeometry3D();
        mesh2.AddPyramid(center, polygon, new Vector3D(0, 3, 2));
        group.Children.Add(mesh2.MakeModel(Brushes.LightBlue));

        // Make a frustum with cutting plane parallel to the base.
        translate.Transform(polygon);
        center = translate.Transform(center);
        MeshGeometry3D mesh3 = new MeshGeometry3D();
        mesh3.AddFrustum(center, polygon, new Vector3D(0, 4, 0), 2);
        group.Children.Add(mesh3.MakeModel(Brushes.LightGreen));

        // Make a frustum with cutting plane not parallel to the base.
        translate.Transform(polygon);
        center = translate.Transform(center);
        MeshGeometry3D mesh4 = new MeshGeometry3D();
        Point3D planePt = center + new Vector3D(0, 2, 0);
        Vector3D planeN = new Vector3D(1, 1, 1);
        mesh4.AddFrustum(center, polygon, new Vector3D(0, 4, 0), planePt, planeN);
        group.Children.Add(mesh4.MakeModel(Brushes.Orange));

        // Show the axes.
        MeshExtensions.AddAxes(group);
    }
```

The code starts by calling the `MakePolygonPoints` method described in the section "Adding Regular Polygons" in Chapter 10. This example uses the method to generate points that make a hexagon in the XZ plane.

The code then defines a `TranslateTransform3D` object that it will later use to move the hexagon's points three units in the -Z direction. It does that between building each of the scene's objects so they appear in different locations.

Next, the code creates a mesh, calls `AddPyramid` to create a basic pyramid, and turns it into a pink model.

The code then uses the `TranslateTransform3D` object to move the hexagon's points and the point `center` to a new location. It creates a second mesh, uses its `AddPyramid` method to make a skewed pyramid, and turns it into a blue model.

The code repeats roughly the same steps to create a green frustum defined by an axis length and an orange frustum defined by a cutting plane.

The code finishes by displaying the coordinate axes and origin cube.

Figure 13-8 shows the Pyramids example program in action.

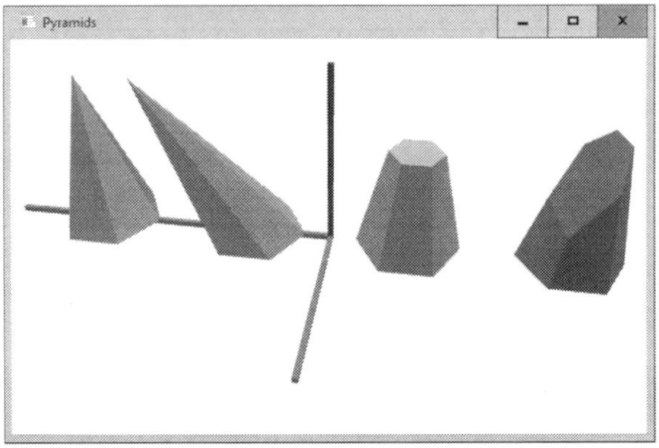

Figure 13-7: The Pyramids example program displays two pyramids and two frustums.

Summary

A cone is similar to a pyramid where the base "polygon" is an ellipse. Of course in practice the program doesn't really draw ellipses, it draws polygons with small sides so it looks like an ellipse. That means the `AddPyramid` and `AddFrustum` methods can already draw cones and frustums of cones (sort of).

Chapter 14 shows how you can modify those methods to give the results smoother sides so they look even more like cones and conic frustums.

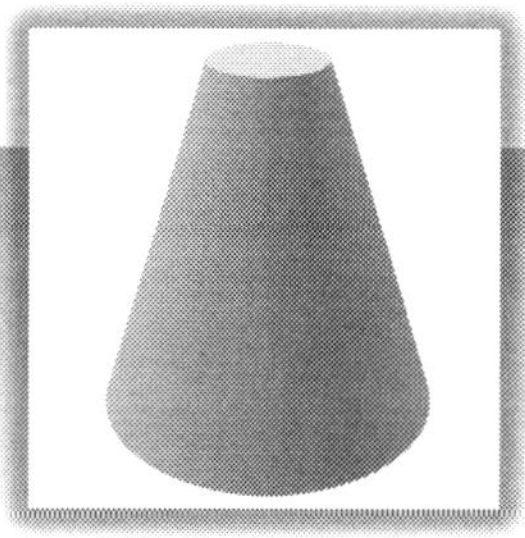

Chapter 14

Cones

As I mentioned at the end of Chapter 13, a cone is basically a pyramid with an elliptical base. The `AddPyramid` method described in that chapter can do a decent job of drawing a cone as long as the base polygon uses enough sides to approximate an ellipse. Figure 14-1 shows a pyramid with a 20-sided base.

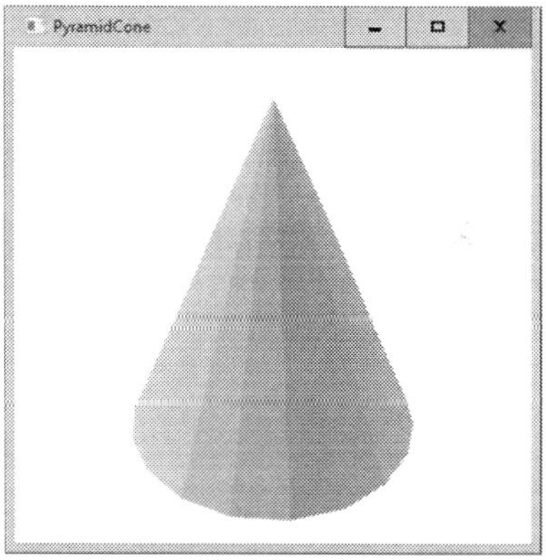

Figure 14-1: A pyramid with enough sides looks like a cone.

This result is pretty good, but we can do even better if we make the cone's sides share vertices so the drawing system smooths them out.

The next section explains how you can modify the `AddPolygon` method to smooth a cone's edges. The sections after that explain how the program can use the modified version of `AddPolygon` to make smooth cones and conic frustums.

Modifying AddPolygon

You may recall the technique of using a point dictionary from way back in Chapter 10. When the program needs to use a point, it checks the dictionary and reuses the point if it already exists. Sharing the point smooths the edge between the polygons that share it.

Unfortunately, the `AddPyramid` and `AddFrustum` methods use the `AddPolygon` method to draw their polygons, and `AddPolygon` doesn't take a point dictionary as a parameter. In fact, `AddPolygon` assumes that the points that make up the polygon should be shared to smooth the polygon, so it makes its own point dictionary internally.

The following code shows a new version of the `AddPolygon` method with the changes highlighted. Other variations of `AddPolygon` call this version to do all of the real work.

```
public static void AddPolygon(this MeshGeometry3D mesh,
    Point3D[] points, Dictionary<Point3D, int> pointDict = null,
    Point[] textureCoords = null)
{
    // Make a point dictionary.
    if (pointDict == null) pointDict = new Dictionary<Point3D, int>();

    // Get the first two point indices.
    int indexA, indexB, indexC;
```

```
        if (textureCoords == null)
            indexA = mesh.PointIndex(points[0].Round(), pointDict);
        else
            indexA = mesh.PointIndex(points[0].Round(), textureCoords[0], pointDict);

        if (textureCoords == null)
            indexC = mesh.PointIndex(points[1].Round(), pointDict);
        else
            indexC = mesh.PointIndex(points[1].Round(), textureCoords[1], pointDict);

        // Make triangles.
        for (int i = 2; i < points.Length; i++)
        {
            indexB = indexC;

            if (textureCoords == null)
                indexC = mesh.PointIndex(points[i].Round(), pointDict);
            else
                indexC = mesh.PointIndex(points[i].Round(), textureCoords[i], pointDict);

            if ((indexA != indexB) &&
                (indexB != indexC) &&
                (indexC != indexA))
            {
                mesh.TriangleIndices.Add(indexA);
                mesh.TriangleIndices.Add(indexB);
                mesh.TriangleIndices.Add(indexC);
            }
        }
    }
```

The previous version of the method created a point dictionary. The new version only creates that dictionary if it doesn't receive one as a parameter. The rest of the method is exactly the same as before.

Now other methods can use this new version to smooth edges between adjacent polygons if desired.

Modifying AddPyramid and AddFrustum

The new version of `AddPolygon` allows you to smooth the edges of adjacent polygons. The next step is to modify the `AddPyramid` and `AddFrustum` methods so they can take advantage of this new feature. The following code shows the new version of the `AddPyramid` method with the changes highlighted.

```
    public static void AddPyramid(this MeshGeometry3D mesh,
        Point3D center, Point3D[] polygon, Vector3D axis,
        bool smoothSides = false)
    {
        // Find the apex.
        Point3D apex = center + axis;

        // If we should smooth the sides, make the point dictionary.
        Dictionary<Point3D, int> pointDict = null;
```

```
        if (smoothSides) pointDict = new Dictionary<Point3D, int>();

        // Make the sides.
        int numPoints = polygon.Length;
        for (int i = 0; i < polygon.Length; i++)
        {
            int i1 = (i + 1) % numPoints;
            mesh.AddPolygon(pointDict, polygon[i], polygon[i1], apex);
        }

        // Make the bottom.
        Point3D[] bottom = new Point3D[numPoints];
        Array.Copy(polygon, bottom, numPoints);
        Array.Reverse(bottom);
        mesh.AddPolygon(bottom);
    }
```

The method declares the variable `pointDict` and sets it to `null`. Then, if the method's `smoothSides` parameter is `true`, the method sets `pointDict` equal to a new point dictionary.

The method then loops through the base polygon's points to make the sides. As it does, it passes `pointDict`, which is either `null` or pointing to a point dictionary, into the new version of `AddPolygon`.

The rest of the method is unchanged.

The changes to the two versions of the `AddFrustum` method are similar. Each creates a variable to hold a point dictionary and then sets it to either `null` or to a new dictionary, depending on the value of the `smoothSides` parameter. The changes are so similar to those in the `AddPyramid` method that I don't want to take the space to show them here. Download the Cones example program to see the details.

Adding Cones

The updated versions of the `AddPolygon`, `AddPyramid`, and `AddFrustum` methods make building cones easy. To make the process even easier, I created the following methods to make cones and frustums of cones.

```
// These methods delegate their work to pyramid and frustum methods.
public static void AddCone(this MeshGeometry3D mesh,
    Point3D center, Point3D[] polygon, Vector3D axis,
    bool smoothSides = false)
{
    mesh.AddPyramid(center, polygon, axis, true);
}
public static void AddConeFrustum(this MeshGeometry3D mesh,
    Point3D center, Point3D[] polygon, Vector3D axis, double length,
    bool smoothSides = false)
{
    mesh.AddFrustum(center, polygon, axis, length, true);
}
```

```
public static void AddConeFrustum(this MeshGeometry3D mesh,
    Point3D center, Point3D[] polygon, Vector3D axis,
    Point3D planePt, Vector3D n, bool smoothSides = false)
{
    mesh.AddFrustum(center, polygon, axis, planePt, n, true);
}
```

These methods simply call the appropriate `AddPyramid` and `AddFrustum` methods, setting their `smoothSides` parameters to `true`.

Example Program

The Cones example program uses the following code to define its model.

```
private void DefineModel(Model3DGroup group)
{
    // Define a polygon in the XZ plane.
    Point3D center = new Point3D(0, 0, 4.5);
    Point3D[] polygon = G3.MakePolygonPoints(6, center,
        new Vector3D(1, 0, 0), new Vector3D(0, 0, -1));

    // Make a transform to move the polygon in the -Z direction.
    TranslateTransform3D translate = new TranslateTransform3D(0, 0, -3);

    // Make a right cone.
    MeshGeometry3D mesh1 = new MeshGeometry3D();
    mesh1.AddCone(center, polygon, new Vector3D(0, 3, 0));
    group.Children.Add(mesh1.MakeModel(Brushes.Pink));

    // Make a skewed cone.
    translate.Transform(polygon);
    center = translate.Transform(center);
    MeshGeometry3D mesh2 = new MeshGeometry3D();
    mesh2.AddCone(center, polygon, new Vector3D(0, 3, 2));
    group.Children.Add(mesh2.MakeModel(Brushes.LightBlue));

    // Make a conic frustum with cutting plane parallel to the base.
    translate.Transform(polygon);
    center = translate.Transform(center);
    MeshGeometry3D mesh3 = new MeshGeometry3D();
    mesh3.AddConeFrustum(center, polygon, new Vector3D(0, 4, 0), 2);
    group.Children.Add(mesh3.MakeModel(Brushes.LightGreen));

    // Make a conic frustum with cutting plane not parallel to the base.
    translate.Transform(polygon);
    center = translate.Transform(center);
    MeshGeometry3D mesh4 = new MeshGeometry3D();
    Point3D planePt = center + new Vector3D(0, 2, 0);
    Vector3D planeN = new Vector3D(1, 1, 1);
    mesh4.AddConeFrustum(center, polygon, new Vector3D(0, 4, 0), planePt, planeN);
    group.Children.Add(mesh4.MakeModel(Brushes.Orange));

    // Show the axes.
    MeshExtensions.AddAxes(group);
}
```

This code is very similar to the code used by the Pyramids example program described in the Chapter 13 except it creates cones instead of pyramids. It first creates a polygon in the XZ plane. This time the polygon has 20 sides and approximates a circle.

The code creates a transformation to move the points and then creates a cone. It translates the base polygon's points and makes a skewed cone.

The method translates the base polygon again and makes a conic frustum. It translates the polygon a final time and makes a conic frustum defined by a cutting plane.

The code finishes by making the coordinate axes and origin cube.

Figure 14-2 shows the Cones example program displaying its cones and frustums. They use the same number of sides as the cone shown in Figure 14-1, but vertex sharing lets them produce a much smoother result.

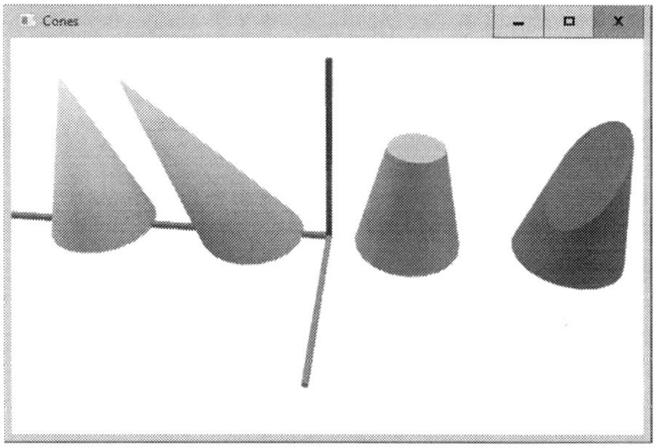

Figure 14-2: The Cones example program draws two cones and two conic frustums.

If you look very closely where the cones' sides meet their bottoms, you may be able to make out the edges of the polygonal base. This is common when you use shared vertices to smooth edges. The interior of the shape looks smooth, but the actual triangles may be visible on the object's profile.

Summary

A cylinder is very similar to a conic frustum: both have an elliptical base and polygonal sides. In fact, if the frustum's top and bottom are the same, then it *is* a cylinder.

Chapter 15 explains how you can draw cylinders. (At this point, you may feel confident enough to give it a try on your own before you read that chapter.)

Chapter 15

Cylinders

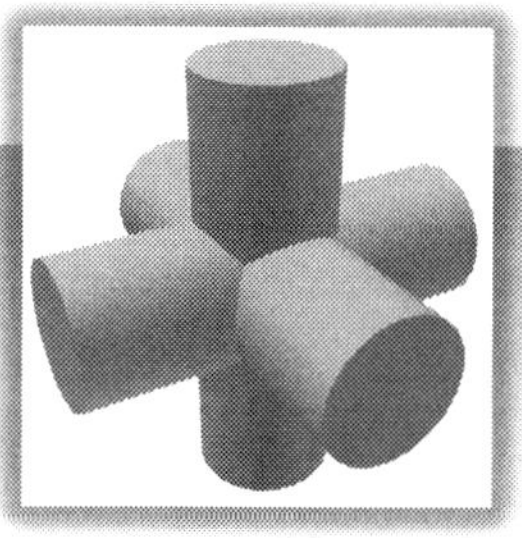

A cylinder is a lot like a pyramid with a flat top that's parallel to its bottom. Yeah, I know that sounds pretty silly. It's kind of like saying, "A cube is like a sphere with flat sides." The point is that you can use code similar to the pyramid-drawing code to draw a cylinder.

The following section explains how you can modify the pyramid-drawing code to draw cylinders.

Adding Cylinders

The code to draw a pyramid loops through the base polygon's points. For each point, it makes a vector from that point to the apex and then uses that vector to define one of the pyramid's edges.

To draw a cylinder, you only need to change the vector used. Instead of going from the polygon's point to the apex, the new vector goes from the polygon's point in the direction of the cylinder's axis.

The following code shows the `AddCylinder` method. The places where this code differs from the pyramid code are highlighted.

```
// Add a cylinder defined by a polygon and an axis vector.
// The cylinder should be oriented toward its axis.
public static void AddCylinder(this MeshGeometry3D mesh,
    Point3D[] polygon, Vector3D axis,
    bool smoothSides = false)
{
    // If we should smooth the sides, make the point dictionary.
    Dictionary<Point3D, int> pointDict = null;
    if (smoothSides) pointDict = new Dictionary<Point3D, int>();

    // Make the top.
    int numPoints = polygon.Length;
    Point3D[] top = new Point3D[numPoints];
    for (int i = 0; i < polygon.Length; i++)
    {
        top[i] = polygon[i] + axis;
    }
    mesh.AddPolygon(top);

    // Make the sides.
    for (int i = 0; i < polygon.Length; i++)
    {
        int i1 = (i + 1) % numPoints;
```

```
            mesh.AddPolygon(pointDict, polygon[i], polygon[i1], top[i1], top[i]);
        }

        // Make the bottom.
        Point3D[] bottom = new Point3D[numPoints];
        Array.Copy(polygon, bottom, numPoints);
        Array.Reverse(bottom);
        mesh.AddPolygon(bottom);
    }
```

The first difference between this code and the cylinder code is the piece that finds the cylinder's top polygon. This code loops through the base polygon's points and adds the cylinder's axis to each to find the corresponding point in the top polygon.

Because the base polygon is oriented upward in the direction of the axis, the new top polygon is also oriented upward so it's outward-oriented.

The other place where this code differs from the pyramid version is where it creates the solid's sides. The pyramid code uses two polygon points and the apex to make a single triangle. The cylinder version uses two points from the base polygon and two from the top polygon to make a quadrilateral. (In fact, it's a parallelogram. You can probably even use your high school geometry skills to prove it's a parallelogram.)

Using Cutting Planes

One of the methods for making a frustum described in Chapter 14 uses a cutting plane to define the frustum's top. The following code modifies that method to make a cylinder that is defined by a polygon, axis, and two cutting planes, one on the top and one on the bottom. The changes to the frustum code are highlighted.

```
// Add a cylinder defined by a polygon, two axis, and two cutting planes.
public static void AddCylinder(this MeshGeometry3D mesh,
    Point3D[] polygon, Vector3D axis,
    Point3D topPlanePt, Vector3D topN,
    Point3D bottomPlanePt, Vector3D bottomN,
    bool smoothSides = false)
{
    // Make the top.
    int numPoints = polygon.Length;
    Point3D[] top = new Point3D[numPoints];
    for (int i = 0; i < polygon.Length; i++)
    {
        // See where this vector intersects the top cutting plane.
        top[i] = IntersectPlaneLine(polygon[i], axis, topPlanePt, topN);
    }
    mesh.AddPolygon(top);

    // Make the bottom.
    Point3D[] bottom = new Point3D[numPoints];
    for (int i = 0; i < polygon.Length; i++)
    {
        // See where this vector intersects the bottom cutting plane.
        bottom[i] = IntersectPlaneLine(polygon[i], axis, bottomPlanePt, bottomN);
```

```
        }

        // If we should smooth the sides, make the point dictionary.
        Dictionary<Point3D, int> pointDict = null;
        if (smoothSides) pointDict = new Dictionary<Point3D, int>();

        // Make the sides.
        for (int i = 0; i < polygon.Length; i++)
        {
            int i1 = (i + 1) % numPoints;
            mesh.AddPolygon(pointDict, bottom[i], bottom[i1], top[i1], top[i]);
        }

        // Make the bottom.
        Array.Reverse(bottom);
        mesh.AddPolygon(bottom);
    }
```

The first difference between this method and the frustum code occurs where the code finds the top polygon. Both versions loop through the defining polygon's points. For each point, the frustum code uses the point and a vector between that point and the apex to define a line. It then finds the point of intersection between that line and the cutting plane.

The cylinder code is the same except it uses the cylinder's axis instead of the vector between each point and the apex.

The second difference between this method and the frustum code occurs where the method finds the bottom polygon. The frustum code uses its polygon parameter as the bottom. The cylinder method uses the bottom cutting plane to find the bottom polygon. The code that finds the bottom polygon is the same as the code that finds the top polygon except it uses the bottom cutting plane instead of the top plane.

> **NOTE:** You could use the same technique to find the bottom for a pyramid or cone, too, if you didn't want to explicitly define the pyramid/cone's base with a polygon.

Example Program

The following code shows how the Cylinders example program defines its scene.

```
    private void DefineModel(Model3DGroup group)
    {
        // Define a polygon in the XZ plane.
        Point3D center = new Point3D(0, -1.5, 2);
        Point3D[] polygon = G3.MakePolygonPoints(20, center,
            new Vector3D(0.5, 0, 0), new Vector3D(0, 0, -0.5));

        // Transform to move the polygon.
        TranslateTransform3D xTranslate = new TranslateTransform3D(-2, 0, 0);
```

```
        // Make a transform to move the polygon in the -Z direction.
        TranslateTransform3D xzTranslate = new TranslateTransform3D(2, 0, -2);

        // Make a smooth skewed cylinder.
        MeshGeometry3D mesh1 = new MeshGeometry3D();
        mesh1.AddCylinder(polygon, new Vector3D(0, 2, -1), true);
        group.Children.Add(mesh1.MakeModel(Brushes.Pink));

        // Make a skewed cylinder.
        MeshGeometry3D mesh2 = new MeshGeometry3D();
        xTranslate.Transform(polygon);
        mesh2.AddCylinder(polygon, new Vector3D(0, 3, -1));
        group.Children.Add(mesh2.MakeModel(Brushes.Pink));

        // Make a smooth right cylinder.
        MeshGeometry3D mesh3 = new MeshGeometry3D();
        xzTranslate.Transform(polygon);
        mesh3.AddCylinder(polygon, new Vector3D(0, 2, 0), true);
        group.Children.Add(mesh3.MakeModel(Brushes.LightGreen));

        // Make a right cylinder.
        MeshGeometry3D mesh4 = new MeshGeometry3D();
        xTranslate.Transform(polygon);
        mesh4.AddCylinder(polygon, new Vector3D(0, 3, 0));
        group.Children.Add(mesh4.MakeModel(Brushes.LightGreen));

        // Make a cylinder defined by cutting planes.
        MeshGeometry3D mesh5 = new MeshGeometry3D();
        xzTranslate.Transform(polygon);
        mesh5.AddCylinder(polygon, new Vector3D(0, 3, 0),
            center + new Vector3D(0, 1, 0), new Vector3D(0, 2, 1),
            center + new Vector3D(0, -0.5, 0), new Vector3D(1, -1, 0),
            true);
        group.Children.Add(mesh5.MakeModel(Brushes.LightBlue));

        // Make a smooth cylinder defined by cutting planes.
        MeshGeometry3D mesh6 = new MeshGeometry3D();
        xTranslate.Transform(polygon);
        mesh6.AddCylinder(polygon, new Vector3D(0, 3, 0),
            center + new Vector3D(0, 2, 0), new Vector3D(0, 2, 1),
            center + new Vector3D(0, -0.5, 0), new Vector3D(1, -1, 0));
        group.Children.Add(mesh6.MakeModel(Brushes.LightBlue));

        // Show the axes.
        MeshExtensions.AddAxes(group);
    }
```

The code starts by creating a 20-sided polygon to define the cylinders' bases. It then makes two transformations so it can later move the polygon around for the different cylinders.

Next, the code makes a smooth-sided cylinder. It moves the polygon and makes a similar cylinder that doesn't have smooth sides.

The code repeats those steps to create two new cylinders, this time with axes that are not perpendicular to the polygon.

The code repeats the same steps one more time to create two cylinders with tops and bottoms defined by cutting planes.

Figure 5-1 shows the Cylinders example program displaying its assorted cylinders.

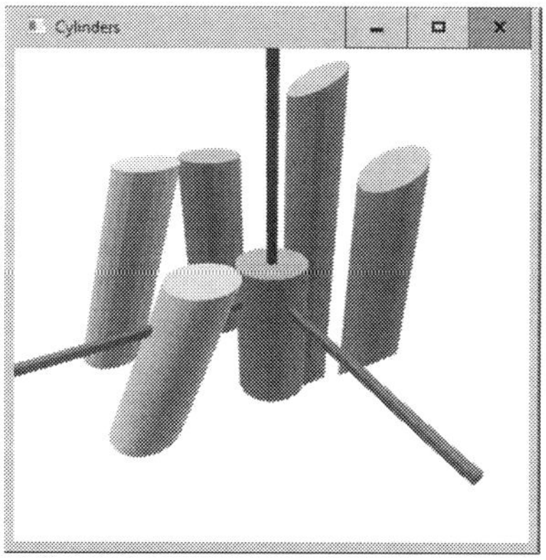

Figure 15-1: The Cylinders example program draws smooth and non-smooth cylinders.

Summary

This chapter and the previous one show how to make smooth-sided cones and cylinders. The next chapter explains how you can draw the ultimate smooth solid: the sphere.

Chapter 16
Spheres

This chapter explains how to draw smooth and non-smooth spheres, with and without textures.

The following section shows how to build a simple, untextured sphere. The section after that explains how to add textures and solve a rather odd problem that they create.

Adding Spheres

Adding an untextured sphere to a mesh isn't too hard; you just need to do some bookkeeping to keep track of which points make up the sphere's polygons. The following code makes a smooth or non-smooth sphere.

```
// Add a sphere without texture coordinates.
public static void AddSphere(this MeshGeometry3D mesh,
    Point3D center, double radius, int numTheta, int numPhi,
    bool smooth = false)
{
    // Make a point dictionary if needed.
    Dictionary<Point3D, int> pointDict = null;
    if (smooth) pointDict = new Dictionary<Point3D, int>();

    // Generate the points.
    double dtheta = 2 * Math.PI / numTheta;
    double dphi = Math.PI / numPhi;
    double theta = 0;
    for (int t = 0; t < numTheta; t++)
    {
        double phi = 0;
        for (int p = 0; p < numPhi; p++)
        {
            // Find this piece's points.
            Point3D[] points =
            {
                G3.SpherePoint(center, radius, theta, phi),
                G3.SpherePoint(center, radius, theta, phi + dphi),
                G3.SpherePoint(center, radius, theta + dtheta, phi + dphi),
                G3.SpherePoint(center, radius, theta+ dtheta, phi),
            };

            // Make the polygon.
            mesh.AddPolygon(pointDict, points);

            phi += dphi;
        }
```

```
            theta += dtheta;
        }
    }
```

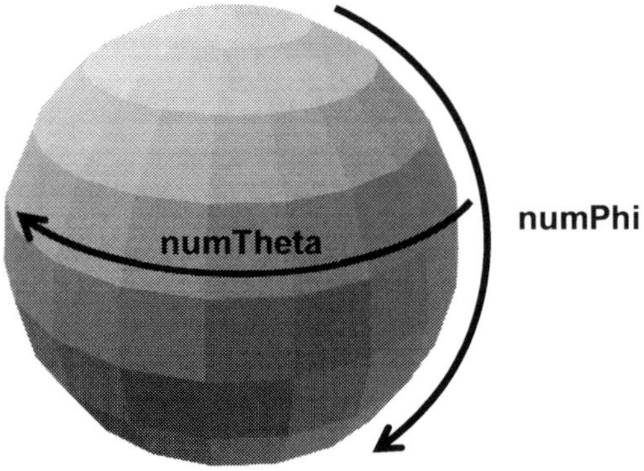

Figure 16-1: The `numTheta` and `numPhi` parameters determine the number of pieces used to represent the sphere.

The method's `center` and `radius` parameters are reasonably straightforward. The values `numTheta` and `numPhi` indicate the number of horizontal and vertical divisions, respectively, that we should use to approximate the sphere. Figure 16-1 shows how those values apply to the sphere.

For example, if `numTheta` is 20 and `numPhi` is 10, then the program should use 10×20=200 polygons. Most of those polygons are trapezoids, but the areas closest to the north and south poles are triangles.

The following code shows the basic `AddSphere` method.

```
// Add a sphere without texture coordinates.
public static void AddSphere(this MeshGeometry3D mesh,
    Point3D center, double radius, int numTheta, int numPhi,
    bool smooth = false)
{
    // Make a point dictionary if needed.
    Dictionary<Point3D, int> pointDict = null;
    if (smooth) pointDict = new Dictionary<Point3D, int>();

    // Generate the points.
    double dtheta = 2 * Math.PI / numTheta;
    double dphi = Math.PI / numPhi;
    double theta = 0;
    for (int t = 0; t < numTheta; t++)
    {
        double phi = 0;
        for (int p = 0; p < numPhi; p++)
        {
            // Find this piece's points.
            Point3D[] points =
            {
                G3.SpherePoint(center, radius, theta, phi),
                G3.SpherePoint(center, radius, theta, phi + dphi),
                G3.SpherePoint(center, radius, theta + dtheta, phi + dphi),
                G3.SpherePoint(center, radius, theta + dtheta, phi),
            };

            // Make the polygon.
            mesh.AddPolygon(pointDict, points);

            phi += dphi;
        }
        theta += dtheta;
    }
}
```

If the smooth parameter is true, the method creates a point dictionary so the polygons it makes it can share points.

The method then makes the variables t (for theta) and p (for phi) loop from 0 to numTheta and numPhi, respectively. The program uses the variables theta and phi to keep track of each point's polar coordinate values θ and φ on the sphere.

The code uses the SpherePoint method described shortly to find the Cartesian coordinates for the points. It then uses those coordinates to define a polygon. Figure 16-2 shows how the variables theta and phi define one of those polygons.

The code adds the points to the points array and then passes it to the AddPolygon method to create the triangles that represent the polygon.

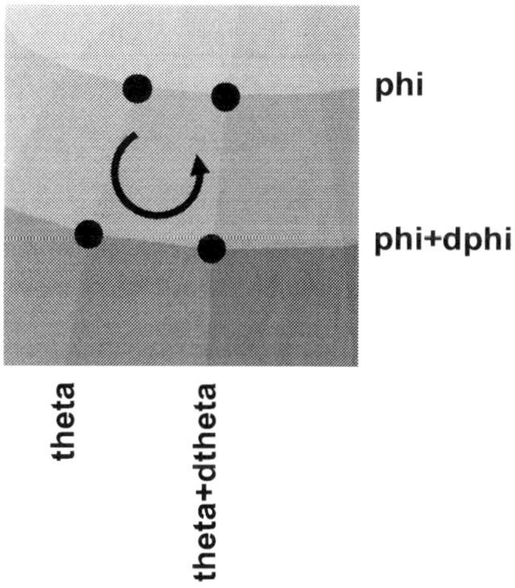

Figure 16-2: Variables theta and phi determine where an area's points are.

The following code shows the SpherePoint method.

```
// Return a point on a sphere.
public static Point3D SpherePoint(Point3D center, double r, double theta, double phi)
{
    double y = r * Math.Cos(phi);
    double h = r * Math.Sin(phi);
    double x = h * Math.Sin(theta);
    double z = h * Math.Cos(theta);
    return center + new Vector3D(x, y, z);
}
```

This method translates a point's spherical coordinates into Cartesian coordinates. If you don't remember how this calculation works, see the section "Spherical Mathematics" in Chapter 5.

> **NOTE:** I put the SpherePoint method in the G3 class so it would be easy to reuse later.

Adding Textured Spheres

If you simply add texture coordinates to the areas created by the previous version of the AddSphere method, you run into two problems, one big and one small. The following sections explain the problems and how to solve them.

The Big Problem

To understand this problem, you need to remember how the drawing system makes a smooth shape. If adjacent triangles share vertices, then the system averages the triangles' surface normals at those vertices. The drawing system then uses the normals to determine how the triangles are shaded. Because the triangles share a normal, they receive the same shading at that point so they blend smoothly together and you get a smooth surface.

That's fine in areas where the texture coordinates vary continuously, but there are places on a sphere where two adjacent points have very different texture coordinates.

For example, suppose you wrap a texture around a sphere. The texture coordinates vary smoothly until you come to the edge of the texture. At that point, one triangle displays points on one side of the texture and its neighbors display points on the other.

Take a look at Figure 16-3 and suppose you want to map the texture on the left onto the sphere on the right. The points A and B are close together on the sphere, but their texture coordinates are far apart.

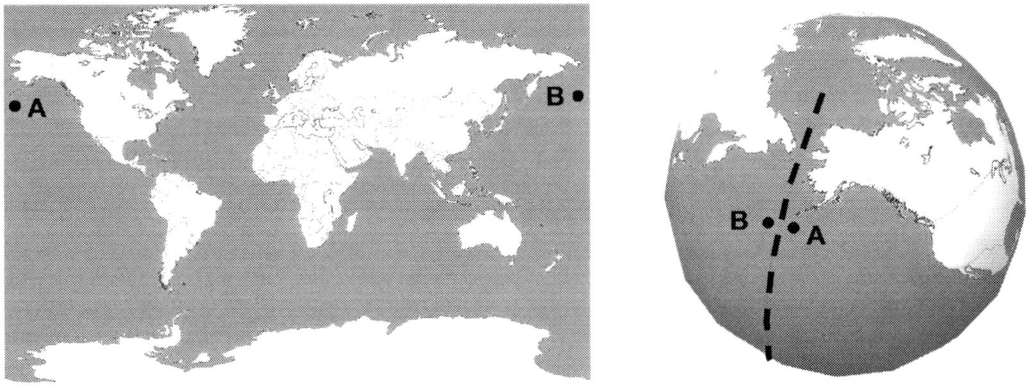

Figure 16-3: Points that are close on a solid may be far apart in texture coordinates.

Remember that texture coordinates are usually called U and V coordinates and they range from 0 to 1. In Figure 16-3, point A has U coordinate close to 0 and point B has U coordinate close to 1.

Unfortunately, texture coordinates are stored on a point-by-point basis. The 17th point has coordinates stored in the mesh's 17th `Positions` entry and texture coordinates stored in its 17th `TextureCoordinates` entry. That means if two triangles share a point, they also share its texture coordinates. In Figure 16-3, if point A and B are exactly on the edge of the texture, then their triangles would share those points, but then what texture coordinates should they share?

This same problem occurs at the sphere's poles. Horizontally the triangles must span the entire range $0 \leq u \leq 1$. If they share the point at the pole, then they can't all have the correct texture coordinates at that point. The result makes the top row of triangles look twisted.

> **NOTE:** You could try texturing a sphere in this way as an experiment. You'll find that one set of triangles near the edge is forced to span a huge range of texture coordinates. They will have some corners near U=0 and other corners near U=1. That means they will cram the entire texture into a narrow strip. It's pretty mystifying if you don't know what's going on.

One way to solve this problem is to give up on the idea of sharing points and specify each point's normal explicitly. Then, because A and B have separate entries in the mesh's `Positions`, `Normals`, and `TextureCoordinates` arrays, they can use copies of the same normal but still have different texture coordinates.

The following `AddTexturedSphere` method uses this approach. It's a bit longer than the `AddSphere` method, but it's still fairly straightforward.

```
// Add a sphere with texture coordinates.
public static void AddTexturedSphere(this MeshGeometry3D mesh,
    Point3D center, double radius, int numTheta, int numPhi,
    bool smooth = false)
{
    double dtheta = 2 * Math.PI / numTheta;
    double dphi = Math.PI / numPhi;
    double theta = 0;
    for (int t = 0; t < numTheta; t++)
    {
        double phi = 0;
        for (int p = 0; p < numPhi; p++)
        {
            // Find this piece's points.
            Point3D point1 =
                G3.SpherePoint(center, radius, theta, phi).Round();
            Point3D point2 =
                G3.SpherePoint(center, radius, theta, phi + dphi).Round();
            Point3D point3 =
                G3.SpherePoint(center, radius, theta + dtheta, phi + dphi).Round();
            Point3D point4 =
                G3.SpherePoint(center, radius, theta + dtheta, phi).Round();

            // Find this piece's texture coordinates.
            Point coords1 =
                new Point((double)t / numTheta, (double)p / numPhi);
            Point coords2 =
                new Point((double)t / numTheta, (double)(p + 1) / numPhi);
            Point coords3 =
                new Point((double)(t + 1) / numTheta, (double)(p + 1) / numPhi);
            Point coords4 =
                new Point((double)(t + 1) / numTheta, (double)p / numPhi);
```

```
                // Find this piece's normals.
                Vector3D normal1 = (Vector3D)G3.SpherePoint(
                    D3.Origin, 1, theta, phi).Round();
                Vector3D normal2 = (Vector3D)G3.SpherePoint(
                    D3.Origin, 1, theta, phi + dphi).Round();
                Vector3D normal3 = (Vector3D)G3.SpherePoint(
                    D3.Origin, 1, theta + dtheta, phi + dphi).Round();
                Vector3D normal4 = (Vector3D)G3.SpherePoint(
                    D3.Origin, 1, theta + dtheta, phi).Round();

                // Make the first triangle.
                int index = mesh.Positions.Count;
                mesh.Positions.Add(point1);
                if (smooth) mesh.Normals.Add(normal1);
                mesh.TextureCoordinates.Add(coords1);

                mesh.Positions.Add(point2);
                if (smooth) mesh.Normals.Add(normal2);
                mesh.TextureCoordinates.Add(coords2);

                mesh.Positions.Add(point3);
                if (smooth) mesh.Normals.Add(normal3);
                mesh.TextureCoordinates.Add(coords3);

                mesh.TriangleIndices.Add(index++);
                mesh.TriangleIndices.Add(index++);
                mesh.TriangleIndices.Add(index++);

                // Make the second triangle.
                mesh.Positions.Add(point1);
                if (smooth) mesh.Normals.Add(normal1);
                mesh.TextureCoordinates.Add(coords1);

                mesh.Positions.Add(point3);
                if (smooth) mesh.Normals.Add(normal3);
                mesh.TextureCoordinates.Add(coords3);

                mesh.Positions.Add(point4);
                if (smooth) mesh.Normals.Add(normal4);
                mesh.TextureCoordinates.Add(coords4);

                mesh.TriangleIndices.Add(index++);
                mesh.TriangleIndices.Add(index++);
                mesh.TriangleIndices.Add(index++);

                phi += dphi;
            }
            theta += dtheta;
        }
    }
```

This method loops over `theta` and `phi` values just as the `AddSphere` method does. For each location on the sphere, the code calculates information about the quadrilateral at that location. (See Figure 16-2 again.)

The code uses the `SpherePoint` method to find each point's Cartesian coordinates. It rounds the results so points on adjacent triangles match exactly.

Next, the code calculates the locations' texture coordinates by simply mapping the `theta` and `phi` values into U and V texture coordinate values.

The method then finds the points' surface normals. For spheres, this is easy because all of the normals point outward away from the sphere's center. To find the normals, the program uses the `SpherePoint` method again. This time it uses the origin as the method's center so the normals radiate outward. The `SpherePoint` method returns a `Point3D`, so the code casts it into a `Vector3D`.

After it gathers the points' information, the method creates the `Positions`, `Normals`, and `TextureCoordinates` entries. The only trick here is making sure to create the points in the correct order to make the triangles outwardly-oriented.

Revising Transformations

Way back in Chapter 9, I added two `ApplyTransformation` extension methods to the `MeshExtensions` class. Those methods apply a `Matrix3D` or a `Transform3D` to the mesh by transforming the mesh's points. Now that we're using explicit normals, we need to modify those methods to transform the normals, too. If we don't make that change, then you could transform the shape so it no longer matches its normals.

For example, suppose you build a scene containing a textured sphere illuminated by a directional light point downward so the top of the sphere is bright and the bottom is dark. Now suppose you rotate the sphere 90° around the X axis. If you don't modify the sphere's normals, then the sphere's north pole, which now points toward the Z axis, still has a normal pointing upward. The drawing system sees that the normal points toward the light, so it makes that part of the sphere bright. Now the sphere is bright on the side toward the Z axis and dark toward the -Z axis.

The BadNormals example program shown in Figure 16-4 demonstrates this problem. The program rotates the sphere on the right but doesn't rotate its normals.

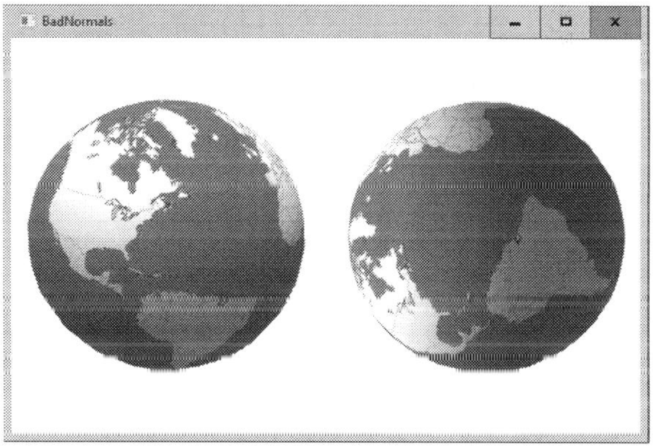

Figure 16-4: If you transform a mesh and not its normals, you may get incorrect lighting.

The following code shows revised `ApplyTransformation` methods that solve this problem. The new code is highlighted.

```
// Apply a transformation Matrix3D or transformation class.
public static void ApplyTransformation(this MeshGeometry3D mesh,
```

```
        Matrix3D transformation)
    {
        Point3D[] points = mesh.Positions.ToArray();
        transformation.Transform(points);
        mesh.Positions = new Point3DCollection(points);

        Vector3D[] normals = mesh.Normals.ToArray();
        transformation.Transform(normals);
        mesh.Normals = new Vector3DCollection(normals);
    }

    public static void ApplyTransformation(this MeshGeometry3D mesh,
        Transform3D transformation)
    {
        Point3D[] points = mesh.Positions.ToArray();
        transformation.Transform(points);
        mesh.Positions = new Point3DCollection(points);

        Vector3D[] normals = mesh.Normals.ToArray();
        transformation.Transform(normals);
        mesh.Normals = new Vector3DCollection(normals);
    }
```

The new code simply applies the transformations to the mesh's normal vectors in addition to its points.

The Small Problem

The big problem is really big. If you use shared vertices instead of explicit normals, the result looks terrible.

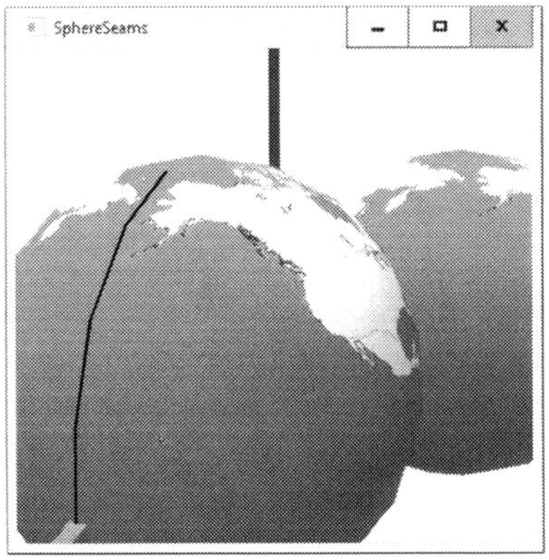

Figure 16-5: You can prevent the "seam," by adding a point with texture u = 1.01.

The small problem is small enough that you could ignore it. In fact, you might not even notice it if you don't look very closely. It's particularly hard to spot if you're using a complicated texture.

If you look at the nearer sphere in Figure 16-5, you can see a thin vertical line that looks like a seam running between Alaska and Russia. I've darkened it in the figure so it's more obvious. It's fainter but still present when you run the program.

I'm not sure what causes this. My hypothesis is that it's caused by the drawing system's "helpfully" scaling the texture. (Remember the complicated way a brush's viewbox and viewport determine a texture's appearance? If you want a refresher, see the section "Texture Scaling" in Chapter 7.)

One way you can fix this is to adjust the texture coordinates so the visible points don't go all the way to U=1.0. For example, you can add a new point that isn't used in any of the visible triangles with U=1.01. That makes the drawing system rescale the texture just enough to prevent the seam from appearing.

After drawing the farther sphere in Figure 16-5, the program uses the following code to hide the sphere's seam.

```
// Add a point to redefine the texture area to hide the "seam."
mesh2.Positions.Add(new Point3D());
mesh2.TextureCoordinates.Add(new Point(1.01, 1.01));
```

This code adds a single point with texture coordinates (1.01, 1.01) to the sphere's mesh, and that prevents the seam from appearing.

Figure 16-5 was produced by the SphereSeams example program. If you like, you can download it and experiment with the seam. (If you find a better way to prevent it, or if you figure out exactly why it is appearing in the first place, please post a comment on the book's web site.)

Example Program

The Spheres example program shown in Figure 16-6 uses the following code to display four spheres.

```
private void DefineModel(Model3DGroup group)
{
    // Make a non-smooth sphere.
    MeshGeometry3D mesh1 = new MeshGeometry3D();
    mesh1.AddSphere(new Point3D(-1.75, 0, 1.75), 1.5, 20, 10);
    group.Children.Add(mesh1.MakeModel(Brushes.Pink));

    // Make a smooth sphere.
    MeshGeometry3D mesh2 = new MeshGeometry3D();
    mesh2.AddSphere(new Point3D(1.75, 0, 1.75), 1.5, 20, 10, true);
    group.Children.Add(mesh2.MakeModel(Brushes.Pink));

    // Make a non-smooth textured sphere.
    MeshGeometry3D mesh3 = new MeshGeometry3D();
    mesh3.AddTexturedSphere(new Point3D(-1.75, 0, -1.75), 1.5, 20, 10);
    group.Children.Add(mesh3.MakeModel("world.jpg"));
    // Add a point to redefine the texture area to hide the "seam."
    mesh3.Positions.Add(new Point3D());
    mesh3.TextureCoordinates.Add(new Point(1.01, 1.01));

    // Make a smooth textured sphere.
    MeshGeometry3D mesh4 = new MeshGeometry3D();
    mesh4.AddTexturedSphere(new Point3D(1.75, 0, -1.75), 1.5, 20, 10, true);
    group.Children.Add(mesh4.MakeModel("world.jpg"));
    // Add a point to redefine the texture area to hide the "seam."
    mesh4.Positions.Add(new Point3D());
    mesh4.TextureCoordinates.Add(new Point(1.01, 1.01));

    // Show the axes.
    MeshExtensions.AddAxes(group);
```

```
}
```

Figure 16-6: The Spheres example program draws four spheres.

This code creates a mesh and calls `AddSphere` to create a non-smooth sphere. It turns the mesh into a pink model and adds it to the program's `Model3DGroup`.

Next, the code repeats those steps, this time passing the `AddSphere` method the final parameter `true` to indicate that it should create a smooth sphere. That makes `AddSphere` use shared vertices to produce the smooth result.

The program then repeats roughly the same steps, except this time it calls `AddTexturedSphere` to make textured spheres. It adds an extra hidden point to both meshes to prevent the "seam" from appearing.

Summary

This chapter showed how you can create spheres. You can make them smooth or non-smooth, textured or untextured. Making a smooth textured sphere requires a bit of extra work, but can produce some very nice results.

The example programs described in this chapter use a texture that holds an image of the globe unwrapped into a rectangle, but this isn't the only way that you can unwrap a globe. It's not even necessarily the best way.

For example, the `AddTexturedSphere` method uses triangles to represent the areas near the poles, but if you use a rectangular texture, those areas should really be represented by increasingly small quadrilaterals.

For other spheres, you may want to use other mapping techniques or other projections of the texture. For example, if you need to show more detail at the poles (such as the routes taken by Peary, Shackleton, and other polarphiles), then you'll probably need to handle the pole areas differently.

To learn more about global mapping than you probably want to know, search the internet for "globe projection."

Making a smoothly textured sphere requires some work, but the sphere is still a relatively simple object. The next chapter explains how you can build a more complicated solid: the torus. It also shows how you can use techniques similar to those used in this chapter to make smooth and textured tori.

Chapter 17

Tori

This chapter explains how to draw smooth and non-smooth tori.

> **NOTE:** "Tori" (pronounced "tor-eye") is the plural of "torus." Torus is fancy math-speak for the donut shape.
>
> Does this kind of "tori" have anything to do with the Japanese tori gate? (Here "tori" is pronounced tor-ee.) Take a look at Figure 17-1 and then you decide.
>
> 
>
> **Tori** **Tori gate** **Stargate**
>
> **Figure 17-1: Tori, tori gate, and stargate. Coincidence or alien conspiracy?**

The following section explains a bit more about the geometry of the torus. The two sections after that explain how you can draw textured and untextured tori.

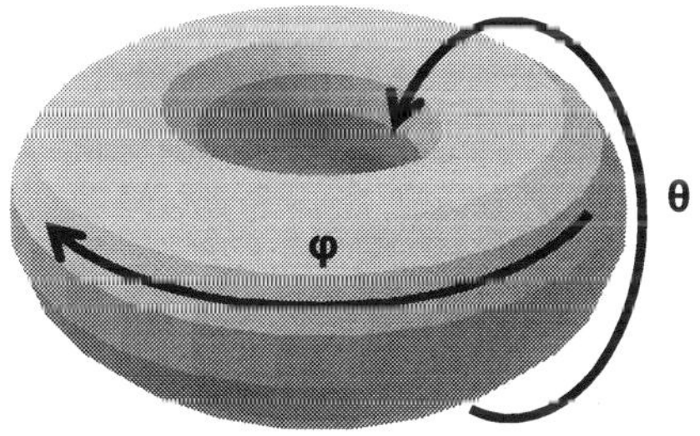

Figure 17-2: You can represent points in a torus with θ and φ values.

Understanding Tori

A torus doesn't look much like a sphere, but the two shapes have several features in common. For example, you can use variables θ and φ to represent points on both a sphere and a torus. Figure 17-2 shows how θ and φ determine points on a torus.

In a torus, the θ direction is called the *poloidal*

direction and the φ direction is called the *toroidal* direction.

> **NOTE:** The term "poloidal" (yet another impressive vocabulary word) means having to do with a toroidal magnetic field. If you were to run a current through a wire curled into a loop, then the poloidal direction is the direction of the magnetic field. That direction would point along the θ arrow in Figure 17-2. You can even use the right-hand rule in the figure to verify the field's direction.

To draw a torus, you can use code that is similar to the code you use to draw a sphere. Both can loop through `theta` and `phi` values to find the solids' points. Both can also use `numTheta` and `numPhi` variables to determine how many pieces are used to represent the solids.

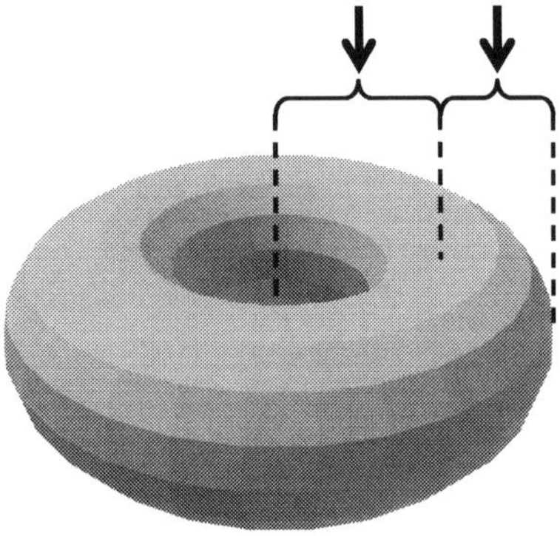

Figure 17-3: A torus has a major radius and a minor radius.

Even the big and small problems described in Chapter 16 apply to tori as well as spheres, and you can solve them in the same ways.

To define a sphere, you only need to specify its radius. To define a torus, you need to specify two radii: a major radius and a minor radius. The *major radius*, which is often denoted R, is the distance from the center of the torus to the center of its "tube." The *minor radius*, denoted r, is the radius of the tube. Figure 17-3 shows a torus's two radii.

The ratio R/r is called the torus's *aspect ratio*.

You can group tori into three categories depending on the relative lengths of their major and minor axes. If the major axis is longer than the minor axis, you get a normal donut shape. (In a classic donut shape, the aspect ratio is around 3/2.)

If the major axis and minor axis are equal, you get a shape where the hole in the center of the donut is just barely closed. This is called a *horn torus* because the central area makes a horn if you cut the torus in half horizontally.

If the major axis is shorter than the minor axis, then the torus's opposite sides intersect each other. This is called a *spindle torus* because the central area looks sort of like the yarn on an old-fashioned spindle like the one shown in Figure 17-4.

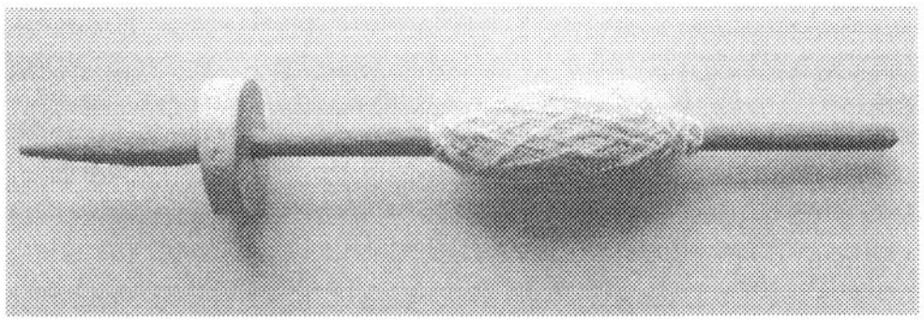

Figure 17-4: A spindle torus's center looks like yarn on a spindle.

The TorusTypes example program shown in

Figure 17-5 displays examples of the three kinds of tori. The versions closer to the viewing position have been split in half horizontally so you can see their interiors.

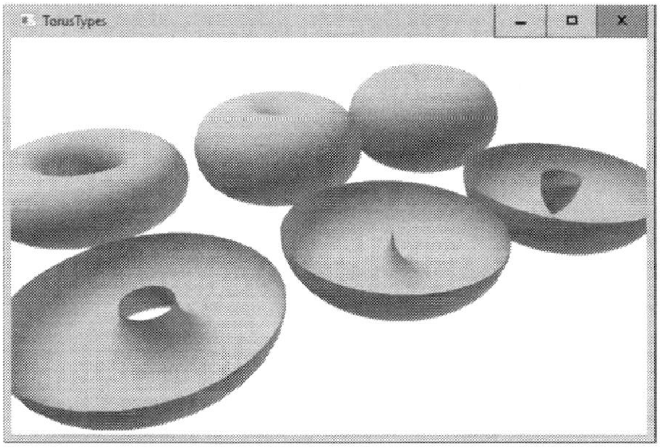

Figure 17-5: The TorusTypes example program draws normal, horn, and spindle tori.

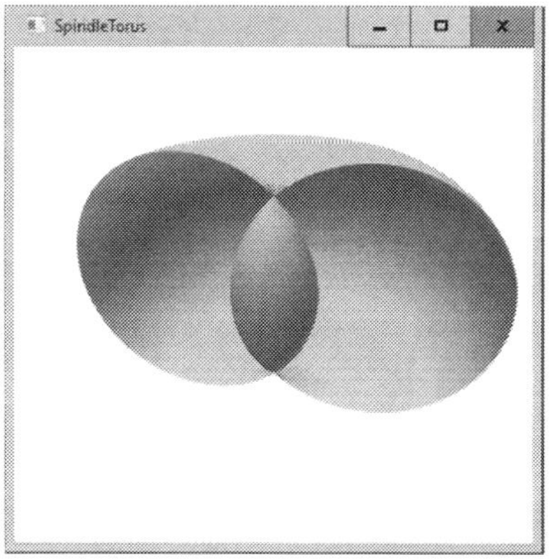

Figure 17-6: The SpindleTorus example program draws a spindle torus split vertically.

The SpindleTorus example program shown in Figure 17-6 shows a spindle torus cut in half vertically so it's easier to see the spindle.

> **NOTE:** Mathematicians sometimes call the exterior surface of a spindle torus the "apple" and the interior spindle part the "lemon." I can only assume they invented those terms during lunch.

The following sections explain how you can build untextured and textured tori.

Adding Tori

The following `AddTorus` method creates an untextured torus. This code is very similar to the `AddSphere` method described in Chapter 16. The differences are highlighted.

```
public static void AddTorus(this MeshGeometry3D mesh,
    Point3D center, double R, double r, int numTheta, int numPhi,
    bool smooth = false)
{
    // Make a point dictionary if needed.
    Dictionary<Point3D, int> pointDict = null;
    if (smooth) pointDict = new Dictionary<Point3D, int>();

    // Generate the points.
    double dtheta = 2 * Math.PI / numTheta;
    double dphi = 2 * Math.PI / numPhi;
    double theta = 0;
    for (int t = 0; t < numTheta; t++)
    {
```

```
            double phi = 0;
            for (int p = 0; p < numPhi; p++)
            {
                // Find this piece's points.
                Point3D[] points =
                {
                    G3.TorusPoint(center, R, r, theta + dtheta, phi),
                    G3.TorusPoint(center, R, r, theta + dtheta, phi + dphi),
                    G3.TorusPoint(center, R, r, theta, phi + dphi),
                    G3.TorusPoint(center, R, r, theta, phi),
                };

                // Make the polygon.
                mesh.AddPolygon(pointDict, points);

                phi += dphi;
            }
            theta += dtheta;
        }
    }
```

This methods loops through `theta` and `phi` values much as the `AddSphere` method did. This time, however, the value `phi` must range from 0 to 2π to make a complete circle around the torus's tube.

The only other difference between `AddTorus` and `AddSphere` is that `AddTorus` calls the `TorusPoint` method instead of the `SpherePoint` method to find locations on the torus. The following code shows the `TorusPoint` method.

```
    public static Point3D TorusPoint(Point3D center, double R, double r,
        double theta, double phi)
    {
        return new Point3D(
            center.X + (R + r * Math.Cos(theta)) * Math.Cos(phi),
            center.Y + r * Math.Sin(theta),
            center.Z + (R + r * Math.Cos(theta)) * Math.Sin(phi));
    }
```

This code plugs `theta` and `phi` into the equations for a torus. You can find those equations at Wikipedia (`tinyurl.com/njf99fs`) or Wolfram MathWorld (`tinyurl.com/3k2fe`). To save space, I'm not going to include the derivation here. If you really want to see if, search the internet.

Adding Textured Tori

In Chapter 16, I explained two problems in texturing a sphere. The big problem is that you cannot use shared triangle vertices because points that are close together on the sphere may have texture coordinates that are far apart. The smaller problem is that the drawing system's scaling methods seem to create a thin line on the sphere.

To solve those problems, the `AddTexturedSphere` method uses explicit normals instead of shared vertices, and it includes an extra point with texture coordinates (1.01, 1.01). The following `AddTexturedTorus` method uses the same techniques.

```
public static void AddTexturedTorus(this MeshGeometry3D mesh,
    Point3D center, double R, double r, int numTheta, int numPhi,
    bool smooth = false)
{
    double dtheta = 2 * Math.PI / numTheta;
    double dphi = 2 * Math.PI / numPhi;
    double theta = Math.PI;         // Puts the texture's top/bottom on the inside.
    for (int t = 0; t < numTheta; t++)
    {
        double phi = 0;
        for (int p = 0; p < numPhi; p++)
        {
            // Find this piece's points.
            Point3D point1 = G3.TorusPoint(center, R, r, theta, phi).Round();
            Point3D point2 = G3.TorusPoint(center, R, r, theta + dtheta, phi).Round();
            Point3D point3 = G3.TorusPoint(center, R, r, theta + dtheta,
                phi + dphi).Round();
            Point3D point4 = G3.TorusPoint(center, R, r, theta, phi + dphi).Round();

            // Find this piece's normals.
            Vector3D normal1 = G3.TorusNormal(D3.Origin, R, r, theta, phi);
            Vector3D normal2 = G3.TorusNormal(D3.Origin, R, r, theta + dtheta, phi);
            Vector3D normal3 = G3.TorusNormal(D3.Origin, R, r, theta + dtheta,
                phi + dphi);
            Vector3D normal4 = G3.TorusNormal(D3.Origin, R, r, theta, phi + dphi);

            // Find this piece's texture coordinates.
            Point coords1 = new Point(
                1 - (double)p / numPhi,
                1 - (double)t / numTheta);
            Point coords2 = new Point(
                1 - (double)p / numPhi,
                1 - (double)(t + 1) / numTheta);
            Point coords3 = new Point(
                1 - (double)(p + 1) / numPhi,
                1 - (double)(t + 1) / numTheta);
            Point coords4 = new Point(
                1 - (double)(p + 1) / numPhi,
                1 - (double)t / numTheta);

            // Make the first triangle.
            int index = mesh.Positions.Count;
            mesh.Positions.Add(point1);
            if (smooth) mesh.Normals.Add(normal1);
            mesh.TextureCoordinates.Add(coords1);

            mesh.Positions.Add(point2);
            if (smooth) mesh.Normals.Add(normal2);
            mesh.TextureCoordinates.Add(coords2);

            mesh.Positions.Add(point3);
            if (smooth) mesh.Normals.Add(normal3);
            mesh.TextureCoordinates.Add(coords3);
```

```
                mesh.TriangleIndices.Add(index++);
                mesh.TriangleIndices.Add(index++);
                mesh.TriangleIndices.Add(index++);

                // Make the second triangle.
                mesh.Positions.Add(point1);
                if (smooth) mesh.Normals.Add(normal1);
                mesh.TextureCoordinates.Add(coords1);

                mesh.Positions.Add(point3);
                if (smooth) mesh.Normals.Add(normal3);
                mesh.TextureCoordinates.Add(coords3);

                mesh.Positions.Add(point4);
                if (smooth) mesh.Normals.Add(normal4);
                mesh.TextureCoordinates.Add(coords4);

                mesh.TriangleIndices.Add(index++);
                mesh.TriangleIndices.Add(index++);
                mesh.TriangleIndices.Add(index++);

                phi += dphi;
            }
            theta += dtheta;
        }

        // Add texture coordinates 1.01 to prevent "seams."
        mesh.Positions.Add(new Point3D());
        mesh.TextureCoordinates.Add(new Point(1.01, 1.01));
    }
```

This code follows the same basic approach as the `AddTexturedSphere` method. It loops over `theta` and `phi` values and uses them to calculate points and normals on the solid's surface. It then uses the points and normals to make the pieces of the sphere.

The code uses the `TorusPoint` method described in the preceding section to find points on the torus. It uses the following `TorusNormal` method to find the points' normals.

The following code shows the `TorusNormal` method.

```
    public static Vector3D TorusNormal(Point3D center, double R, double r,
        double theta, double phi)
    {
        return (Vector3D)TorusPoint(center, 0, r, theta, phi);
    }
```

This code simply calls the `TorusPoint` method setting the `R` argument to 0. It's not obvious why this works, but it makes sense if you think about the geometry of the situation. If you set `R` = 0, the torus degenerates so its tube is centered at the origin. Then a vector from the origin to a point on the tube gives the normal vector at that point.

The `TorusPoint` method returns a point instead of a vector, so the `TorusNormal` method casts the result into a `Vector3D` before returning it.

Example Program

The Tori example program uses the following code to build its scene.

```
private void DefineModel(Model3DGroup group)
{
    const int numTheta = 15;
    const int numPhi = 30;

    // Make a non-smooth torus.
    MeshGeometry3D mesh1 = new MeshGeometry3D();
    Point3D center = new Point3D(-1, 1, 2);
    mesh1.AddTorus(center, 1, 0.5, numTheta, numPhi);
    group.Children.Add(mesh1.MakeModel(Brushes.LightGreen));

    // Make a smooth torus.
    MeshGeometry3D mesh2 = new MeshGeometry3D();
    center = new Point3D(1, 0, 2);
    mesh2.AddTorus(center, 1, 0.5, numTheta, numPhi, true);
    group.Children.Add(mesh2.MakeModel(Brushes.LightGreen));

    // Make a non-smooth textured torus.
    MeshGeometry3D mesh3 = new MeshGeometry3D();
    center = new Point3D(-1, 1, -2);
    mesh3.AddTexturedTorus(center, 1, 0.5, numTheta, numPhi);
    mesh3.ApplyTransformation(D3.Rotate(D3.YVector(), center, -150));
    mesh3.Positions.Add(new Point3D());
    mesh3.TextureCoordinates.Add(new Point(1.01, 1.01));
    group.Children.Add(mesh3.MakeModel("world.jpg"));

    // Make a smooth textured torus.
    MeshGeometry3D mesh4 = new MeshGeometry3D();
    center = new Point3D(1, 0, -2);
    mesh4.AddTexturedTorus(center, 1, 0.5, numTheta, numPhi, true);
    mesh4.ApplyTransformation(D3.Rotate(D3.YVector(), center, -150));
    mesh4.Positions.Add(new Point3D());
    mesh4.TextureCoordinates.Add(new Point(1.01, 1.01));
    group.Children.Add(mesh4.MakeModel("world.jpg"));

    // Show the axes.
    MeshExtensions.AddAxes(group);
}
```

This code creates a mesh and uses its `AddTorus` method to make a non-smooth green torus without a texture. It repeats those steps to make a smooth green torus.

The method then repeats the same steps two more times, this time calling `AddTexturedTorus` to create non-smooth and smooth textured tori.

Figure 17-7 shows the result.

Figure 17-7: The Tori example program draws four tori.

Summary

This chapter explained how to build smooth and non-smooth tori with or without textures. The code parallels the code used in Chapter 16 to draw spheres.

Both the spheres described in Chapter 16 and the tori described in this chapter are inherently smooth-sided solids. The next several chapters show how to draw a group of solids that have polygonal sides: the Platonic solids.

Chapter 18 Tetrahedrons

The *Platonic solids* are all of the regular convex three-dimensional solids. To be *regular*, the solid's faces must be congruent (the same size and shape) and regular (all edges have the same length and all angles are the same). The faces must also meet with the same angles, and the same number of faces must meet at each vertex.

> **NOTE:** The Platonic solids were named after the Greek philosopher Plato (c. 428 - 348 BC) who hypothesized that the classical elements earth, air, fire, water, and aether were made from these solids.

In three dimensions, there are only five regular solids: the tetrahedron, cube, octahedron, dodecahedron, and icosahedron. This chapter explains how to build a tetrahedron. The chapters that follow explain how to build the other Platonic solids.

Tetrahedron Vertices

A tetrahedron has four faces that are equilateral triangles. In an equilateral triangle, the sides have the same lengths and they meet at 60° angles. Figure 18-1 shows a tetrahedron.

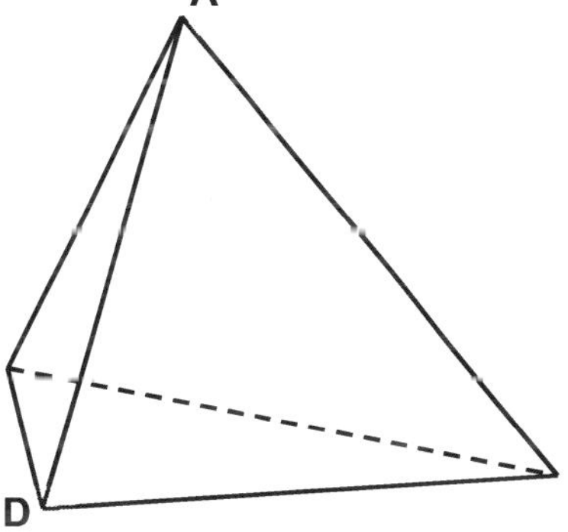

Figure 18-1: A tetrahedron has four sides that are equilateral triangles.

It is a trigonometric fact that a triangle with angles of 30°, 60°, and 90° has sides with relative lengths of 1, 2, and $\sqrt{3}$ as shown in Figure 18-2. These lengths are not absolute—they are relative to each other. For example, if the short side has length 4, the other sides have lengths 4×2 and $4 \times \sqrt{3}$.

Now imagine you're looking at the tetrahedron from the top as shown in Figure 18-3. By symmetry, the projections of the sides of the tetrahedron bisect the angles in the solid's base. Those angles are each 60°, so the bisected halves of the angles are 30°.

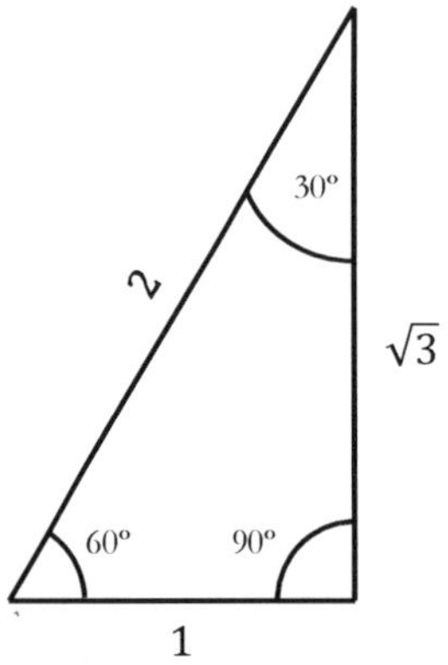

Figure 18-2: A 30-60-90 triangle has side length ratios $1, 2, \sqrt{3}$.

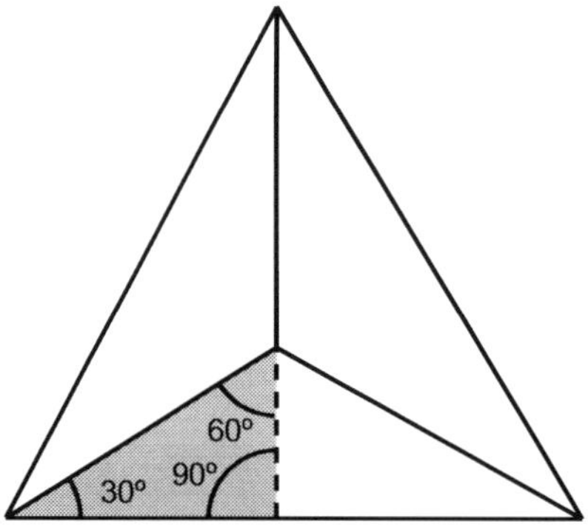

Figure 18-3: The shaded triangle is a 30-60-90 triangle.

Since one of the other angles in this smaller triangle (one of them is shaded in Figure 18-3) is 90°, the remaining angle must be 180-90-30=60°. That means the shaded triangle is a 30-60-90 triangle.

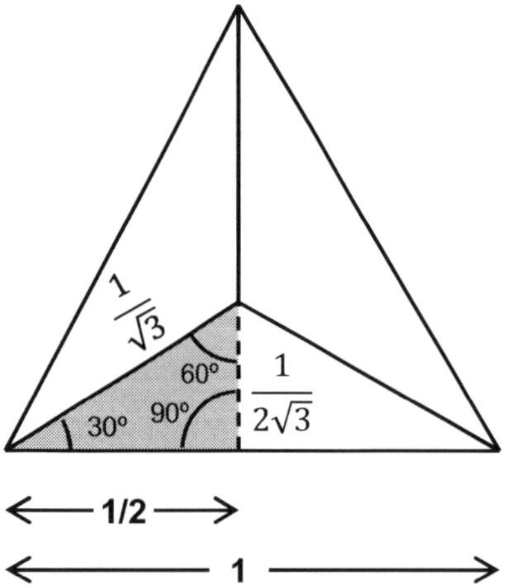

Figure 18-4: The shaded triangle's sides have lengths $\frac{1}{2}, \frac{1}{\sqrt{3}},$ and $\frac{1}{2\sqrt{3}}$.

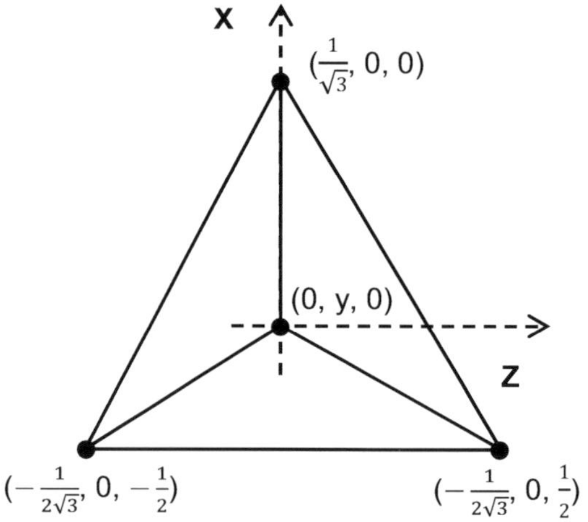

Figure 18-5: Only the Y coordinate for the top vertex is missing.

If the sides of the tetrahedron have length 1, then the shaded triangle's bottom side has length 1/2. Because this is a 30-60-90 triangle, the other sides must have lengths $1/\sqrt{3}$ and $1/2\sqrt{3}$ as shown in Figure 18-4.

Now suppose you want the tetrahedron's top vertex to lie on the vertical Y axis and the bottom face to lie in the X-Z plane. Then the values shown in Figure 18-4 give the coordinates of all four vertices except for the Y coordinate of the top vertex as shown in Figure 18-5.

Now imagine viewing the tetrahedron from the side, looking parallel to the Z axis. Figure 18-6 shows the tetrahedron from close to this angle. The view is turned just a little so you can still see all four sides.

The tetrahedron's edges have length 1, so the shaded triangle in Figure 18-6 has side lengths 1, $1/\sqrt{3}$ (see Figure 18-4), and y. Because this is a right triangle, you can use the Pythagorean theorem to calculate the value y.

$$y = \sqrt{1^2 - \left(\frac{1}{\sqrt{3}}\right)^2} = \sqrt{1 - \frac{1}{3}} = \sqrt{\frac{2}{3}}$$

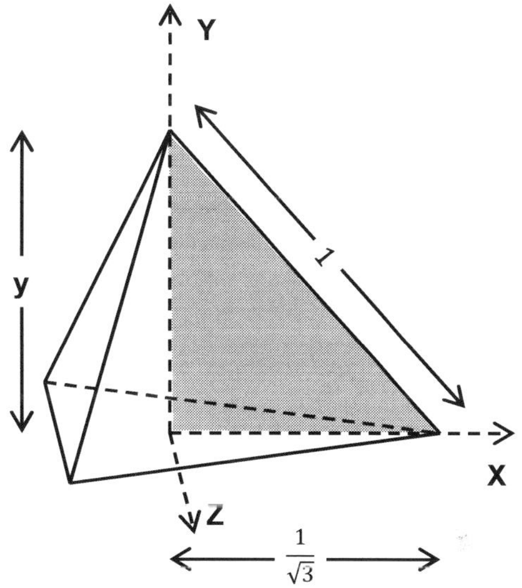

Figure 18-6: The shaded triangle has side lengths 1, $^1/_{\sqrt{3}}$, and y.

This gives the final coordinate that we need. The coordinates of the tetrahedron's four vertices are the following.

$$A = \left(0, \sqrt{\frac{2}{3}}, 0\right)$$

$$B = \left(\frac{1}{\sqrt{3}}, 0, 0\right)$$

$$C = \left(-\frac{1}{2\sqrt{3}}, 0, -\frac{1}{2}\right)$$

$$D = \left(-\frac{1}{2\sqrt{3}}, 0, \frac{1}{2}\right)$$

That gives the coordinates for a tetrahedron sitting on the XZ plane. If you want to center the solid at the origin, you need to move the solid down slightly. To do that, it helps to know what a circumsphere is.

A *circumsphere* (or *circumscribed sphere*) is a sphere that encloses a solid and touches each of its vertices. The sphere's radius is called the solid's *circumradius*, and its center is called the solid's *circumcenter*. (More interesting vocabulary words!)

By symmetry, the center of the tetrahedron is at the average of its vertices. If you add up the four vertices' components, the X and Z values cancel out leaving 0. Only point A has a nonzero Y component, so the sphere's center is at (y+0+0+0)/4=y/4.

That means the tetrahedron's circumcenter is at the following point.

$$\text{Center} = \left(0, \frac{\sqrt{2/3}}{4}, 0\right)$$

To center the tetrahedron at the origin, you move it so its circumcenter is at the origin. To do that, simply subtract $\frac{\sqrt{2/3}}{4}$ from each point's Y coordinate.

The tetrahedron's circumradius is the distance from the circumcenter to any one of its vertices. In particular, you can use point A's Y coordinate for the circumradius.

If you move the circumcenter to the origin, then point A's Y component is the following.

$$\sqrt{\frac{2}{3}} - \frac{\sqrt{2/3}}{4} = \sqrt{\frac{2}{3}}\left(1 - \frac{1}{4}\right) = \frac{3}{4}\sqrt{\frac{2}{3}}$$

That gives us the circumradius.

$$\text{Circumradius} = \frac{3}{4}\sqrt{\frac{2}{3}}$$

The circumsphere is useful for centering the tetrahedron. You don't really need to know about the insphere, but I'll describe it for completeness.

An *insphere* (or *inscribed sphere*) is a sphere that is completely inside the solid and that is tangent to each of the solid's faces. This sphere's radius is called the solid's *inradius*, and its center is called the solid's *incenter*.

The distance from the tetrahedron's center to its bottom face gives the inradius. When you translate tetrahedron's circumcenter to the origin, the points that define the bottom face have the following Y coordinate.

$$-\frac{\sqrt{2/3}}{4}$$

The inradius is the negative of that value.

$$\text{Inradius} = \frac{\sqrt{2/3}}{4}$$

The equations shown in this section let you understand the tetrahedron's geometry. The next section describes code that you can use to draw tetrahedrons.

Adding Tetrahedrons

The G3 class includes the following code to work with tetrahedrons.

```
public static void TetrahedronPoints(
    out Point3D A, out Point3D B, out Point3D C, out Point3D D,
    bool centered)
{
    double dy = 0;
    if (centered) dy = 0.25 * Math.Sqrt(2.0 / 3.0);

    A = new Point3D(0, Math.Sqrt(2.0 / 3.0) - dy, 0);
    B = new Point3D(1.0 / Math.Sqrt(3.0), -dy, 0);
    C = new Point3D(-1.0 / (2 * Math.Sqrt(3.0)), -dy, -1.0 / 2.0);
    D = new Point3D(-1.0 / (2 * Math.Sqrt(3.0)), -dy, 1.0 / 2.0);
}
public static double TetrahedronCircumradius()
{
    return Math.Sqrt(2.0 / 3.0) * 0.75;
}
public static double TetrahedronInradius()
{
    return Math.Sqrt(2.0 / 3.0) * 0.25;
}
```

The `TetrahedronPoints` method returns the points that make up a tetrahedron with side lengths 1. If the `centered` parameter is `true`, the code sets variable `dy` to the offset needed to move the tetrahedron down to center it at the origin. The method then uses the equations shown earlier to define the tetrahedron's vertices.

As you can guess from their names, the `TetrahedronCircumradius` and `TetrahedronInradius` methods return the tetrahedron's circumradius and inradius. You can use those to scale the tetrahedron if you like. For example, if you want to fit the tetrahedron inside a unit sphere, you can scale it by a factor of 1/circumradius.

The `MeshExtensions` class defines the following `AddTetrahedron` method.

```
public static void AddTetrahedron(this MeshGeometry3D mesh, bool centered = true)
{
    // Get the points.
    Point3D A, B, C, D;
    G3.TetrahedronPoints(out A, out B, out C, out D, centered);

    // Make the faces.
    mesh.AddPolygon(A, B, C);
    mesh.AddPolygon(A, C, D);
    mesh.AddPolygon(A, D, B);
    mesh.AddPolygon(D, C, B);
}
```

This method calls the `TetrahedronPoints` method to find the tetrahedron's vertex coordinates and then uses the mesh's `AddPolygon` method to create the tetrahedron's faces.

Drawing Tetrahedrons

The OneTetrahedron example program uses the following code to display a single tetrahedron.

```
private void DefineModel(Model3DGroup group)
{
    // Make a tetrahedron.
    const double scale = 5;
    MeshGeometry3D mesh = new MeshGeometry3D();
    mesh.AddTetrahedron();
    mesh.ApplyTransformation(new ScaleTransform3D(scale, scale, scale));
    group.Children.Add(mesh.MakeModel(Brushes.LightBlue));

    // Show the axes.
    MeshExtensions.AddAxes(group);
}
```

This method defines a `scale` value that it will later use to scale the tetrahedron. It creates a mesh and uses its `AddTetrahedron` method to create a tetrahedron. The code does not pass the `AddTetrahedron` method a parameter telling it whether it should center the tetrahedron at the origin. That parameter defaults to `true`, so the tetrahedron is centered.

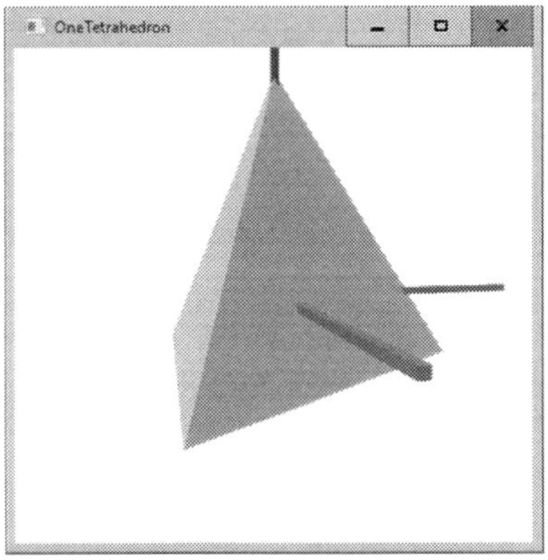

Figure 18-7: The OneTetrahedron example program draws a tetrahedron centered at the origin.

Next, the code converts the mesh into a light blue model and saves it in the program's `Model3DGroup`. The program finishes by displaying the coordinate axes.

Figure 18-7 shows the OneTetrahedron program displaying its scene. The result is similar to the picture shown in Figure 18-6.

Because the tetrahedron is the simplest of the Platonic solids, it's worth spending a little time studying it before moving on to the more complicated solids described in the following chapters. The following sections show how you can display circumspheres, inspheres, and duals for tetrahedrons. When you read the following chapters, you can use the same techniques to do the same for more complicated solids.

Before I talk about those topics, however, I should say a few things about translucent materials.

Translucent Materials

Up until now, I haven't talked about translucent materials. It turns out that you can use them in a three-dimensional program as long as you order the objects properly.

When it displays a scene, the drawing system organizes the scene's objects in a *z-order* that determines each object's distance from the viewing position. Objects farther from the viewing position are lower in the z-order. The system then draws the objects in the order in which they were added to the program's `Model3DGroup`.

When it considers an object, the system checks the z-order to see if the object lies behind another object that has already been drawn. If it is behind some other object, the system doesn't draw it.

To see how this can be a problem, suppose a program creates a tetrahedron and then a translucent circumsphere surrounding it. The drawing system first considers the tetrahedron and draws it. Next, it considers the sphere. Because the tetrahedron does not obscure the tetrahedron, the system draws it, too. Because the sphere is translucent, you can still see the tetrahedron inside it. So far, so good.

Now suppose the program creates the circumsphere first and then the tetrahedron. The drawing system considers the sphere and draws it. Next, the system considers the tetrahedron. It checks the z-order and discovers that the tetrahedron is inside the sphere. (Actually, it discovers that the tetrahedron is behind the front of the sphere.) It concludes that the tetrahedron is obscured so it doesn't draw the tetrahedron. Ideally the tetrahedron would be visible inside the sphere, but in this scenario, the tetrahedron doesn't appear.

The moral of the story is that you need to add translucent objects to the program's `Model3DGroup` *after* you add solid objects that may be obscured by them.

Unfortunately, that's not always easy. In the current example, the tetrahedron is inside the sphere so the sphere obscures the tetrahedron no matter what viewing direction you use. As long as you create the sphere second, the tetrahedron is always drawn.

However, suppose you had two translucent non-overlapping spheres. Then there are some viewing positions that put the first behind the second and other positions that put the second behind the first. There is no possible ordering in the `Model3DGroup` that can display them correctly from every viewing position.

One other problem with translucent materials is that you cannot see a solid's faces by looking through itself. For example, if you build a translucent cube, you won't be able to see the edges between any of its faces by looking through the cube.

Circumspheres and Inspheres

Now that you know how to use translucent materials, we can use them to show a tetrahedron with its circumsphere and insphere. The Tetrahedron example program uses the following code to build its scene.

```
private void DefineModel(Model3DGroup group)
```

```
{
    // Show the axes.
    MeshExtensions.AddAxes(group);

    const double scale = 5;

    // Make a solid insphere.
    MeshGeometry3D mesh1 = new MeshGeometry3D();
    mesh1.AddSphere(D3.Origin, G3.TetrahedronInradius(), 60, 30, true);
    mesh1.ApplyTransformation(new ScaleTransform3D(scale, scale, scale));
    group.Children.Add(mesh1.MakeModel(Brushes.Red));

    // Make a translucent tetrahedron.
    MeshGeometry3D mesh2 = new MeshGeometry3D();
    mesh2.AddTetrahedron();
    mesh2.ApplyTransformation(new ScaleTransform3D(scale, scale, scale));
    Brush brush = new SolidColorBrush(Color.FromArgb(128, 128, 255, 128));
    MaterialGroup group2 = D3.MakeMaterialGroup(
        new DiffuseMaterial(brush),
        new SpecularMaterial(Brushes.White, 100));
    group.Children.Add(mesh2.MakeModel(group2));

    // Make a translucent circumsphere.
    MeshGeometry3D mesh3 = new MeshGeometry3D();
    mesh3.AddSphere(D3.Origin, G3.TetrahedronCircumradius(), 60, 30, true);
    mesh3.ApplyTransformation(new ScaleTransform3D(scale, scale, scale));
    MaterialGroup group3 = D3.MakeMaterialGroup(
        new DiffuseMaterial(brush),
        new SpecularMaterial(Brushes.White, 100));
    group.Children.Add(mesh3.MakeModel(group3));
}
```

This code first displays the coordinate axes. It then defines a `scale` constant that it will use to scale its other solids so they fit nicely on the display.

Next, the code creates a sphere with radius equal to the tetrahedron's inradius. It scales the sphere and turns it into a solid red model.

The code then makes a tetrahedron and scales it. It makes a translucent brush and uses it to create a diffuse material. The code then creates a specular material and passes the two materials into the following `MakeMaterialGroup` method.

```
public static MaterialGroup MakeMaterialGroup(params Material[] materials)
{
    MaterialGroup group = new MaterialGroup();
    foreach (Material material in materials)
        group.Children.Add(material);
    return group;
}
```

This method simply creates a `MaterialGroup` and adds a list of materials to it.

Next, the `DefineModel` method calls the following version of `MakeModel` to convert a mesh and a material group into a model.

```
public static GeometryModel3D MakeModel(this MeshGeometry3D mesh,
    MaterialGroup material)
```

```
    {
        return new GeometryModel3D(mesh, material);
    }
```

This method simply creates and returns a `GeometryModel3D`. The `DefineModel` method could just create the model directly instead of calling `MakeModel`, but I've included this method to make the code more consistent.

Having created an insphere and tetrahedron, the program creates a circumsphere. The code gives the new sphere translucent diffuse and specular materials and adds it to the program's `Model3DGroup`.

Figure 18-8 shows the Tetrahedron example program displaying its scene. Download the example and experiment with it. You may need to rotate the scene around a bit to convince yourself that the insphere touches the tetrahedron's faces and that the tetrahedron's vertices touch the circumsphere.

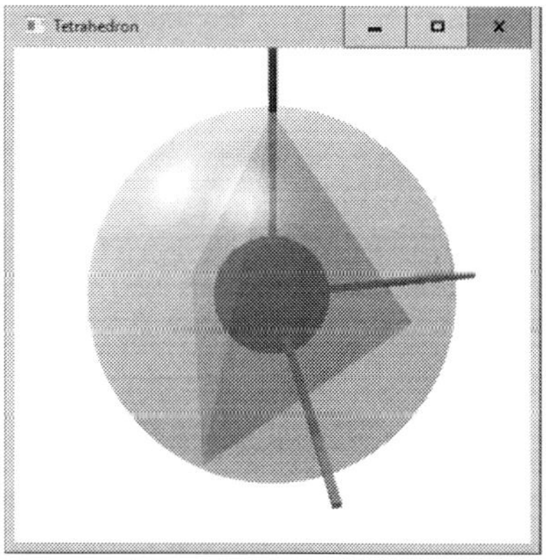

Figure 18-8: The Tetrahedron program draws a tetrahedron, insphere, and circumsphere.

Duals

A *polyhedron* is a solid with plane faces such as a cube or icosahedron. The *dual* or *reciprocal* of a polyhedron is another polyhedron that has faces and vertices that are arranged in a complementary fashion to the original polyhedron. Where the original solid has a face, the dual has a vertex and vice versa.

The dual of a Platonic solid is another Platonic solid. For example, the dual of a cube is an octahedron with vertices placed in the center of the cube's faces. Note that the dual of a dual is the original solid. For example, the dual of a cube is an octahedron and the dual of an octahedron is a cube.

The tetrahedron differs from the other Platonic solids in that it is its own dual.

The DualTetrahedron example program uses the following code to display a tetrahedron and its dual.

```
private void DefineModel(Model3DGroup group)
{
    // Show the axes.
    MeshExtensions.AddAxes(group);

    const double scale = 2;

    // Make a solid tetrahedron.
    MeshGeometry3D mesh1 = new MeshGeometry3D();
    mesh1.AddTetrahedron(true);
```

```
        mesh1.ApplyTransformation(new ScaleTransform3D(scale, scale, scale));
        mesh1.ApplyTransformation(D3.Rotate(D3.YVector(), D3.Origin, 180));
        mesh1.ApplyTransformation(D3.Rotate(D3.XVector(), D3.Origin, 180));
        group.Children.Add(mesh1.MakeModel(Brushes.LightBlue));

        // Make a translucent tetrahedron.
        MeshGeometry3D mesh2 = new MeshGeometry3D();
        mesh2.AddTetrahedron(true);
        mesh2.ApplyTransformation(new ScaleTransform3D(scale * 3, scale * 3, scale * 3));
        Brush brush = new SolidColorBrush(Color.FromArgb(128, 128, 255, 128));
        MaterialGroup group3 = D3.MakeMaterialGroup(
            new DiffuseMaterial(brush),
            new SpecularMaterial(Brushes.White, 100));
        group.Children.Add(mesh2.MakeModel(group3));

        // Mark both tetrahedrons' vertices.
        MeshGeometry3D mesh3 = new MeshGeometry3D();
        foreach (Point3D point in mesh1.Positions)
            mesh3.AddSphere(point, 0.1, 20, 10, true);
        foreach (Point3D point in mesh2.Positions)
            mesh3.AddSphere(point, 0.1, 20, 10, true);
        group.Children.Add(mesh3.MakeModel(Brushes.Red));
    }
```

This code displays the coordinate axes. It then creates a solid, scaled tetrahedron centered at the origin.

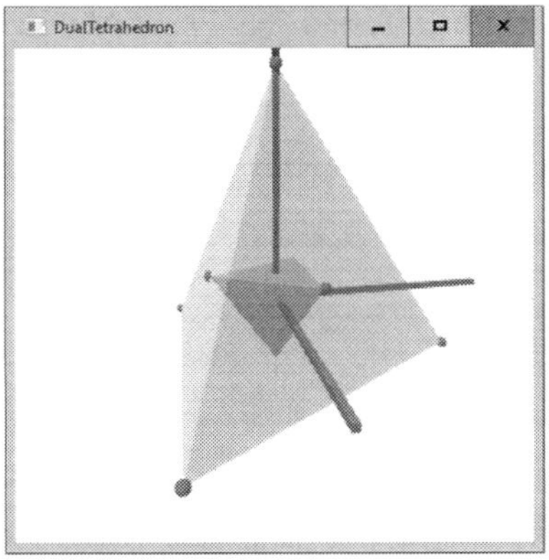

Figure 18-9: The tetrahedron is its own dual.

Next, the code creates another tetrahedron three times as big as the first so its inradius equals the first tetrahedron's circumradius. (If you look again at the formulas for the inradius and circumradius in the section "Tetrahedron Vertices" earlier in this chapter, you'll see that the circumradius is three times the inradius.)

The first tetrahedron's circumsphere touches its vertices, and the second tetrahedron's insphere is tangent to its sides. Because those two spheres have the same radius, that means the first tetrahedron's vertices touch the second tetrahedron's sides so the two are duals. (At least after the code rotates the first tetrahedron to put it into position.)

The program gives the second tetrahedron a translucent material so you can see the first shape inside it.

The code finishes by creating a third mesh containing small spheres at the tetrahedrons' vertices. That makes it easier to see that the inner tetrahedron's vertices lie in the outer tetrahedron's faces

Figure 18-9 shows the DualTetrahedron example program in action. You may need to download the example and rotate the scene around a bit to convince yourself that the two tetrahedrons are duals.

NOTE: At the end of the section on translucent materials I mentioned that you can't see the sides of a translucent solid by looking through the solid. Figure 18-9 provides an example. You cannot see the edge where the outer tetrahedron's back face meets its bottom because that edge is obscured by the tetrahedron's body.

Summary

This chapter explained what the Platonic solids are and gave some information about them such as their dual relationships. It showed how you can find the vertices for a tetrahedron and provided code to build tetrahedrons.

Although the tetrahedron has the fewest faces among the Platonic solid, calculating the positions of its vertices is relatively difficult. The next chapter covers the second Platonic solid: the cube. After finding the vertices for the tetrahedron, finding them for the cube is refreshingly easy.

Chapter 19

Cubes

If you thought the description of tetrahedrons in Chapter 18 was long and complicated, you'll be pleased to know that this chapter's description of cubes is short and simple. The following extra-short section explains how to find the cube's vertices, inradius, and circumradius. The section after that describes C# code for working with cubes.

Cube Vertices

As I'm sure you know, a cube has six faces that are squares. Figure 19-1 shows a cube with its vertices labeled.

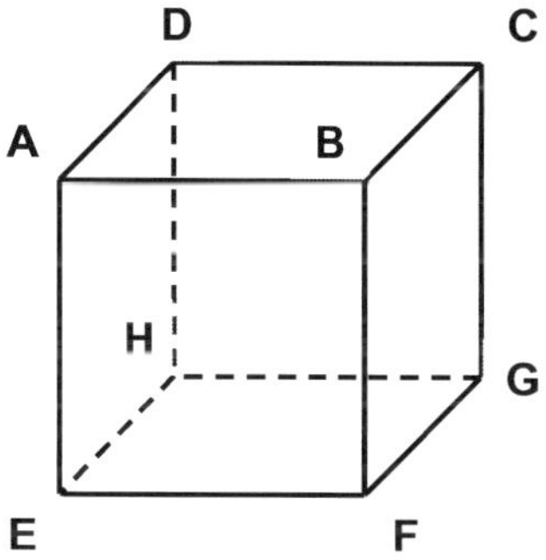

Figure 19-1: A cube has six faces and eight vertices.

Chapter 18 creates a tetrahedron with edges of length one. A cube's mathematics is slightly easier if the cube's edges have length two, so for now I'll assume that the cube's vertices have coordinates $(\pm1, \pm1, \pm1)$.

The cube's inradius is 1. Its circumradius is the distance from the origin to any of its vertices. For example, the distances to the point (1, 1, 1) is given by the following.

$$\text{Circumradius} = \sqrt{1^2 + 1^2 + 1^2} = \sqrt{3}$$

The following section describes code that you can use to build cubes.

Example Program

The G3 class includes the following code to work with cubes.

```
public static void CubePoints(
    out Point3D A, out Point3D B, out Point3D C, out Point3D D,
    out Point3D E, out Point3D F, out Point3D G, out Point3D H)
{
    A = new Point3D(-1, +1, +1);
    B = new Point3D(+1, +1, +1);
    C = new Point3D(+1, +1, -1);
    D = new Point3D(-1, +1, -1);
    E = new Point3D(-1, -1, +1);
    F = new Point3D(+1, -1, +1);
    G = new Point3D(+1, -1, -1);
    H = new Point3D(-1, -1, -1);
```

```
}
public static double CubeCircumradius()
{
    return Math.Sqrt(3.0);
}
public static double CubeInradius()
{
    return 1;
}
```

The `CubePoints` method returns the points that make up a cube arranged as shown in Figure 19-1.

As you can guess from their names, the `CubeCircumradius` and `CubeInradius` methods return the cube's circumradius and inradius.

The `MeshExtensions` class defines the following `AddCube` method.

```
public static void AddCube(this MeshGeometry3D mesh)
{
    // Get the points.
    Point3D A, B, C, D, E, F, G, H;
    G3.CubePoints(out A, out B, out C, out D, out E, out F, out G, out H);

    // Make the faces.
    mesh.AddPolygon(A, B, C, D);
    mesh.AddPolygon(A, D, H, E);
    mesh.AddPolygon(A, E, F, B);
    mesh.AddPolygon(G, C, B, F);
    mesh.AddPolygon(G, F, E, H);
    mesh.AddPolygon(G, H, D, C);
}
```

This method calls `CubePoints` to get the cube's vertices and then uses the mesh's `AddPolygon` method to create the cube's faces.

The Cube example program uses the following code to create its scene.

```
private void DefineModel(Model3DGroup group)
{
    // Show the axes.
    MeshExtensions.AddAxes(group);

    const double scale = 2;

    // Make a solid insphere.
    MeshGeometry3D mesh1 = new MeshGeometry3D();
    mesh1.AddSphere(D3.Origin, G3.CubeInradius(), 60, 30, true);
    mesh1.ApplyTransformation(new ScaleTransform3D(scale, scale, scale));
    group.Children.Add(mesh1.MakeModel(Brushes.Red));

    // Make a translucent cube.
    MeshGeometry3D mesh2 = new MeshGeometry3D();
    mesh2.AddCube();
    mesh2.ApplyTransformation(new ScaleTransform3D(scale, scale, scale));
    Brush brush = new SolidColorBrush(Color.FromArgb(128, 128, 255, 128));
    MaterialGroup group2 = D3.MakeMaterialGroup(
        new DiffuseMaterial(brush),
```

```
            new SpecularMaterial(Brushes.White, 100));
        group.Children.Add(mesh2.MakeModel(group2));

        // Make a translucent circumsphere.
        MeshGeometry3D mesh3 = new MeshGeometry3D();
        mesh3.AddSphere(D3.Origin, G3.CubeCircumradius(), 60, 30, true);
        mesh3.ApplyTransformation(new ScaleTransform3D(scale, scale, scale));
        MaterialGroup group3 = D3.MakeMaterialGroup(
            new DiffuseMaterial(brush),
            new SpecularMaterial(Brushes.White, 100));
        group.Children.Add(mesh3.MakeModel(group3));
    }
```

This code displays the coordinate axes and defines a `scale` constant that it will use to scale its other solids.

Next, the code creates a sphere with radius equal to the cube's inradius. It scales the sphere and turns it into a red model.

The code then makes a scaled translucent cube and finally a scaled translucent circumsphere.

Figure 19-2 shows the Cube example program displaying its scene. You may want to download the example and view its scene from different angles to convince yourself that the insphere touches the cube's faces and that the cube's vertices touch the circumsphere.

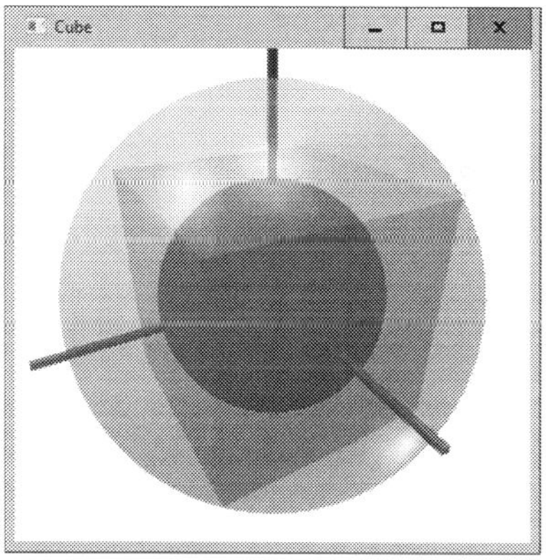

Figure 19-2: The Cube example program draws a cube, its insphere, and its circumsphere.

Summary

See? I told you the cube was easy!

This chapter explained how to draw a cube and how to calculate its inradius and circumradius.

The dual of a cube is an octahedron. Chapter 20 explains how to work with octahedrons. They're a little more complicated than cubes, but they're still much simpler than the dreaded tetrahedron!

Chapter 20 Octahedrons

The octahedron is a bit more complicated than a cube, but nowhere near as complicated as the tetrahedron. The following section explains how to find the octahedron's vertices, inradius, and circumradius.

Octahedron Vertices

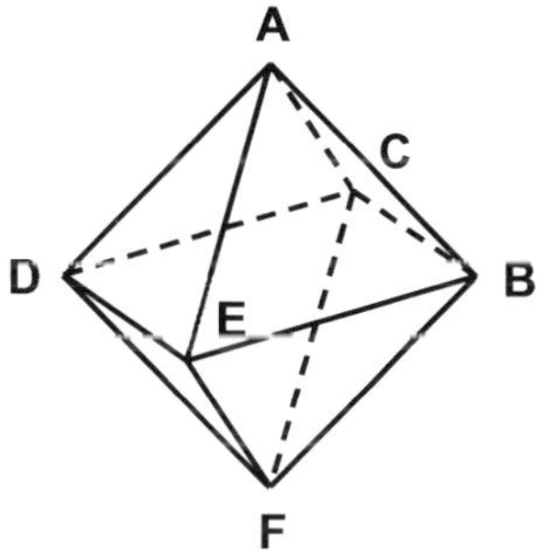

Figure 20-1: An octahedron has eight faces and six vertices.

An octahedron has eight faces that are equilateral triangles. Figure 20-1 shows an octahedron with its vertices labeled.

You can align the octahedron so each of its vertices lies on a coordinate axis. In Figure 20-1, vertex A lies on the Y axis, B lies on the X axis, and E lies on the Z axis. The other vertices lie on the negative axes.

With that arrangement, each vertex has a single non-zero coordinate. For simplicity, I'll set that coordinate equal to 1 so the vertices are (±1, 0, 0), (0, ±1, 0), and (0, 0, ±1).

Because each of the octahedron's vertices is one unit away from the origin along one of the coordinate axes, it's easy to see that the octahedron's circumradius is 1.

The inradius is the distance from the center of one of the octahedron's faces to the origin. You can find the center of a face by averaging the coordinates of the three points that define it. For example, if you average the coordinates of points A, B, and E, you get the following point.

$$\left(\frac{0+1+0}{3}, \frac{1+0+0}{3}, \frac{0+0+1}{3}\right) = \left(\frac{1}{3}, \frac{1}{3}, \frac{1}{3}\right)$$

Then the inradius is the distance from the origin to that point and is given by the following equation.

$$\text{Inradius} = \sqrt{\left(\frac{1}{3}\right)^2 + \left(\frac{1}{3}\right)^2 + \left(\frac{1}{3}\right)^2} = \sqrt{\frac{3}{9}} = \frac{1}{\sqrt{3}}$$

The following section describes code that you can use to build octahedrons.

Example Program

The `G3` class includes the following code to work with octahedrons.

```
public static void OctahedronPoints(out Point3D A, out Point3D B,
    out Point3D C, out Point3D D, out Point3D E, out Point3D F)
{
    A = new Point3D(0, 1, 0);
    B = new Point3D(1, 0, 0);
    C = new Point3D(0, 0, -1);
    D = new Point3D(-1, 0, 0);
    E = new Point3D(0, 0, 1);
    F = new Point3D(0, -1, 0);
}
public static double OctahedronCircumradius()
{
    return 1;
}
public static double OctahedronInradius()
{
    return 1.0 / Math.Sqrt(3.0);
}
```

The `OctahedronPoints` method returns the points that make up an octahedron arranged as shown in Figure 20-1.

As you would expect, the `OctahedronCircumradius` and `OctahedronInradius` methods return the octahedron's circumradius and inradius.

The `MeshExtensions` class defines the following `AddOctahedron` method.

```
public static void AddOctahedron(this MeshGeometry3D mesh)
{
    // Get the points.
    Point3D A, B, C, D, E, F;
    G3.OctahedronPoints(out A, out B, out C, out D, out E, out F);

    // Make the faces.
    mesh.AddPolygon(A, B, C);
    mesh.AddPolygon(A, C, D);
    mesh.AddPolygon(A, D, E);
    mesh.AddPolygon(A, E, B);
    mesh.AddPolygon(F, B, E);
    mesh.AddPolygon(F, C, B);
    mesh.AddPolygon(F, D, C);
    mesh.AddPolygon(F, E, D);
}
```

This method calls `OctahedronPoints` to get the octahedron's vertices and then uses the mesh's `AddPolygon` method to create the octahedron's faces.

The Octahedron example program uses the following code to create its scene.

```
private void DefineModel(Model3DGroup group)
{
    // verify the octahedron calculations.
    MeshExtensions.VerifyOctahedron();

    // Show the axes.
    MeshExtensions.AddAxes(group);

    const double scale = 3;

    // Make a solid insphere.
    MeshGeometry3D mesh1 = new MeshGeometry3D();
    mesh1.AddSphere(D3.Origin, G3.OctahedronInradius(), 60, 30, true);
    mesh1.ApplyTransformation(new ScaleTransform3D(scale, scale, scale));
    group.Children.Add(mesh1.MakeModel(Brushes.Red));

    // Make a translucent octahedron.
    MeshGeometry3D mesh2 = new MeshGeometry3D();
    mesh2.AddOctahedron();
    mesh2.ApplyTransformation(new ScaleTransform3D(scale, scale, scale));
    Brush brush = new SolidColorBrush(Color.FromArgb(128, 128, 255, 128));
    MaterialGroup group2 = D3.MakeMaterialGroup(
        new DiffuseMaterial(brush),
        new SpecularMaterial(Brushes.White, 100));
    group.Children.Add(mesh2.MakeModel(group2));

    // Make a translucent circumsphere.
    MeshGeometry3D mesh3 = new MeshGeometry3D();
    mesh3.AddSphere(D3.Origin, G3.OctahedronCircumradius(), 60, 30, true);
    mesh3.ApplyTransformation(new ScaleTransform3D(scale, scale, scale));
    MaterialGroup group3 = D3.MakeMaterialGroup(
        new DiffuseMaterial(brush),
        new SpecularMaterial(Brushes.White, 100));
    group.Children.Add(mesh3.MakeModel(group3));
}
```

Like the Tetrahedron and Cube examples described in the preceding two chapters, this example displays axes, a solid insphere, a translucent solid (this time an octahedron), and a translucent circumsphere. Figure 20-2 shows the Octahedron example program displaying its scene.

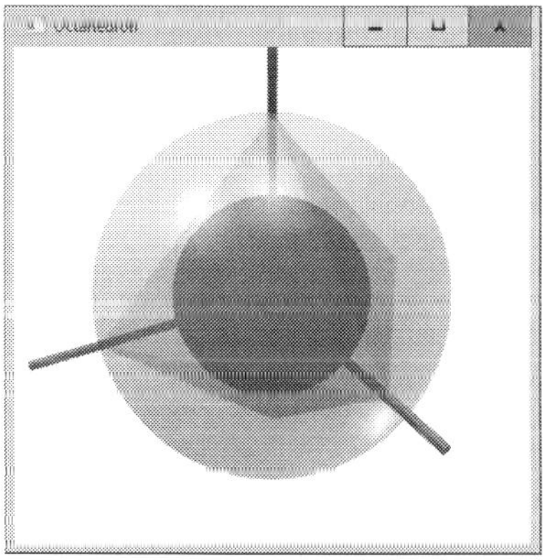

Figure 20-2: The Octahedron example program draws an octahedron, insphere, and circumsphere.

As I mentioned in Chapter 19, the dual of a cube is an octahedron. The DualCubeOctahedron example program displays a cube, its dual (an octahedron), and its dual (a cube)

The program uses the following code to create its scene.

```
private void DefineModel(Model3DGroup group)
{
    // Show the axes.
    MeshExtensions.AddAxes(group);
```

```
        const double scale = 0.75;

        // Make a solid cube.
        MeshGeometry3D mesh1 = new MeshGeometry3D();
        mesh1.AddCube();
        mesh1.ApplyTransformation(new ScaleTransform3D(scale, scale, scale));
        group.Children.Add(mesh1.MakeModel(Brushes.Red));

        // Make a translucent octahedron.
        MeshGeometry3D mesh2 = new MeshGeometry3D();
        mesh2.AddOctahedron();
        double octScale = scale * G3.CubeCircumradius() / G3.OctahedronInradius();
        mesh2.ApplyTransformation(new ScaleTransform3D(octScale, octScale, octScale));
        Brush brush = new SolidColorBrush(Color.FromArgb(128, 128, 255, 128));
        MaterialGroup group2 = D3.MakeMaterialGroup(
            new DiffuseMaterial(brush),
            new SpecularMaterial(Brushes.White, 100));
        group.Children.Add(mesh2.MakeModel(group2));

        // Make a translucent cube.
        MeshGeometry3D mesh3 = new MeshGeometry3D();
        mesh3.AddCube();
        double cubeScale = octScale * G3.OctahedronCircumradius() / G3.CubeInradius();
        mesh3.ApplyTransformation(new ScaleTransform3D(cubeScale, cubeScale, cubeScale));
        MaterialGroup group3 = D3.MakeMaterialGroup(
            new DiffuseMaterial(brush),
            new SpecularMaterial(Brushes.White, 100));
        group.Children.Add(mesh3.MakeModel(group3));
    }
```

This method creates the coordinate axes as usual and then creates a cube.

Next, it makes a translucent octahedron scaled by the cube's circumradius divided by the octahedron's inradius. That makes the octahedron have an inradius equal to the cube's circumradius so its faces touch the cube's vertices.

The code then makes a translucent cube scaled so its faces touch the drawn octahedron's vertices. Figure 20-3 shows the DualCubeOctahedron example program in action.

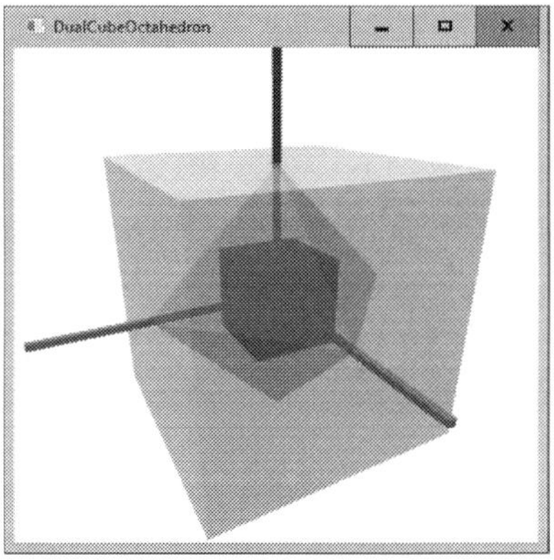

Figure 20-3: Cubes and octahedrons are duals.

Summary

An octahedron isn't as simple as a cube, but it's certainly simpler than the tetrahedron. Chapter 21 describes the next Platonic solid: the 12-sided dodecahedron. Finding its vertices requires you to break out some mad trigonometric skillz.

Chapter 21

Dodecahedrons

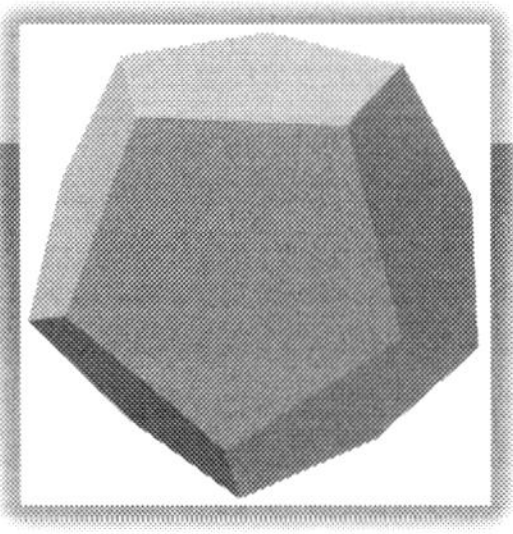

A dodecahedron has 20 vertices and 12 faces, each of which is a pentagon. Figure 21-1 shows a dodecahedron with backfaces removed.

The following section explains how to find the dodecahedron's vertices. Be warned that this requires some heavy-duty high school mathematics, particularly trigonometry. If you don't like that sort of thing, you might want to skim that section and resume careful reading with the section after that.

Dodecahedron Vertices

Figure 21-2 shows a dodecahedron with its vertices labeled, hidden edges drawn with dashed lines, and the coordinate axes drawn in gray.

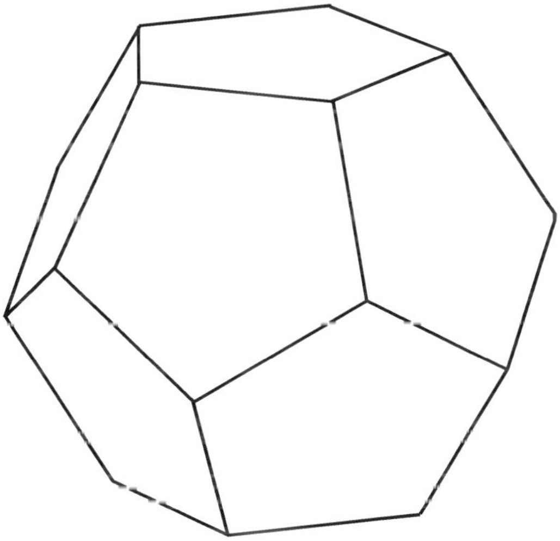

Figure 21-1: A dodecahedron has 12 faces and 20 vertices.

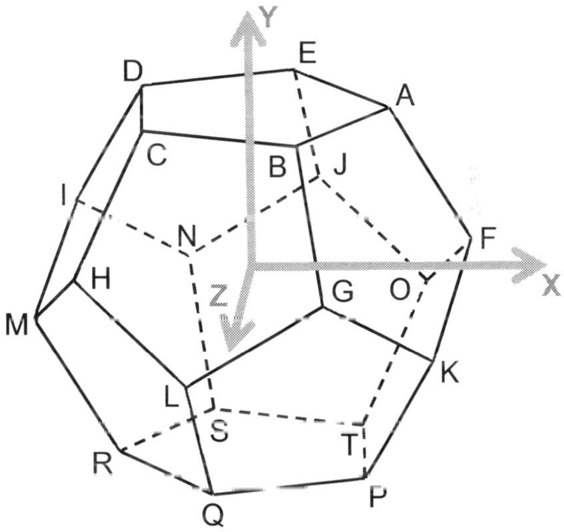

Figure 21-2: This picture shows how you can label a dodecahedron's vertices.

The dodecahedrons in Figures 21-1 and 21-2 are centered at the origin. Vertices A, F, R, and M lie in the XY plane so they have Z coordinate 0.

Figure 21-3 shows the dodecahedron from the top. You can use this figure to calculate the X and Z coordinates of vertices A through E.

The first step is to calculate the angles labeled t1 through t4. Because a pentagon has five sides, $t1=2\pi/5$ radians. Angle t4 is half as big, so $t4=\pi/5$.

The angle between the X and Z axes is 90° or $\pi/2$ radians. Because that angle also equals t1+t2, we know that $t1+t2=\pi/2$. Solving for t2 gives the following.

$$t2 = \pi/2 - t1 = \pi/2 - 2\pi/5 = \pi/10$$

Finally, $t1 = t2 + t3$, so we can write the following equation for t3.

$$t3 = t1 - t2 = 2\pi/5 - \pi/10 = 3\pi/10$$

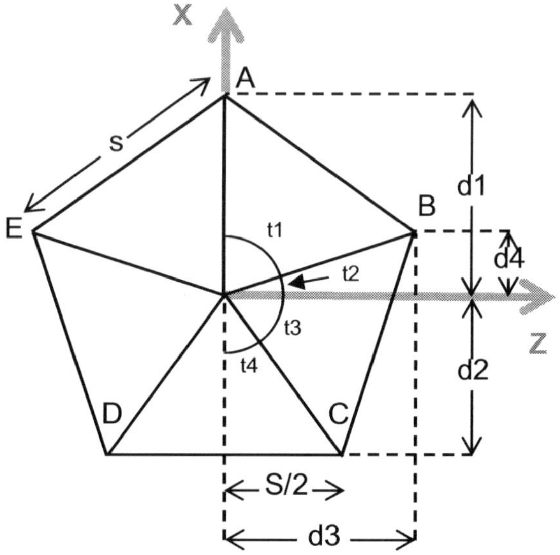

Figure 21-3: This view shows the dodecahedron from the top.

Note that all of the distances from the center of the pentagon to its vertices are the same. The distance from the center to vertex A is labeled d1 in Figure 21-3, so all of the vertices A through E are distance d1 from the center of the pentagon.

Now you can use trigonometry to calculate the values in the following table.

Variable	Value
t1	$2\pi/5$
t2	$\pi/10$
t3	$3\pi/10$
t4	$\pi/5$
d1	$s/2/\sin(t4)$
d2	$d1\cdot\cos(t4)$
d3	$d1\cdot\cos(t2)$
d4	$d1\cdot\sin(t2)$

Figure 21-4 shows the complete dodecahedron from the top. You can see from the figure that the bottom face P-Q-R-S-T is the same as the top face but rotated 180°. Using that fact and the values in the table, you can find the X and Z coordinates for vertices P through T.

The segment AF is one of the dodecahedron's edges, so it has length s. Then you can use the distance formula and square the results to get the following equation.

$$|AF|^2 = s^2 = (Ax - Fx)^2 + (Ay - Fy)^2 + (Az - Fz)^2$$

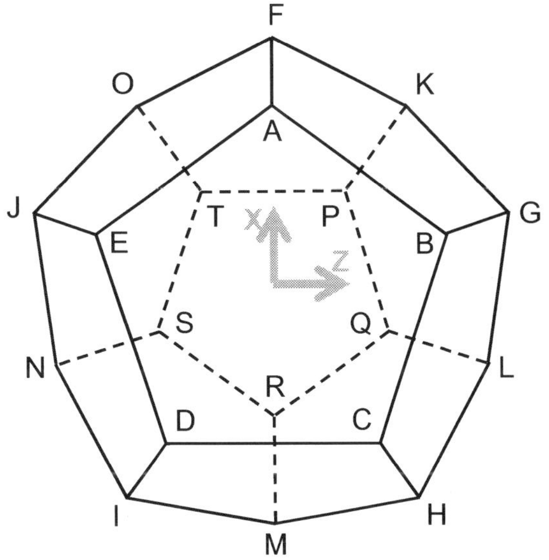

Figure 21-4: A dodecahedron's bottom is similar to its top rotated 180°.

Figures 21-2, 21-3, and 21-4 show that values Az=Fz=0, Ax=d1, Bx=d4, Bz=d3, and Ay=By. If you define d5=Ay-Fy, then you can rewrite the preceding equation as the following.

$$s^2 = (d1 - Fx)^2 + d5^2 \qquad (1)$$

Next, if you look at Figure 21-4, you can see that segments BF and EB both cut across one corner of a side's pentagon so they must have the same length. Figure 21-3 shows that |BF| is 2×d3, so the distance formula lets you write the following equation.

$$|BF|^2 = (2 \cdot d3)^2 = (Bx - Fx)^2 + (By - Fy)^2 + (Bz - Fz)^2$$

Now you can plug in Bx=d4, Bz=d3, Fz=0, and d5=Ay-Fy=By-Fy to get the following.

$$(2 \cdot d3)^2 = (d4 - Fx)^2 + d5^2 + d3^2 \qquad (2)$$

Subtracting equation 2 from equation 1 gives the following.

$$\begin{aligned} s^2 - (2 \cdot d3)^2 &= (d1 - Fx)^2 - (d4 - Fx)^2 - d3^2 \\ &= (d1^2 - 2 \cdot d1 \cdot Fx + Fx^2) - (d4^2 - 2 \cdot d4 \cdot Fx + Fx^2) - d3^2 \\ &= 2 \cdot Fx \cdot (d4 - d1) + (d1^2 - d3^2 - d4^2) \end{aligned}$$

The previous table gives values for d1, d3, and d4, so this equation only has one remaining unknown value: Fx. Solving for Fx gives the following.

$$\mathrm{Fx} = [\mathrm{s}^2 - (2 \cdot \mathrm{d3})^2 - (\mathrm{d1}^2 - \mathrm{d3}^2 - \mathrm{d4}^2)]/[2 \cdot (\mathrm{d4} - \mathrm{d1})]$$

This is a bit messy, but you know all of the values on the right hand side so you can calculate Fx.

Now if you add the equations for $|AF|^2$ and $|BF|^2$, you get the following.

$$\mathrm{s}^2 + (2 \cdot \mathrm{d3})^2 = (\mathrm{d1} - \mathrm{Fx})^2 + 2 \cdot \mathrm{d5}^2 + (\mathrm{d4} - \mathrm{Fx})^2 + \mathrm{d3}^2$$

You can solve this for d5.

$$\mathrm{d5} = \sqrt{\frac{1}{2}(\mathrm{s}^2 + (2 \cdot \mathrm{d3})^2 - (\mathrm{d1} - \mathrm{Fx})^2 - (\mathrm{d4} - \mathrm{Fx})^2 + \mathrm{d3}^2)}$$

This is another messy expression, but at this point you know all of the values necessary to calculate d5.

If you look closely at Figure 21-4, you'll see that vertices F-G-H-I-J form a hexagon similar to the one shown in Figure 21-3 except it's bigger. The only difference is the distance from the pentagon's center to its vertices. For vertices F though J, this distance is Fx. By using that fact and trigonometry similar to that shown in Figure 21-3, you can find the X and Z coordinates of vertices F through J.

By using symmetry, you can find the X and Z coordinates for vertices K through O.

All you need to do now is find the vertices' Y coordinates.

By symmetry, every vertex must be the same distance from the origin. In particular, vertices A an F must be the same distance from the origin. That means the following.

$$\mathrm{Ax}^2 + \mathrm{Ay}^2 + \mathrm{Az}^2 = \mathrm{Fx}^2 + \mathrm{Fy}^2 + \mathrm{Fz}^2$$

Earlier calculations showed that d5=Ay-Fy. Substituting Fz=0, Ax=d1, Az=0, and Ay=d5+Fy into this equation gives the following.

$$\mathrm{d1}^2 + (\mathrm{d5} + \mathrm{Fy})^2 = \mathrm{Fx}^2 + \mathrm{Fy}^2$$

You know Fx at this point, so you can solve this equation for its only unknown value Fy.

$$\mathrm{d1}^2 + \mathrm{d5}^2 + 2 \cdot \mathrm{d5} \cdot \mathrm{Fy} + \mathrm{Fy}^2 = \mathrm{Fx}^2 + \mathrm{Fy}^2$$

$$2 \cdot \mathrm{d5} \cdot \mathrm{Fy} = \mathrm{Fx}^2 - \mathrm{d1}^2 - \mathrm{d5}^2$$

$$\text{Fy} = (\text{Fx}^2 - \text{d1}^2 - \text{d5}^2)/(2 \cdot \text{d5})$$

From these values and symmetry you can calculate the remaining vertex coordinates. The following table shows the remaining intermediate values that you need.

Variable	Value
Fx	$[s^2 - (2 \cdot d3)^2 - (d1^2 - d3^2 - d4^2)]/[2 \cdot (d4 - d1)]$
d5	$\sqrt{\frac{1}{2}(s^2 + (2 \cdot d3)^2 - (d1 - Fx)^2 - (d4 - Fx)^2 - d3^2)}$
Fy	$(Fx^2 - d1^2 - d5^2)/(2 \cdot d5)$
Ay	$d5 + Fy$

The following table shows the final coordinates for all of the vertices.

Vertex	X	Y	Z
A	d1	Ay	0
B	d4	Ay	d3
C	-d2	Ay	s/2
D	-d2	Ay	-s/2
E	d4	Ay	-d3
F	Fx	Fy	0
G	Fx sin(t2)	Fy	Fx cos(t2)
H	-Fx sin(t3)	Fy	Fx cos(t3)
I	-Fx sin(t3)	Fy	-Fx cos(t3)
J	Fx sin(t2)	Fy	-Fx cos(t2)
K	Fx sin(t3)	-Fy	Fx cos(t3)
L	-Fx sin(t2)	-Fy	Fx cos(t2)
M	-Fx	-Fy	0
N	-Fx sin(t2)	-Fy	-Fx cos(t2)
O	Fx sin(t3)	-Fy	-Fx cos(t3)
P	d2	-Ay	s/2
Q	-d4	-Ay	d3

R	-d1	-Ay	0
S	-d4	-Ay	-d3
T	d2	-Ay	-s/2

After all of that, calculating the inradius and circumradius is easy.

The dodecahedron's inradius is the distance from the origin to one of the solid's faces. The Y coordinate of the upper face is Ay so the inradius is Ay.

The dodecahedron's circumradius is the distance from the origin to one of the solid's vertices. You can use the distance formula with any of the vertices to calculate this distance, but vertex A has some of the simplest coordinates so I'll use it. The following equation shows the circumradius.

$$\text{Circumradius} = \sqrt{\text{d1}^2 + \text{Ay}^2}$$

Example Program

If you skipped the preceding section (and I can't blame you), welcome back!

The `G3` class includes the following code to work with octahedrons.

```
// Dodecahedron intermediate values.
private static double ds = 2;
//private static double dt1 = 2 * Math.PI / 5;     // Not actually used.
private static double dt2 = Math.PI / 10;
private static double dt3 = 3 * Math.PI / 10;
private static double dt4 = Math.PI / 5;
private static double dd1 = ds / 2 / Math.Sin(dt4);
private static double dd2 = dd1 * Math.Cos(dt4);
private static double dd3 = dd1 * Math.Cos(dt2);
private static double dd4 = dd1 * Math.Sin(dt2);
private static double dFx =
    (ds * ds - (2 * dd3) * (2 * dd3) -
        (dd1 * dd1 - dd3 * dd3 - dd4 * dd4)) /
    (2 * (dd4 - dd1));
private static double dd5 = Math.Sqrt(
    0.5 * (ds * ds + (2 * dd3) * (2 * dd3) -
        (dd1 - dFx) * (dd1 - dFx) -
        (dd4 - dFx) * (dd4 - dFx) - dd3 * dd3));
private static double dFy = (dFx * dFx - dd1 * dd1 -
    dd5 * dd5) / (2 * dd5);
private static double dAy = dd5 + dFy;

// Calculate the dodecahedron vertices.
public static void DodecahedronPoints(
    out Point3D A, out Point3D B, out Point3D C, out Point3D D,
    out Point3D E, out Point3D F, out Point3D G, out Point3D H,
    out Point3D I, out Point3D J, out Point3D K, out Point3D L,
    out Point3D M, out Point3D N, out Point3D O, out Point3D P,
    out Point3D Q, out Point3D R, out Point3D S, out Point3D T)
{
```

```
        // Make the points.
        A = new Point3D(dd1, dAy, 0);
        B = new Point3D(dd4, dAy, dd3);
        C = new Point3D(-dd2, dAy, ds / 2);
        D = new Point3D(-dd2, dAy, -ds / 2);
        E = new Point3D(dd4, dAy, -dd3);
        F = new Point3D(dFx, dFy, 0);
        G = new Point3D(dFx * Math.Sin(dt2), dFy, dFx * Math.Cos(dt2));
        H = new Point3D(-dFx * Math.Sin(dt3), dFy, dFx * Math.Cos(dt3));
        I = new Point3D(-dFx * Math.Sin(dt3), dFy, -dFx * Math.Cos(dt3));
        J = new Point3D(dFx * Math.Sin(dt2), dFy, -dFx * Math.Cos(dt2));
        K = new Point3D(dFx * Math.Sin(dt3), -dFy, dFx * Math.Cos(dt3));
        L = new Point3D(-dFx * Math.Sin(dt2), -dFy, dFx * Math.Cos(dt2));
        M = new Point3D(-dFx, -dFy, 0);
        N = new Point3D(-dFx * Math.Sin(dt2), -dFy, -dFx * Math.Cos(dt2));
        O = new Point3D(dFx * Math.Sin(dt3), -dFy, -dFx * Math.Cos(dt3));
        P = new Point3D(dd2, -dAy, ds / 2);
        Q = new Point3D(-dd4, -dAy, dd3);
        R = new Point3D(-dd1, -dAy, 0);
        S = new Point3D(-dd4, -dAy, -dd3);
        T = new Point3D(dd2, -dAy, -ds / 2);
    }
    public static double DodecahedronCircumradius()
    {
        // Get intermediate values.
        return Math.Sqrt(dd1 * dd1 + dAy * dAy);
    }
    public static double DodecahedronInradius()
    {
        return dAy;
    }
```

At 60 lines, this is significantly longer than the 18 lines of code needed by the octahedron.

The code begins by calculating the dodecahedron's intermediate values. I prefixed them with d so I can use some of the variable names again in the next chapter when we're working with icosahedrons. For example, instead of calling the side length variable `s`, I've called it `ds`.

The `DodecahedronPoints` method uses the intermediate values to find the dodecahedron's vertices. The `DodecahedronCircumradius` and `DodecahedronInradius` methods use the values to calculate the circumradius and inradius.

The OneDodecahedron example program uses the following code to define its scene.

```
    private void DefineModel(Model3DGroup group)
    {
        // Show the axes.
        MeshExtensions.AddAxes(group);

        // Make a dodecahedron.
        MeshGeometry3D mesh2 = new MeshGeometry3D();
        mesh2.AddDodecahedron();
        group.Children.Add(mesh2.MakeModel(Brushes.LightGreen));
    }
```

This code first creates the coordinate axes. It then creates a mesh, uses its `AddDodecahedron` extension method to create a dodecahedron, converts it into a light green model, and adds the result to the program's `Model3DGroup`.

Figure 21-5 shows the OneDodecahedron program displaying its scene.

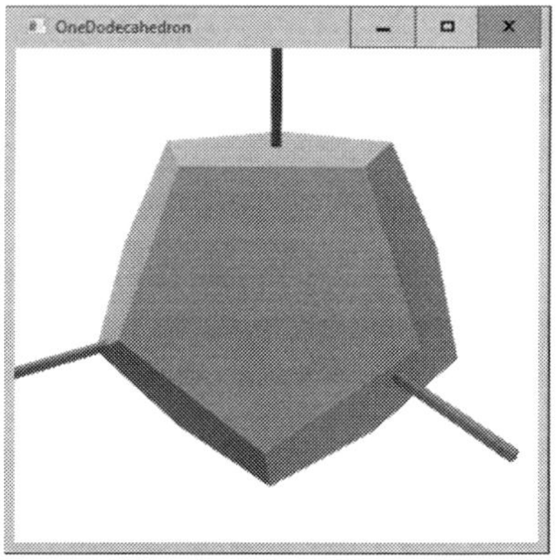

Figure 21-5: The OneDodecahedron program displays a dodecahedron.

The Dodecahedron example program uses the following code to define a scene similar to the ones described in previous chapters that include a solid together with its insphere and circumsphere.

```
private void DefineModel(Model3DGroup group)
{
    // Show the axes.
    MeshExtensions.AddAxes(group);

    const double scale = 1.25;

    // Make a solid insphere.
    MeshGeometry3D mesh1 = new MeshGeometry3D();
    mesh1.AddSphere(D3.Origin, G3.DodecahedronInradius(), 60, 30, true);
    mesh1.ApplyTransformation(new ScaleTransform3D(scale, scale, scale));
    group.Children.Add(mesh1.MakeModel(Brushes.Red));

    // Make a translucent dodecahedron.
    MeshGeometry3D mesh2 = new MeshGeometry3D();
    mesh2.AddDodecahedron();
    mesh2.ApplyTransformation(new ScaleTransform3D(scale, scale, scale));
    Brush brush = new SolidColorBrush(Color.FromArgb(128, 128, 255, 128));
    MaterialGroup group2 = D3.MakeMaterialGroup(
        new DiffuseMaterial(brush),
        new SpecularMaterial(Brushes.White, 100));
    group.Children.Add(mesh2.MakeModel(group2));

    // Make a translucent circumsphere.
    MeshGeometry3D mesh3 = new MeshGeometry3D();
    mesh3.AddSphere(D3.Origin, G3.DodecahedronCircumradius(), 60, 30, true);
    mesh3.ApplyTransformation(new ScaleTransform3D(scale, scale, scale));
    MaterialGroup group3 = D3.MakeMaterialGroup(
        new DiffuseMaterial(brush),
        new SpecularMaterial(Brushes.White, 100));
    group.Children.Add(mesh3.MakeModel(group3));
}
```

This is basically the same code used by previous examples but modified to draw a dodecahedron. It creates a solid insphere, a translucent dodecahedron, and then a translucent circumsphere.

Figure 21-6 shows the Dodecahedron example program displaying its scene.

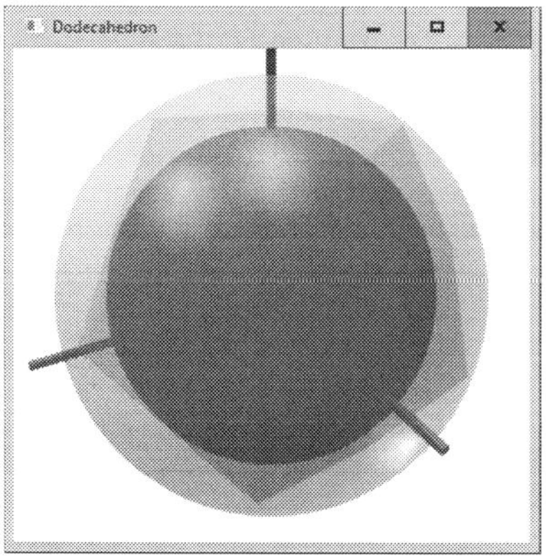

Figure 21-6: The Dodecahedron program draws a dodecahedron, insphere, and circumsphere.

Summary

I warned you that calculating the dodecahedron's vertices was harder than finding the vertices for the previous Platonic solids.

This chapter explained how to draw a dodecahedron and how to calculate its inradius and circumradius. Chapter 22 describes the dual of the dodecahedron and the final Platonic solid: the icosahedron. An icosahedron has a lot of faces (20) and vertices (12), so the calculations are a bit on the longish side, but they're much simpler than the calculations for the dodecahedron.

Chapter 22
Icosahedrons

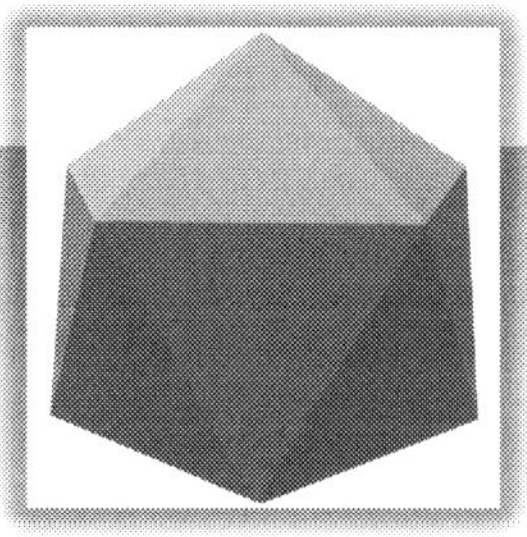

An icosahedron has 12 vertices and 20 faces, each of which is an equilateral triangle. Figure 22-1 shows an icosahedron with its backfaces removed.

The following section explains how to find the icosahedron's vertices. The icosahedron has a lot of vertices so there are a lot of values to calculate, but the calculations are simpler than those needed to find a dodecahedron's vertices. Still, if you're not keen on mathematics, you can skim that section and rejoin our program with the section after that.

Icosahedron Vertices

Figure 22-2 shows an icosahedron with its vertices labeled, hidden edges drawn with dashed lines, and the coordinate axes drawn in gray.

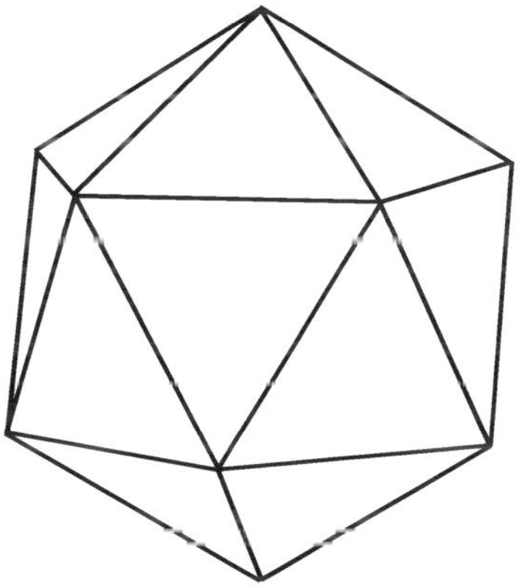

Figure 22-1: An icosahedron has 20 faces and 12 vertices.

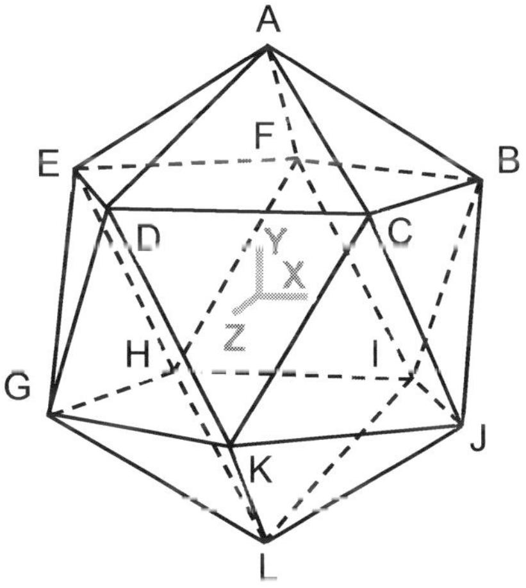

Figure 22-2: This picture shows how you can label an Icosahedron's vertices.

The icosahedron is centered at the origin, so vertices A and L lie on the Y axis and have X and Z coordinate 0. Vertices B and G lie in the XY plane so they have Z coordinate 0.

Let y1 be the Y coordinate of vertex A and let y2 be the Y coordinate of vertices B through F. By symmetry, the Y coordinate of vertex L is -y1 and the Y coordinate of vertices G through K are -y2.

To calculate the vertices' X and Z coordinates, look at the icosahedron from the top. Consider only the positions of vertices B through F and G through K as shown in Figure 22-3. The two pentagons that contain those vertices allow you to calculate their X and Z coordinates.

Let s be the length of the icosahedron's edges and consider just the right half of the pentagon shown in Figure 22-4. You can use the angles t1, t2, t3, and t4 to calculate the points' coordinates.

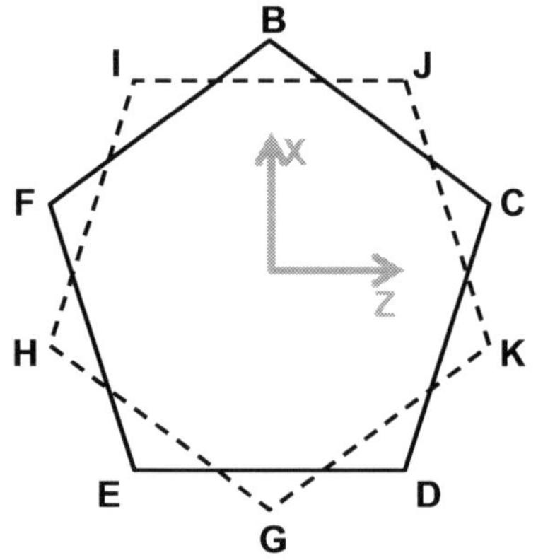

Figure 22-3: To find X and Y coordinates, view the solid from the top.

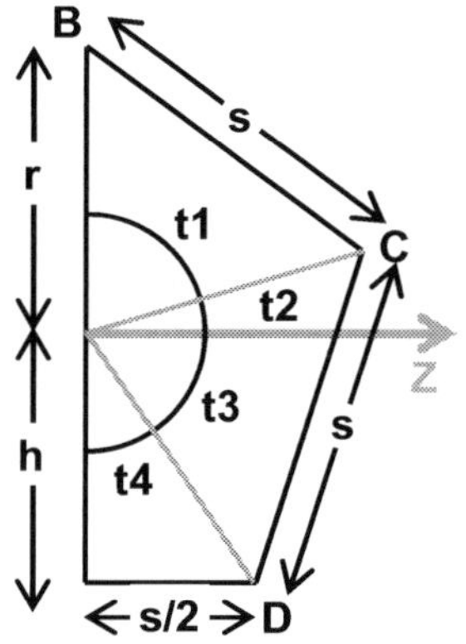

Figure 22-4: To find X and Y coordinates, view the solid from the top.

Because the nodes are arranged in a pentagon, t1=2π/5 radians. Then you can use that value to calculate t2.

$$t2 = \frac{\pi}{2} - t1 = \frac{\pi}{2} - \frac{2\pi}{5} = \frac{\pi}{10}$$

Angle t4 is half as big as t1, so t4=t1/2=π/5, and you can use that value to calculate t3.

$$t3 = -\left(\frac{\pi}{2} - t1\right) = -\left(\frac{\pi}{2} - \frac{\pi}{5}\right) = -\frac{3\pi}{10}$$

Using the trigonometry of the t4 triangle shown in Figure 22-4, you get sin(t4)=(s/2)/r, so r=(s/2)/sin(t4).

Then using the same triangle, cos(t4)=h/r, so h=r cos(t4).

At this point, you know that B=(r, y2, 0) and D=(-h, y2, s/2).

Similarly, you can use trigonometry to calculate that the X and Z coordinates of point C are r sin(t2) and r cos(t2). For notational convenience, let those values be Cx and Cz.

Now using the symmetry shown in Figure 22-3, you can calculate the X and Z coordinates for all of the rest of the points. The only values left to calculate are y1 and y2.

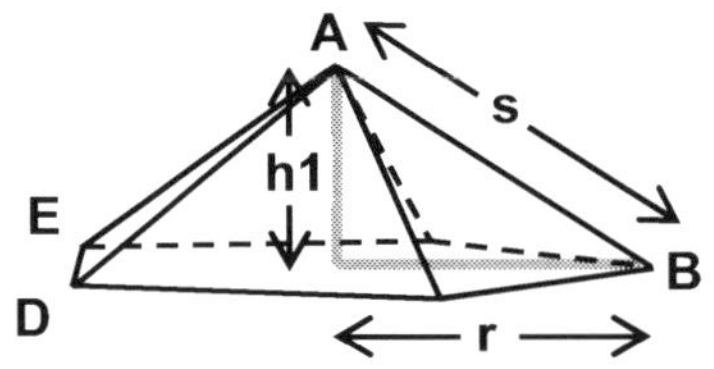

Figure 22-5: This picture can help you find Y coordinates.

Consider the top of the icosahedron as shown in Figure 22-5. Look again at Figure 22-4 to see how the value r fits into this picture.

We know s and r, so we can calculate h1.

$$h1 = \sqrt{s^2 - r^2}$$

Now consider the pentagon on the side that contains the points A-C-J-I-F as shown in Figure 22-6. Let h2 be the vertical distance between points A and I. We already know that the X coordinate of point I is h, so the horizontal distance along the X-axis between these points is h as shown in the figure.

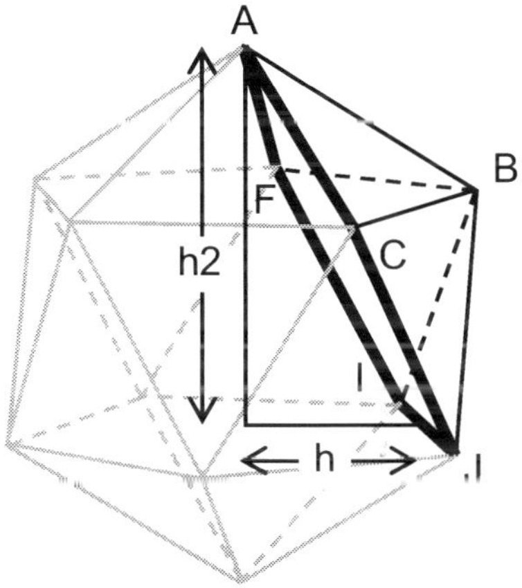

Figure 22-6: Consider the highlighted pentagon.

The hypotenuse of the triangle with sides h and h2 is the height of the pentagon A-C-J-I-F. Figure 22-4 shows that this distance is h+r. You can use those values to solve for h2.

$$h2 = \sqrt{(h + r)^2 - h^2}$$

Now you can finally use the values of h1 and h2 to calculate y1 and y2.

$$y2 = (h2 - h1)/2$$

$$y1 = y2 + h1$$

The following table shows the intermediate values used to calculate the points' coordinates.

Variable	Value

t1	$2\pi/5$
t2	$\pi/10$
t4	$\pi/5$
t3	$-3\pi/10$
r	$(s/2)/\sin(t4)$
h	$r \cdot \cos(t4)$
h1	$\sqrt{s^2 - r^2}$
h2	$\sqrt{(h + r)^2 - h^2}$
Cx	$r \cdot \sin(t2)$
Cz	$r \cdot \cos(t2)$
y1	$y2 + h1$
y2	$(h2 - h1)/2$

The following table shows the icosahedron's vertex coordinates.

Vertex	X	Y	Z
A	0	y1	0
B	r	y2	0
C	Cx	y2	Cz
D	-h	y2	s/2
E	-h	y2	-s/2
F	Cx	y2	-Cz
G	-r	-y2	0
H	-Cx	-y2	-Cz
I	h	-y2	-s/2
J	h	-y2	s/2
K	-Cx	-y2	Cz
L	0	-y1	0

The icosahedron's circumradius is the distance from the origin to any of its points. That distance for point A is simply its Y coordinate y1.

The inradius is the distance from the origin to the center of any of the icosahedron's faces. You can find the center point of triangle ABC by averaging the coordinates of points A, B, and C.

$$\text{ABC center point} = \left(\frac{r + Cx}{3}, \frac{y1 + y2 + y2}{3}, \frac{Cz}{3}\right)$$

Now you can use the distance formula to find the distance between that point and the origin. The result is the inradius.

$$\text{Inradius} = \sqrt{\left(\frac{r + cx}{3}\right)^2 + \left(\frac{y1 + y2 + y2}{3}\right)^2 + \left(\frac{cz}{3}\right)^2}$$

$$= \frac{1}{3}\sqrt{(r + cx)^2 + (y1 + y2 + y2)^2 + (cz)^2}$$

Adding Icosahedrons

The `G3` class includes the following code to work with octahedrons.

```
// Icosahedron intermediate values.
private static double s = 2;
//private static double t1 = 2 * Math.PI / 5;     // Not actually used.
private static double t2 = Math.PI / 10;
private static double t4 = Math.PI / 5;
//private static double t3 = -3 * Math.PI / 10;   // Not actually used.
private static double r = (s / 2) / Math.Sin(t4);
private static double h = r * Math.Cos(t4);
private static double h1 = Math.Sqrt(s * s - r * r);
private static double h2 = Math.Sqrt((h + r) * (h + r) - h * h);
private static double cx = r * Math.Sin(t2);
private static double cz = r * Math.Cos(t2);
private static double y2 = (h2 - h1) / 2;
private static double y1 = y2 + h1;

// Calculate the icosahedron vertices.
public static void IcosahedronPoints(
    out Point3D A, out Point3D B, out Point3D C, out Point3D D,
    out Point3D E, out Point3D F, out Point3D G, out Point3D H,
    out Point3D I, out Point3D J, out Point3D K, out Point3D L)
{
    // Make the points.

    A = new Point3D(0, y1, 0);
    B = new Point3D(r, y2, 0);
    C = new Point3D(cx, y2, cz);
    D = new Point3D(-h, y2, s / 2);
    E = new Point3D(-h, y2, -s / 2);
    F = new Point3D(cx, y2, -cz);
    G = new Point3D(-r, -y2, 0);
```

```
        H = new Point3D(-cx, -y2, -cz);
        I = new Point3D(h, -y2, -s / 2);
        J = new Point3D(h, -y2, s / 2);
        K = new Point3D(-cx, -y2, cz);
        L = new Point3D(0, -y1, 0);
    }
    public static double IcosahedronCircumradius()
    {
        // Get intermediate values.
        return y1;
    }
    public static double IcosahedronInradius()
    {
        return 1.0 / 3.0 * Math.Sqrt(
            (r + cx) * (r + cx) +
            (y1 + y2 + y2) * (y1 + y2 + y2) +
            (cz) * (cz));
    }
```

The code begins by calculating the icosahedron's intermediate values. (I was going to prefix them with `i`, but C# has problems with a variable named `is`, so I just left the names alone.)

The `IcosahedronPoints` method uses the intermediate values to find the icosahedron's vertices. The `IcosahedronCircumradius` and `IcosahedronInradius` methods use the values to calculate the circumradius and inradius.

OneIcosahedron

The OneIcosahedron example program shown in Figure 22-7 uses the following code to draw a single icosahedron centered at the origin.

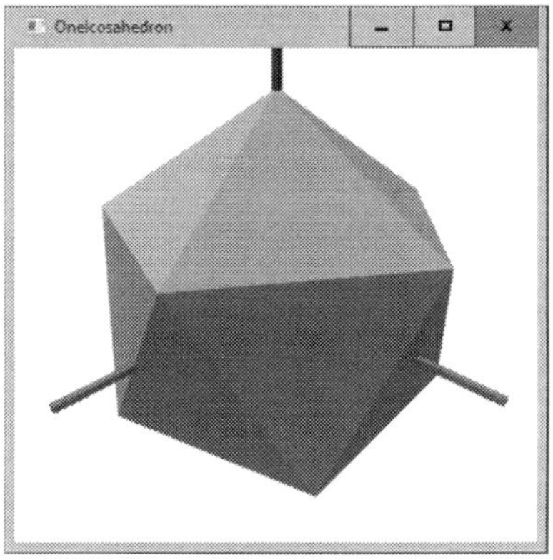

Figure 22-7: The OneIcosahedron program draws an icosahedron.

```
    private void DefineModel(Model3DGroup group)
    {
        // Show the axes.
        MeshExtensions.AddAxes(group);

        const double scale = 1.75;

        // Make an icosahedron.
        MeshGeometry3D mesh2 = new MeshGeometry3D();
        mesh2.AddIcosahedron();
        mesh2.ApplyTransformation(new ScaleTransform3D(scale, scale, scale));
        group.Children.Add(mesh2.MakeModel(Brushes.LightGreen));
    }
```

This code creates the coordinate axes. It then makes a mesh and calls its `AddIcosahedron` method to make an icosahedron. It scales the icosahedron, converts it into a light green model, and adds the model to the program's `Model3DGroup`.

Icosahedron

The Icosahedron example program uses the following code to define its scene.

```
private void DefineModel(Model3DGroup group)
{
    // Show the axes.
    MeshExtensions.AddAxes(group);

    const double scale = 1.75;

    // Make a solid insphere.
    MeshGeometry3D mesh1 = new MeshGeometry3D();
    mesh1.AddSphere(D3.Origin, G3.IcosahedronInradius(), 60, 30, true);
    mesh1.ApplyTransformation(new ScaleTransform3D(scale, scale, scale));
    group.Children.Add(mesh1.MakeModel(Brushes.Red));

    // Make a translucent icosahedron.
    MeshGeometry3D mesh2 = new MeshGeometry3D();
    mesh2.AddIcosahedron();
    mesh2.ApplyTransformation(new ScaleTransform3D(scale, scale, scale));
    Brush brush = new SolidColorBrush(Color.FromArgb(128, 128, 255, 128));
    MaterialGroup group2 = D3.MakeMaterialGroup(
        new DiffuseMaterial(brush),
        new SpecularMaterial(Brushes.White, 100));
    group.Children.Add(mesh2.MakeModel(group2));

    // Make a translucent circumsphere.
    MeshGeometry3D mesh3 = new MeshGeometry3D();
    mesh3.AddSphere(D3.Origin, G3.IcosahedronCircumradius(), 60, 30, true);
    mesh3.ApplyTransformation(new ScaleTransform3D(scale, scale, scale));
    MaterialGroup group3 = D3.MakeMaterialGroup(
        new DiffuseMaterial(brush),
        new SpecularMaterial(Brushes.White, 100));
    group.Children.Add(mesh3.MakeModel(group3));
}
```

This code follows the pattern used by earlier examples but this time with an icosahedron. It creates a solid insphere, a translucent icosahedron, and then a translucent circumsphere. Figure 22-8 shows the Icosahedron example program displaying its scene.

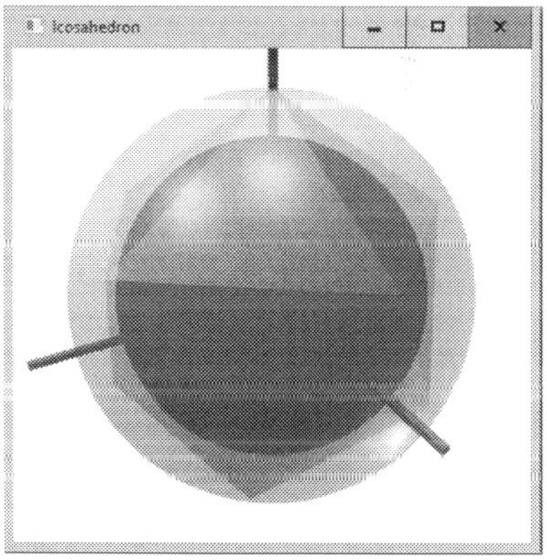

Figure 22-8: The Icosahedron program draws an icosahedron, insphere, and circumsphere.

DualDodecahedronIcosahedron

As I mentioned in Chapter 21, the dual of a dodecahedron is an icosahedron and vice versa. The DualDodecahedronIcosahedron example program displays a dodecahedron, its dual (an icosahedron), and the dual's dual (another dodecahedron). The program uses the following code to create its scene.

```
private void DefineModel(Model3DGroup group)
{
    //// Verify the icosahedron calculations.
    //MeshExtensions.VerifyIcosahedron();

    // Show the axes.
    MeshExtensions.AddAxes(group);

    const double scale = 0.8;

    // Make a solid dodecahedron.
    MeshGeometry3D mesh1 = new MeshGeometry3D();
    mesh1.AddDodecahedron();
    mesh1.ApplyTransformation(new ScaleTransform3D(scale, scale, scale));
    group.Children.Add(mesh1.MakeModel(Brushes.Red));

    // Make a translucent icosahedron.
    MeshGeometry3D mesh2 = new MeshGeometry3D();
    mesh2.AddIcosahedron();
    double icoScale = scale * G3.DodecahedronCircumradius() / G3.IcosahedronInradius();
    mesh2.ApplyTransformation(new ScaleTransform3D(icoScale, icoScale, icoScale));
    mesh2.ApplyTransformation(D3.Rotate(D3.YVector(), D3.Origin, 180));
    Brush brush = new SolidColorBrush(Color.FromArgb(128, 128, 255, 128));
    MaterialGroup group2 = D3.MakeMaterialGroup(
        new DiffuseMaterial(brush),
        new SpecularMaterial(Brushes.White, 100));
    group.Children.Add(mesh2.MakeModel(group2));

    // Make a translucent dodecahedron.
    MeshGeometry3D mesh3 = new MeshGeometry3D();
    mesh3.AddDodecahedron();
    double dodScale =
        icoScale * G3.IcosahedronCircumradius() / G3.DodecahedronInradius();
    mesh3.ApplyTransformation(new ScaleTransform3D(dodScale, dodScale, dodScale));
    MaterialGroup group3 = D3.MakeMaterialGroup(
        new DiffuseMaterial(brush),
        new SpecularMaterial(Brushes.White, 100));
    group.Children.Add(mesh3.MakeModel(group3));
}
```

This method creates the coordinate axes as usual and then creates a solid dodecahedron.

Next, the program makes a translucent icosahedron. It scales this object by the dodecahedron's circumradius divided by the icosahedron's inradius so the icosahedron has an inradius equal to the dodecahedron's circumradius. That makes its faces touch the dodecahedron's vertices.

The code then makes a translucent dodecahedron. This time it scales the dodecahedron by the icosahedron's circumradius divided by the dodecahedron's inradius. Note that it multiples the value returned by `G3.OctahedronCircumradius` by the previous solid's scale so the dodecahedron's faces touch the drawn icosahedron's vertices.

Figure 22-8 shows the DualCubeOctahedron example program in action. You may want to download the example and view the scene from different angles to verify that each object's vertices touch the faces of its enclosing object.

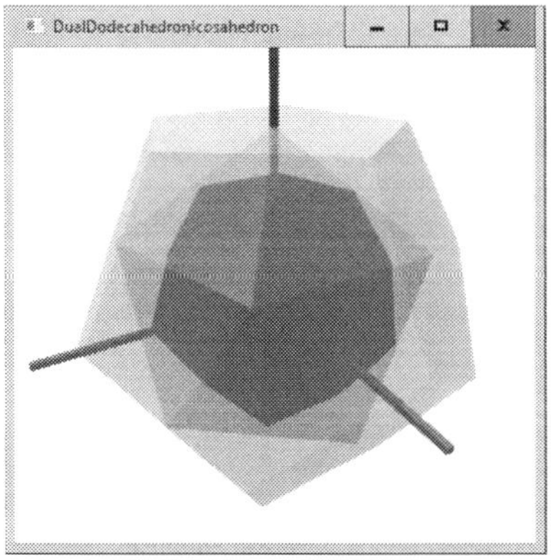

Figure 22-8: Dodecahedrons and Icosahedrons are each other's duals.

Summary

This chapter explained how to draw the final Platonic solid: the icosahedron. Solids such as the Platonic solids look pretty good when you draw them normally. Their sides point in different enough directions that they stand out reasonably well if you pick your lights carefully.

Sometimes, however, a shape may be easier to visualize as a wireframe. For example, a subtly varying surface may only show its structure in a wireframe. The next chapter explains how you can add wireframes and other line-like objects to a scene.

Chapter 23 Wireframes

A *wireframe* is a skeletal model that represents a shape with vertices and line segments. Sometimes it's useful to display an object as a wireframe, either by itself or overlaid on top of the original object. That can highlight subtle changes in the object's surface that may not be as obvious with lighting alone.

This chapter explains how you can build wireframes for objects. The following section explains how you can draw a single piece of wire. The later sections explain how you can use that wire to build simple and not-so-simple methods for drawing wireframes under different circumstances.

Segments

In order to draw a wireframe, you need to be able to draw the wires. You can use long, skinny boxes the way we earlier drew coordinate axes, but the coordinate axes are nicely aligned vertically and horizontally, so it's easy to find vectors representing their lengths, breadths, and heights. This time the boxes might need to point in any direction.

The following `AddSegment` extension method makes a box connecting two points and pointing in any direction.

```
// Make a thin line segment.
public static void AddSegment(this MeshGeometry3D mesh,
    double thickness, Point3D point1, Point3D point2)
{
    // Get a vector between the points.
    Vector3D v = point2 - point1;

    // Get perpendicular vectors.
    Vector3D vz, vx;
    double angle = Vector3D.AngleBetween(v, D3.YVector());
    if ((angle > 10) && (angle < 170))
        vz = Vector3D.CrossProduct(v, D3.YVector());
    else
        vz = Vector3D.CrossProduct(v, D3.ZVector());
    vx = Vector3D.CrossProduct(v, vz);

    // Give the perpendicular vectors length thickness.
    vx *= thickness / vx.Length;
    vz *= thickness / vz.Length;

    // Make the box.
    mesh.AddBox(point1 - vx / 2 - vz / 2, vx, v, vz);
```

```
}
```

You may remember the `AddBox` method described in Chapter 12. That method takes as parameters a corner point and three vectors that define the box's edges. When drawing a segment, the box's long edge can be the vector between the two points. The real trick is finding the other two vectors so they have the correct lengths and so all three vectors are mutually perpendicular.

The `AddSegment` method starts by finding the first vector `v` between the two points.

Next, the method should take the cross product of that vector and a temporary vector to find a vector perpendicular to the first. Normally you might use the Y axis as the temporary vector. That's more or less what a camera does with its "up" vector.

But what if vector v is parallel to the Y axis? In that case, the cross product isn't defined.

To handle that situation, the method uses `Vector3D.AngleBetween` to find the angle between vector `v` and the Y axis. If the angle is *not* close to 0° or 180°, then it's safe to use the Y axis as the temporary vector, so the method does so.

If the angle is close to 0° or 180°, then vector `v` and the Y axis are close to parallel. In that case, the method uses the Z axis as the temporary vector.

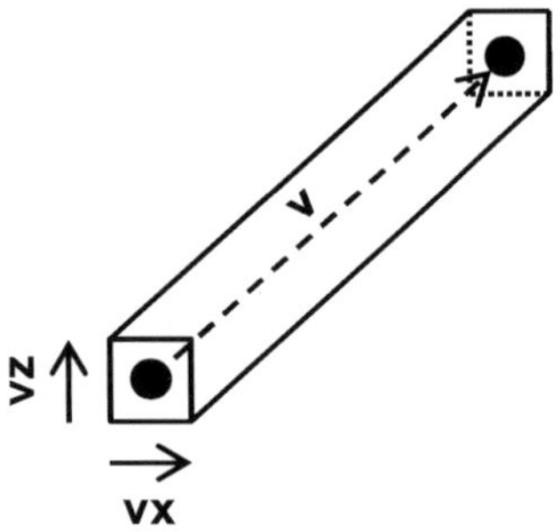

Figure 23-1: Vectors v, vx, and vz are mutually perpendicular.

At this point, the method has two perpendicular vectors: `v` and `vz`. It takes their cross product to find the third perpendicular vector `vx`.

Next, the code divides vectors `vx` and `vz` by their lengths and multiples them by `thickness` so they are as long as the desired segment's thickness. Figure 23-1 shows the vectors greatly enlarged. Vector `v` points along the length of the segment. Vectors `vx` and `vz` are perpendicular to `v`.

The method is then ready to call `AddBox`. It sets the box's corner to the starting point `point1` minus half of the vectors `vx` and `vz` so the box is centered on the line between the two points. The other parameters to `AddBox` are simply the three vectors.

Now a program can add a segment to a mesh by calling the `AddSegment` extension method as in the following code.

```
mesh.AddSegment(0.05, new Point3D(-1, -1, -1), new Point3D(1, 1, 1));
```

Edges

You can use the `AddSegment` method described in the preceding section to draw line segments. If you're not careful, however, you'll end up duplicating a lot of segments. For example, every edge on a closed polygonal solid is shared by two faces. If you simply make a segment for every edge, then you'll create every edge twice.

One way to avoid duplicates is to keep track of the points that you have connected and then skip segments that would connect the same two points again.

You can use the following `Edge` class to store information about an edge.

```
// An object to prevent duplicate wireframe edges.
public class Edge : IEquatable<Edge>, IComparable<Edge>
{
    public Point3D Point1, Point2;
    public Edge(Point3D point1, Point3D point2)
    {
        // Put them in order so Point1 <= Point2.
        bool p1smaller =
            (point1.X < point2.X) ||
            ((point1.X == point2.X) && (point1.Y < point2.Y)) ||
            ((point1.X == point2.X) && (point1.Y == point2.Y) &&
                (point1.Z < point2.Z));
        if (p1smaller)
        {
            Point1 = point1;
            Point2 = point2;
        }
        else
        {
            Point1 = point2;
            Point2 = point1;
        }
    }

    public bool Equals(Edge other)
    {
        if (ReferenceEquals(other, null)) return false;
        if ((Point1 == other.Point1) && (Point2 == other.Point2)) return true;
        return false;
    }
    public static bool operator ==(Edge edge1, Edge edge2)
    {
        if (ReferenceEquals(edge1, edge2)) return true;
        if ((edge1 == null)) return false;
        return edge1.Equals(edge2);
    }
    public static bool operator !=(Edge edge1, Edge edge2)
    {
        return !(edge1 == edge2);
    }
    public override bool Equals(object obj)
    {
        if (!(obj is Edge)) return false;
        return Equals(obj as Edge);
    }

    public override int GetHashCode()
    {
        return Point1.GetHashCode() ^ Point2.GetHashCode();
```

```
        }

        public override string ToString()
        {
            return Point1.ToString() + " --> " + Point2.ToString();
        }

        // Return:
        //      -1 if Point1 < Point2
        //       0 if Point1 == Point2
        //       1 if Point1 > Point2
        public int CompareTo(Edge other)
        {
            if (Point1.X < Point2.X) return -1;
            if (Point1.X > Point2.X) return 1;
            if (Point1.Y < Point2.Y) return -1;
            if (Point1.Y > Point2.Y) return 1;
            if (Point1.Z < Point2.Z) return -1;
            if (Point1.Z > Point2.Z) return 1;
            return 0;
        }
    }
```

The class first defines two public `Point3D` variables `Point1` and `Point2`. That's all it really needs to store information about an edge. The reason the class doesn't end there is that it implements two interfaces: `IEquatable` and `IComparable`. The `IComparable` interface isn't really necessary right now, but it may be useful later (depending on how you use this class) and it's not hard to add.

The class's constructor lexicographically orders the points so `Point1` comes before `Point2`. That will make comparing edges easier.

The `Equals` method compares this `Edge` object with another one to determine whether they are equal. If their points match, the method returns `true`. Otherwise it returns `false`. Because the `Edge` class orders its points lexicographically, the `Equals` method doesn't need to worry about whether the points are in the same order in the two objects.

The == operator checks for `null` values and then invokes the `Equals` method. The `!=` operator invokes == and negates the result.

If a class overrides == and `!=`, then Microsoft says it should also override the `Equals(object)` and `GetHashCode` methods. This class's `Equals(object)` method simply invokes the earlier version of `Equals`.

The `GetHashCode` method is actually important in this example because it is used by dictionary objects to compare `Edge` objects more quickly. This version of `GetHashCode` takes the hash values of the `Edge` object's two points and combines them with the bitwise XOR operator.

Next, the class overrides its `ToString` method. That may help with later debugging if you need to examine the contents of some `Edge` objects.

Finally, the class implements the `CompareTo` method that is required by the `IComparable` interface.

Because the `Edge` class implements `IEquatable`, the `Dictionary` and `HashSet` classes can quickly locate the `Edge` objects that they contain.

> **NOTE:** If you haven't used the `HashSet` class before, it's sort of like a `Dictionary` that only contains keys without associated values. You can use it to see if something is already present in the set.

Now that we have an `Edge` class, we can use a `HashSet` containing `Edge` objects to see if we have already added a particular `Edge` to a mesh. This is similar to the way we've been using point dictionaries since Chapter 10 to see if a point is already present in a mesh.

If a point is already present, we can use a dictionary to get its index in the mesh's `Positions` list. Now we don't need to find an edge's index; we just need to know whether we've created the same edge before.

The following `AddEdge` method uses a `HashSet` to avoid adding duplicate edges.

```
// Add a wireframe edge to this mesh.
public static void AddEdge(this MeshGeometry3D mesh,
    HashSet<Edge> edges, double thickness, Point3D point1, Point3D point2)
{
    // If the points are the same, skip it.
    if (point1 == point2) return;

    // See if the edge is already in the HashSet.
    Edge edge = new Edge(point1, point2);
    if (edges.Contains(edge)) return;

    // Add the edge.
    edges.Add(edge);
    mesh.AddSegment(thickness, point1, point2);
}
```

The method first compares the two points that it should connect and, if they are the same, it returns without doing anything.

> **NOTE:** It's generally a good idea to avoid making empty objects such as triangles with two identical vertices or zero-length segments because the WPF drawing system doesn't handle those situations very well. For example, I've seen bugs where a program mysteriously makes pieces of triangles appear and disappear when you move the camera. The problem was caused by some unrelated triangles that had duplicate vertices and was very hard to find.

Next, the method makes a new `Edge` to connect `point1` and `point2`. It then checks the `HashSet` named `edges` and returns if the `Edge` is already present in the set.

If the `Edge` is not already present, the method adds it to the `HashSet` and calls the `AddSegment` method described earlier to make the new segment.

Polygons

Occasionally you may want to draw a single edge, but most of the programs I've described so far in this book draw triangles or larger polygons. The following `AddPolygonEdge` method makes drawing the edges of those polygons easier.

```
// Add a polygon's wireframe to this mesh.
public static void AddPolygonEdges(this MeshGeometry3D mesh,
    HashSet<Edge> edges, double thickness, params Point3D[] points)
{
    for (int i = 0; i < points.Length; i++)
    {
        int i1 = (i + 1) % points.Length;
        mesh.AddEdge(edges, thickness, points[i], points[i1]);
    }
}
```

This method simply loops through the points in the polygon and calls `AddEdge` to connect them with edges.

Mesh to Wireframe

The `AddPolygonEdges` method makes it easy to convert an existing mesh into a wireframe. The `ToWireframe` method shown in the following code does that.

```
// Convert a mesh into a new mesh containing a wireframe.
public static MeshGeometry3D ToWireframe(this MeshGeometry3D mesh, double thickness)
{
    // Make a dictionary of edges.
    HashSet<Edge> edges = new HashSet<Edge>();

    // Make the wireframe pieces.
    MeshGeometry3D result = new MeshGeometry3D();
    for (int i = 0; i < mesh.TriangleIndices.Count; i += 3)
    {
        Point3D point1 = mesh.Positions[mesh.TriangleIndices[i]];
        Point3D point2 = mesh.Positions[mesh.TriangleIndices[i + 1]];
        Point3D point3 = mesh.Positions[mesh.TriangleIndices[i + 2]];
        result.AddPolygonEdges(edges, thickness, point1, point2, point3);
    }
    return result;
}
```

Recall that the `TriangleIndices` collection contains triples of indices of points that makeup the mesh's triangles. This method loops through the `TriangleIndices` collection.

For each triple, it gets the Point3D objects that make up the corresponding triangle. It then passes those points into the AddPolygonEdges method to make edges for the triangle.

The IcosahedronWireframe example program uses the following code to draw an icosahedron with a wireframe.

```
private void DefineModel(Model3DGroup group)
{
    // Make an icosahedron.
    MeshGeometry3D mesh1 = new MeshGeometry3D();
    mesh1.AddIcosahedron();
    mesh1.ApplyTransformation(new TranslateTransform3D(-2, 0, 0));
    group.Children.Add(mesh1.MakeModel(Brushes.LightGreen));

    // Copy the icosahedron.
    MeshGeometry3D mesh2 = mesh1.Clone();
    mesh2.ApplyTransformation(new TranslateTransform3D(4, 0, 0));
    group.Children.Add(mesh2.MakeModel(Brushes.LightGreen));

    // Make a wireframe for the new icosahedron.
    MeshGeometry3D mesh3 = new MeshGeometry3D();
    mesh3 = mesh2.ToWireframe(0.05);
    group.Children.Add(mesh3.MakeModel(Brushes.Green));
}
```

This code creates a mesh and uses its AddIcosahedron method to make an icosahedron. It moves the mesh and then adds it to the program's Model3DGroup.

Next, the code clones the first mesh and moves it to a new position. It then uses the ToWireframe method to convert the new mesh into a wireframe.

Figure23-2 shows the IcosahedronWireframe example program displaying its two icosahedrons. The lighting makes the edges between the upper faces hard to see in the icosahedron on the left. The one on the right displays a wireframe so it's much easier to see those edges.

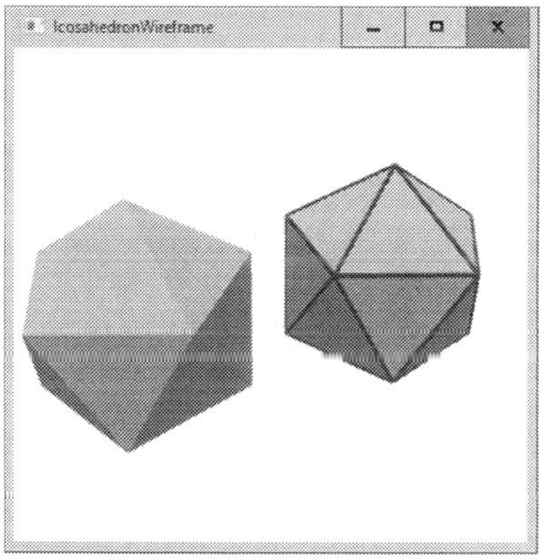

Figure 23-2: This example displays icosahedrons with and without wireframes.

General Wireframes

Unfortunately, the AddWireframe method only works well if the mesh is logically made up of triangles. All meshes are made up of triangles at some level, but often those triangles are used to build larger polygons.

For example, a dodecahedron has faces that are pentagons. Because all three-dimensional objects are built from triangles in WPF, each of those pentagons is made up of three triangles. If you use the ToWireframe method to convert a dodecahedron into a wireframe, the result outlines all of those triangles and looks rather disappointing.

The triangles *do* show the structure of the dodecahedron, so in that sense they are correct. The result may be reasonable for a large, smooth surface such as the graph of the function y=Sin(x+z), but for a solid such as a dodecahedron, the triangles look strange.

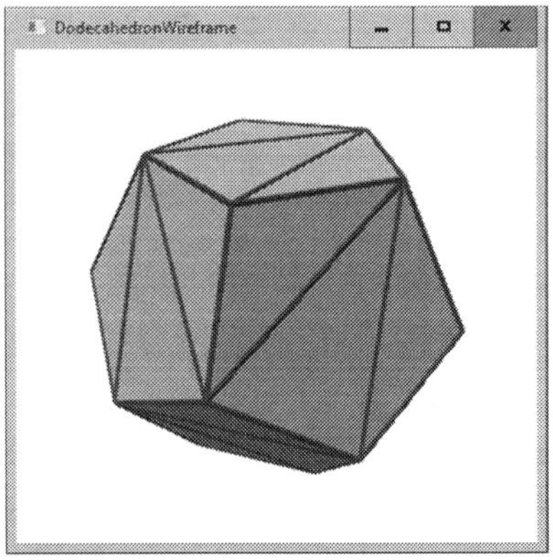

Figure 23-3: The `ToWireframe` method makes triangles not polygons.

The DodecahedronWireframe example program shown in Figure 23-3 uses the `ToWireframe` method to display edges.

The `AddPolygonEdges` method can create edges to represent a polygon, so you can use it to fix this issue. There are a couple of approaches that you could take.

For example, you could write new versions of the `AddBox`, `AddCube`, `AddDodecahedron` and the other mesh extension methods so they used `AddPolygonEdges` to outline polygons instead of drawing them. Unfortunately, that would require you to have several nearly identical methods. That would greatly increasing the amount of code that you need to write, debug, and maintain.

The approach that I've taken is to look at a lower level in the drawing process. Methods such as `AddDodecahedron` eventually call the `AddPolygon` method to create their polygons. That method is the lowest level where polygons are treated as polygons and not triangles. The `AddPolygon` method converts a polygon into triangles and adds the triangles to the mesh.

The following code shows a new version of the `AddPolygon` method that either adds triangles or edges to the mesh depending on whether its `edges` parameter is `null`.

```
public static void AddPolygon(this MeshGeometry3D mesh,
    Dictionary<Point3D, int> pointDict = null,
    HashSet<Edge> edges = null, double thickness = 0.1,
    Point[] textureCoords = null, params Point3D[] points)
{
    if (edges != null)
    {
        // Make a wireframe polygon.
        mesh.AddPolygonEdges(edges, thickness, points);
    }
    else
    {
        // Make a wireframe polygon.
        mesh.AddPolygonTriangles(pointDict,textureCoords, points);
    }
}
```

The new `edges` parameter is a `HashSet` containing `Edge` objects. If this parameter is not `null`, then the method assumes that you want to create edges instead of triangles. In that case, it calls the `AddPolygonEdges` method described earlier in this chapter, passing it the `HashSet` so it can avoid making duplicate edges.

If the `edges` parameter is `null`, then the method calls the new `AddPolygonTriangles` method. That method simply contains all of the code that the old version of the `AddPolygon` method did.

That's all there is to the new edge-adding code, but you need to make some other modifications to the other extension methods so they can pass a `HashSet` down the call chain into the new version of `AddPolygon`.

For example, the `AddDodecahedron` method must now take an optional `HashSet` parameter to pass into `AddPoylgon`. The following code snippet shows the new method signature.

```
public static void AddDodecahedron(this MeshGeometry3D mesh,
    HashSet<Edge> edges = null, double thickness = 0.1)
{
   ...
}
```

The only difference to the omitted code is that it passes the `edges HashSet` and the `thickness` value into its calls to `AddPolygon`.

Now the main program passes a `HashSet<Edge>` into the `AddDodecahedron` method so that method can pass it down the chain.

The DodecahedronWireframe2 example program uses the following code to build its scene.

```
private void DefineModel(Model3DGroup group)
{
    // Make a dodecahedron.
    MeshGeometry3D mesh1 = new MeshGeometry3D();
    mesh1.AddDodecahedron();
    group.Children.Add(mesh1.MakeModel(Brushes.LightGreen));

    // Make a wireframe for the dodecahedron.
    MeshGeometry3D mesh2 = new MeshGeometry3D();
    HashSet<Edge> edges = new HashSet<Edge>();
    double thickness = 0.05;
    mesh2.AddDodecahedron(edges, thickness);
    group.Children.Add(
        mesh2.MakeModel(Brushes.Green));
}
```

This method first creates a mesh and a dodecahedron as usual. It then creates a second mesh, makes a `HashSet<Edge>`, and calls the new mesh's `AddDodecahedron` method passing in the `HashSet`. This time `AddDodecahedron` passes the `HashSet` along to the `AddPolygon` method, and `AddPolygon` creates edges instead of triangles.

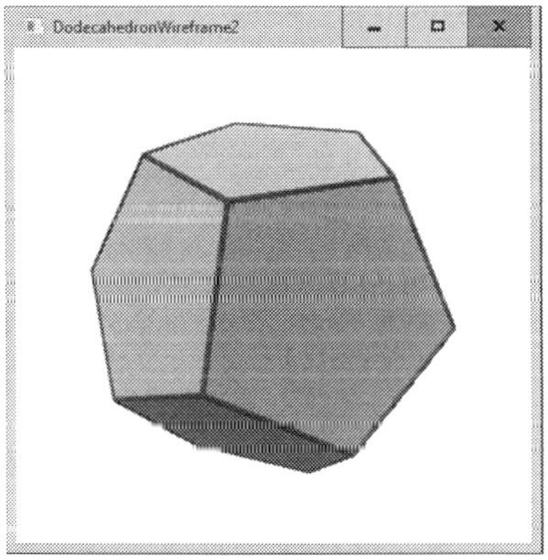

Figure 23-4: This example makes wireframe polygons instead of triangles.

Figure23-4 shows the DodecahedronWireframe2

example program using the new methods to display a dodecahedron. The result is much cleaner than the version shown in Figure 23-3.

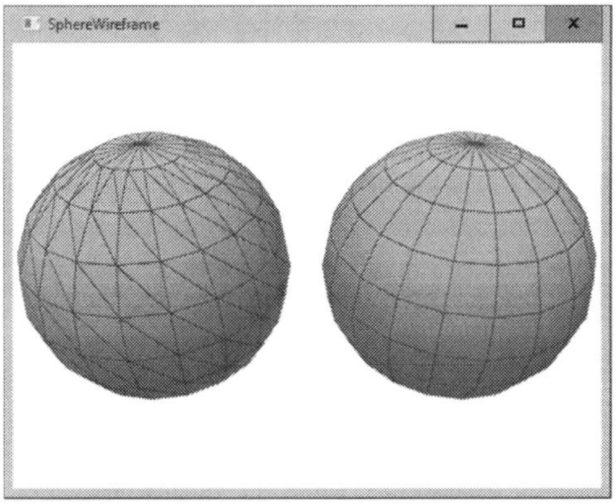

Figure 23-5: Sphere wireframes look better with polygons instead of triangles.

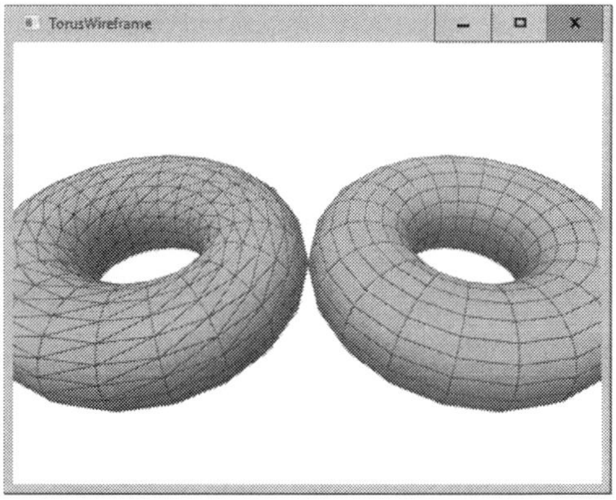

Figure 23-6: Torus wireframes also look better with polygons instead of triangles.

The difference is even more obvious for regular, smooth shapes such as spheres and tori. The example programs SphereWireframe and TorusWireframe shown in Figures 23-5 and 23-6 demonstrate triangular and polygonal wireframes. The polygonal versions are generally less cluttered and easier to understand.

> **NOTE:** I didn't make new versions of methods that add textured objects such as `AddTexturedSphere` and `AddTexturedTorus`. Because those methods need to set points' normal vectors, they create their points directly instead of calling `AddPolygon`.
>
> You can modify those methods if you like, but if you're drawing a wireframe anyway, you may as well just use the non-textured version of those methods such as `AddSphere` and `AddTorus`. I did create new versions of those variations.

Example Programs

In addition to the examples described earlier in this chapter, I made two others that are related to wireframes. First, I made the AllSolids example program shown in Figure 23-7 to verify that I didn't mess up anything while modifying the mesh extension methods to draw wireframes.

I made the AllWireframes example program shown in Figure 23-8 to demonstrate the new wireframe methods. The program doesn't display textured vesions of objects because those don't have wireframe versions.

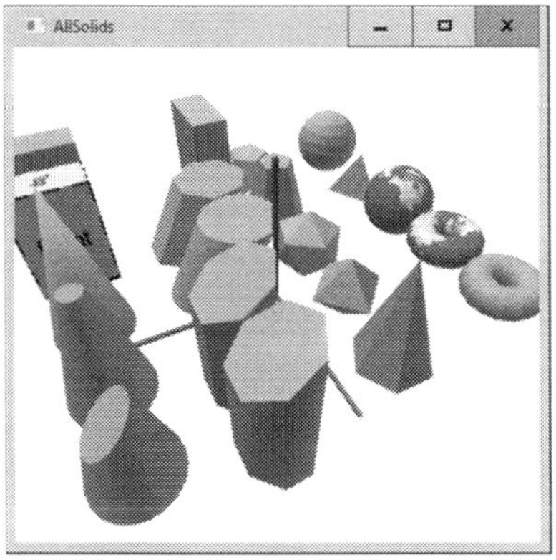

Figure 23-7: The AllSolids example program draws solids.

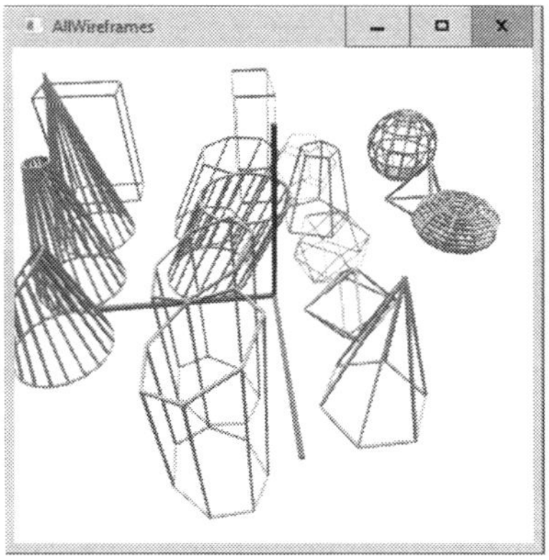

Figure 23-8: The AllWireframes example program draws wireframes.

These examples are relatively long but straightforward. Download them to see how they work.

> **NOTE:** If you scale a wireframe, the thickness of the "wires" changes, too. To avoid that, scale the original points before you use them to generate the wireframe.

Summary

This chapter explained how to draw wireframes. The `ToWireframe` method is extremely easy to use, although it converts a mesh's triangles directly into wireframe segments so it doesn't always produce the best result. For example, that method converts a dodecahedron's pentagonal sides into three triangles each.

Modifying the low-level `AddPolygon` method allows other methods to create wireframes that look better.

Wireframes are particularly handy for emphasizing subtle differences in parts of smooth objects such as spheres and tori. The next chapter explains how to make another kind of object that is sometimes easiest to understand with a wireframe: the geodesic sphere.

Part III

Investigating Advanced Topics

The first part of this book explained the basics that you need to know to create any sort of three-dimensional scene. The second part provided examples that showed how to create different kinds of three-dimensional objects.

The chapters in the third part of the book cover more advanced topics. They show how to create more complicated objects such as geodesic solids, parametric surfaces, surfaces of transformation, and complex models created by other three-dimensional drawing applications. These chapters also show how to display text, either as part of three-dimensional objects or overlaid two-dimensionally behind or on top of a scene.

This part of the book also explains new ways to control objects. It shows how to allow the user to select and move objects, and how to use skeletons to control complex objects such as people, robots, animals, or vehicles.

Chapter 24

Geodesic Spheres

The geodesic dome was invented by Walther Bauersfeld in 1922. They were later popularized by R. Buckminster Fuller who coined the term *geodesic* in the late 1940s.

A *geodesic polyhedron* is a solid made up of triangles that approximate a sphere. It's surprisingly easy to construct a geodesic polyhedron starting from any simpler solid such as a cube or dodecahedron. This chapter explains how to build a geodesic sphere starting from an icosahedron.

Triangles

To build a geodesic sphere, you start with a simpler shape such as a dodecahedron or icosahedron. If the solid does not have triangular faces, subdivide the faces into triangles, preferably as close to equilateral triangles as possible.

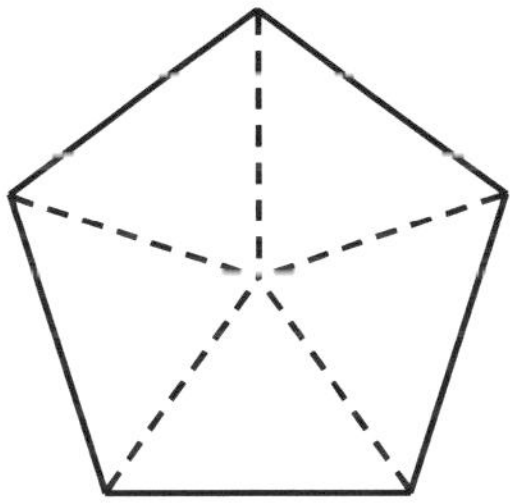

Figure 24-1: You can subdivide a pentagon into five triangles.

For example, suppose you start with a dodecahedron. Each of a dodecahedron's faces is a pentagon. You can divide the pentagons into triangles as shown in Figure 24-1.

If you start with an initial solid that has triangular faces, you can skip the first step and just use those triangles. For example, an icosahedron's faces are already triangles so you don't need to subdivide its faces.

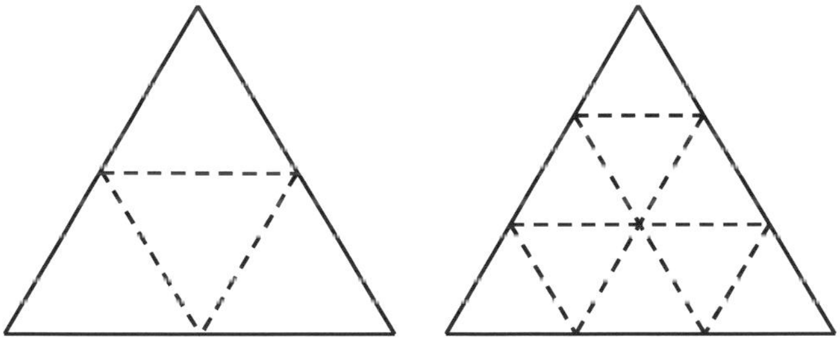

Figure 24-2: These patterns subdivide a triangle into four or nine smaller triangles.

After you convert the initial solid into one with triangular faces, you subdivide the triangles into more triangles. Figure 24-2 shows two ways that you can subdivide a triangle into smaller triangles.

You can refine the pattern shown in Figure 24-2 to subdivide the triangles into as many smaller triangles as you like. The more triangles you use, the closer the final solid will be to approximating a sphere.

After you finish subdividing the solid's triangles, you *project* or push the vertices of the triangles outward until they rest on a sphere. You can use any sphere centered at the original solid's center, such as the solid's circumsphere.

Figure 24-3 shows the projection for a single subdivided triangle. The vertices of the gray triangles are projected along the dotted lines until they reach the sphere where they form the dark triangles.

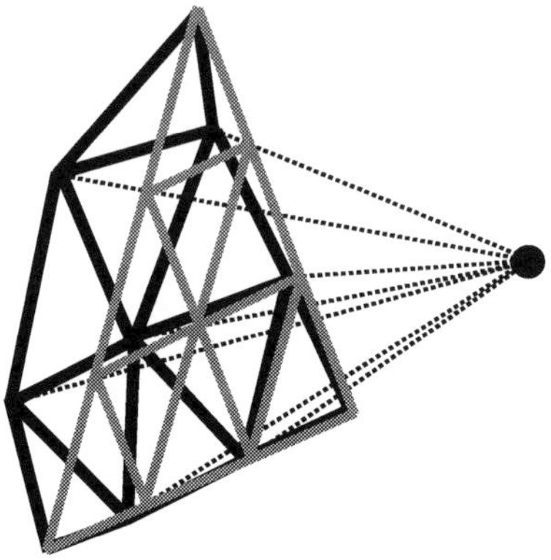

Figure 24-3: Project the vertices onto the sphere.

After you project all of the vertices for all of the solid's triangles, the result is a new solid made up of triangles that approximate the sphere.

> **NOTE:** The sub-triangles in Figure 24-2 are equilateral triangles, at least if the larger triangle is equilateral. However, projecting the vertices onto the sphere distorts them slightly so they are no longer equilateral.

Subdivision

It's pretty easy to use vector arithmetic and the patterns shown in Figure 24-2 to subdivide triangles. Think of the subdivisions as occurring in rows and columns, where the columns are angled to the side as shown in Figure 24-4.

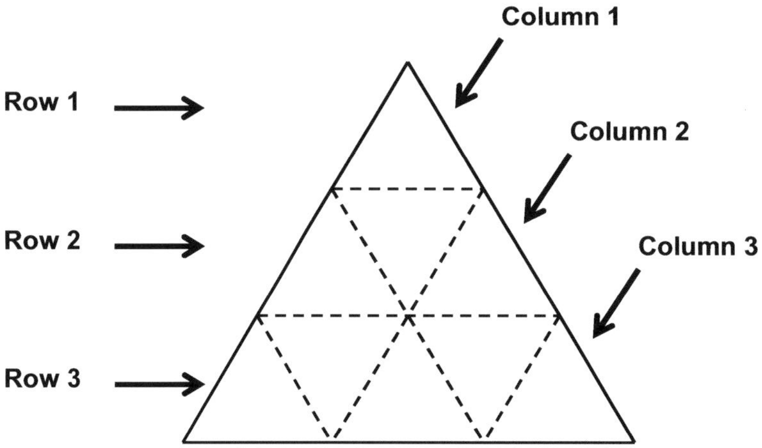

Figure 24-4: You can think of the smaller triangles as coming in rows and columns.

To find the smaller triangles, loop through the rows. For each row, loop through that row's columns, noting that row number R also has R columns. For each row and column, you can use vector arithmetic to find the points that define its smaller triangles.

To see how that works, consider the situation shown in Figure 24-5. The points A, B, and C define the larger triangle that we must subdivide. Now suppose we're trying to find the triangles in row number `row` and column number `col`.

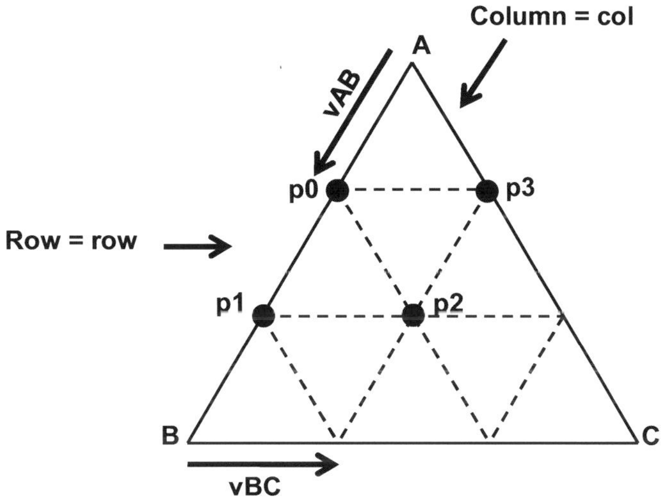

Figure 24-5: You can use vector arithmetic to find points p1, p2, p3, and p4.

The first step is to find vectors that you can use to calculate the points `p0`, `p1`, `p2`, and `p3`. Subtract point `A` from point `B` and divide the result by the number of rows to get the vector `vAB`. That vector points from point `A` toward point `B` but is only long enough to move from one row to the next in the subdivision. You can see that vector in Figure 24-5.

Similarly, find vector `vBC` pointing from point `B` toward point `C` and long enough to move from one column to the next.

Now it's easy to use vector arithmetic to find points `p0`, `p1`, `p2`, and `p3`.

```
p0 = A + row * vAB + col * vBC
p1 = p0 + vAB
p2 = p1 + vBC
p3 = p0 + vBC
```

Having found the points that subdivide the triangles, the next step in building the geodesic sphere is projecting the triangle vertices onto the sphere.

Projection

Projecting a point away from the center of a sphere is relatively simple. First find the vector from the sphere's center to the point. Scale the vector so its length equals the sphere's radius. Then adding that vector to the center point gives the original point's projection.

To make this calculation easier, I added the following `SetDistanceFrom` method to the `Point3DExtensions` class.

```
public static Point3D SetDistanceFrom(this Point3D point, Point3D center,
    double distance)
{
    Vector3D v = point - center;
    return center + v / v.Length * distance;
}
```

This code finds the vector from a center point to a target point, divides that vector by its length, and then multiplies it by the desired distance from the center point (the sphere's radius). The method adds the result to the center point and returns the result.

Subdivision Code

To make subdividing triangles easier, I created the following `Triangle` class.

```
// Hold three points that make up a triangle.
public class Triangle
{
    public List<Point3D> Points = null;

    // Copy the points into the Points list.
    public Triangle(params Point3D[] points)
    {
        Points = new List<Point3D>(points);
    }

    // Divide this triangle into triangles for use in geodesic spheres.
    public List<Triangle> DivideGeodesic(Point3D center, double radius, int numRows)
    {
        // Make vectors 1/numDivisions of the length along the triangle's edges.
        Vector3D vAB = (Points[1] - Points[0]) / numRows;
        Vector3D vBC = (Points[2] - Points[1]) / numRows;

        // Use vector arithmetic to create the points.
        List<Triangle> triangles = new List<Triangle>();
        for (int row = 0; row < numRows; row++)
        {
            for (int col = 0; col <= row; col++)
            {
                // Make the points we will need.
                Point3D p0 = Points[0] + row * vAB + col * vBC;
                Point3D p1 = p0 + vAB;
                Point3D p2 = p1 + vBC;
                Point3D p3 = p0 + vBC;
```

```
                // Project the points onto the sphere.
                p0 = p0.SetDistanceFrom(center, radius);
                p1 = p1.SetDistanceFrom(center, radius);
                p2 = p2.SetDistanceFrom(center, radius);
                p3 = p3.SetDistanceFrom(center, radius);

                // Make the lower triangle.
                triangles.Add(new Triangle(p0, p1, p2));
                if (col == row) break;

                // Make the upper triangle.
                triangles.Add(new Triangle(p0, p2, p3));
            }
        }
        return triangles;
    }
}
```

The `Points` list holds the triangle's points. The class's constructor simply copies its parameters into that list.

The interesting part is the `DivideGeodesic` method that divides the triangle into smaller triangles. It starts by finding vectors `vAB` and `vBC` as described earlier and shown in Figure 24-5. It then loops over the subdivision's rows and columns.

For each row and column, the method uses the vector arithmetic described earlier to find the points `p0`, `p1`, `p2`, and `p3`. It then calls each point's `SetDistanceFrom` method to move the point to the edge of the sphere.

Next, the code creates the lower triangle defined by points `p0`, `p1`, and `p2` in Figure 24-5 and adds it to the `triangles` list. If this is the last column in the row, then that is the only triangle in this column so the code breaks out of its `for` loop. (You may want to look at Figure 24-5 again to verify that this makes sense.)

If the code doesn't break out of the loop, it create the upper triangle defined by points `p0`, p2, and `p3` and adds it to the `triangles` list. (Again, you may want to look at Figure 24-5.)

After it finishes processing all of the rows, the method returns the list of new triangles.

Geodesic Sphere Code

The following `AddGeodesicSphere` method uses the preceding `DivideGeodesic` method to create a geodesic sphere. This method is long but also straightforward.

```
public static void AddGeodesicSphere(this MeshGeometry3D mesh,
    Point3D center, double radius, int numDivisions,
    HashSet<Edge> edges = null, double thickness = 0.1)
{
    // Create an icosahedron.
    // Get the points.
    Point3D A, B, C, D, E, F, G, H, I, J, K, L;
```

```
            G3.IcosahedronPoints(
                out A, out B, out C, out D, out E, out F,
                out G, out H, out I, out J, out K, out L);

            // Scale the icosahedron to the proper radius and center it.
            double scale = radius / G3.IcosahedronCircumradius();
            ScaleTransform3D scaleT = new ScaleTransform3D(scale, scale, scale);
            TranslateTransform3D translateT =
                new TranslateTransform3D(center.X, center.Y, center.Z);
            Transform3DGroup groupT = new Transform3DGroup();
            groupT.Children.Add(scaleT);
            groupT.Children.Add(translateT);
            A = groupT.Transform(A);
            B = groupT.Transform(B);
            C = groupT.Transform(C);
            ...
            L = groupT.Transform(L);

            // Make the icosahedron's faces.
            List<Triangle> triangles = new List<Triangle>();
            triangles.Add(new Triangle(A, C, B));
            triangles.Add(new Triangle(A, D, C));
            triangles.Add(new Triangle(A, E, D));
            ...
            triangles.Add(new Triangle(L, K, G));

            // Subdivide the faces as desired.
            List<Triangle> newTriangles = new List<Triangle>();
            foreach (Triangle triangle in triangles)
            {
                // Subdivide this triangle and add the results to newTriangles.
                newTriangles.AddRange(triangle.DivideGeodesic(center, radius, numDivisions));
            }

            // Create the geodesic sphere.
            foreach (Triangle triangle in newTriangles)
            {
                mesh.AddPolygon(edges, thickness, triangle.Points.ToArray());
            }
        }
```

This method uses the `G3` class's `IcosahedronPoints` method to get the points that define an icosahedron. It scales and translates the points to give the final result the desired position and radius. (To save space, I've omitted shown some of the statements that transform the points.)

Next, the code uses the points to build the icosahedron's 20 triangular faces. (Again, I've omitted some of those statements to save space.) It then loops through the triangles and calls their `DivideGeodesic` methods. It takes each triangle's returned list of smaller triangles and adds it to the `newTriangles` list.

The method finishes by looping through the new triangles and adding them to the mesh.

Example Program

The GeodesicSphere example program uses the following remarkably short code to build a scene containing nine geodesic spheres with different levels of refinement.

```
private void DefineModel(Model3DGroup group)
{
    MeshGeometry3D mesh0 = new MeshGeometry3D();
    double radius = 1;
    double spacing = 2 * radius + 0.1;
    int numRows = 1;
    for (int i = 0; i < 3; i++)
    {
        for (int j = 0; j < 3; j++)
        {
            Point3D center = new Point3D((i - 1) * spacing, 0, (j - 1) * spacing);
            mesh0.AddGeodesicSphere(center, radius, numRows++);
        }
    }
    group.Children.Add(mesh0.MakeModel(Brushes.LightBlue));

    MeshGeometry3D mesh1 =
        mesh0.ToWireframe(0.01);
    group.Children.Add(
        mesh1.MakeModel(Brushes.Blue));
}
```

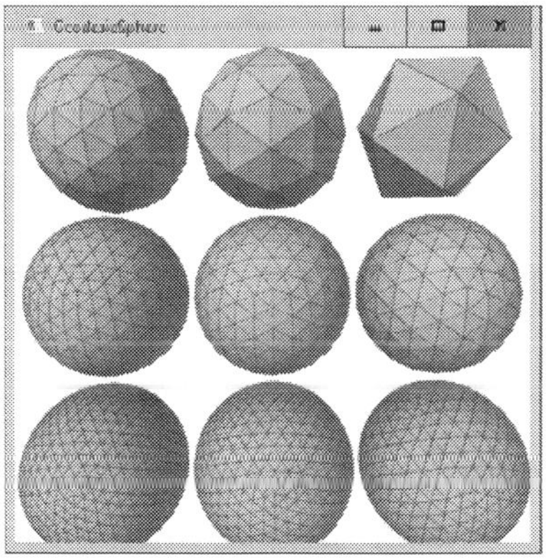

Figure 24-6: This program displays nine geodesic spheres.

This method creates a mesh and defines some constants. It then loops over variables `i` and `j` to make three rows and columns. For each `i` and `j` value, the code makes a geodesic sphere with one more row of subdivisions than the previous one. Figure 25-6 shows the GeodesicSphere program displaying its scene.

The least subdivided version is in the upper right corner. In that solid, the number subdivision rows was one, so each of the icosahedron's faces was divided into a single triangle, leaving the original icosahedron unchanged.

The most subdivided solid is in the lower left corner. In that solid, the number subdivision rows was nine, so each of the icosahedron's faces was divided into 9×9=81 sub-triangles. That gives the solid a total of 20×81=1,620 faces.

NOTE: If you look closely at a geodesic solid, you can find the places where the original triangles were subdivided. For example, in an icosahedron, the corners are places where five triangles meet. When you subdivide a triangle, the new sub-triangles meet in groups of six instead of five. If you look for them, you can still find the places where original sets of five triangles meet.

Figure 24-7 shows an icosahedron and a geodesic version with two subdivision rows. The thick lines show the sub-triangles that correspond to one of the icosahedron's original faces.

Corners that correspond to those in the original icosahedron are shared by five triangles. Corners that do not correspond to original corners are shared by six triangles.

You can find similar meeting places for geodesic spheres of higher degrees or built with different originating solids.

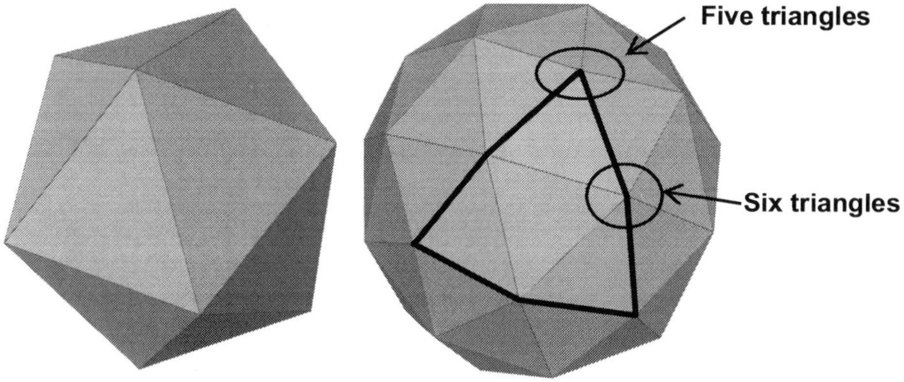

Figure 24-7: If you look closely, you can spot the original icosahedron's triangles.

Summary

This chapter explained how to create geodesic spheres. The idea may seem complicated at first, but the `Triangle` class's `DivideGeodesic` method makes it fairly easy. In fact, you should be able to use that method to make your own routines for creating geodesic spheres starting from tetrahedrons or octahedrons. With a little extra work, you should also be able to make geodesic spheres starting from cubes or dodecahedrons.

One of the key techniques for building geodesic spheres is projecting points from a center onto a sphere. The next chapter uses a similar technique to make stellate solids: solids where the faces have been drawn out to form peaks, giving the solid a star-like appearance.

Chapter 25

Stellate Solids

Without getting too technical, a *stellate polyhedron* is a solid where each of the faces has been replaced with a pyramid to make a star-like solid. The following section discusses stellate polyhedrons in general. The rest of the chapter explains how you can make different kinds of stellate polyhedrons in WPF.

Stellate Polyhedrons

More precisely, a stellate polyhedron is a solid where the edges or faces are extended until they meet to create a new shape. For example, you can extend the faces of an octahedron to create the stellate octahedron shown in Figure 25-1.

Figure 25-1: You can extend an octahedron's faces to make a stellate version.

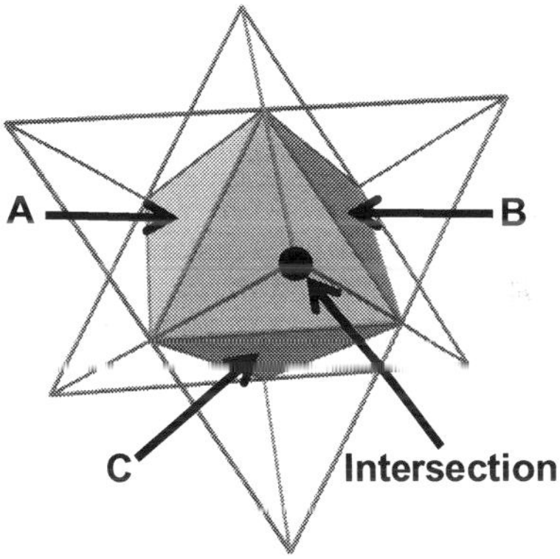

Figure 25-2: Three non-parallel planes intersect at a single point.

Figure 25-2 shows the original octahedron shaded and the stellate version as a wireframe. The octahedron's faces labeled A, B, and C intersect at the indicated point. That point forms one of the vertices of the stellate octahedron.

> **NOTE:** This is pretty hard to visualize on a two-dimensional picture. To understand it better, you could dig out your old *Dungeons & Dragons*

equipment and take a good look at the eight-sided dice. While you're at it, you may as well look at the 12- and 20-sided dice, too.

If you use the technical definition that uses intersecting faces, you cannot make a stellate tetrahedron. Because all of its faces are already touching, you cannot extend them to make them intersect in new ways.

You also cannot make a stellate cube because the faces that are not already touching are parallel so their extensions can't intersect.

There's only one way to make a stellate octahedron and it's shown in Figure 25-1.

NOTE: If you're collecting interesting vocabulary words, the stellate octahedron is also called the *stella octangula*, which sounds to me like the nightmare offspring of an octopus and a tarantula.

There are three ways you can make stellate dodecahedrons and 58 ways you can make a stellate icosahedron, depending on which faces you extend. The following table summarizes the number of stellate polyhedrons you can make for each of the Platonic solids. The URLs in the final column lead to Wolfram MathWorld pages that show pictures of the stellations.

Platonic Solid	Number of Stellations	Reference
Tetrahedron	0	
Cube	0	
Octahedron	1	`tinyurl.com/km5w7p7`
Dodecahedron	3	`tinyurl.com/ya9s9m9o`
Icosahedron	58	`tinyurl.com/ya3qfdft`

Note that in some of the stellations the faces are extended *into* the original solid instead of outward away from it. That produces some interesting concave shapes.

Technically, you build stellate solids by extending the faces until they intersect, but that's fairly hard to do in general. For the octahedron, you need to find the equations representing the planes containing the appropriate trios of faces, find their points of intersection, and use them to build the new faces. For the icosahedron, even figuring out which faces to intersect would be difficult.

A much easier strategy is to replace the solid's faces with pyramids or inverted pyramids. That lets you create some of the stellate Platonic solids and easily produce some results that are interesting even if not technically stellate. The rest of this chapter explains how you can build those kinds of solids.

Pyramids

The previous chapter projected the vertices of sub-triangles onto a sphere. You can use a similar technique to make pyramids to replace a solid's faces.

First, find the center of a face by averaging its vertices. Next, project that point some distance away from the center of the original solid to get the pyramid's apex. Now use the apex and the original face's vertices to build the pyramid.

This is pretty easy for the octahedron and icosahedron where the faces are triangles. You can use the same technique to build a pseudo-stellate version of the tetrahedron.

You could even modify the `Triangle` class described in the previous chapter so a `Triangle` object could make the face pyramids. Unfortunately, the cube and dodecahedron don't have triangular faces, so putting this functionality in the `Triangle` class won't help with them. To make working with the cube and dodecahedron easier, I created the following new `Polygon` class.

```
// Hold points that make up a polygon.
public class Polygon
{
    public List<Point3D> Points = null;

    // Copy the points into the Points list.
    public Polygon(params Point3D[] points)
    {
        Points = new List<Point3D>(points);
    }

    // Create triangles for stellation.
    public List<Triangle> MakeStellateTriangles(Point3D center, double radius)
    {
        // Find the polygon's center.
        Point3D pgonCenter = Center;

        // Find the unit vector from the stellar center to the polygon's center.
        Vector3D v = pgonCenter - center;

        // Find the pyramid's apex.
        Point3D apex = center + v / v.Length * radius;

        // Make a pyramid with this polygon as its base and the calculated apex.
        List<Triangle> triangles = new List<Triangle>();
        int numPoints = Points.Count;
        for (int i = 0; i < numPoints; i++)
        {
            int i1 = (i + 1) % numPoints;
            triangles.Add(new Triangle(Points[i], Points[i1], apex));
        }
```

```
            return triangles;
        }

        // Find the polygon's center by averaging its vertices.
        public Point3D Center
        {
            get
            {
                Point3D center = new Point3D();
                foreach (Point3D point in Points)
                {
                    center.X += point.X;
                    center.Y += point.Y;
                    center.Z += point.Z;
                }
                int numPoints = Points.Count;
                center.X /= numPoints;
                center.Y /= numPoints;
                center.Z /= numPoints;
                return center;
            }
        }
    }
```

This class holds its vertices in a list of `Point3D` structures. Its constructor simply copies a variable number of points into that list.

The `MakeStellateTriangles` method creates the triangles that define a pyramid for the polygon. The `center` parameter indicates the center of the solid. The `radius` parameter indicates the distance away from the solid's center that the pyramid's apex should be moved.

The method first uses the `Center` property described shortly to find the polygon's center. It subtracts the solid's center to get a vector pointing from the solid's center to the polygon's center.

The code then scales that vector so it has the length `radius`, the desired distance from the solid's center to the pyramid's apex. The method then adds the vector to the solid's center to find the apex point.

Next, the method loops through the polygon's vertices, using them to create the pyramid's triangles. (This is very similar to the technique used by the `AddPyramid` method described in Chapter 13. If it's not clear, look at the section "Adding Pyramids" in that chapter.) The method finishes by returning the list of pyramid triangles.

The `Polygon` class's `Center` property simply returns the average of the points' X, Y, and Z coordinates. It loops through the points, adds their corresponding coordinates, divides the totals by the number of points, and returns a new point with those coordinates. This gives a point at the center of the polygon.

> **NOTE:** If the polygon's points are all coplanar, and they should be if this is truly a polygon and not some sort of bent potato chip shape, then the center point is in the same plane as the polygon's points.

Now that you have a `Polygon` class that can build pyramids, using it is easy. The following sections explain how you can use that class to build stellate octahedrons, dodecahedrons, and geodesic spheres.

Stellate Octahedrons

The `Polygon` class makes it pleasantly easy to build stellate polyhedrons. The following code shows the `AddStellateOctahedron` mesh extension method.

```
public static void AddStellateOctahedron(this MeshGeometry3D mesh,
    double starRadius, HashSet<Edge> edges = null, double thickness = 0.1)
{
    // Get the octahedron's points.
    Point3D A, B, C, D, E, F;
    G3.OctahedronPoints(out A, out B, out C, out D, out E, out F);

    // Make face polygons.
    List<Polygon> polygons = new List<Polygon>();
    polygons.Add(new Polygon(A, B, C));
    polygons.Add(new Polygon(A, C, D));
    polygons.Add(new Polygon(A, D, E));
    polygons.Add(new Polygon(A, E, B));
    polygons.Add(new Polygon(F, B, E));
    polygons.Add(new Polygon(F, C, B));
    polygons.Add(new Polygon(F, D, C));
    polygons.Add(new Polygon(F, E, D));

    // Stellify the faces.
    List<Triangle> triangles = new List<Triangle>();
    foreach (Polygon polygon in polygons)
    {
        triangles.AddRange(polygon.MakeStellateTriangles(D3.Origin, starRadius));
    }

    // Add triangles to the mesh.
    foreach (Triangle triangle in triangles)
        mesh.AddPolygon(edges, thickness, triangle.Points.ToArray());
}
```

This method parallels the `AddOctahedron` method closely. In fact, I considered modifying that method to allow it to make stellate solids, but I felt that would have made the method too complicated and unfocused.

The code first calls `G3.OctahedronPoints` to get the points that make up an octahedron. Next, the code makes a list of `Polygon` objects representing the octahedron's faces. This code is very similar to the code that the `AddOctahedron` method uses to create the octahedron's face triangles.

The code then loops through the polygons and calls their `MakeStellateTriangles` methods to make their pyramids. It adds the pyramids' triangular faces to the new `triangles` list.

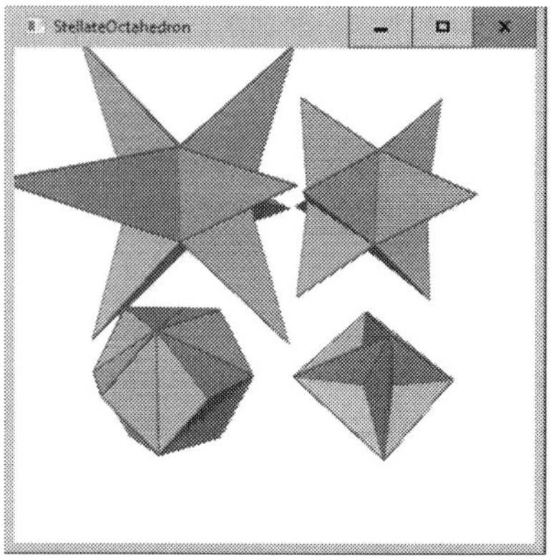

Figure 25-3: These stellate octahedrons use star radii of three, two, one, and 0.3.

Finally, the method loops through the triangles and adds them to the mesh. The result is the stellate solid.

Figure 25-3 shows the StellateOctahedron example program displaying four stellate octahedrons. The solid in the upper left pushes its outer vertices a distance of three from the center of the solid. This is relatively far compared to the distance of one between the octahedron's vertices and the origin, so the result is relatively spiky.

The solid in the upper right uses a star radius of two, so the result is still fairly spiky. This is only slightly farther than the distance used to make the technically correct stellate octahedron so it looks a lot like the stella octangula.

The third solid has an outer radius of one, so the pyramids only poke up a bit beyond the faces of the original octahedron.

The final solid has a star radius of 0.3, so the pyramids push inward and make concavities in the original octahedron.

Stellate Dodecahedrons

The `AddStellateDodecahedron` method shown in the following code uses the same technique used by the `AddStellateOctahedron` methhod.

```
public static void AddStellateDodecahedron(this MeshGeometry3D mesh,
    double starRadius, HashSet<Edge> edges = null, double thickness = 0.1)
{
    // Get the points.
    Point3D A, B, C, D, E, F, G, H, I, J, K, L, M, N, O, P, Q, R, S, T;
    G3.DodecahedronPoints(
        out A, out B, out C, out D, out E,
        out F, out G, out H, out I, out J,
        out K, out L, out M, out N, out O,
        out P, out Q, out R, out S, out T);

    // Make face polygons.
    List<Polygon> polygons = new List<Polygon>();
    polygons.Add(new Polygon(E, D, C, B, A));
    polygons.Add(new Polygon(A, B, G, K, F));
    polygons.Add(new Polygon(A, F, O, J, E));
    polygons.Add(new Polygon(E, J, N, I, D));
```

```
        polygons.Add(new Polygon(D, I, M, H, C));
        polygons.Add(new Polygon(C, H, L, G, B));
        polygons.Add(new Polygon(K, P, T, O, F));
        polygons.Add(new Polygon(O, T, S, N, J));
        polygons.Add(new Polygon(N, S, R, M, I));
        polygons.Add(new Polygon(M, R, Q, L, H));
        polygons.Add(new Polygon(L, Q, P, K, G));
        polygons.Add(new Polygon(P, Q, R, S, T));

        // Stellify the faces.
        List<Triangle> triangles = new List<Triangle>();
        foreach (Polygon polygon in polygons)
        {
            triangles.AddRange(polygon.MakeStellateTriangles(D3.Origin, starRadius));
        }

        // Add triangles to the mesh.
        foreach (Triangle triangle in triangles)
            mesh.AddPolygon(edges, thickness, triangle.Points.ToArray());
    }
```

This code uses the `G3.DodecahedronPoints` method to get the dodecahedron's vertices. It then adds them to a list of `Polygon` objects representing the solid's faces. It loops through the `Polygon` objects, calls their `MakeStellateTriangles` methods, and adds the resulting triangles to a list. Finally, it loops through the list, adding the triangles to the mesh.

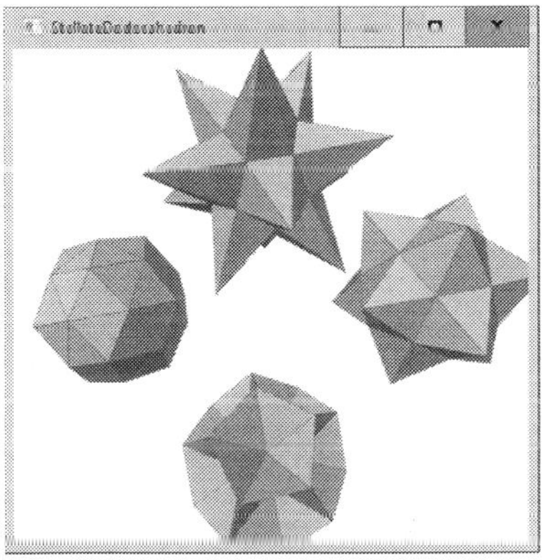

Figure 25-4: These stellate octahedrons use star radii of six, four, three, and one.

The StellateDodecahedron example program shown in Figure 25-4 builds four stellate dodecahedrons using star radii of six, four, three, and one.

Notice that the solid on the left looks a lot like a geodesic sphere. Its star radius, three, is close to the circumradius of the dodecahedron so it is close to a geodesic sphere built starting with a dodecahedron.

Stellate Geodesic Spheres

The code described in the previous sections makes stellate solids by starting with Platonic solids and replacing their faces with pyramids. There's no reason why you can't use the same approach to make any other solid stellate. The following method uses the same basic approach as the previous methods, this time to build a stellate geodesic sphere.

```
    // Make a stellate geodesic sphere without texture coordinates or smoothing.
    public static void AddStellateGeodesicSphere(this MeshGeometry3D mesh,
        Point3D center, double radius, int numDivisions, double starRadius,
        HashSet<Edge> edges = null, double thickness = 0.1)
    {
```

```
        // Create an icosahedron.
        // Get the points.
        Point3D A, B, C, D, E, F, G, H, I, J, K, L;
        G3.IcosahedronPoints(
            out A, out B, out C, out D, out E, out F,
            out G, out H, out I, out J, out K, out L);

        // Scale the icosahedron to the proper radius and center it.
        double scale = radius / G3.IcosahedronCircumradius();
        ScaleTransform3D scaleT = new ScaleTransform3D(scale, scale, scale);
        TranslateTransform3D translateT =
            new TranslateTransform3D(center.X, center.Y, center.Z);
        Transform3DGroup groupT = new Transform3DGroup();
        groupT.Children.Add(scaleT);
        groupT.Children.Add(translateT);
        A = groupT.Transform(A);
        B = groupT.Transform(B);
        ...
        L = groupT.Transform(L);

        // Make the icosahedron's faces.
        List<Triangle> triangles = new List<Triangle>();
        triangles.Add(new Triangle(A, C, B));
        triangles.Add(new Triangle(A, D, C));
        triangles.Add(new Triangle(A, E, D));
        ...
        triangles.Add(new Triangle(L, K, G));

        // Subdivide the faces as desired.
        List<Triangle> newTriangles = new List<Triangle>();
        foreach (Triangle triangle in triangles)
        {
            // Subdivide this triangle and add the results to newTriangles.
            newTriangles.AddRange(triangle.DivideGeodesic(center, radius, numDivisions));
        }

        // Convert the triangles into polygons.
        List<Polygon> polygons = new List<Polygon>();
        foreach (Triangle triangle in newTriangles)
            polygons.Add(new Polygon(triangle.Points.ToArray()));

        // Stellify the triangles.
        List<Triangle> stellateTriangles = new List<Triangle>();
        foreach (Polygon polygon in polygons)
        {
            stellateTriangles.AddRange(polygon.MakeStellateTriangles(center, starRadius));
        }

        // Add triangles to the mesh.
        foreach (Triangle triangle in stellateTriangles)
            mesh.AddPolygon(edges, thickness, triangle.Points.ToArray());
    }
```

The code starts by using the `G3.IcosahedronPoints` method to get points to define an icosahedron. It positions and scales the points to put them where they should go.

Next, the code creates `Triangle` objects to represent the icosahedron's faces. It loops through the triangles and calls their `DivideGeodesic` methods to create the triangles that make up the geodesic sphere. So far, this code is similar to the code used by the `AddGeodesicSphere` method to create a geodesic sphere.

At this point, the code converts the triangles into `Polygon` objects. It then loops through the polygons, calling their `MakeStellateTriangles` methods and adding the resulting triangles to a new list. Finally, the code loops through the list and adds the triangles to the mesh.

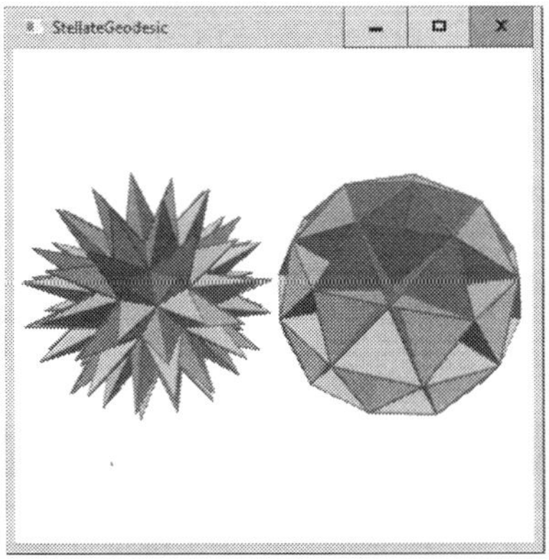

Figure 25-5: These stellate geodesic spheres use star radii of 2 and 0.5.

The StellateGeodesicSphere example program shown in Figure 25-5 uses this method to make two stellate solids with star radii two and 0.5.

Example Program

The three example programs, StellateOctahedron, StellateDodecahedron, and StellateGeodesicSphere, use similar code to build their scenes. The following code shows how the `StellateGeodesicSphere` program makes its objects. The other programs are similar.

```
private void DefineModel(Model3DGroup group)
{
    MeshGeometry3D mesh1 = new MeshGeometry3D();
    mesh1.AddStellateGeodesicSphere(new Point3D(-2, 0, 0), 1, 2, 2);
    group.Children.Add(mesh1.MakeModel(Brushes.LightBlue));
    MeshGeometry3D mesh1a = mesh1.ToWireframe(0.02);
    group.Children.Add(mesh1a.MakeModel(Brushes.Blue));

    MeshGeometry3D mesh2 = new MeshGeometry3D();
    mesh2.AddStellateGeodesicSphere(new Point3D(2, 0, 0), 2, 2, 0.5);
    group.Children.Add(mesh2.MakeModel(Brushes.LightBlue));
    MeshGeometry3D mesh2a = mesh2.ToWireframe(0.02);
    group.Children.Add(mesh2a.MakeModel(Brushes.Blue));
}
```

This code creates a mesh and then calls the `AddStellateGeodesicSphere` method. It centers the resulting solid at (-2, 0, 0), gives the initial sphere a radius of 1, and uses two rows of subdivisions when building the geodesic sphere. The final "2" in the argument list gives the star radius. Because that radius is greater than the sphere's radius of one, the final solid is spiky.

After it creates the first solid, the code turns it into a light blue model. It then calls the mesh's `ToWireframe` method to build a wireframe for the solid and makes that into a blue model.

The program then repeats the same steps to make a second solid with geodesic sphere radius 2 and star radius 0.5. Because the star radius is smaller than the geodesic sphere radius, the stellate pyramids poke down into the solid and make concavities.

Summary

This chapter showed how to use a technique similar to the one used to make geodesic spheres to add stellation to a solid. The technique described here doesn't necessarily produce "true" stellation because it doesn't extend the solid's faces to find their points of intersection, but it does produce some interesting results.

The next chapter leaves the topic of polyhedrons for the moment to describe surfaces.

Chapter 26
Surfaces

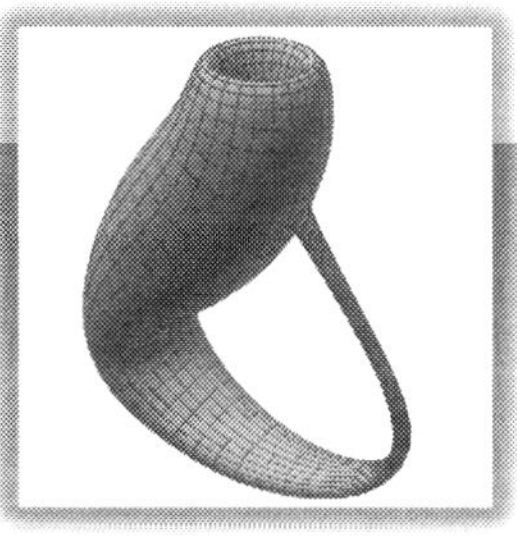

Mathematically speaking, a *surface* is a set of points that has length and breadth but no thickness. A surface can define two sides like a sheet, or it can enclose one or more volumes like the surface of a balloon.

This chapter explains how you can display surfaces in WPF. It also describes some fairly interesting examples.

Surfaces

Chapter 7 showed practically in passing how to create a surface so it could demonstrate a textured material on a large area. Figure 26-1 shows Chapter 7s Materials example program displaying a surface with a diffuse texture and a specular material.

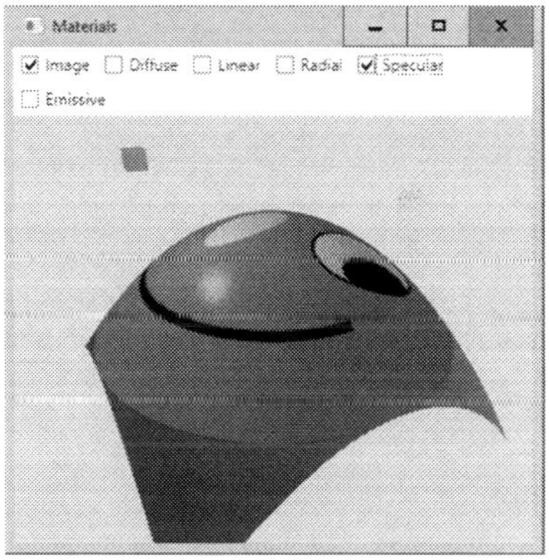

Figure 26-1: This example applies a texture to a surface.

The following `AddSurface` method uses a similar technique to add a surface to a mesh.

```
public static void AddSurface(this MeshGeometry3D mesh,
    Func<double, double, Point3D> F,
    double xmin, double xmax, int numX,
    double zmin, double zmax, int numZ,
    bool smooth = false,
    HashSet<Edge> edges = null, double thickness = 0.1,
    Point[] textureCoords = null)
{
    // Make a point dictionary if desired.
    Dictionary<Point3D, int> pointDict = null;
    if (smooth) pointDict = new Dictionary<Point3D, int>();

    // Generate the surface's points.
    double dx = (xmax - xmin) / numX;
    double dz = (zmax - zmin) / numZ;
    double x = xmin;
    for (int ix = 0; ix < numX; ix++)
    {
        double z = zmin;
        for (int iz = 0; iz < numZ; iz++)
        {
            Point3D p1 = F(x, z);
            Point3D p2 = F(x, z + dz);
            Point3D p3 = F(x + dx, z + dz);
            Point3D p4 = F(x + dx, z);
```

```
                mesh.AddPolygon(pointDict, edges, thickness,
                    textureCoords, p1, p2, p3, p4);
                z += dz;
            }
            x += dx;
        }
    }
```

The method's first parameter is the mesh that is executing the method. The second parameter `F` has the type `Func`. This is a generic type defined in the `System` namespace that represents a method that returns some value. The generic parameters give the data types of the method's parameters and return type. In this example, the parameter declaration `Func<double, double, Point3D> F` means `F` is a method that takes two `double` parameters and returns a `Point3D`.

You can think of `F` as a function F(x, z) that returns a Y coordinate for a point on a surface above the point (x, z). You'll see later in this chapter that this doesn't always need to be the case, but that assumption makes it easier to visualize how the `AddSurface` method works.

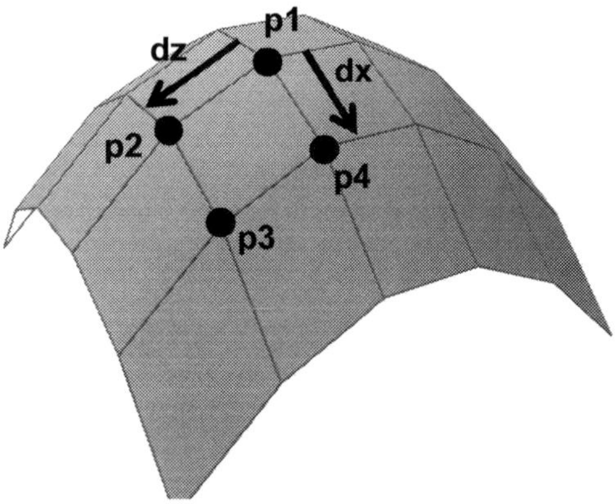

Figure 26-2: Vectors dx and dz let you find X and Z coordinates for the points p2, p3, and p4.

The rest of the method's parameters give the bounds over which X and Z should range, the number of pieces the surface should be broken into in the X and Z directions, and other values that should be familiar from previous examples.

If the method should draw a smooth surface, it starts by creating a point dictionary. It then calculates vectors `dx` and `dz` that it can use to move in the X and Z directions to break the area into the desired number of pieces.

The code then loops over the desired number of steps in the X and Z directions. As the loops progress, the code updates variables `x` and `z` to keep track of a point within the XZ plane. For each such point, the method uses the function `F` to get the point on the surface above that position and at three nearby positions as shown in Figure 26-2. The code then uses the `AddPolygon` method to add the four points `p1`, `p2`, `p3`, and `p4` to the mesh. The `AddPolygon` method makes the surface smooth and produces a wireframe if desired.

> **NOTE:** The four points in Figure 26-2 look like they make up a rectangle, or at least a trapezoid, but in general they will not be coplanar so they actually define a sort of bent potato chip shape.

Notice that the four points p1, p2, p3, and p4 are "upward oriented" in Figure 26-2. That means the triangles that they define will be visible when seen from the top. If you want to be able to view the surface from the bottom, or if the function `F` produces points in the opposite orientation, you need to set the model's `BackMaterial` property. You'll see some examples of that later in this chapter.

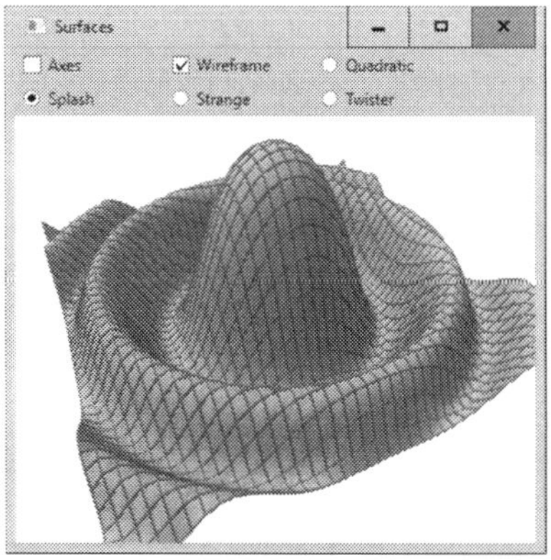

Figure 26-3: The Surfaces example program uses the AddSurface method to display several surfaces.

The `AddSurface` method is not only relatively straightforward but it's also quite flexible. The Surfaces example program shown in Figure 26-3 uses it to display a variety of surfaces. When you check or uncheck one of the program's checkboxes, or when you click on a radio button, the program rebuilds its scene so it includes the items that you've selected. Download the example and experiment with it to see what the other surfaces look like.

The following code snippet shows how the Surfaces example program displays the items that you've selected.

```
private void DefineModel()
{
    // Remove non-light models.
    for (int i = ModelGroup.Children.Count - 1; i >= 0; i--)
    {
        if (!(ModelGroup.Children[i] is Light))
            ModelGroup.Children.RemoveAt(i);
    }

    // Axes.
    if (axesCheckBox.IsChecked.Value)
        MeshExtensions.AddAxes(ModelGroup);

    // Add the selected surface.
    HashSet<Edge> edges = new HashSet<Edge>();
    MeshGeometry3D mesh1 = new MeshGeometry3D();
    MeshGeometry3D mesh1a = new MeshGeometry3D();
    if (quadraticRadioButton.IsChecked.Value)
    {
        ...
    }
    else if (splashRadioButton.IsChecked.Value)
    {
        if (wireframeCheckBox.IsChecked.Value)
        {
            mesh1.AddSurface(Splash, -3, 3, 40, -3, 3, 40, true);
            mesh1a.AddSurface(Splash, -3, 3, 40, -3, 3, 40, false, edges, 0.02);
        }
```

```
            else
                mesh1.AddSurface(Splash, -3, 3, 100, -3, 3, 100, true);
        }
        else if (strangeRadioButton.IsChecked.Value)
        {
            ...
        }
        else if (twisterRadioButton.IsChecked.Value)
        {
            ...
        }

        ModelGroup.Children.Add(mesh1.MakeModel(Brushes.LightBlue));
        if (wireframeCheckBox.IsChecked.Value)
            ModelGroup.Children.Add(mesh1a.MakeModel(Brushes.Blue));
    }
```

The method first loops through the children of the program's main model group and removes any children that are not lights. That gets rid of the previously displayed axes, surface, and wireframe.

Notice that the code loops through the children from the back of the collection to the front. That allows it to remove some children without messing up the indices of the remaining children.

Next, if the axes checkbox is checked, the code builds the coordinate axes.

The code then creates a `HashSet` of edges in case it needs it. It also makes two meshes, one for the surface and one for the wireframe.

The method then performs a sequence of `if-then-else` tests to see which surface you selected. They're all pretty similar so I've omitted their code except for the splash surface.

If the Splash radio button is selected, the code checks the Wireframe checkbox. If that box is checked, the program calls `AddSurface` twice, once to build the surface mesh and once to make the wireframe. If the Wireframe checkbox is not checked, the program only builds the surface mesh.

Notice that the code passes the `Splash` method into `AddSurface` as a parameter. That method is shown shortly.

Notice also that the parameters are not the same in the two calls that build the surface. When the wireframe is present, the program divides the X and Z values into 40 pieces and the result looks smooth enough because the wireframe covers small bumps. If the wireframe is omitted, the program divides the X and Z values into 100 pieces to make the surface look smoother.

The method finishes by adding whichever meshes it created to the main model group.

The following code shows the functions that the Surfaces program uses to generate its surfaces.

```
private Point3D Quadratic(double x, double z)
{
    double y = 3.0 - (x * x + z * z) / 5.0;
    return new Point3D(x, y, z);
}

private Point3D Splash(double x, double z)
{
    double r2 = x * x + z * z;
    double y = 1 + 4 * Math.Cos(r2) / (2 + r2);
    return new Point3D(x, y, z);
}

private Point3D Strange(double x, double z)
{
    double r2 = (x * x + z * z) / 4;
    double r = Math.Sqrt(r2);

    double theta = Math.Atan2(z, x);
    double y = 3 * Math.Exp(-r2) * Math.Sin(2 * Math.PI * r) * Math.Cos(3 * theta);
    return new Point3D(x, y, z);
}

private Point3D Twister(double u, double v)
{
    double r2 = (u * u + v * v) / 4;
    double r = Math.Sqrt(r2);

    double y = 2 - 1 / (r + 0.0001);
    double x = u * Math.Cos(r) - v * Math.Sin(r);
    double z = u * Math.Sin(r) + v * Math.Cos(r);
    return new Point3D(x, y, z);
}
```

You can look over these methods to see how they generate the points on their surfaces. Download the Surfaces example program to see additional details about how it works and to see what the different surfaces look like.

Data Surfaces

Sometimes you may not have a function y = F(x, z) that generates a surface. Instead, you may have an array containing points that should be converted into a surface. The following version of the AddSurface method performs the conversion.

```
// Make a surface defined by a 2D array of points.
public static void AddSurface(this MeshGeometry3D mesh,
    Point3D[,] points, bool smooth = false,
    HashSet<Edge> edges = null, double thickness = 0.1,
    Point[] textureCoords = null)
{
    // Make a point dictionary if desired.
    Dictionary<Point3D, int> pointDict = null;
    if (smooth) pointDict = new Dictionary<Point3D, int>();

    // See how many pieces there are.
```

```
        int numX = points.GetUpperBound(0);
        int numZ = points.GetUpperBound(1);

        // Build the pieces.
        for (int ix = 0; ix < numX; ix++)
        {
            for (int iz = 0; iz < numZ; iz++)
            {
                Point3D p1 = points[ix, iz];
                Point3D p2 = points[ix, iz + 1];
                Point3D p3 = points[ix + 1, iz + 1];
                Point3D p4 = points[ix + 1, iz];
                mesh.AddPolygon(pointDict, edges, thickness, textureCoords,
                    p1, p2, p3, p4);
            }
        }
    }
```

This method uses roughly the same approach as the previous version. If it should produce a smooth surface, it creates a point dictionary. It then loops through the values and calls the mesh's `AddPolygon` extension method to create the surface's polygons.

This may be a brute-force approach, but it's also very flexible. Depending on the application, it may be a lot of work building the array of points, but this method lets you position every point exactly where you want it.

Parametric Surfaces

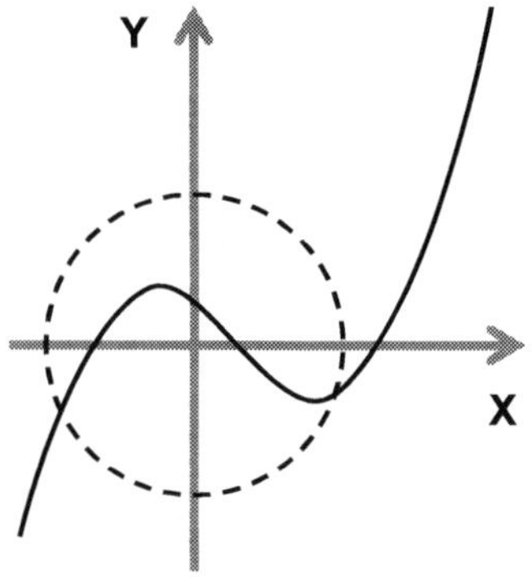

Figure 26-4: The solid curve is a function but the dashed curve is not.

The Surfaces example program displays surfaces that are mathematical functions of the form y = F(x, z) for some function F, although F can admittedly can be a rather complicated function.

However, surfaces don't always need to follow that simple format. The method that you pass into `AddSurface` as a parameter returns a `Point3D` and not a simple Y coordinate. That means the surface doesn't really need to be a simple function of two variables in the mathematical sense.

If that seems confusing, drop down to two dimensions for a moment and consider the two-dimensional graph shown in Figure 26-4. The solid curve is a function y = F(x). For each x value, there is (at most) one y value.

The dashed curve is not a function of the form y = F(x) because, for each x value, it may have more than one y value. It's also not a function of the form x = F(y) because, for each y value, it may have more than one x value.

You cannot write the dashed curve as a function, but you can write is as a parametric curve. In a *parametric curve*, you use separate equations to define the X and Y coordinates of the points on the curve. For the circle shown in Figure 26-4, you could use the following parametric equations.

$$x(t) = \cos(t)$$

$$y(t) = \sin(t)$$

Here t is the parameter of the equations. If you plug in values for t, you can generate points on the curve.

For a closed curve such as this one, you can generate the whole curve by plugging in values for t ranging from 0 to 2π. If you go beyond that range, the curve repeats.

Now let's jump back up to three dimensions. Just as you can use two parametric equations to define a curve in two dimensions, you can also use three parametric equations to define a surface in three dimensions.

For example, the following equations generate a sphere with radius R.

$$x = R\cos(\theta)\sin(\varphi)$$

$$y = R\sin(\theta)\sin(\varphi)$$

$$z = R\cos(\varphi)$$

Here the parameters θ and φ range over the values $0 \le \theta \le 2\pi$ and $0 \le \varphi \le \pi$. If you use more values for θ and φ, you just generate duplicates of points that you've already seen. (Just like you repeat points on the circle x=cos(t), y=sin(t) if t exceeds its range 0 to 2π.)

By using parametric equations of two variables, you can generate three-dimensional surfaces. The next section explains how you can do that in a WPF program.

Complex Surfaces

You can use parametric equations with two parameters to generate surfaces. The `AddSurface` method already takes as a parameter a function that uses two parameters as inputs and produces a point as an output. That means the `AddSurface` method is already set up to generate parametric surfaces.

The method calls its parameters `x` and `z`, but it doesn't really matter what they are called inside the parametric function. They could represent θ and φ or `t1` and `t2` if that makes more sense for a particular parametric surface, but the `AddSurface` method can still call them `x` and `z`.

For example, the following parametric equations generate an ellipsoid.

$$x(\theta, \varphi) = 3\cos(\theta)\cos(\varphi)$$

$$y(\theta, \varphi) = 1\sin(\theta)$$

$$z(\theta, \varphi) = 2\cos(\theta)\sin(\varphi)$$

Where $-\pi/2 \leq \theta \leq \pi/2$ and $-\pi \leq \varphi \leq \pi$.

The following method uses those equations to convert `theta` and `phi` values into points on the surface.

```
private Point3D Ellipsoid(double theta, double phi)
{
    double x = 3 * Math.Cos(theta) * Math.Cos(phi);
    double y = 1 * Math.Sin(theta);
    double z = 2 * Math.Cos(theta) * Math.Sin(phi);

    return new Point3D(x, y, z);
}
```

The `AddSurface` method passes `x` and `z` values into the method. Internally the method treats those values as `theta` and `phi` and carries out its business with `AddSurface` none the wiser.

The ParametricSurfaces example program shown in Figure 26-5 uses this approach to generate its surfaces. The code is almost exactly the same as the code used by the Surfaces program except it uses different surface functions and different parameters for the `AddSurface` method.

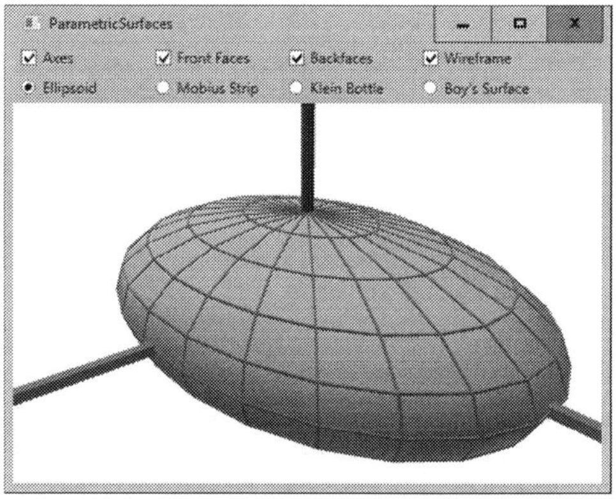

Figure 26-5: This program displays parametric surfaces.

Non-Orientable Surfaces

The surfaces shown so far have been relatively well-behaved in the senses that their generating functions can return triangles that are oriented consistently. For example, the Splash surface shown in Figure 26-3 has a clear top and bottom. Similarly, the ellipsoid shown in Figure 26-5 has a clear inside and outside.

Because you can define consistent surface normals for these surfaces, they are called *orientable surfaces*.

Some surfaces, however, have no consistent orientation. For example, you may be familiar with the Möbius strip shown in Figure 26-6. If you stand on the center of the strip and start walking down its surface lengthwise, you would wrap around to the "other side" of the strip and end up standing upside down opposite the point where you started. If you continued walking, you would eventually come back to your starting point, having traversed "both" sides of the strip.

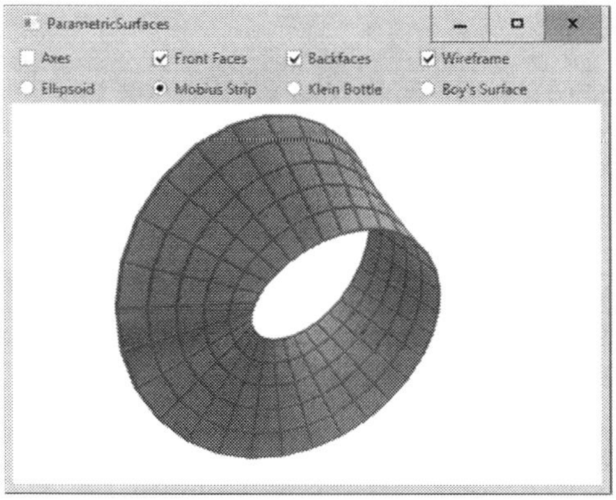

Figure 26-6: The Möbius strip is non-orientable.

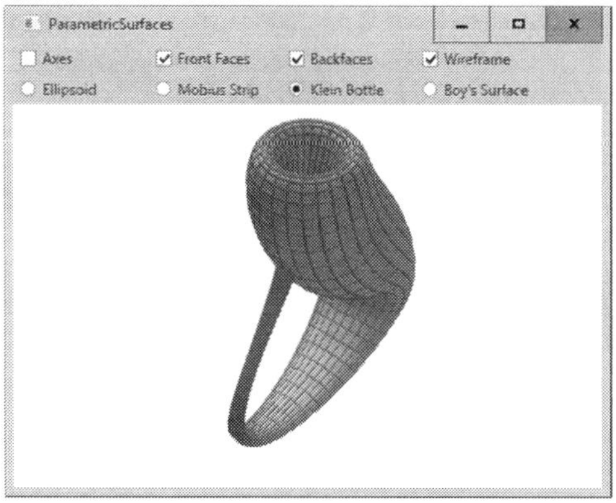

Figure 26-7: The Klein bottle is also non-orientable.

This means you cannot define a consistent "top" and "bottom" for the Möbius strip. If you start walking on the "top" of the strip, then you eventually also end up walking on its other side so that must also be the "top." This kind of surface that you cannot orient is, predictably enough, called a *non-orientable surface*.

NOTE: The Möbius strip is named after the German mathematician August Ferdinand Möbius who discovered it in 1858. Apparently another German mathematician, Johann Benedict Listing, discovered the strip independently a few months earlier, but the surface bears Möbius's name. (Perhaps he had a better public relations firm.)

For a neat party trick, you can build a Möbius strip by taking a strip of paper, twisting the ends so they are offset by 180°, and then taping the ends together. This works best if you use a fairly long piece of paper (perhaps newspaper) about two inches wide and you tape the entire seam on both sides.

Next, put the strip on a table and place a pencil on the middle of the strip. Hold the pencil down as you slide the strip between the pencil and the table. You should be able to draw all the way around the strip and return to your starting point without lifting the pencil. At this point, show everyone that "both" sides of the paper have been marked and wait for the gasps of amazement to die down. Then say, "But wait, there's more!"

Tell people that you are going to take a pair of scissors and cut down the middle of the paper along the line that you drew. Ask people what they think will happen. In particular, will the paper fall into two pieces?

When you try it, you'll find that the result is a single, longer loop of paper with two full twists in it. Now ask for predictions and then draw along one side of the strip again. This time you return to your starting point *without* covering both sides of the paper. Now the strip truly has two sides so it is orientable.

Ask for predictions again (if everyone hasn't wandered off to find snacks) and cut the strip in half again lengthwise. This time you're left with two separate strips that are interlocked in a complicated way. They are also each similar to the loop that you just cut: they each have two sides and two twists.

The Klein bottle shown in Figure 26-7 is also non-orientable because it doesn't have an identifiable inside and outside. Imagine standing on the "outside" of the bottle near the top and then walking along the surface into the opening. That opening leads into the thin tube on the left, so you end up walking on the inside of the tube. That tube curves around to become the bigger part of the bottle's body, so eventually you wind up walking on the "inside" of the larger part, near the "outside" point where you started. If you continue walking in a "straight" line (if you can define "straight" on a Klein bottle), you eventually end up back where you started.

You can't do that on a sphere. No matter where you start and no matter in what directions you walk, you cannot walk from the outside to the inside of a sphere.

NOTE: The Klein bottle is named after the German mathematician Felix Klein who described it in 1882.

The Klein bottle is also said to be a *closed surface* because, unlike the Möbius strip, it has no edges.

Figures 26-8 and 26-9 show two views of another non-orientable closed surface: Boy's surface. Like the Klein bottle, it is self-intersecting, although it's much harder to visualize exactly how the surface penetrates itself.

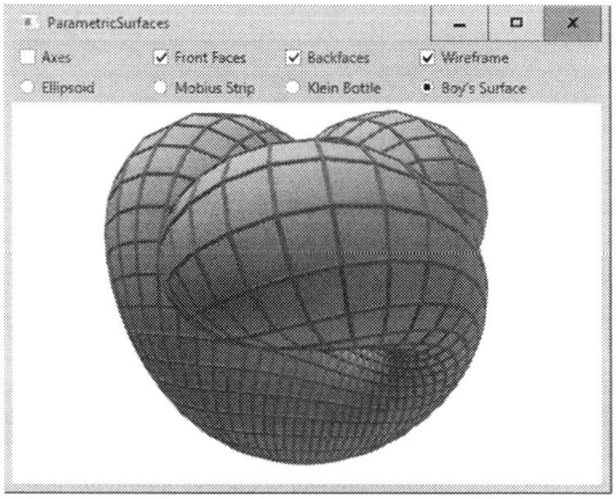

Figure 26-8: Boy's surface is non-orientable.

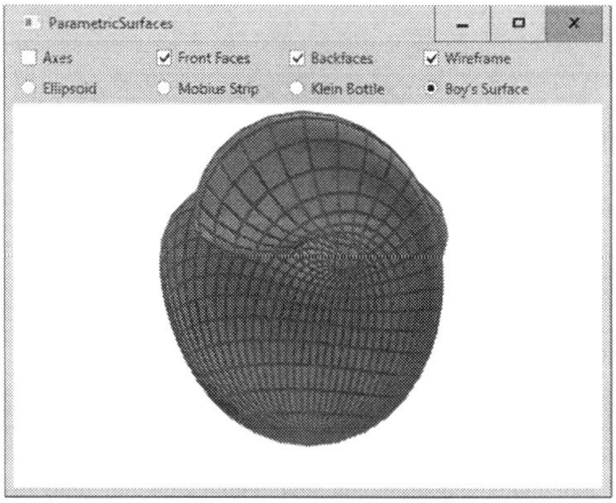

Figure 26-9: In Boy's surface, each "tube" burrows under the next.

In Figure 26-8, you may be able to see that the basic structure involves three bulging "tubes" that cross the exterior of the object. Each of those tubes burrows under the next tube to form a hole below it. In Figure 26-9, you can see the hole where the tube on the upper right emerges.

If you enter one of the holes and follow its tube back into the object, you find yourself in the large chamber below.

Probably the best way to really understand Boy's surface is to download and run the ParametricSurfaces example program. Maximize the program to make it as large as possible. Then turn off the axes and solid triangles so only the wireframe remains. Now rotate the image around with the mouse to see how the pieces fit together.

> **NOTE:** Boy's surface is named after yet another German mathematician, Werner Boy. He discovered it in 1901 at the relatively tender young age of 22, so he practically was still a boy.

As I mentioned earlier, the ParametricSurfaces example program shown in Figures 26-5 through 26-9 is very similar to the Surfaces program, so I won't show its code here. You can download it to see all of the details. The main differences are in the parametric functions that generate the surfaces. They are messy and their details aren't really important to this discussion, so I won't go over them either.

What *is* important is the fact that the Möbius strip, Klein bottle, and Boy's surface are non-orientable. That means there's no true definition for "outward" to use when outwardly orienting the surfaces' triangles. In turn, that means that some of the surfaces' triangles will be culled as backfaces if you view the surfaces from different orientations.

For example, if you orient the triangles so those on the "outside" of the Klein bottle are outwardly oriented, then when you look down into the bottle's opening, the triangles on the inside are removed as backfaces.

The moral is, if you want to see every part of a non-orientable surface, then you must give its model a `BackMaterial`. The ParametricSurfaces example program uses the following code to give its models a `BackMaterial`.

```
GeometryModel3D model1 = mesh1.MakeModel(Brushes.LightBlue);
model1.BackMaterial = model1.Material;
ModelGroup.Children.Add(model1);
```

Using a `BackMaterial` slows the drawing engine slightly, but you really have no choice for these surfaces.

Example Program

I've already mentioned the Surfaces and ParametricSurfaces example programs. There's one more example that I want to discuss in this chapter: the ParametricSurfaces2 example program. That program is similar to the ParametricSurfaces program, except it displays the parametric surfaces shown in the following table.

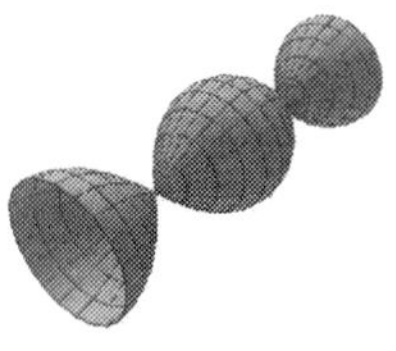 Bonbon	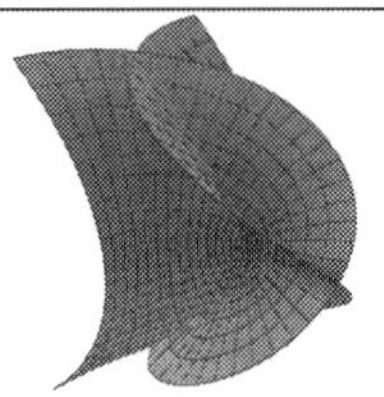 Catalan	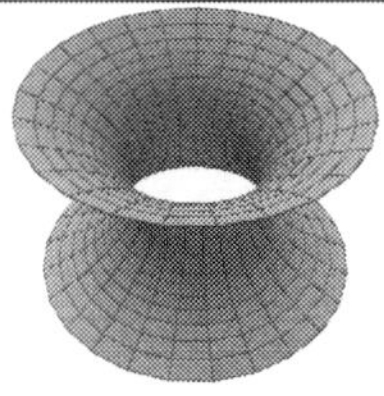 Catenoid	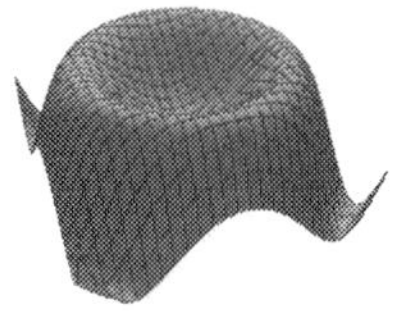 Cosinus
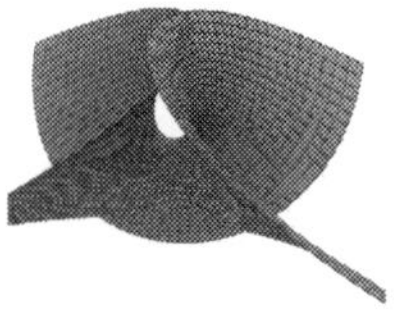 Enneper	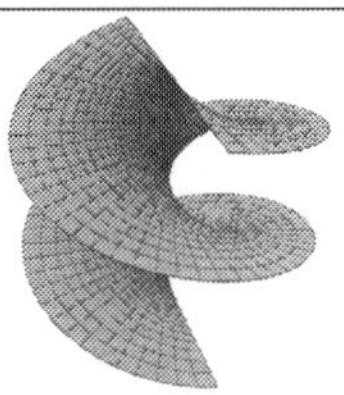 Helicoidal	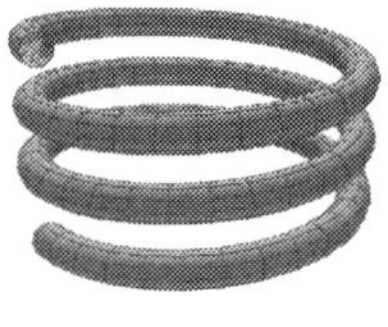 Helix	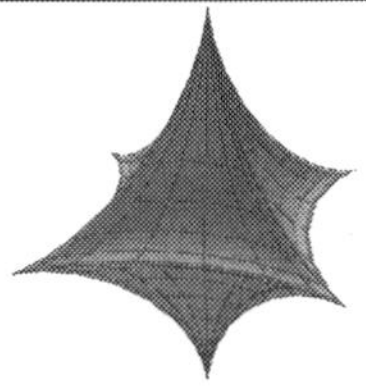 Hexaedron
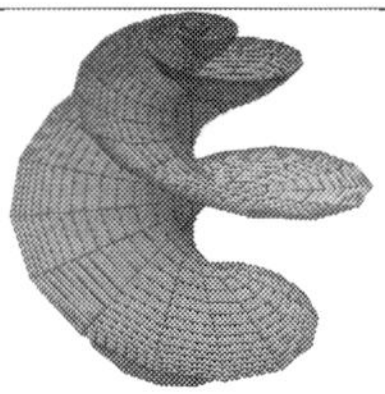 Hyperhelicoidal	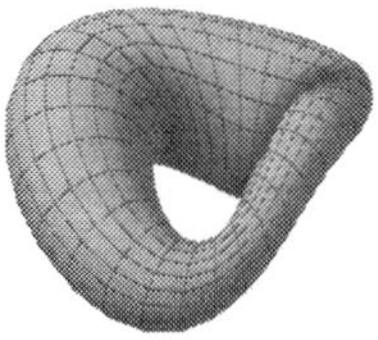 Klein	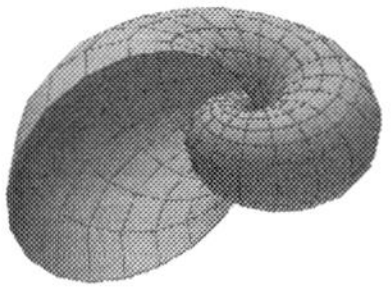 Shell	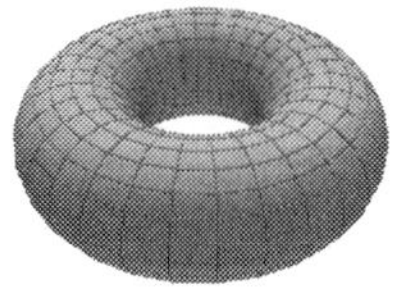 Torus

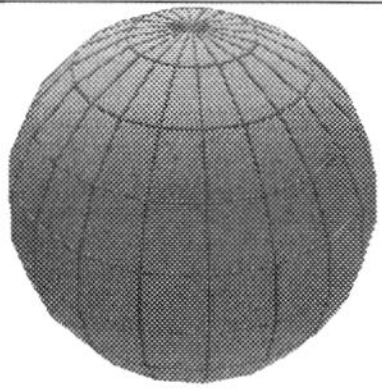 Sphere	 Breather		

I found most of these surfaces on a Blender wiki page at `tinyurl.com/ydyrrwgj`. (Blender is a free and open source 3D toolkit. You can get more information at `blender.org`.)

The Sphere surface is just a sphere similar to the ones you've seen before. I added it to show that a sphere is simply another kinds of parametric surface.

The final surface, Breather, I found on Xah Lee's web page `tinyurl.com/y7qqpbbt`.

The following table shows the surfaces that the ParametricSurfaces2 program displays and the names given to them by their web pages.

Download the ParametricSurfaces2 example program to see details about how it works. Visit the two web pages mentioned earlier to learn a bit more about the surfaces themselves.

Summary

This chapter showed how to draw surfaces defined either as functions y = F(x, z) or as a set of parametric equations. Some of the more complicated surfaces are much easier to understand if you display a wireframe. For example, Figures 26-10 and 26-11 show the Twister surface. Without the wireframe, it looks like a funnel. The wireframe in Figure 26-11 makes it more obvious how the surface twists around its center.

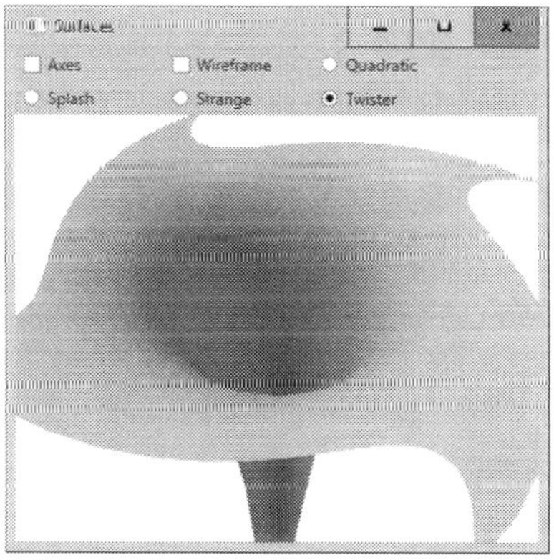

Figure 26-10: The Twister surface looks like a funnel.

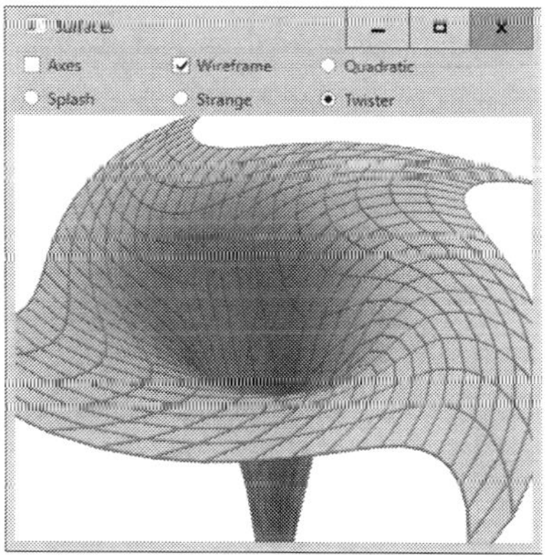

Figure 26-11: A wireframe reveals that the Twister is actually a vortex of death.

Take a few minutes to download the chapter's examples and experiment with them. The pictures in the book don't do justice to the more complicated shapes. In particular, it would be hard to understand the Boy's Surface unless you manipulate it interactively.

Wireframes and direct manipulation make it easier to understand some surfaces. The next chapter shows how you can add another visualization tool to make understanding certain surfaces easier: normals.

Chapter 27

Normals

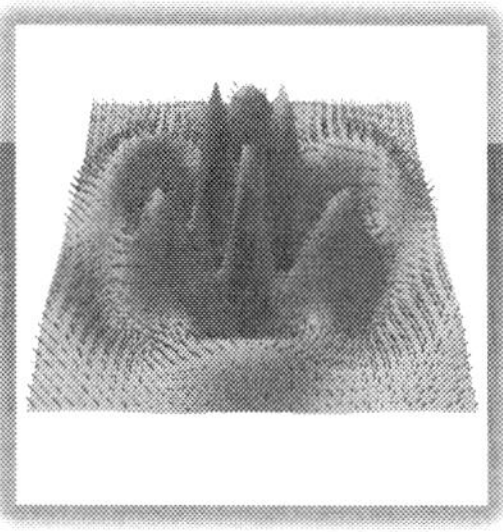

You already know that a normal is a vector perpendicular to a surface. Sometimes it's helpful to display normals on the objects in a scene so you can more easily see the direction that each surface faces.

This chapter describes a fairly simple method for displaying surface normals.

Normals

Creating normals for a mesh isn't too hard. Simply loop through the mesh's triangles and create a segment to represent each triangle's normal.

To find the direction in which the segment should point, you can take the cross product of two vectors that point along the triangle's edges.

The following `ToNormals` method uses this technique to create a new mesh containing normals for an existing mesh.

```
public static MeshGeometry3D ToNormals(this MeshGeometry3D mesh, double thickness,
    double length)
{
    // Make a dictionary of edges.
    HashSet<Edge> edges = new HashSet<Edge>();

    // Loop through the triangles.
    MeshGeometry3D result = new MeshGeometry3D();
    for (int i = 0; i < mesh.TriangleIndices.Count; i += 3)
    {
        // Get vectors.
        Vector3D v01 =
            mesh.Positions[mesh.TriangleIndices[i]] -
            mesh.Positions[mesh.TriangleIndices[i + 1]];
        Vector3D v12 =
            mesh.Positions[mesh.TriangleIndices[i + 1]] -
            mesh.Positions[mesh.TriangleIndices[i + 2]];

        // Find the cross product.
        Vector3D n = Vector3D.CrossProduct(v01, v12);

        // Set the length.
        n = n * length / n.Length;

        // Find the triangle's center.
        Point3D center = new Point3D();
        for (int j = i; j < i + 3; j++)
```

```
            {
                center.X += mesh.Positions[mesh.TriangleIndices[j]].X;
                center.Y += mesh.Positions[mesh.TriangleIndices[j]].Y;
                center.Z += mesh.Positions[mesh.TriangleIndices[j]].Z;
            }
            center.X /= 3.0;
            center.Y /= 3.0;
            center.Z /= 3.0;

            // Add the normal.
            result.AddEdge(edges, thickness, center, center + n);
        }
        return result;
    }
```

The method's parameters indicate the thickness and length that the code should give to the edges used to represent the normals.

The code first creates a `HashSet` to hold edges. It then makes a result mesh and loops through the existing mesh's triangles.

For each existing triangle, the code calculates vectors `v12` from the first point to the second point, and `v23` from the second point to the third point. Figure 27-1 shows those vectors.

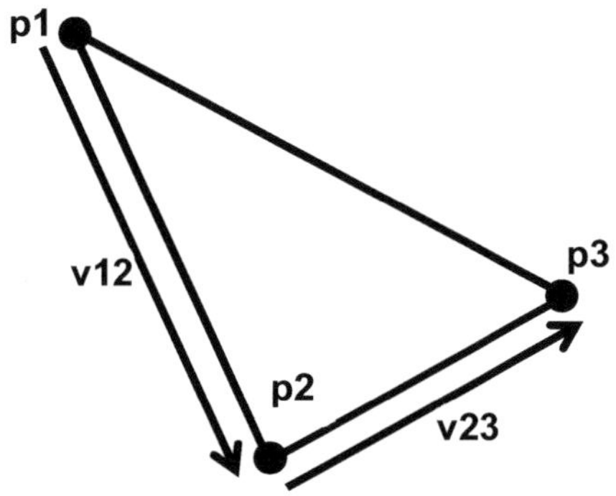

Figure 27-1: The triangle's points define the vectors v12 and v23.

Next, the method takes the cross product of the two vectors to get a new vector that is perpendicular to `v12` and `v23`. The method divides that vector by its current length and multiples by the desired length to get a normal vector with the desired length.

> **NOTE:** Earlier I recommended that you not use meaningless objects such as triangles containing two identical points. Here's another reason why that's important. If two of the triangle's points are identical, then either one of the vectors `v12` and `v23` has zero length or the two vectors are the same. In either case, the cross product is undefined.

The code then averages the coordinates of the triangle's three points to find the center of the triangle.

The method finishes by creating an edge starting at the triangle's center point and moving in the direction of the normal vector.

After it finishes processing all of the triangles, the method returns the new mesh containing the normal vectors.

Example program

The Normals example program uses the following code snippet to demonstrate the `ToNormals` method when it builds its scene.

```
if (normalsCheckBox.IsChecked.Value)
{
    MeshGeometry3D mesh1b = mesh1.ToNormals(0.01, 1);
    ModelGroup.Children.Add(mesh1b.MakeModel(Brushes.Red));
}
```

If the Normals checkbox is checked, the program calls the surface mesh's `ToNormals` method and saves the result in a new mesh. The parameters that the program sends to the `ToNormals` method make the normals 0.01 units thick (half of the thickness the program uses for its wireframe) and one unit long.

After it creates the normals, the program converts the new mesh into a model and adds it to the main model group.

Figure 27-2 shows the Normals program displaying the Twister surface. The direction of the normals gives an indication of how steeply a region on the surface is tilted toward the vortex in the center.

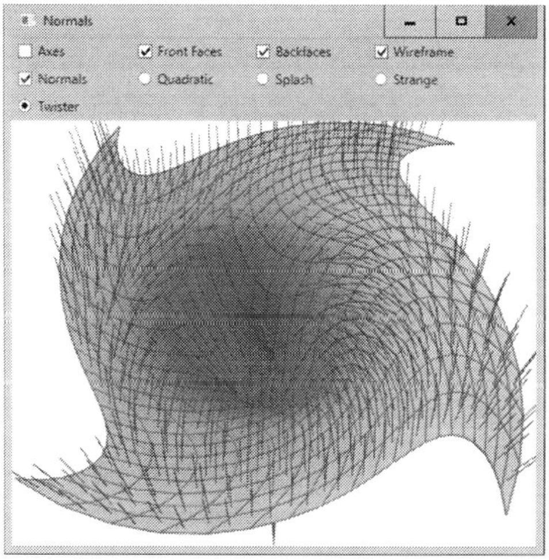

Figure 27-2: The Normals example program can display surface normals.

Summary

By themselves, surface normals don't usually provide enough information to make understanding a surface easy, but they can be a useful addition to surface faces and wireframes. They can be particularly helpful if you can't understand why a particular piece of a scene has an unexpected color or is missing entirely. In those cases, normals can tell you which direction the surface is facing and that may clear up the problem.

The next chapter continues the discussion of surfaces by describing surfaces of transformation.

Chapter 28 Transformation Surfaces

Chapter 26 explained how you can generate surfaces by using a function y=F(x, z) or by using a set of parametric equations. This chapter explains another method for generating surfaces: applying transformations to a shape.

For example, you could start with a curve and rotate it around an axis to create a sort of cylinder with shaped sides. Another approach would be to start with a polygon and then translate it so it follows a path through space, generating a sort of shaped tube. More generally, you could repeatedly apply a transformation matrix to translate, rotate, and scale an initial shape to produce all sorts of interesting results.

Basic Transformations

The basic idea behind this kind of surface is simple. Starting with a set of generator points, transform them to get a modified set. Then connect corresponding points from the two sets to create a surface. Repeat as many times as desired.

For example, Figure 28-1 shows the TranslationSurface example program. It starts with the black hexagon at the bottom of the shape. It then transforms that hexagon six times, performing the following three actions each time.

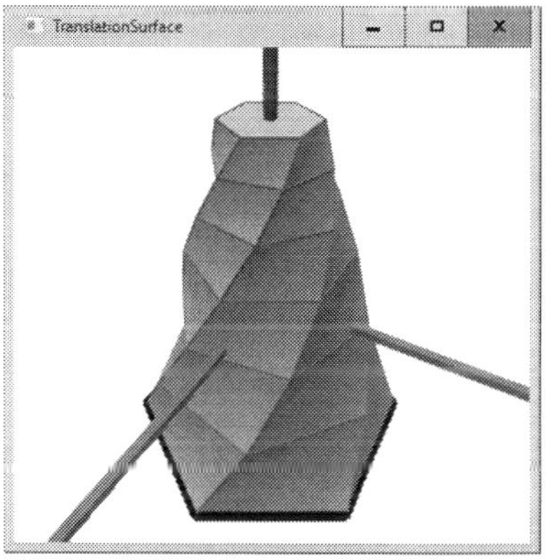

Figure 28-1: This program scales, rotates, and translates a hexagon to make a surface.

1. Scale the hexagon by a factor of 0.8 in the X, Y, and Z directions
2. Rotate the hexagon 20 degrees
3. Translate the hexagon 0.75 units in the Y direction

Each time it performs the combined transformation, the program connects the corresponding parts of the old and new hexagons to make the surface. (The program also builds polygons to cap the surface's ends, but I'll get to that in the next section.)

For now, take a look at the following pieces of the `AddTransformSurface` method, which creates the bulk of the surface.

```
public static void AddTransformSurface(this MeshGeometry3D mesh,
    Point3D[] generator, Transform3D trans, int num,
    bool closeTransStart = false, bool closeTransEnd = false,
    bool closeRotStart = false, bool closeRotEnd = false,
    bool smooth = false,
    HashSet<Edge> edges = null, double thickness = 0.1)
{
    // Make a point dictionary if needed.
    Dictionary<Point3D, int> pointDict = null;
    if (smooth) pointDict = new Dictionary<Point3D, int>();

    // Make two working arrays.
    int numPoints = generator.Length;
    Point3D[] pts1 = new Point3D[generator.Length];
    Point3D[] pts2 = new Point3D[generator.Length];

    // Copy the original generator points into pts2.
    Array.Copy(generator, pts2, numPoints);

    // Apply the transformation.
    for (int i = 0; i < num; i++)
    {
        // Copy the last batch of points into pts1.
        Array.Copy(pts2, pts1, numPoints);

        // Transform the points in pts2.
        trans.Transform(pts2);

        // Build the edges.
        for (int p = 1; p < numPoints; p++)
        {
            Point3D[] sidePts =
            {
                pts1[p - 1], pts1[p], pts2[p], pts2[p - 1],
            };
            mesh.AddPolygon(pointDict: pointDict,
                edges: edges, thickness: thickness, points:sidePts);
        }
    }
    ...
}
```

This piece of code creates the sides of the surface. If its `smooth` parameter is `true`, the method creates a point dictionary as usual.

The code then makes two arrays to hold the points while it manipulates them. It copies the original generator points into the second array.

The code then enters a loop that repeats as many times as we want to perform the transformation. Inside the loop, the method copies the points from `pts2` into `pts1`. That copies the most recently transformed points (which are the original points during the first trip through the loop) into the `pts1` array. A copy of the most recently transformed points is also left in the `pts2` array.

Next, the code applies the transformation to the points in the `pts2` array. It then loops through the points and uses the corresponding points in the two arrays to build the surface's sides.

> **NOTE:** The `AddTransformSurface` method takes a `Transform3D` as a parameter to define the transformation that it applies. The TranslationSurface example program uses a `Transform3DGroup` containing multiple transformations for this parameter. You can use the same technique any time you want the `AddTransformSurface` method to perform more than one transformation.

The rest of the method, which I've left out for now, creates caps on the top and bottom ends of the shape if desired. I'll explain that code in the following two sections.

That explains how the `AddTransformSurface` extension method works, but there is a pretty big restriction on how you use it. You need to be sure that the generator points and the transformation are arranged properly to produce the surface's pieces in the proper orientation. In other words, as variable `p` loops through the points, the points `pts1[p-1]`, `pts1[p]`, `pts2[p]`, and `pts2[p-1]` should be outward-oriented.

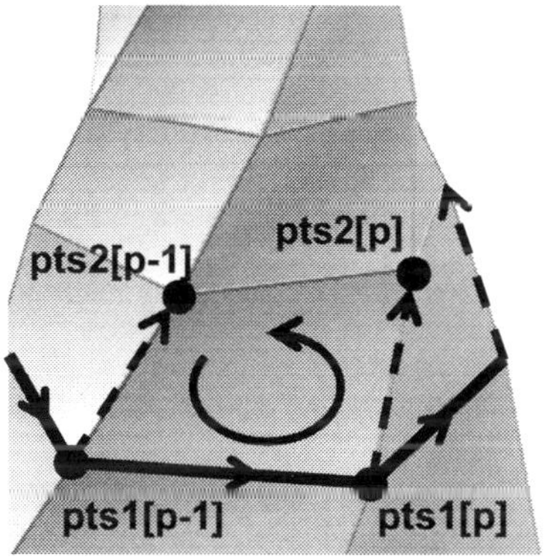

Figure 28-2: The generator and transformation must be properly oriented.

The TranslationSurface example program orients its generator polygon counterclockwise when seen from above, as indicated by the thick lines with arrows shown in Figure 28-2. The transformation is basically upward, as indicated by the dashed arrows. Because of the way the generator and the transformation are arranged, the points are oriented properly.

As you'll see in the next section, it's also useful to have the generator oriented so its normal according to the right-hand rule points into the solid. Because the generator used in Figure 28-2 is oriented counterclockwise when seen from above, its normal points upward into the solid as desired.

> **NOTE:** If you can't get the generator and the transformation oriented properly, you can set the model's `BackMaterial` property equal to its `Material`. You'll also need to do that if you want to see the surface from both sides.

Surfaces of Translation

The TranslationSurface example program uses a closed polygon for a generator and then mostly translates it to build its surface. The result is a sort of tube with open ends. If you look at Figure 28-1 again, you can see the upper end is closed by a cap. (The bottom end is closed, too, but you can't see it in the figure.)

The following code snippet shows the pieces of the `AddTransformSurface` method that builds the caps for the ends.

```
// Close the ends of a surface of translation if desired.
if (closeTransStart)
{
    Point3D[] pts = new Point3D[numPoints];
    Array.Copy(generator, pts, numPoints);
    Array.Reverse(pts);
    mesh.AddPolygon(pointDict: pointDict,
        edges: edges, thickness: thickness, points: pts);
}
if (closeTransEnd)
{
    mesh.AddPolygon(pointDict: pointDict,
        edges: edges, thickness: thickness, points: pts2);
}
```

After it finishes building the sides of the surface as described in the preceding section, the method checks the `closeTransStart` parameter to see if it should make a cap for the start of the surface.

The generator points define the start cap, but they are inwardly oriented. If `closeTransStart` is `true`, the method copies the generator points into a new array, reverses the array's points, and then uses them to build the starting end cap.

Next, the method checks the `closeTransEnd` parameter to see if it should build a cap for the final end of the solid. (The top in Figure 28-1.) Because the generator points are oriented toward the solid's body, they already have the proper orientation for this end cap, so the program simply passes them into `AddPolygon` to make this cap.

The TranslationSurface example program uses the following code to build its scene.

```
private void DefineModel(Model3DGroup group)
{
    // Axes.
    MeshExtensions.AddAxes(group);

    // Make the generator.
    int numTrans = 6;
    double dy = 0.75;
    int numPoints = 6;
    Point3D[] generator = G3.MakePolygonPoints(numPoints,
        new Point3D(0, -numTrans * dy / 2, 0),
        D3.XVector(2), -D3.ZVector(2));
```

```
        // Repeat the first point at the end.
        numPoints++;
        Array.Resize(ref generator, numPoints);
        generator[numPoints - 1] = generator[0];

        // Make the transformation.
        Transform3DGroup transGroup = new Transform3DGroup();
        transGroup.Children.Add(new ScaleTransform3D(0.8, 0.8, 0.8));
        transGroup.Children.Add(D3.Rotate(D3.YVector(), D3.Origin, 20));
        transGroup.Children.Add(new TranslateTransform3D(0, dy, 0));

        // Make the surface of transformation.
        MeshGeometry3D mesh1 = new MeshGeometry3D();
        mesh1.AddTransformSurface(generator, transGroup, numTrans,
            true, true, false, false,
            false);
        group.Children.Add(mesh1.MakeModel(Brushes.LightBlue));

        // Make a wireframe.
        HashSet<Edge> edges = new HashSet<Edge>();
        MeshGeometry3D mesh2 = new MeshGeometry3D();
        mesh2.AddTransformSurface(generator, transGroup, numTrans,
            false, false, false, false,
            false, edges, 0.02);
        group.Children.Add(mesh2.MakeModel(Brushes.Blue));

        // Display the generator.
        edges = new HashSet<Edge>();
        MeshGeometry3D mesh3 = new MeshGeometry3D();
        mesh3.AddPolygonEdges(edges, 0.1, generator);
        group.Children.Add(mesh3.MakeModel(Brushes.Black));
    }
```

This code builds the coordinate axes. It then uses the `G3.MakePolygonPoints` method to create a hexagon that defines the generator points. It moves the polygon down a bit so the final solid will be centered vertically at Y = 0. It uses vectors pointing in the X and -Z directions to define the polygon's plane, so the points will be oriented counterclockwise as seen from above.

Next, the code adds an extra spot to the end of the `generator` array and places a copy of the first point there. The main body of the `AddTransformSurface` method doesn't create a side polygon containing the first and last points, so it won't close the side of the surface unless the generator repeats its first point at its end. You could modify it to do so, but that would make it more complicated if you wanted to make a surface with open sides.

The program then creates a `Transform3DGroup` and adds a scaling, rotation, and translation to it. The code calls the `AddTransformSurface` method, passing it the generator points and the `Transform3DGroup`.

Next, the code calls `AddTransformSurface` again, this time passing it a `HashSet` of edges to produce a wireframe.

Finally, the program creates a new mesh and adds edges to highlight the generator points with thick black segments.

Surfaces of Rotation

The TranslationSurface example program creates a surface by mostly translating its generator points, so it basically creates a tube. Rotation is also useful for producing surfaces. You can take a curve or set of points and rotate them around an axis to produce a surface of rotation.

The RotationSurface example program shown in Figure 28-3 rotates a set of points around the Y axis to make a vase-like shape. The dark strip running up the right side of the vase in Figure 28-3 shows the generator points.

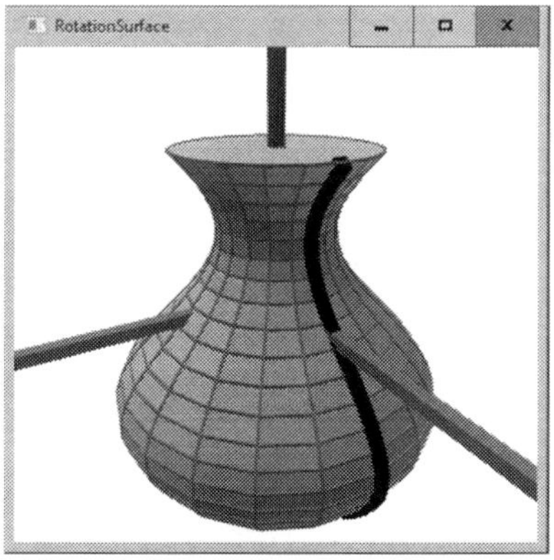

Figure 28-3: The RotationSurface example program rotates a set of points around the Y axis.

When building a surface of rotation, the main body of the `AddTransformSurface` method builds the sides of the solid as usual. It then needs a little extra code to cap the ends just as it does for a surface of translation. The difference is in how it builds those end caps.

In a surface of rotation, the starting end (on the bottom in Figure 28-3) is defined by transforming the first generator point through the shape's sequence of rotations. The finishing end (on the top in the figure) is defined by rotating the last generator point through the rotations.

To make it easier to move a single point through a sequence of rotations, the `MeshExtensions` class defines the following `GetTransformPolygon` helper method to transform a single point and return all of its transformed versions.

```
public static Point3D[] GetTransformPolygon(
    Point3D point, Transform3D trans, int num)
{
    // Make an array to hold the point and its transformations.
    Point3D[] points = new Point3D[num];

    // Transform the point.
    for (int i = 0; i < num; i++)
    {
        points[i] = point;
        point = trans.Transform(point);
    }

    // Return the points.
    return points;
}
```

This method creates an array big enough to hold the transformed points. It then enters a loop where it copies the point into the next array position and then transforms the point.

Earlier I said that the generator and the transformation needed to be properly oriented to produce a surface of translation. The same is true for a surface of rotation. Figure 28-4 shows how the generator and transformation are arranged in the RotationSurface example program. The thick downward-pointing arrows show the ordering of the generator's points. The right-pointing dashed arrows show the direction of rotation. This arrangement gives the points the proper outward orientation.

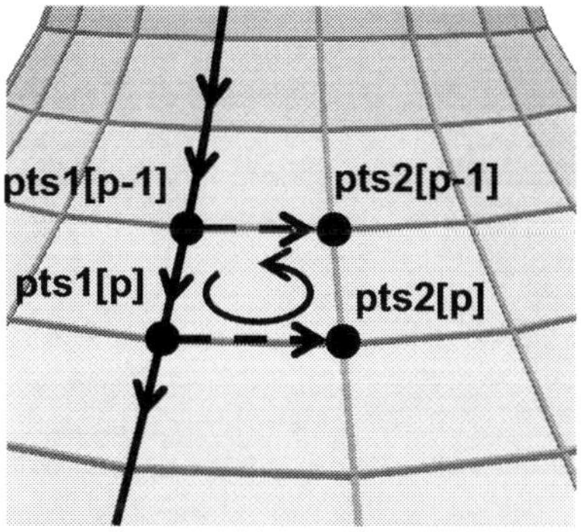

Figure 28-4: The generator and transformation must be properly oriented in a surface of rotation.

This orientation also means that a rotated point produces a sequence of points that is counterclockwise when seen from above. That means the upper cap's transformed points are outwardly oriented and the lower cap's transformed points are inwardly oriented.

The following code snippet shows the part of the `AddTransformSurface` method that makes end caps for a surface of rotation.

```
// Close the ends of a surface of rotation if desired.
if (closeRotStart)
{
    Point3D[] pts = GetTransformPolygon(generator[0], trans, num);
    mesh.AddPolygon(pointDict: pointDict,
        edges: edges, thickness: thickness, generator: pts);
}
if (closeRotEnd)
{
    Point3D[] pts = GetTransformPolygon(generator[numPoints - 1], trans, num);
    Array.Reverse(pts);
    mesh.AddPolygon(pointDict: pointDict,
        edges: edges, thickness: thickness, points: pts);
}
```

If the `closeRotStart` parameter is `true`, the method calls `GetTransformPolygon` to get the transformed versions of the generator's first point. Those points are already outwardly oriented, so the code just passes them to `AddPolygon` to make the upper end cap.

If the `closeRotEnd` parameter is `true`, the method calls `GetTransformPolygon` for the generator's last point. Those points are inwardly oriented, so the code reverses their array and then passes the result to `AddPolygon` to make the lower end cap.

The following code shows how the RotationSurface example program builds its scene.

```
private void DefineModel(Model3DGroup group)
{
    // Axes.
```

```
        MeshExtensions.AddAxes(group);

        // Make the generator.
        const int numPoints = 20;
        const double tmin = 1.1 * Math.PI;
        const double tmax = tmin + 1.8 * Math.PI;
        Point3D[] generator = new Point3D[numPoints];
        double t = tmin;
        double dt = (tmax - tmin) / (numPoints - 1);
        for (int i = 0; i < numPoints; i++)
        {
            generator[i] = new Point3D(1 + 0.5 * Math.Sin(t), 3 - t * 0.5, 0);
            t += dt;
        }

        // Make the transformation.
        const int numRot = 20;
        const double dangle = 360.0 / numRot;
        RotateTransform3D rot = D3.Rotate(D3.YVector(), D3.Origin, dangle);

        // Make the surface of transformation.
        MeshGeometry3D mesh1 = new MeshGeometry3D();
        mesh1.AddTransformSurface(generator, rot, numRot,
            false, false, true, true,
            false);
        group.Children.Add(mesh1.MakeModel(Brushes.LightBlue));

        // Make a wireframe.
        HashSet<Edge> edges = new HashSet<Edge>();
        MeshGeometry3D mesh2 = new MeshGeometry3D();
        mesh2.AddTransformSurface(generator, rot, numRot,
            false, false, true, true,
            false, edges, 0.02);
        group.Children.Add(mesh2.MakeModel(Brushes.Blue));

        // Display the generator.
        edges = new HashSet<Edge>();
        MeshGeometry3D mesh3 = new MeshGeometry3D();
        for (int i = 1; i < numPoints; i++)
            mesh3.AddEdge(edges, 0.1, generator[i - 1], generator[i]);
        group.Children.Add(mesh3.MakeModel(Brushes.Black));
    }
```

The method first creates the coordinate axes. It then uses an equation to create the generator points.

Next, the program creates a transformation that rotates around the Y axis. The amount by which it rotates is 360° divided by the number of times the program will apply the transformation.

The code then calls `AddTransformSurface` to make the surface. It sets `closeRotStart` and `closeRotEnd` to `true` so the method makes the end caps.

The code repeats the call to `AddTransformSurface`, this time including a `HashSet` of edges to produce a wireframe. It finishes by creating a new mesh to display the generator's segments.

Tube Surfaces

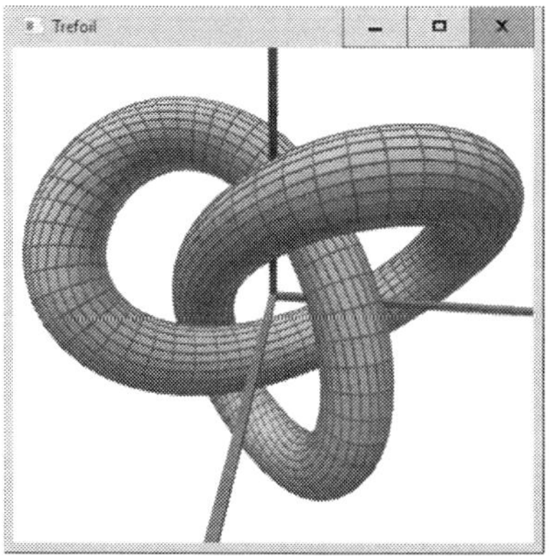

Figure 28-5: Making a circle follow a path creates a tube.

Surfaces of translation and rotation are handy because you can define their transformations in convenient matrices wrapped up in `Transform3D` objects, but those aren't the only possible kinds of transformations. Another interesting surface makes a set of generator points follow a path. For example, the program shown in Figure 28-5 makes a circle follow a path to generate a solid called a *trefoil knot*.

The process of drawing this kind of surface is easiest to understand if you take it in pieces. The following section explains how the program orients the generator along the path. The sections after that explain how the code connects points to make sections of the surface, and how the main `AddPathSurface` method puts it all together.

Translating Generators

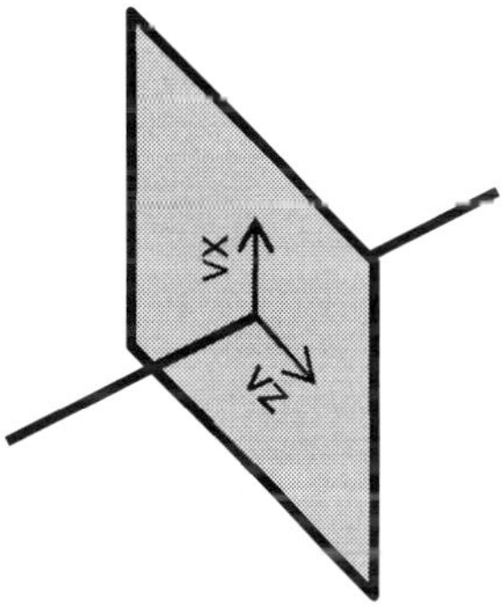

Figure 28-6: Vectors vx and vz help determine the locations of the rectangle's vertices.

To make a tube, the program needs to move the generator points along the path's points. For each point on the path, the program needs to position a copy of the generator suitably transformed so it is centered on the path.

You can orient a polygon on a line segment by making the polygon perpendicular to the segment. Figure 28-6 shows a line segment and a perpendicular rectangle. The rectangle's vertices are defined by the vectors vx and vz, which are perpendicular to the line segment.

You can find one of the perpendicular vectors, say vz, by taking the cross product of a vector along the segment and any other vector that isn't parallel to it. That other vector is often called "up."

After you find vz, you can take the cross product between it and the segment's vector to find the second perpendicular vector vx.

For this program, I'm going to assume that you can define an up vector so that the path is never parallel to it.

It may not be obvious, but the path used in Figure 28-5 does point parallel to the Y axis in two places, so up cannot be parallel to the Y axis. The path also points parallel to the X axis at some locations, so up cannot be parallel to the X axis.

To make that surface, I set "up" equal to a vector parallel to the Z axis. For some curves you may need to use a vector that isn't parallel to any axis, such as <1, 1, 1> or <3, 4, 5>. You should be able to find a usable up vector for all but the most complicated curves.

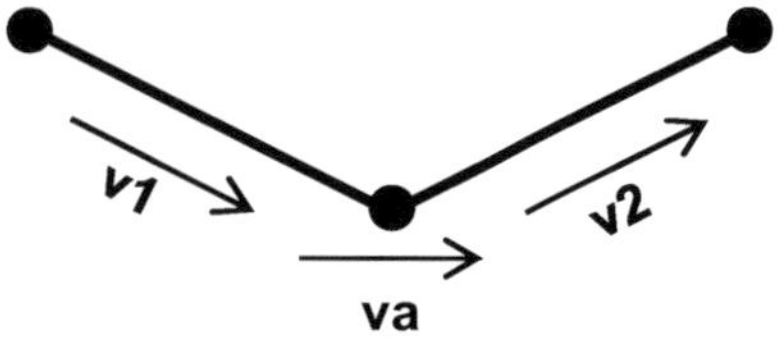

Figure 28-7: The path's direction at a point is the average of its directions on the adjacent segments.

The next question is, "What direction is the path moving when you reach one of its points?" For example, consider the path shown in Figure 28-7. As you follow the path, you get to the point in the middle by moving along the vector v1. However, if you make the generator polygon perpendicular to that vector, the result may look strange.

A better choice is to average the directions of vectors v1 and v2 to determine the official direction of the path at that point.

Now we have a direction va along the path and we have an up vector. You can use them to position the generator points along the path.

The following `GetPathPolygonPoints` method transforms the generator's points so their polygon is perpendicular to the path at one of its points.

```
private static void GetPathPolygonPoints(Point3D[] pts,
    Point3D[] path, int p1, Point3D[] generator, Vector3D up)
{
    // Find the indices of the adjacent points on the path.
    int numPath = path.Length;
    int p0 = p1 - 1;
    int p2 = p1 + 1;

    // Find the path vector.
    Vector3D v1 = path[p1] - path[p0];
    Vector3D v2 = path[p2] - path[p1];
    Vector3D va = (v1 + v2) / 2;

    // Find the polygon's plane vectors.
    Vector3D vz = Vector3D.CrossProduct(va, up);
    Vector3D vx = Vector3D.CrossProduct(va, vz);
    vz.Normalize();
    vx.Normalize();

    // Fill in the points.
    for (int i = 0; i < generator.Length; i++)
    {
        pts[i] = path[p1] + vx * generator[i].X + vz * generator[i].Z;
    }
}
```

The parameter `p1` gives the index of the point along the path where we want to position the generator points. The code first finds the indices of the adjacent points along the path. It uses point `p1` and the two adjacent points to find the vectors along the adjacent segments. It then averages those two vectors to find the official direction `va` of the path at point `p1`.

Next, the method takes the cross product of `va` and `up` to find `vz`. It then crosses vz and `va` to get `vx`. It normalizes `vx` and `vz` so they have length one.

Now the code simply loops through the generator points. A point's transformed version is equal to the point `p1`, plus `vx` times the point's X coordinate value, plus `vz` times the point's Z coordinate value. It's as simple as that!

The vectors `vx` and `vz` produce points in the plane perpendicular to the path at point `p1`. Multiplying them by the generator point's coordinates moves outward from point p1 by the point's distance from the origin.

The HexDonut example program shown in Figure 28-8 creates a wireframe showing a hexagon moving along an octagonal path to produce a sort of torus. The thick octagon in the middle shows the path. The spheres along the path mark the path's points.

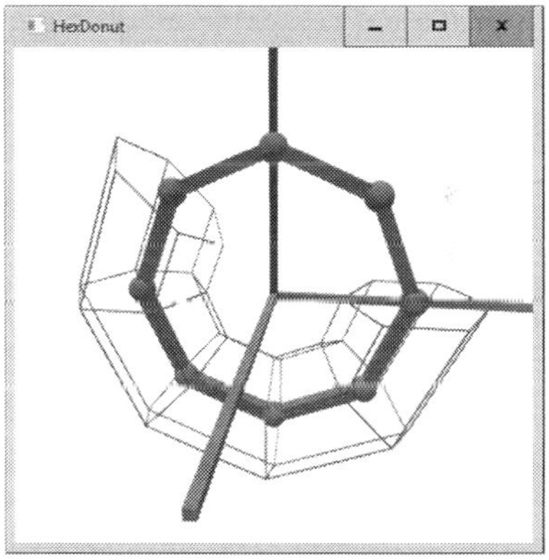

Figure 28-8: The dark octagonal path defines the surface's shape.

You can see in Figure 28-8 that the hexagons are perpendicular to the path's official direction at each of the points.

> **NOTE:** The perspective makes it a bit harder to see that the hexagons are perpendicular to the path at each point. If you download the HexDonut example program and experiment with it, this is obvious.

Building Surface Sections

You've seen several examples that loop through points in two directions and connect them to form the parts of a surface. For example, the programs described in Chapter 26 use that technique to make surfaces for functions y=F(x, z) and parametric surfaces. You can use the same basic technique to make tube surfaces.

The `MakePathRing` method shown in the following code connects the corresponding points on two transformed generator polygons to make a tubular surface between them.

```
private static void MakePathRing(this MeshGeometry3D mesh,
    Point3D[] pts1, Point3D[] pts2,
```

```
        Dictionary<Point3D, int> pointDict,
        HashSet<Edge> edges, double thickness)
    {
        // Loop through the points.
        for (int i = 0; i < pts1.Length - 1; i++)
        {
            Point3D[] points =
            {
                pts1[i], pts2[i],
                pts2[i + 1], pts1[i + 1],
            };

            mesh.AddPolygon(pointDict: pointDict, edges: edges,
                thickness: thickness, points: points);
        }
    }
```

This method simply loops through the points, from the first point to the second-to-last point. For each of those points, it creates a quadrilateral connecting the two polygons between this point and the next one.

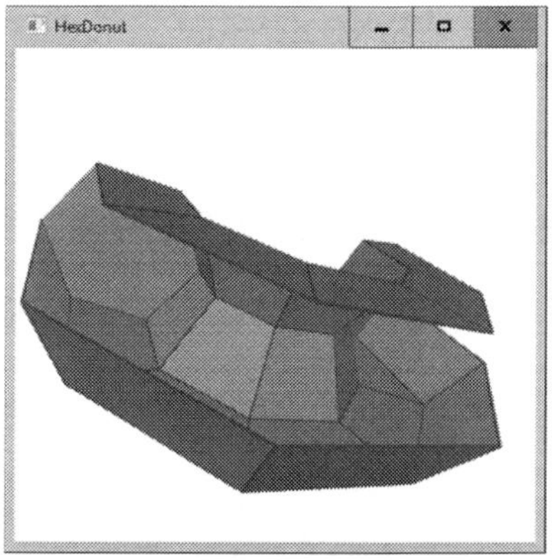

Figure 28-9: To make a closed tube, repeat the generator's first point at its end.

The loop stops with the second-to-last point because there isn't a point after that one to use in making another quadrilateral. You could wrap around and use the first point again, but I decided that you might not always want to close the tube. For example, Figure 28-9 shows the HexDonut example program modified so it doesn't show axes or its path, and so the generator isn't closed.

If you want to close the tube, make the generator repeat its first point at the end so it defines a closed polygon.

Putting it Together

The following `AddPathSurface` method uses the `GetPathPolygonPoints` and `MakePathRing` methods to build the completed tube.

```
    public static void AddPathSurface(this MeshGeometry3D mesh,
        Point3D[] generator, Point3D[] path, Vector3D up,
        bool closeStart = false, bool closeEnd = false,
        bool smooth = false,
        HashSet<Edge> edges = null, double thickness = 0.1)
    {
        // Make a point dictionary if needed.
        Dictionary<Point3D, int> pointDict = null;
        if (smooth) pointDict = new Dictionary<Point3D, int>();

        // Make two work arrays.
        int numGen = generator.Length;
        Point3D[] pts1 = new Point3D[numGen];
        Point3D[] pts2 = new Point3D[numGen];
```

```
        // Get the first set of points.
        GetPathPolygonPoints(pts1, path, 1, generator, up);

        // Loop through the path points.
        int numPath = path.Length;
        for (int p = 2; p <= numPath - 2; p++)
        {
            // Get the set of points at point p.
            GetPathPolygonPoints(pts2, path, p, generator, up);

            // Make a ring between the two sets of points.
            mesh.MakePathRing(pts1, pts2, pointDict, edges, thickness);

            // Switch the arrays.
            Point3D[] temp = pts1;
            pts1 = pts2;
            pts2 = temp;
        }

        // Cap the ends if desired.
        if (closeStart)
        {
            GetPathPolygonPoints(pts1, path, 1, generator, up);
            mesh.AddPolygon(edges, thickness, pts1);
        }
        if (closeEnd)
        {
            GetPathPolygonPoints(pts1, path, numPath - 2, generator, up);
            Array.Reverse(pts1);
            mesh.AddPolygon(edges, thickness, pts1);
        }
    }
```

This method makes a point dictionary if its `smooth` parameter is `true`. Next, it makes two arrays to hold transformed versions of the generator points. The method then calls the `GetPathPolygonPoints` method to initialize the `pts1` array with the generator transformed for point number 1 on the path.

The code then loops through the path points, starting at point number 2 and ending at the second-to-last point in the path. I'll explain why it only loops over those points shortly.

For each of those points, the program uses the `GetPathPolygonPoints` method to get the transformed generator for that point and stores it in the array `pts2`. It then passes the `pts1` and `pts2` arrays to the `MakePathRing` method to build the piece of the tube between those points.

The code then swaps the `pts1` and `pts2` arrays so `pts1` now holds generator points for the more recent path point. The loop then repeats to build the ring for the next section of the path.

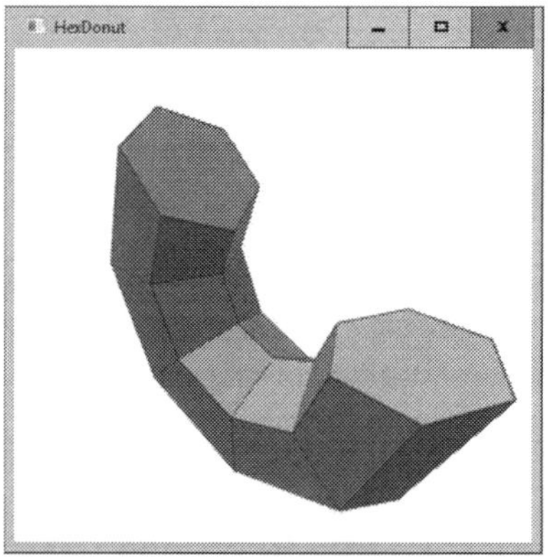

Figure 28-10: The AddPathSurface method makes end caps if desired.

After it finishes the loop, the method builds polygons to cap the tube's ends if desired.

Figure 28-10 shows the HexDonut program displaying a tube with end caps.

So why does the loop not consider the points at the ends of the path? In short, the `GetPathPolygonPoints` method uses endmost points to determine the direction of the path at the second-to-endmost points. See Figure 28-7 again if you want to see the picture.

If you want the tube to be completely closed, repeat the path's first *three* points at its end. To see why you need to repeat three points, look at Figure 28-11. The numbers show the points' indices. The path starts with points 0, 1, 2, and then continues off of the picture in the direction of the dashed line. When the path nears its end, its points have indices N-3, N-2, and N-1, where N is the total number of points in the generator.

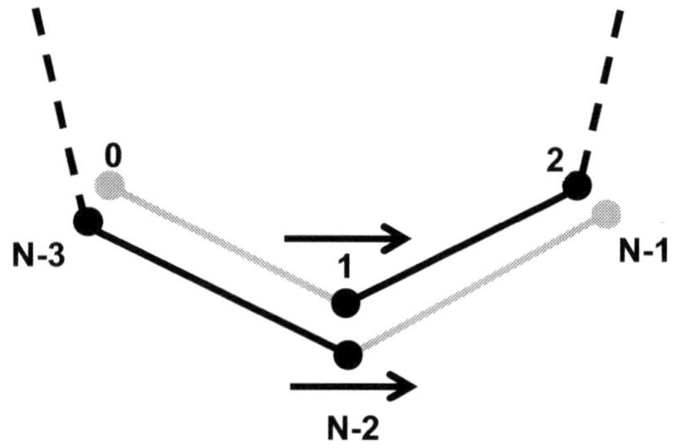

Figure 28-11: To close the tube, make the generator repeat its first three points.

The program uses points 0, 1, and 2 to determine the path's direction at point 1. It can't draw the section between points 0 and 1 because it doesn't have a vector before point 0 to define the path's direction there.

Similarly, at the end of the path, the program uses points N-3, N-2, and N-1 to define the path's direction at point N-2. It can't draw the tube between points N-2 and N-1 because it doesn't have a vector after point N-1 to define the path's direction at that point.

In order to make the tube start at point 1 and finish at point N-2, the points N-3, N-2, and N-1 must repeat points 0, 1, and 2.

Download the HexDonut example program to see additional details. You may want to experiment with its code a bit to change what it displays. For example, you could make it close its tube and display an opaque surface.

Example Program

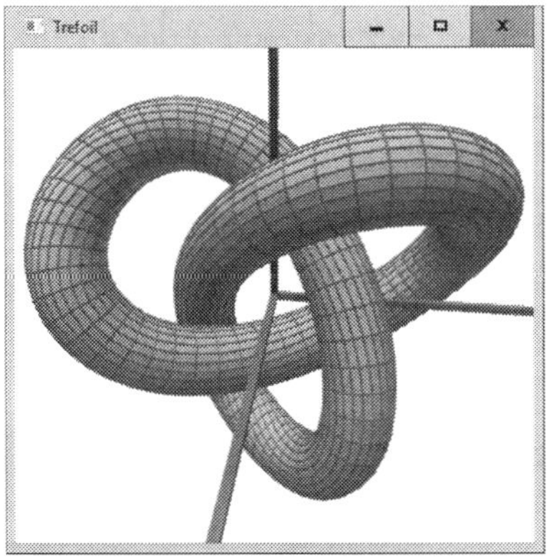

Figure 28-12: The Trefoil example program makes a circle follow a path.

I've already described the key pieces of the TranslationSurface, RotationSurface, and HexDonut example programs. The Trefoil program shown in Figure 28-12 uses the following code to create its tube.

```
private void DefineModel(Model3DGroup group)
{
    // Axes.
    MeshExtensions.AddAxes(group);

    // Make the generator.
    double r = 0.5;
    Point3D[] generator =
        G3.MakePolygonPoints(25, D3.Origin,
            D3.XVector(r), D3.ZVector(r));
    int numGen = generator.Length + 1;
    Array.Resize(ref generator, numGen);
    generator[numGen - 1] = generator[0];

    // Make the path.
    Point3D[] path = G3.MakeTrefoilPoints(100, D3.Origin, D3.XVector(), D3.ZVector());

    // Repeat the first three points.
    int numPath = path.Length + 3;
    Array.Resize(ref path, numPath);
    path[numPath - 3] = path[0];
    path[numPath - 2] = path[1];
    path[numPath - 1] = path[2];

    // Make the surface.
    MeshGeometry3D mesh1 = new MeshGeometry3D();
    mesh1.AddPathSurface(generator, path, D3.ZVector(), false, false, false);
    group.Children.Add(mesh1.MakeModel(Brushes.LightBlue));

    // Make a wireframe.
    HashSet<Edge> edges = new HashSet<Edge>();
    MeshGeometry3D mesh2 = new MeshGeometry3D();
    mesh2.AddPathSurface(generator, path, D3.ZVector(),
        false, false, false, edges, 0.02);
    group.Children.Add(mesh2.MakeModel(Brushes.Blue));
}
```

This code displays the coordinate axes and then uses the `G3.MakePolygonPoints` method to create a circle to act as a generator. It repeats the first point to close the generator.

Next, the code calls the `G3.MakeTrefoilPoints` method, which uses parametric equations to define the path. Download the program to see how that method works. The program repeats the path's first three points to close its tube.

The program passes the generator and path into the `AddPathSurface` method to make the trefoil knot tube. It then calls `AddPathSurface` again to make a wireframe.

The Horn and Snail example programs shown in Figures 28-13 and 28-14 scale, translate, and rotate circles in different ways to produce their scenes. Download the examples and look at their code to see their details.

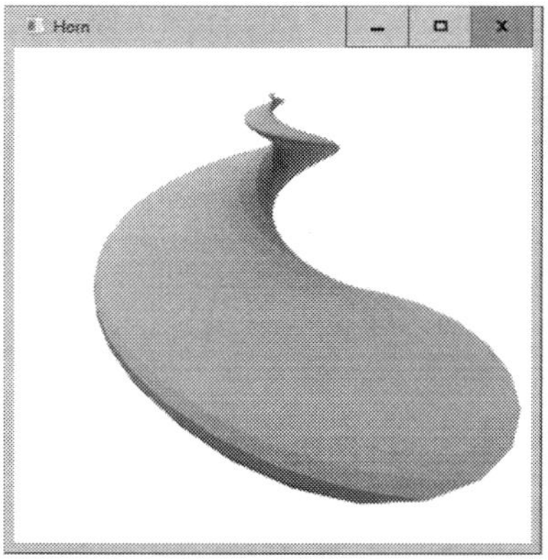

Figure 28-13: The Horn example program scales, translates, and rotates a circle to produce a horn.

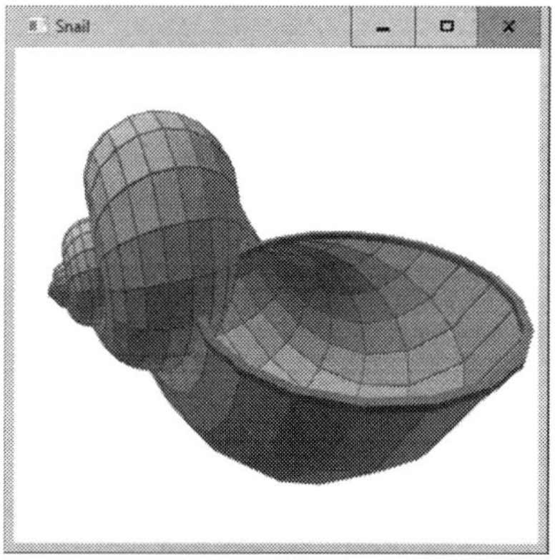

Figure 28-14: The Snail example program uses different transformations to make a snail shell.

Summary

This chapter showed three ways that you can create surfaces of transformation: translation, rotation, and path following. Combinations of transformations can also produce some interesting results. For example, you could make a generator polygon rotate and change size as it follows a path.

All of these surfaces are defined by systematic techniques such a transforming a polygon so they produce generally regular results. The next chapter explains how you can modify basic surfaces to produce fractal terrains that are irregular and that appear almost natural.

Chapter 29

Fractal Surfaces

Chapters 26 and 28 explained how to build several different kinds of surfaces including surfaces defined by functions, parametric equations, and transformations. This chapter explains a method for creating fractal surfaces.

There are a couple of different definitions for fractals. The definition that makes sense for this chapter is, a *fractal* is a shape that is *self-similar* at all levels of magnification. In other words, a piece of the shape looks more or less like the shape as a whole. If you break the piece into smaller pieces, those pieces look more or less like the bigger piece and the whole shape.

In the context of surfaces, a fractal surface is bumpy at all levels of magnification. Fractal surfaces are useful for generating landscapes that look somewhat realistic.

The following section explains the basic midpoint displacement algorithms used by the examples in this chapter.

Midpoint Displacement

The basic idea behind the midpoint displacement algorithm is fairly simple. You start with a quadrilateral that represents part of a surface. You then perform two steps to divide the area into four smaller pieces.

First, you use the area's corners to find values for the midpoints of the edges of the area. You set each midpoint to the average of its neighboring corners plus a random amount added to the midpoint's Y coordinate.

Figure 29-1 shows this step. The left part of the figure shows the area from the top. You know the positions of the black corner points. In the first step, you set the coordinates for the gray points equal to the average of their adjacent black points plus a random Y amount. The arrows show

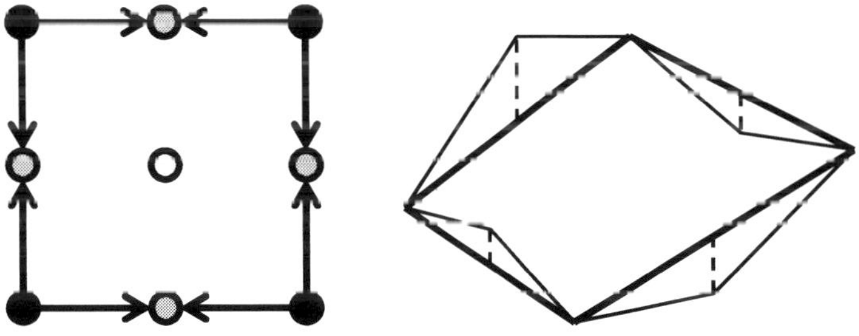

Figure 29-1: First find coordinates for the midpoints. (The gray points on the left.)

which corner points contribute to the midpoints' positions.

The right part of Figure 29-1 shows this step in perspective. Notice that some of the midpoints have been randomly adjusted up and others have been adjusted down.

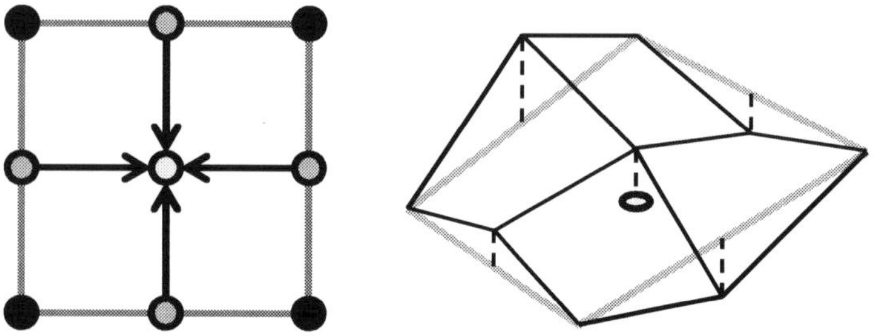

Figure 29-2: Use the midpoints to find the center point's coordinates.

The second step is to find the coordinates for the point in the center of the area. (The white point on the left in Figure 29-1.) To position that point, use the average of the four midpoints and add a random amount to the Y coordinate.

Figure 29-2 shows this step. On the left, the arrows indicate which points contribute to the center point's position. The ellipse on the right shows the location of the average of the midpoints. That location is then adjusted randomly, in this example upward a bit, to produce the final point.

When you perform midpoint adjustment, you increase the number of pieces by a factor of four. In this example, the number of pieces goes from one to four.

If you want to refine the surface further, you can perform the same steps on the four smaller pieces. That would increase the total number of pieces from four to 16.

You can continue refining the surface until you reach the desired level of refinement.

Note that each time you refine the surface, you need to reduce the largest amount by which you might adjust Y coordinates. That lets the earlier steps that deal with large areas make big changes to the surface's shape while later smaller areas provide only local refinements.

Displacement Code

The following `FractalizeSurface` method uses midpoint displacement to refine a surface for a given number of iterations.

```
public static Point3D[,] FractalizeSurface(Point3D[,] surface, int iterations,
    int seed, double minDy, double maxDy)
{
    // Initialize the random number generator with the seed.
    Random rand;
    if (seed < 0) rand = new Random();
    else rand = new Random(seed);

    // Get the middle dy value.
    double midDy = (minDy + maxDy) / 2;
    double dySpread = maxDy - minDy;
```

```
// Repeat for the desired number of iterations.
for (int iteration = 0; iteration < iterations; iteration++)
{
    // Get the middle dy value.
    double midDy = (minDy + maxDy) / 2;

    // Get the array's current and new size.
    int numX1 = surface.GetUpperBound(0) + 1;
    int numZ1 = surface.GetUpperBound(1) + 1;
    int numX2 = numX1 * 2 - 1;
    int numZ2 = numZ1 * 2 - 1;

    // Expand the array.
    Point3D[,] surface2 = new Point3D[numX2, numZ2];

    // Copy the old values into the new array.
    for (int ix = 0; ix < numX1; ix++)
        for (int iz = 0; iz < numZ1; iz++)
            surface2[ix * 2, iz * 2] = surface[ix, iz];

    // Position midpoints.
    for (int ix = 1; ix < numX2; ix += 2)
    {
        for (int iz = 0; iz < numZ2; iz += 2)
        {
            double x = surface2[ix - 1, iz].X + surface2[ix + 1, iz].X;
            double y = surface2[ix - 1, iz].Y + surface2[ix + 1, iz].Y +
                rand.NextDouble(minDy, maxDy);
            double z = surface2[ix - 1, iz].Z + surface2[ix + 1, iz].Z;
            surface2[ix, iz] = new Point3D(x / 2, y / 2, z / 2);
        }
    }
    for (int iz = 1; iz < numZ2; iz += 2)
    {
        for (int ix = 0; ix < numX2; ix += 2)
        {
            double x = surface2[ix, iz - 1].X + surface2[ix, iz + 1].X;
            double y = surface2[ix, iz - 1].Y + surface2[ix, iz + 1].Y +
                rand.NextDouble(minDy, maxDy);
            double z = surface2[ix, iz - 1].Z + surface2[ix, iz + 1].Z;
            surface2[ix, iz] = new Point3D(x / 2, y / 2, z / 2);
        }
    }

    // Position center points.
    for (int ix = 1; ix < numX2; ix += 2)
    {
        for (int iz = 1; iz < numZ2; iz += 2)
        {
            double x =
                surface2[ix, iz - 1].X + surface2[ix, iz + 1].X +
                surface2[ix - 1, iz].X + surface2[ix + 1, iz].X;
            double y =
                surface2[ix, iz - 1].Y + surface2[ix, iz + 1].Y +
                surface2[ix - 1, iz].Y + surface2[ix + 1, iz].Y +
                    rand.NextDouble(minDy, maxDy);
            double z =
```

```
                    surface2[ix, iz - 1].Z + surface2[ix, iz + 1].Z +
                    surface2[ix - 1, iz].Z + surface2[ix + 1, iz].Z;
                surface2[ix, iz] = new Point3D(x / 4, y / 4, z / 4);
            }
        }

        // Replace surface with surface2.
        surface = surface2;

        // Reduce the spread of random values.
        dySpread /= 2;
        minDy = midDy - dySpread / 2;
        maxDy = midDy + dySpread / 2;
    } // End looping for iterations.

    // Return the latest surface.
    return surface;
}
```

The method first creates a `Random` object to generate random numbers. If the `seed` parameter is negative, the method does not pass a seed into the `Random` class's constructor.

If seed is `greater` than or equal to 0, the code passes the seed into the constructor. That lets the program generate a repeatable sequence of "random" numbers. If you start with the same initial points and use the same seed, then the method produces the same fractal surface every time.

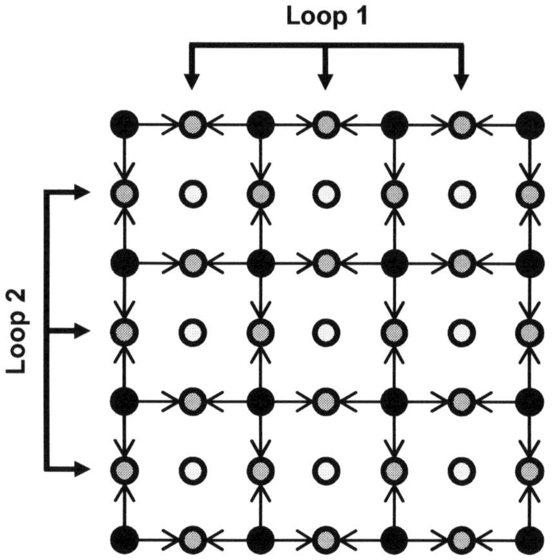

Figure 29-3: First, use the corners to find the midpoints' positions.

Next, the code calculates the average and spread of the values `minDy` and `maxDy`. These give the minimum and maximum amounts that the program will add to a point's Y coordinate.

The method then enters a loop that runs for the desired number of iterations.

Inside the loop, the code gets the array's bounds. It needs to make a new, larger array to hold the divided surface's new points, so it calculates the size of the enlarged array. The code creates the new larger array and then copies the old values into their positions in the new array.

Next, the method uses two double loops to calculate the midpoint values. Figure 29-3 shows this step. The first double loop positions the midpoints along the horizontal edges, which are and indicated by the "Loop 1" label in Figure 29-3. The second double loop positions the remaining "Loop 2" midpoints.

The method then uses a third double loop to position the white, center points. Figure 29-4 shows this step.

After it has positioned all of the new points, the method must prepare for its next iteration. To do that, it replaces the surface array with the enlarged surface2 array.

The code then divides the spread of the random Y amounts dySpread by 2. That makes later iterations adjust new Y coordinates by a smaller amount so the surface settles down. If you don't do this, the surface's Y values vary wildly and create an unnatural, spiky result.

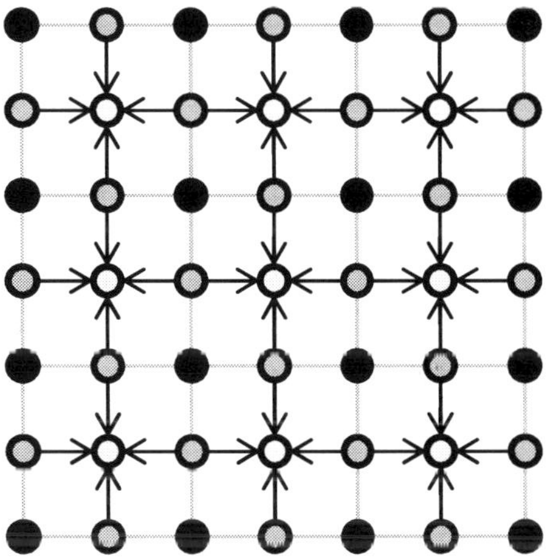

Figure 29-4: Use the midpoints to position the center points.

The code uses the new dySpread value to calculate new minDy and maxDy values, which determine the minimum and maximum amounts added to new Y coordinates.

The method repeats the midpoint displacement process until it has performed the desired number of iterations. It then returns the most recent version of the surface array.

There's one detail in this code that I skipped. When it positions a new point, the code uses the Random class's NextDouble method to find a random value between minDy and maxDy.

Unfortunately, the Random class's NextDouble method returns a value between 0.0 (inclusive) and 1.0 (exclusive) and not a value within a range. To fix this omission, I created the following RandomExtensions class.

```
public static class RandomExtensions
{
    // Return a double between min inclusive and max exclusive.
    public static double NextDouble(this Random rand, double min, double max)
    {
        return min + rand.NextDouble() * (max - min);
    }
}
```

This code defines a NextDouble extension method that returns a value within a range.

NOTE: This NextDouble extension method can come in handy in many other programs, so you might want to add it to your programming toolkit.

RandomSurfaces

The RandomSurfaces example program demonstrates the `FractalizeSurface` method. It uses the following code to define its scene.

```
private void DefineModel()
{
    // Remove non-light models.
    for (int i = MainGroup.Children.Count - 1; i >= 0; i--)
        if (!(MainGroup.Children[i] is Light))
            MainGroup.Children.RemoveAt(i);

    // Axes.
    MeshExtensions.AddAxes(MainGroup);

    // Make the initial surface.
    Point3D[,] surface =
    {
        {
            new Point3D(-3, 2, -3),
            new Point3D(-3, 0, 3),
        },
        {
            new Point3D(3, 0, -3),
            new Point3D(3, -1, 3),
        }
    };

    // Fractalize.
    surface = G3.FractalizeSurface(surface, 5, -1, -2, 2);

    // Make the mesh.
    MeshGeometry3D mesh1 = new MeshGeometry3D();
    mesh1.AddSurface(surface);
    MainGroup.Children.Add(mesh1.MakeModel(Brushes.LightBlue));

    // Make a wireframe.
    HashSet<Edge> edges = new HashSet<Edge>();
    MeshGeometry3D mesh2 = new MeshGeometry3D();
    mesh2.AddSurface(surface, false, edges, 0.005);
    MainGroup.Children.Add(mesh2.MakeModel(Brushes.Blue));
}
```

The program calls this method whenever you click its Generate button, so the method starts by removing any previous surface. It does that by looping through the main `Model3DGroup` object's `Children` collection and removing any objects that are not lights.

Next, the code creates the coordinate axes. It then defines a two-by-two array containing the four points (-3, 2, -3), (-3, 0, 3), (3, 0, -3), and (3, -1, 3). Those points define the four corners of the initial surface.

The code then passes the point array into the `FractalizeSurface` method. The second parameter indicates that the method should perform five iterations. That means the final surface will contain 4^5=1,024 areas that will eventually be represented by 2×1,024=2,048 triangles.

The third parameter to `FractalizeSurface` is -1, indicating that the method should not use a seed when creating its `Random` object. That allows the program to create a different random surface every time you click the button.

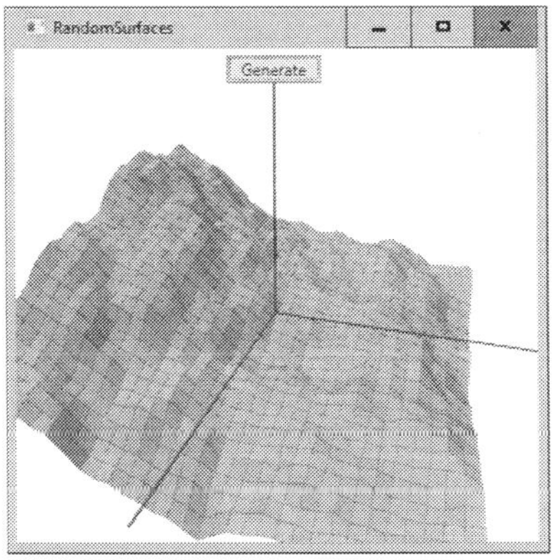

Figure 29-5: The RandomSurfaces example program displays random fractal surfaces.

The final two parameters, -2 and 2, make the method adjust new Y coordinates by amounts between -2 and 2. Remember that these values apply only to the first round of midpoints. Each time the surface's area is divided, the amount by which the new Y coordinates might be adjusted is divided by two.

After it finishes fractalizing the points, the program creates a mesh and calls its `AddSurface` extension method to turn the `surface` array into a surface mesh. It creates a second mesh and calls `AddSurface` again, this time passing it a `HashSet` of edges to create a wireframe.

Figure 29-5 shows the RandomSurfaces example program displaying a surface.

FractalLandscape

The RandomSurfaces example program creates some interesting surfaces, but they hardly look like landscapes. The FractalLandscape example program shown in Figure 29-6 does some extra processing to make the result look a bit more natural.

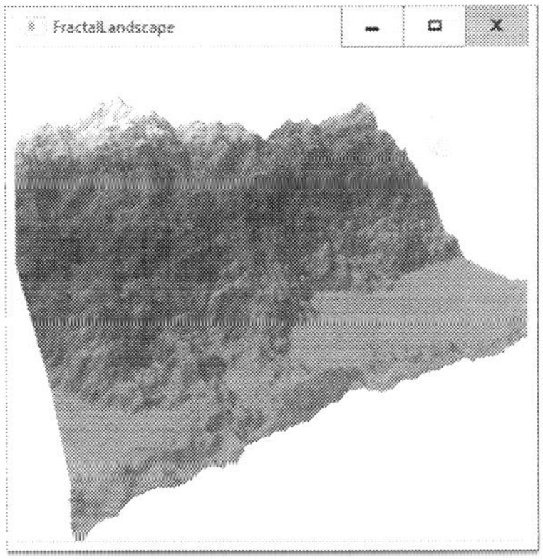

Figure 29-6: The FractalLandscape example program builds a more natural fractal landscape.

If you download the program and run it, you'll see that the landscape uses colors to suggest a more realistic landscape. The flat areas on the bottom are blue so they look like water. The sides of the mountain range shade through green, brown, gray, and white. You probably won't mistake the image for a photograph, but it's not hard to imagine it representing a mountain scene.

The following code shows how this program creates its landscape.

```
private void DefineModel(Model3DGroup group)
{
    // Make the initial surface.
```

```
        int numX = 10;
        int numZ = 10;
        Point3D[,] surface = G3.InitSurface(0, numX, -3, 3, numZ, -3, 3);

        // Add some interest.
        Random rand = new Random(0);
        for (int ix = 0; ix < numX; ix++)
        {
            for (int iz = 0; iz < numZ; iz++)
            {
                double x = surface[ix, iz].X;
                double z = surface[ix, iz].Z;
                surface[ix, iz].Y = 1 - Math.Sin(x) + Math.Sin(z) / 5;
            }
        }

        // Fractalize.
        surface = G3.FractalizeSurface(surface, 4, 12345, -0.4, 0.4);

        // Limit Y.
        G3.LimitY(surface, minY: 0.15);

        // Make the mesh.
        MeshGeometry3D mesh1 = new MeshGeometry3D();
        mesh1.AddSurface(surface);

        // Apply a height map.
        double minY = surface[0, 0].Y;
        double maxY = minY;
        foreach (Point3D point in surface)
        {
            if (minY > point.Y) minY = point.Y;
            if (maxY < point.Y) maxY = point.Y;
        }
        mesh1.ApplyHeightMap(0, 1, minY, maxY);

        GradientStopCollection stops = new GradientStopCollection();
        stops.Add(new GradientStop(Colors.Blue, 0));
        stops.Add(new GradientStop(Colors.Blue, 0.001));
        stops.Add(new GradientStop(Colors.Chartreuse, 0.002));
        stops.Add(new GradientStop(Colors.Chartreuse, 0.2));
        stops.Add(new GradientStop(Colors.OliveDrab, 0.4));
        stops.Add(new GradientStop(Colors.Gray, 0.7));
        stops.Add(new GradientStop(Colors.White, 0.9));
        stops.Add(new GradientStop(Colors.White, 1));
        LinearGradientBrush brush =
            new LinearGradientBrush(stops, new Point(0, 0), new Point(1, 1));

        GeometryModel3D model = mesh1.MakeModel(brush);
        model.BackMaterial = new DiffuseMaterial(Brushes.Gray);
        group.Children.Add(model);
    }
```

The method first calls `InitSurface` (described shortly) to create an initial flat surface within the area $-3 \leq \{x, z\} \leq 3$, and with $y=0$.

It then loops over the points and sets their Y coordinates to the result of an equation that gives the surface its basic structure. The result so far is sort of a wavy ridge along the back of the viewing area and a valley in the front.

The method then calls `FractalizeSurface` to add randomness. It calls the `LimitY` method (also described shortly) to set a lower limit on the surface's Y values. That adds some water-like features to the terrain.

The code then converts the surface into a mesh as before.

To give the result some more realistic coloring, the program then creates a height map. First, it loops through the points and finds the minimum and maximum Y values. It calls `ApplyHeightMap` (yet another method described shortly) to give the points texture coordinates that depend on their Y coordinates.

Next, the program creates a linear gradient brush with colors that shade through blue, chartreuse, olive drab, gray, and white. The code finishes by converting the mesh into a model that uses the brush. The points' texture coordinates, which depend on the points' Y coordinates, give the points their correct colors.

The following sections describe the program's helper methods.

InitSurface

The `InitSurface` method shown in the following code makes it easier to create a flat surface.

```
public static Point3D[,] InitSurface(double y,
    int numX, double xmin, double xmax,
    int numZ, double zmin, double zmax)
{
    double dx = (xmax - xmin) / (numX - 1);
    double dz = (zmax - zmin) / (numZ - 1);
    Point3D[,] surface = new Point3D[numX, numZ];
    for (int ix = 0; ix < numX; ix++)
    {
        double x = xmin + ix * dx;
        for (int iz = 0; iz < numX; iz++)
        {
            double z = zmin + iz * dz;
            surface[ix, iz] = new Point3D(x, y, z);
        }
    }
    return surface;
}
```

This method calculates the dimensions `dx` and `dz` that the pieces of the surface will have. It then allocates an array to hold the surface's points and loops over them, assigning their coordinates. It sets the points' X and Z coordinates to make them divide the surface evenly. It sets the points' Y coordinates to the `y` value passed in as a parameter.

LimitY

The `LimitY` method shown in the following code ensures that a surface's Y coordinates lie between upper and lower bounds.

```
public static void LimitY(Point3D[,] surface,
    double minY = double.MinValue, double maxY = double.MaxValue)
{
    int numX = surface.GetUpperBound(0) + 1;
    int numZ = surface.GetUpperBound(1) + 1;
    for (int ix = 0; ix < numX; ix++)
    {
        for (int iz = 0; iz < numZ; iz++)
        {
            double y = surface[ix, iz].Y;
            if (y < minY) y = minY;
            if (y > maxY) y = maxY;
            surface[ix, iz].Y = y;
        }
    }
}
```

This method simply loops through the points, compares their Y coordinates to `minY` and `maxY`, and updates any coordinates that fall outside of the allowed range.

ApplyHeightMap

The `ApplyHeightMap` method shown in the following code gives texture coordinates to a mesh's points depending on their Y values.

```
public static void ApplyHeightMap(this MeshGeometry3D mesh,
    double minV, double maxV, double minY, double maxY)
{
    double ydiff = maxY - minY;
    double vdiff = maxV - minV;
    mesh.TextureCoordinates.Clear();
    for (int i = 0; i < mesh.Positions.Count; i++)
    {
        double v = minV + (mesh.Positions[i].Y - minY) * vdiff / ydiff;
        mesh.TextureCoordinates.Add(new Point(0, v));
    }
}
```

This code loops through the mesh's points and sets their texture coordinates. If a point has Y value close to `minY`, it gives that point a texture coordinate with V value close to `minV`. Similarly, if a point's Y coordinate is close to `maxY`, it gives the point a texture coordinate with V close to `maxV`.

Moonscape

The Moonscape example program shown in Figure 29-7 draws a scene that's intended to look something like the lunar surface. This example is somewhat similar to the FractalLandscape example but it uses a different technique for building the underlying scene that is then randomized. (It also uses different colors. I don't think there are blue lakes and green trees on the moon.)

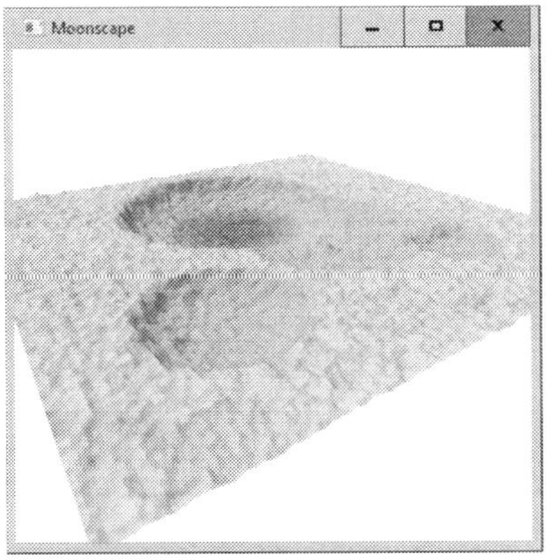

Figure 29-7: The Moonscape example program displays a surface with fractal craters.

The following code shows how the program builds its scene.

```
private void DefineModel(Model3DGroup group)
{
    // Make the initial surface.
    int numX = 40;
    int numZ = 40;
    Point3D[,] surface =
        G3.InitSurface(0, numX, -3, 3, numZ, -3, 3);

    // Add some craters.
    AddCrater(surface, -1, 0, 1.5, 0.3);
    AddCrater(surface, 1.6, -1.5, 0.5, 0.4);
    AddCrater(surface, 1.5, 1.5, 0.75, 0.3);
    AddCrater(surface, 0.5, -0.6, 1.25, 0.1);

    // Add some relatively large-scale randomness to random points.
    Random rand = new Random(0);
    for (int i = 0; i < 10; i++)
    {
        int ix = rand.Next(0, numX);
        int iz = rand.Next(0, numZ);
        surface[ix, iz].Y += rand.NextDouble(-0.1, 0.1);
    }

    // Fractalize.
    surface = G3.FractalizeSurface(surface, 2, 1, -0.05, 0.05);

    // Translate to center better.
    TranslateTransform3D trans = new TranslateTransform3D(0, 1, 0);
    numX = surface.GetUpperBound(0) + 1;
    numZ = surface.GetUpperBound(1) + 1;
    for (int ix = 0; ix < numX; ix++)
        for (int iz = 0; iz < numZ; iz++)
            surface[ix, iz] = trans.Transform(surface[ix, iz]);

    // Make the mesh.
    MeshGeometry3D mesh1 = new MeshGeometry3D();
    mesh1.AddSurface(surface);

    // Apply a height map.
    double minY = surface[0, 0].Y;
    double maxY = minY;
    foreach (Point3D point in surface)
    {
        if (minY > point.Y) minY = point.Y;
        if (maxY < point.Y) maxY = point.Y;
    }
    mesh1.ApplyHeightMap(0, 1, minY, maxY);

    GradientStopCollection stops = new GradientStopCollection();
```

```
        stops.Add(new GradientStop(Colors.Gray, 0));
        stops.Add(new GradientStop(Colors.LightGray, 0.25));
        stops.Add(new GradientStop(Colors.LightGray, 0.75));
        stops.Add(new GradientStop(Colors.White, 1));
        LinearGradientBrush brush =
            new LinearGradientBrush(stops, new Point(0, 0), new Point(1, 1));
        group.Children.Add(mesh1.MakeModel(brush));
    }
```

This code uses the `InitSurface` method to create an initial surface. This time it uses many more divisions in the X and Z directions to better show the shape of the craters created next.

The code calls the `AddCrater` method described shortly to add some circular dents to the surface. If the initial surface doesn't contain a relatively large number of points, then the craters don't look round.

Next, the program picks some random points and adjusts their Y coordinates by up to 0.1 up or down. This gives the surface a few spots that are a bit less uniform.

The program then fractalizes the surface and translates its points up a bit to center the surface in the program's viewport.

The code then converts the point data into a mesh containing a surface and creates a height map much as the FractalLandscape example program did. This program uses a linear gradient brush that shades from gray to light gray to white.

The following code shows the `AddCrater` method.

```
    private void AddCrater(Point3D[,] surface, double cx, double cz,
        double radius, double yscale)
    {
        int numX = surface.GetUpperBound(0) + 1;
        int numZ = surface.GetUpperBound(1) + 1;
        for (int ix = 0; ix < numX; ix++)
        {
            for (int iz = 0; iz < numZ; iz++)
            {
                double dx = surface[ix, iz].X - cx;
                double dz = surface[ix, iz].Z - cz;
                double y = -yscale * Math.Sqrt(radius * radius - (dx * dx + dz * dz));
                if (surface[ix, iz].Y > y) surface[ix, iz].Y = y;
            }
        }
    }
```

This code loops over the X and Z coordinates of the points on the surface. If a point is within distance `radius` of the center point (`cx`, `cz`), the code subtracts a value from the point's Y coordinate. The value it subtracts is the distance of the point from the crater's center multiplied by a scale factor. The result is a roughly circular indentation.

Random Sphere

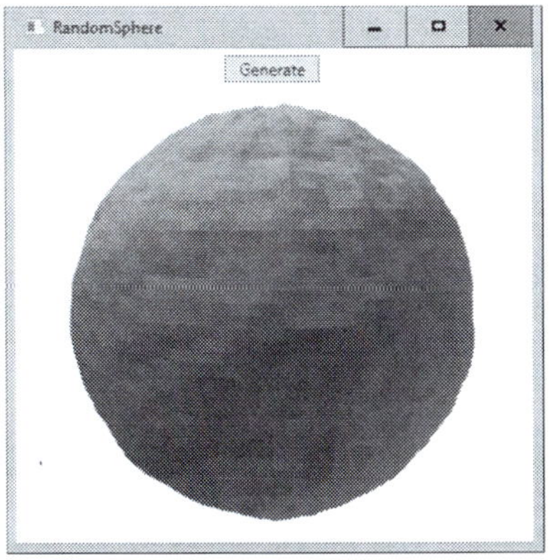

Figure 29-8: The RandomSphere example program randomizes a sphere's surface.

The previous examples use midpoint displacement to randomize a flat surface, but with a little extra work, you can apply the same techniques to just about any surface. For example, the RandomSphere example program shown in Figure 29-8 uses this method to make a sphere with a bumpy surface. You can adjust the parameters passed into the `FractalizeSurface` method to change the sphere's bumpiness.

The program uses the following code to create its scene.

```
private void DefineModel()
{
    // Remove non-light models.
    for (int i = MainGroup.Children.Count - 1; i >= 0; i--)
        if (!(MainGroup.Children[i] is Light))
            MainGroup.Children.RemoveAt(i);

    // Make an initial sphere with coordinates theta, r, phi.
    const double minTheta = 0;
    const double maxTheta = Math.PI * 2;
    const int numTheta = 20;
    const double dTheta = (maxTheta - minTheta) / numTheta;
    const double minPhi = 0;
    const double maxPhi = Math.PI;
    const int numPhi = 10;
    const double dPhi = (maxPhi - minPhi) / numPhi;
    const double r = 3;
    Point3D[,] surface = new Point3D[numTheta + 1, numPhi + 1];
    double theta = minTheta;
    for (int it = 0; it <= numTheta; it++)
    {
        double phi = minPhi;
        for (int ip = 0; ip <= numPhi; ip++)
        {
            surface[it, ip] = new Point3D(theta, r, phi);
            phi += dPhi;
        }
        theta += dTheta;
    }

    // Fractalize.
    surface = G3.FractalizeSurface(surface, 3, -1, -0.125, 0.125);

    // Make the edges match.
    int numT = surface.GetUpperBound(0);
    for (int j = 0; j <= surface.GetUpperBound(1); j++)
    {
        surface[numT, j] = surface[0, j];
    }
```

```
        // Convert the points into Cartesian coordinates.
        for (int i = 0; i <= surface.GetUpperBound(0); i++)
        {
            for (int j = 0; j <= surface.GetUpperBound(1); j++)
            {
                surface[i, j] = SphericalToCartesian(
                    surface[i, j].Y, surface[i, j].X, surface[i, j].Z);
            }
        }

        // Make the mesh.
        MeshGeometry3D mesh1 = new MeshGeometry3D();
        mesh1.AddSurface(surface);
        MainGroup.Children.Add(mesh1.MakeModel(Brushes.LightBlue));

        // Make a wireframe.
        HashSet<Edge> edges = new HashSet<Edge>();
        MeshGeometry3D mesh2 = new MeshGeometry3D();
        mesh2.AddSurface(surface, false, edges, 0.005);
        MainGroup.Children.Add(mesh2.MakeModel(Brushes.Blue));
    }
```

The method removes any previous objects that are not lights. It then initializes the `surface` array to hold points on the sphere in spherical coordinates. The `Point3D` structures hold the points' θ, radius, and φ values.

Next, the code calls `FractalizeSurface` to displace the points' Y coordinates. The Y coordinates hold the points' radii in spherical coordinates, so it is the radii that are displaced.

The sphere is a closed solid so the points with $\theta=0$ should be the same as those with $\theta=2\pi$. After the values have been randomly displaced, however, that is no longer true. To fix that, the code loops through the values where $\theta=2\pi$ and sets them equal to the corresponding values where $\theta=0$.

The code then loops through the values and converts them from spherical to Cartesian coordinates. It calls `AddSurface` to turn the points into a surface and displays the result.

Summary

This chapter explains how to use the midpoint displacement algorithm. Because you use the same technique, suitably scaled, at different levels of resolution, the result has a fractal structure that can give the surface a natural appearance. Color can make the surface appear even more natural. If you want to make the illusion even more complete, you can add objects such as rocks, trees, and bushes to the scene.

Applying midpoint displacement to objects such as spheres gives them a textured appearance. Another way to change an object's appearance is to give it a textured material. The next chapters explains how you can define a specific kind of texture: those containing text.

Chapter 30 Three-Dimensional Text

This chapter explains how you can display text in a three-dimensional scene.

The simplest way to display three-dimensional text is to create an image containing the text and then use that image to texture an object. Unfortunately, that method has a couple of drawbacks.

First, it has limited resolution. If you zoom in far enough on an object displaying a texture, you will eventually see the pixels that make up the texture. That's not the end of the world, but it's somewhat annoying.

A bigger problem is that this technique makes it hard to change the text at runtime.

Fortunately, there's a simple approach that handles both of those problems. Create a `VisualBrush` and use it to make the object's material. As its name implies, a `VisualBrush` displays the contents of a `Visual` object. The `Visual` class is an ancestor for the huge number of classes that render graphics, and that includes controls such as `Label` and `TextBlock` that can display text.

> **NOTE:** A `VisualBrush` is remarkably flexible, but that flexibility comes with reduced performance. The following list shows WPF's brush types in order of decreasing performance.
>
> `SolidColorBrush` Fastest
>
> `LinearGradientBrush`
>
> `ImageBrush`
>
> `DrawingBrush` (cached)
>
> `VisualBrush` (cached)
>
> `RadialGradientBrush`
>
> `DrawingBrush` (uncached)
>
> `VisualBrush` (uncached) Slowest

> Usually you can ignore the performance differences, but you may need to use the simpler brushes if you want to display many thousands of objects.

The biggest problem with this approach is an embarrassment of riches. WPF's visual controls provide so much flexibility that it can be hard to figure out the best way to arrange the controls that create the text.

The two following sections explain different methods for displaying relatively simple three-dimensional text on a rectangle. The section after that shows how to display text on a more complicated surface.

Fitted Text

Often you might like to display text that is scaled to be as large as possible within some area. The `AddFittedText` method shown in the following code takes that approach.

```
public static GeometryModel3D AddFittedText(this MeshGeometry3D mesh,
    string text, Point3D ll, Point3D lr, Point3D ur, Point3D ul,
    Brush bgBrush, Brush fgBrush, TextAlignment textAlign = TextAlignment.Center,
    FontFamily fontFamily = null)
{
    Point3D[] points = { ll, lr, ur, ul };
    Point[] textureCoords =
    {
        new Point(0, 1),
        new Point(1, 1),
        new Point(1, 0),
        new Point(0, 0),
    };
    mesh.AddPolygon(points: points, textureCoords: textureCoords);

    // Make a material holding the text.
    double width = (ur - ul).Length;
    double height = (ul - ll).Length;
    Material material = mesh.MakeFittedTextMaterial(text,
        width, height, bgBrush, fgBrush, textAlign, fontFamily);

    // Make a model and return it.
    return new GeometryModel3D(mesh, material);
}
```

This method's `ll`, `lr`, `ur`, and `ul` parameters give the lower left, lower right, upper right, and upper left corners of the rectangle that should hold the text. The code creates a corresponding texture coordinate array and calls the `AddPolygon` method to create the rectangle.

Next, the code uses vector arithmetic to calculate the width and height of the rectangle and calls the `MakeFittedTextMaterial` method (described shortly) to make a material to fit the rectangle. The method finishes by creating a new `GeometryModel3D` for the mesh and material.

Before I describe the `MakeFittedTextMaterial` method, I want to explain the controls that it uses to create its `VisualBrush`. The most obvious controls for displaying text are the `Label` and `TextBlock` controls. The `TextBlock` control has better alignment features, so that's the control I decided to use.

By itself, a `TextBlock` displays text at a specific size, so it won't resize the text to fit an area. Fortunately, the `Viewbox` control can resize whatever control it contains. It even provides several resize modes. The one used here enlarges the control's contents as much as possible without causing distortion.

Unfortunately, if you use a `Viewbox` control as a brush, it will only fill the area behind its resized contents. For example, Figure 30-1 shows a `Viewbox` inside a rectangle. The `Viewbox` enlarged the text as much as possible without distorting it, so the text fills the width of the rectangle. The `Viewbox` only occupies the space behind the text, so the top and bottom parts of the rectangle are not colored by the `Viewbox` control's background.

Figure 30-1: A `Viewbox` only fills the area behind its contents.

This is a problem for three-dimensional drawing. If you use a `Viewbox` to define the material for a rectangle, then parts of the rectangle will be transparent.

To work around this problem, the `MakeFittedTextMaterial` method places the `Viewbox` inside a `Grid` control, and that control fills the background.

To summarize, the `Grid` provides a background, the `TextBlock` draws the text, and the `Viewbox` makes the `TextBlock` as large as possible.

The following code shows the `MakeFittedTextMaterial` method.

```
public static Material MakeFittedTextMaterial(this MeshGeometry3D mesh,
    string text, double width, double height, Brush bgBrush, Brush fgBrush,
    TextAlignment textAlign = TextAlignment.Center,
    FontFamily fontFamily = null)
{
    // Make a grid to hold everything and display the background.
    Grid grid = new Grid();
    grid.Background = bgBrush;
    grid.Width = width;          // Size to fit the area.
    grid.Height = height;

    // Make a viewbox to scale the text to fit.
    Viewbox box = new Viewbox();
    grid.Children.Add(box);
```

```
        box.Width = grid.Width;     // Size to fit the area.
        box.Height = grid.Height;

        // Make a TextBlock to display the text.
        TextBlock block = new TextBlock();
        box.Child = block;
        block.Text = text;
        block.Foreground = fgBrush;
        block.TextAlignment = textAlign;
        if (fontFamily != null) block.FontFamily = fontFamily;
        block.Margin = new Thickness(block.FontSize / 10);

        // Make a brush.
        VisualBrush brush = new VisualBrush(grid);
        brush.Stretch = Stretch.Fill;

        // Make the brush into a material and return it.
        return new DiffuseMaterial(brush);
    }
```

This method creates a `Grid` control and sets its background. It gives the `Grid` the same width and height as the rectangle that it should fill.

Next, the code creates a `Viewbox` and places it inside the `Grid`. It gives the `Viewbox` the same width and height as the `Grid`.

The method then creates a `TextBlock` and places it inside the `Viewbox`. It sets the `TextBlock` control's text, foreground brush, and text alignment. If the method's parameters include a font family, the code also sets that property. The code then sets the control's `Margin` property.

> **NOTE:** If you don't include some margin, then the text seems to extend slightly beyond the edges of the `Grid` control. As a result, the `Grid` doesn't fill the `VisualBrush` all the way to its edges, so the rectangle has thin transparent pieces along some of its edges.

The method then uses the `Grid` to make a `VisualBrush`. It sets the brush's `Stretch` property to `Fill` so the brush resizes its contents (the `Grid`) to fill the brush.

Finally, the method uses the brush to make a new `DiffuseMaterial` and returns it.

The FittedText example program shown in Figure 30-2 demonstrates the `AddFittedText` method. It displays the text "3D Text" three times in rectangles with transparent background brushes. First, it creates the rectangle in the middle, then the one in front, and then the one in back. The program draws thin segments around each of its rectangles so you can see where they are.

If you look closely, you can see that the middle rectangle's text is visible through the rectangle in front. The text in the back, however, is covered by the other two rectangles even though they have transparent backgrounds.

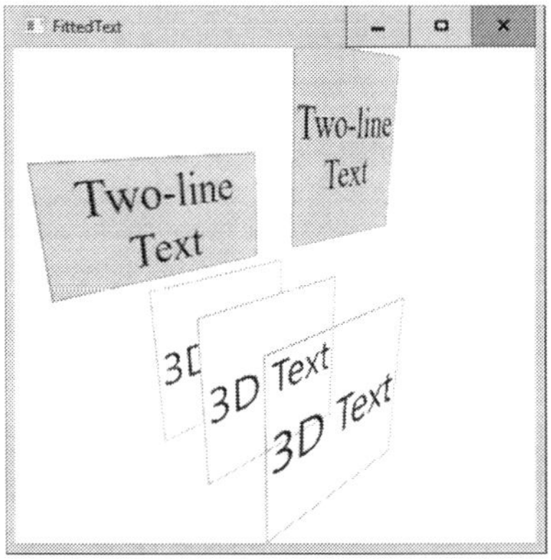

Figure 30-2: The FittedText example program demonstrates the `AddFittedText` method.

You may recall from the section "Translucent Materials" in Chapter 18 that this is an issue in WPF. The renderer draws objects ordered by their z-order. When it draws an object, it determines whether parts of the object are blocked by objects that were drawn earlier. In this example, that happens when the program draws the third rectangle, which is behind the other two. The renderer decides that it is blocked by the other rectangles, so it doesn't draw all of that rectangle.

After it draws the first three rectangles, the FittedText example program draws two more rectangles with solid backgrounds. Those rectangles display multiline text and are sized to show how the `AddFittedText` method can center text vertically or horizontally.

Fixed-Sized Text

Often you will want to draw text as large as possible as described in the preceding section, but sometimes that would produce strange results. For example, suppose you want to draw a three-dimensional graph (Chapter 34 describes graphs) and you want to label parts of the graph with the names of the months. If each label's text is enlarged to fit rectangles of the same size, then "May" will be enlarged much more than "November." Different labels will be drawn with different font sizes producing an inconsistent result.

The following `AddSizedText` method solves this problem by drawing text at a specified font size.

```
public static GeometryModel3D AddSizedText(this MeshGeometry3D mesh, string text,
    double fontSize, double matWidth, double matHeight,
    Point3D ll, Point3D lr, Point3D ur, Point3D ul,
    Brush bgBrush, Brush fgBrush,
    HorizontalAlignment hAlign = HorizontalAlignment.Center,
    VerticalAlignment vAlign = VerticalAlignment.Center,
    FontFamily fontFamily = null)
{
    Point3D[] points = { ll, lr, ur, ul };
    Point[] textureCoords =
    {
        new Point(0, 1),
        new Point(1, 1),
        new Point(1, 0),
```

```
            new Point(0, 0),
        };
        mesh.AddPolygon(points: points, textureCoords: textureCoords);

        // Make a material holding the text.
        double width = (ur - ul).Length;
        double height = (ul - ll).Length;
        Material material = mesh.MakeSizedTextMaterial(text,
            fontSize, matWidth, matHeight,
            bgBrush, fgBrush, hAlign, vAlign, fontFamily);

        // Make a model and return it.
        return new GeometryModel3D(mesh, material);
    }
```

This method works much as does the `AddFittedText` method described in the preceding section. The main difference is that it calls the following `MakeSizedTextMaterial` method to make its material.

```
    public static Material MakeSizedTextMaterial(this MeshGeometry3D mesh, string text,
        double fontSize, double matWidth, double matHeight,
        Brush bgBrush, Brush fgBrush,
        HorizontalAlignment hAlign = HorizontalAlignment.Center,
        VerticalAlignment vAlign = VerticalAlignment.Center,
        FontFamily fontFamily = null)
    {
        // Make a grid to hold everything and display the background.
        Grid grid = new Grid();
        grid.Background = bgBrush;
        grid.Width = matWidth;          // Size to fit the area.
        grid.Height = matHeight;

        // Make a TextBlock to display the text.
        TextBlock block = new TextBlock();
        grid.Children.Add(block);
        block.FontSize = fontSize;
        block.Text = text;
        block.Foreground = fgBrush;
        if (fontFamily != null) block.FontFamily = fontFamily;
        block.HorizontalAlignment = hAlign;
        block.VerticalAlignment = vAlign;
        block.Margin = new Thickness(fontSize / 10);

        // Make a brush.
        VisualBrush brush = new VisualBrush(grid);
        brush.Stretch = Stretch.Fill;

        // Make the brush into a material and return it.
        return new DiffuseMaterial(brush);
    }
```

This method makes a `Grid` control much as the `MakeFittedTextMaterial` method did. Instead of making a `Viewbox` that holds a `TextBlock`, this method places its `TextBlock` directly inside the `Grid`.

It sets the TextBlock properties largely as before. This time, however, it also sets the control's HorizontalAlignment and VerticalAlignment properties to position the TextBlock inside the Grid.

The method finishes as before by making a VisualBrush and using it to create a DiffuseMaterial.

The SameSizedText example program shown in Figure 30-3 uses the AddSizedText method to draw nine rectangles displaying text with various horizontal and vertical alignments. (The figure shows the rectangles viewed head-on so the result looks two-dimensional.)

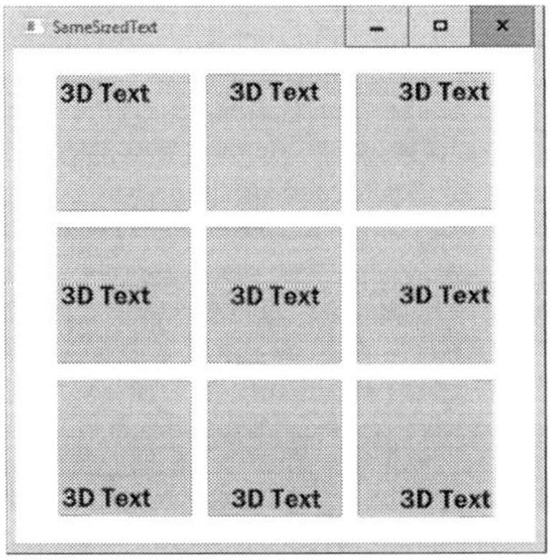

Figure 30-3: The SameSizedText example program demonstrates the AddSizedText method.

The following code fragment shows how the SameSizedText example program draws the piece of text on the upper left.

```
FontFamily fontFamily = new FontFamily("Franklin Gothic Demi");
const double fontSize = 0.4;
const double matWidth = 2;
const double matHeight = 2;
const string text = "3D Text";
double y = 1.25;
double z = 1.25;

MeshGeometry3D mesh1 = new MeshGeometry3D();
MainGroup.Children.Add(mesh1.AddSizedText(text,
    fontSize, matWidth, matHeight,
    new Point3D(0, y, z + 2), new Point3D(0, y, z),
    new Point3D(0, y + 2, z), new Point3D(0, y + 2, z + 2),
    Brushes.LightGreen, Brushes.Black,
    HorizontalAlignment.Left, VerticalAlignment.Top, fontFamily));
z -= 2.25;
```

This code creates a new font family, a font size, and some variables to make positioning the rectangles easier.

Notice that the font size it quite small at 0.4. Normally Windows programs specify font size in points, but sizes that make sense in a three-dimensional program depend on the scale of the drawing. The rectangles used in this example are only two units on a side, so the font must be relatively small to fit. If the program used a 12-point font, only a tiny piece of the text would be visible.

The code then creates a mesh and uses its AddSizedText extension method to create the text. It adds the result to the main Model3DGroup and decreases the variable z to position the next rectangle.

Download the example program to see additional details.

Text Textures

The FittedText and SameSized Text example programs show how to draw text on a rectangle. There's no reason why you can't use similar techniques to draw text on more complicated objects. The TextTextures example program shown in Figure 30-4 uses the following code to do just that.

Figure 30-4: The TextTextures example program draws text on a surface.

```
private void DefineModel()
{
    MeshGeometry3D mesh = new MeshGeometry3D();
    mesh.AddSurface(Quadratic,
        -2, 2, 0, 1, 20,
        -2, 2, 0, 1, 20, true);
    Material mat = mesh.MakeFittedTextMaterial(
        "A day without\nsunshine\nis like,\nyou know, night.",
        1, 1, Brushes.LightBlue, Brushes.Black);
    GeometryModel3D model = new GeometryModel3D(mesh, mat);
    MainGroup.Children.Add(model);
}
```

This code makes a mesh and calls its `AddSurface` extension method to add a surface to it. It passes the `Quadratic` function described shortly into `AddSurface` to produce an inverted bowl shape. The other parameters define the surface over the values $-2 \leq \{x, z\} \leq 2$ and give the points texture coordinate ranging from 0 to 1.

The method then calls the `MakeFittedTextMaterial` method described earlier in this chapter to make a material one unit wide and one unit tall that contains the text. It uses the mesh and material to create a model and adds the model to the main `Model3DGroup`.

The following code shows the `Quadratic` method.

```
private Point3D Quadratic(double x, double z)
{
    double y = 3.0 - (x * x + z * z) / 5.0;
    return new Point3D(x, y, z);
}
```

This method simply uses the following equation to create a point for a given x and z value.

$$y = 3 - \frac{x^2 + z^2}{5}$$

Download the example to see additional details.

Summary

The basic idea behind three-dimensional text is fairly simple: use a `VisualBrush` to create a material and then cover a three-dimensional object with it. This chapter showed how to handle two particularly useful situations: text sized to fit a rectangle and text created at a specific size.

Those aren't the only possible ways that you can arrange text, however. By using different combinations of controls and alignment properties, you can arrange one or more pieces of text in almost any way imaginable. Often the hard part is figuring out exactly how you want to arrange the controls that define the brush.

In fact, this method works not only with text but also with just about any visual control that you place inside a `VisualBrush`. For example, you could fill the brush with a `Grid` holding an assortment of `Label`, `Image`, and `Polygon` controls.

You can even make a brush containing a `MediaElement` that plays video. The VideoTexture example program shown in Figure 30-5 creates a quadratic surface that displays a looping video of a bear standing in a stream. Download the example to see how it works.

Figure 30-5: The VideoTexture example program maps a video onto a surface.

Three-dimensional text can be useful in some applications and it certainly looks cool, but sometimes it's better to use simple two-dimensional text drawn on top of a three-dimensional scene. For example, that lets you create a heads-up display that doesn't move even when the viewing angle changes. The following chapter explains how to create that kind of text.

Chapter 31

Two-Dimensional Text

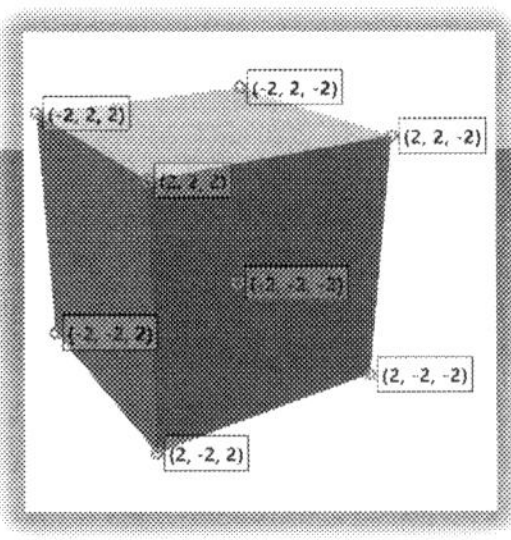

Chapter 30 explained how to draw three-dimensional text. Three-dimensional text looks cool and can provide useful information in some applications, but sometimes it's better to display two-dimensional text on top of a three-dimensional scene. Unlike three-dimensional text, this kind of text always faces the camera even if you change the viewing position.

For example, you could use two-dimensional text to create a heads-up display showing summary information. Or you could use two-dimensional text to label objects in the scene.

This chapter explains how to draw two-dimensional text in a three-dimensional scene.

> **NOTE:** You can extend this notion further to perform more general two-dimensional annotations of a scene. For example, you might like to draw a circle around part of a scene to highlight that part. The techniques described in this chapter will let you do that, also.

The following section explains the relatively easy problem of drawing text above or below the scene in fixed positions. The sections after that explain the much harder problem of displaying text at positions defined by the objects in the scene.

Text in Fixed Positions

Displaying text in a fixed position o the viewport is easy. Simply add controls to the program to display the text. The only catch is that you must ensure that the controls appear in the proper position in the application's stacking order. Controls that come before the `Viewport3D` object in the XAML code are drawn behind the scene. Controls that come after the `Viewport3D` are drawn above the scene.

For example, the following XAML code defines two `Canvas` controls, one behind the viewport and one in front of it. Each of the `Canvas` controls contains a `Label` that displays some text.

```
<Grid Name="MainGrid" Background="White">
    <Canvas Name="backCanvas" HorizontalAlignment="Stretch"
        VerticalAlignment="Stretch">
        <Label Content="Text in Back" FontSize="30" Canvas.Top="50"/>
    </Canvas>
```

```
        <Border Name="MainBorder">
            <Viewport3D Name="mainViewport"/>
        </Border>

        <Canvas Name="foreCanvas" HorizontalAlignment="Stretch"
            VerticalAlignment="Stretch">
            <Label Content="Text on Top" FontSize="30" Canvas.Top="100"/>
        </Canvas>
    </Grid>
```

As you can probably guess, the `Label` contained in `backCanvas` is drawn behind the viewport and the `Label` contained in `foreCanvas` is drawn in front of the viewport.

The easiest way to draw text in C# code behind is to create a container control and then place the text in that. For example, the preceding code creates two `Canvas` controls, `backCanvas` and `foreCanvas`. The following code adds new `Label` controls to those `Canvas` controls.

```
// Define the model.
private void DefineModel()
{
    // Make a cube.
    MeshGeometry3D mesh = new MeshGeometry3D();
    mesh.AddBox(new Point3D(-2, -2, -2), D3.XVector(4), D3.YVector(4), D3.ZVector(4));
    MainGroup.Children.Add(mesh.MakeModel(Brushes.LightBlue));

    // Add some two-dimensional text.
    AddLabel(backCanvas, 0, 150, "More Text in Back", 30);
    AddLabel(foreCanvas, 0, 200, "More Text on Top", 30);
}

// Add a Label control inside a Canvas control.
private void AddLabel(Canvas canvas, double left, double top, string text,
    double fontsize)
{
    Label label = new Label();
    canvas.Children.Add(label);
    Canvas.SetLeft(label, left);
    Canvas.SetTop(label, top);
    label.Content = text;
    label.FontSize = fontsize;
}
```

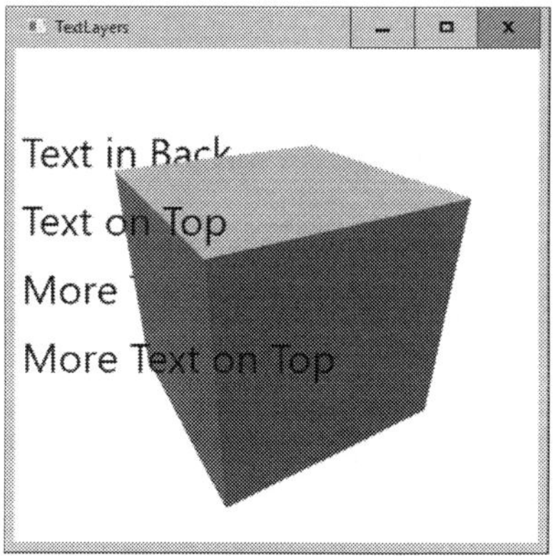

Figure 31-1: The TextLayers example program uses both XAML and C# to draw text below and above the scene.

The code first creates a box. It then calls the `AddLabel` method to add `Label` controls to the `Canvas` controls.

The `AddLabel` method creates a new `Label` control, adds it to the appropriate `Canvas` parent, and sets its `Canvas.Left`, `Canvas.Top`, `Text`, and `FontSize` properties. The position of the `Canvas` controls in the stacking order ensures that the text is drawn above or below the viewport as desired.

The TextLayers example program shown in Figure 31-1

uses the previous XAML and C# code to draw text both at design time and at runtime.

> **NOTE:** If the scene is complicated, it may be hard to see labels sitting on top of three-dimensional objects. You can make that easier by giving the labels a non-transparent background.
>
> You can make the background translucent if you want allow the scene to show through. For example, you could set a label's background color to the translucent white returned by `Color.FromArgb(128, 255, 255, 255)`.

Positioned Text

Placing text at a fixed position on the viewport is easy. Positioning text relative to the objects in a three-dimensional scene is much harder.

To do that, you need to figure out where the three-dimensional object is drawn on the two-dimensional viewport. You would think this would be easy. After all, WPF's drawing system needs to make that sort of calculation so it knows where three-dimensional objects belong on the screen. It should be simple enough for it to make that calculation available to your programs.

Unfortunately, those calculations are hidden inside the drawing system. If you want to transform three-dimensional points into two dimensions, you need to do it yourself.

The following section provides an overview of how the process of converting from three to two dimensions works. The sections after that describe the transformation matrices that perform that conversion.

> **NOTE:** The discussion in the next few sections is probably the most complex and challenging part of the book, so you may need to read it several times to absorb it all. (There's a reason why this chapter is in the "Investigating Advanced Topics" part of the book.)
>
> If you find that no amount of caffeine can keep you focused, you may want to skim the discussion and resume careful reading at the section "Locating Points" later in this chapter. That section explains how you can use the methods that map points from three to two dimensions. Building the transformations is complicated but using them isn't.

Projection Overview

Before you learn how to map three-dimensional positions to two-dimensional locations, you need to understand the full projection process. In principle, you can directly find a transformation to project the points that make up a scene with respect to a particular camera position and orientation. In practice, however, it's much easier to think of the transformation as a combination of several simpler transformations.

The following list briefly describes the coordinate systems through which the three-dimensional data moves during its trip to the two-dimensional screen.

1. *Model space*—In some applications, a model is initially built in its own coordinate system, often centered at the origin. For example, you could define a sphere at the origin intending to move it into some other position. Each object would have a *world transform* (also called an *object transform* or *model transform*) that moves the object into its final position in world space.
2. *World space*—These are the three-dimensional coordinates that determine the relationships among the scene's objects. For example, you might create several spheres, all centered at the origin in model space and then use a different world transform for each to move the spheres into their final positions. Next, you use a *view transform* to moves the objects from world space to view space.

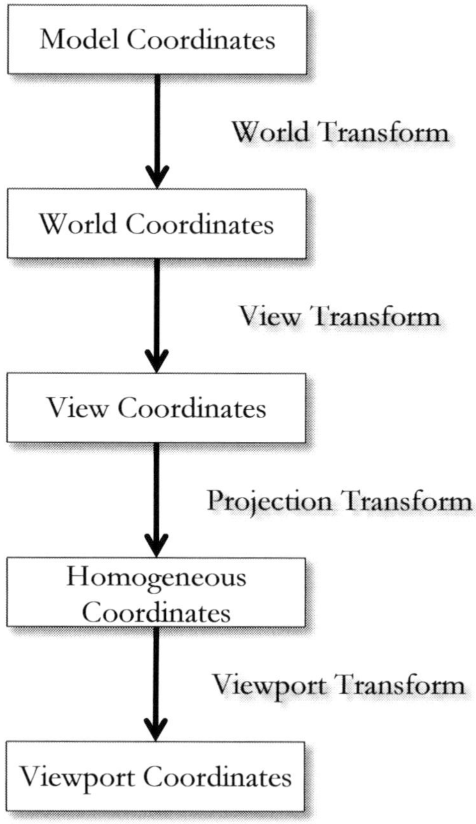

Figure 31-2: You can think of projection as a sequence of transformations.

3. *View space*—This space defines coordinates relative to the camera's position and viewing direction. Typically view space, which is also called *camera space*, repositions objects to simplify the camera's location and orientation. For example, the view transform might move the camera to the origin and make it look down the -Z axis. The next step is to use a *projection transform* to move the objects into homogeneous coordinate space.

4. *Homogeneous coordinate space*—The projection transform flattens the objects as seen from the camera's position in view space. Homogeneous coordinate space is also sometimes called *clip space* because it is at this point that you can easily clip objects that fall outside of the viewing frustum. In an orthographic projection, this transform might be as simple as removing the objects' Z coordinates. In a perspective transformation, the projection transform scales the objects' X and Y coordinates depending on their distances from the camera's position at the origin. The final step is to use a *viewport transform* to map the objects into viewport space.
5. *Viewport space*—The projection transform typically maps objects so their X and Y positions in homogeneous coordinates are between 0 and 1. The viewport transform performs the final mapping to viewport space or *device space*, which has coordinates that match those of the display area on the screen.

Figure 31-2 shows the complete sequence of transformations. I don't want to take room to explain *how* each of the transforms work, but you do need to be able to calculate them to map three-dimensional points onto the viewport, so the following sections explain how you can calculate each of these transforms.

> **NOTE:** Understanding what each of the transformations does is useful, so I felt you should see it. However, the way the transformations work is pretty confusing. If you find your eyes glazing over during the following sections, it's still not too late to skip to the section "Locating Points" later in this chapter.

World Transform

The world transform depends on your application. It lets you transform standard objects such as cubes, spheres, or cones from their standard positions (often at the origin) into whatever positions you need them to occupy in your scene.

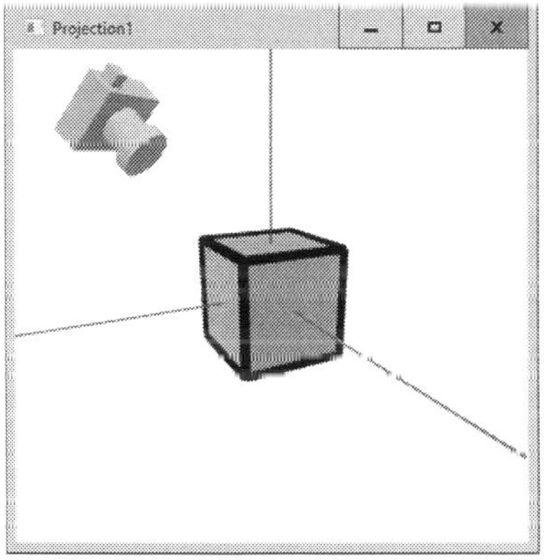

Figure 31-3: The world transform maps objects from standard starting positions to their final positions.

For example, consider the scene shown in Figure 31-3. The "camera" in the upper left is built out of a couple of boxes and a couple of cylinders. It's just there to give you a sense of how the scene is being viewed and is not part of the "real" scene.

In theory you could create the "camera's" cubes and cylinders floating out in space with their desired final orientation, but in practice that would be hard. For this program I created the "camera" objects at the origin and then rotated and translated the whole group into their final positions.

> **NOTE:** Here I'm putting "camera" in quotes to differentiate the fake camera drawn in the scene from the real camera that displays the scene. Although "real" should probably be in quotes, too, because the "real" camera is really just an abstraction and isn't any more real than the fake "camera." Hopefully you get the idea.

In a three-dimensional WPF program, a mesh's `Positions` entries are in world coordinates. That means you need to apply the world transform before you turn the rendering engine loose on your data.

> **NOTE:** Some three-dimensional drawing applications may handle the world transform differently. For example, they may let you define an object and then give it a transformation to be applied before rendering.
>
> Some applications also let you group objects into larger objects. For example, you could combine the boxes and cylinders in Figure 31-3 into a single object. Then you could manipulate the combined object as a single unit.

The target box at the origin in Figure 31-3 includes two meshes: one defining a cube and one holding a black wireframe for the cube.

The Projection1 example program creates the scene shown in Figure 31-3. The code that builds the program's scene isn't very interesting, so it isn't shown here. Download the example to see the details.

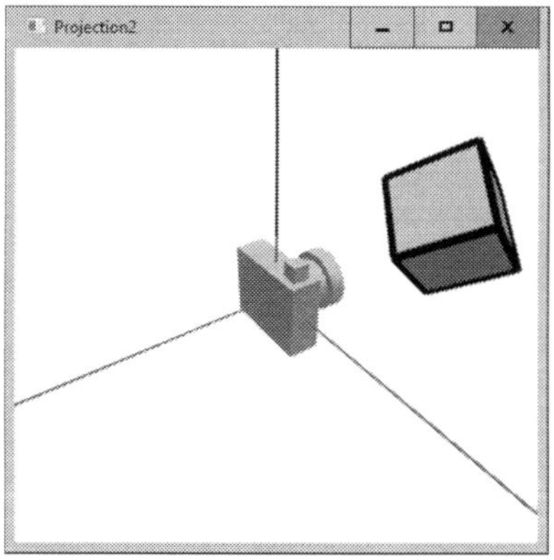

Figure 31-4: WPF's view transform moves the camera to the origin and points it along the -Z axis.

View Transform

The view transform moves the objects in the scene into a standard position and orientation to make projection easier in the next step. In WPF, the view transform moves the camera to the origin and orients it so it points down the Z axis with the Y axis as its "up" direction as shown in Figure 31-4.

You can construct a view transform out of a sequence of rotations and translations. (It's actually an interesting exercise.) The following `GetViewMatrix` method creates a matrix to represent the view transformation in a single step. This code works for projection cameras, which include both perspective and orthographic cameras.

```
public static Matrix3D GetViewMatrix(Point3D position,
    Vector3D lookDirection, Vector3D upDirection)
{
    Vector3D zaxis = -lookDirection;
    zaxis.Normalize();
    Vector3D xaxis = Vector3D.CrossProduct(upDirection, zaxis);
    xaxis.Normalize();
    Vector3D yaxis = Vector3D.CrossProduct(zaxis, xaxis);

    Vector3D positionDirection = (Vector3D)position;
    double offsetX = -Vector3D.DotProduct(xaxis, positionDirection);
    double offsetY = -Vector3D.DotProduct(yaxis, positionDirection);
    double offsetZ = -Vector3D.DotProduct(zaxis, positionDirection);

    return new Matrix3D(
        xaxis.X, yaxis.X, zaxis.X, 0,
        xaxis.Y, yaxis.Y, zaxis.Y, 0,
        xaxis.Z, yaxis.Z, zaxis.Z, 0,
        offsetX, offsetY, offsetZ, 1);
}
```

As I mentioned earlier, I'm not going to explain this calculation.

The following overloaded version of the method returns the view transform for an actual `ProjectionCamera` object.

```
public static Matrix3D GetViewMatrix(ProjectionCamera camera)
{
    return GetViewMatrix(camera.Position, camera.LookDirection, camera.UpDirection);
}
```

There is another kind of camera that I haven't covered in this book: `MatrixCamera`. A `MatrixCamera` defines a camera by explicitly specifying its view and projection matrices. Of course that begs the question, "How do you find those matrices in the first place?" (That's why I haven't covered this type of camera.)

If you *do* have a `MatrixCamera`, however, you can get its view transform by simply reading its `ViewMatrix` property.

The following version of the `GetViewMatrix` method returns a view transform matrix for all three kinds of cameras: perspective, orthographic, or matrix.

```
public static Matrix3D GetViewMatrix(Camera camera)
{
    if (camera is ProjectionCamera)
        return GetViewMatrix(camera as ProjectionCamera);
    if (camera is MatrixCamera)
        return (camera as MatrixCamera).ViewMatrix;
    throw new ArgumentException("Unknown camera type " +
        camera.GetType().FullName, "camera");
}
```

The Projection2 example program shown in Figure 31-4 uses the following code to demonstrate the view transform.

```
private void DefineModel()
{
    // Axes.
    MeshExtensions.AddAxes(MainGroup);

    // Make the objects.
    MeshGeometry3D cameraMesh, boxMesh, edgeMesh;
    Point3D cameraCenter;
    MakeObjects(out cameraMesh, out boxMesh, out edgeMesh, out cameraCenter);

    // Get the view transform.
    Matrix3D viewMat = Cameras.GetViewMatrix(
        new Point3D(cameraCenter.X, cameraCenter.Y, cameraCenter.Z),
        new Vector3D(-cameraCenter.X, -cameraCenter.Y, -cameraCenter.Z),
        D3.YVector());

    // Apply the view transform.
    cameraMesh.ApplyTransformation(viewMat);
    boxMesh.ApplyTransformation(viewMat);
    edgeMesh.ApplyTransformation(viewMat);
}
```

The code first creates models to display the coordinate axes as usual. It then creates `MeshGeometry3D` variables to define the scene's objects. It also defines a `Point3D` variable to keep track of the center of the scene's "camera" object. The program then passes those variables into the `MakeObjects` method.

The `MakeObjects` method, which is also used by the Projection1 example program, defines the scene's objects and applies a world transform to move the "camera" into an interesting position. The method is fairly long and not very interesting so it's not shown here. As always, you can download the example to see its details.

I've placed the `GetViewMatrix` method in a new static class called `Cameras`, so the code then calls `Cameras.GetViewMatrix` to get the view transform for a camera located where the "camera" object is in the scene.

The code finishes by applying that transform to the objects in the scene. That moves the "camera" to the origin and aims it down the negative Z axis. The other objects in the scene (the cube and its wireframe) are also moved by the transformation.

NOTE: The "real" camera is still out there displaying the fake "camera" and the target cube. If you download the Projection2 example program and run it, you can rotate the scene as usual to see what it looks like from different angles. In particular, you can verify that the fake "camera" is located at the origin and pointing down the -Z axis.

Projection Transform

After the scene's objects are transformed into the standard viewing position and orientation, the next step is to project the objects. For an orthographic projection, this is trivial; you simply ignore each point's Z coordinate.

For a perspective projection, the system must scale each point's X and Y coordinates depending on their distance from the camera. Objects closer to the camera appear larger and those farther away appear smaller.

> **NOTE:** Because the view transform moved the "camera" to the origin and made it point along the -Z axis, a point's distance from the camera at this point is basically the negative of its Z coordinate.

After this projection, an object's Z coordinate isn't really necessary because the object has been projected down to two dimensions. In practice, however, many systems do not bother to set each point's Z coordinate to 0. Instead they leave the Z value alone or scale it so the program can use the Z coordinates to tell which objects are closer to the camera than others.

After performing the actual projection, the transform rescales the points' X and Y coordinates to normalize them. For example, they may scale the points within the bounding volume so they have coordinates $-1 \leq \{x, y\} \leq 1$.

How you find the projection transform in WPF depends on the type of camera. The following `GetOrthographicProjectionMatrix` method works with an orthographic camera.

```
private static Matrix3D GetOrthographicProjectionMatrix(double width,
    double nearPlaneDistance, double farPlaneDistance, double aspectRatio)
{
    double w = width;
    double h = w / aspectRatio;
    double zn = nearPlaneDistance;
    double zf = farPlaneDistance;
    double m33 = 1 / (zn - zf);
    double m43 = zn * m33;
    return new Matrix3D(
        2 / w,     0,   0, 0,
            0, 2 / h,   0, 0,
            0,     0, m33, 0,
            0,     0, m43, 1);
}
```

The following `GetProjectionMatrix` method uses the preceding one to make finding the transform a bit easier if you are working with an actual `OrthographicCamera` object.

```
private static Matrix3D GetProjectionMatrix(OrthographicCamera camera,
```

```
        double aspectRatio)
    {
        return GetOrthographicProjectionMatrix(camera.Width,
            camera.NearPlaneDistance, camera.FarPlaneDistance, aspectRatio);
    }
```

The following `GetPerspectiveProjectionMatrix` method returns a perspective projection transform.

```
    public static Matrix3D GetPerspectiveProjectionMatrix(double fieldOfView,
        double nearPlaneDistance, double farPlaneDistance, double aspectRatio)
    {
        fieldOfView = DegreesToRadians(fieldOfView);
        double zn = nearPlaneDistance;
        double zf = farPlaneDistance;
        double xScale = 1 / Math.Tan(fieldOfView / 2);
        double yScale = aspectRatio * xScale;
        double m33 = (zf == double.PositiveInfinity) ? -1 : (zf / (zn - zf));
        double m43 = zn * m33;
        return new Matrix3D(
            xScale,      0,   0,  0,
                 0, yScale,   0,  0,
                 0,      0, m33, -1,
                 0,      0, m43,  0);
    }
```

The following overloaded version of `GetProjectionMatrix` uses the preceding method to find the transform for a `PerspectiveCamera` object.

```
    public static Matrix3D GetProjectionMatrix(PerspectiveCamera camera,
        double aspectRatio)
    {
        return GetPerspectiveProjectionMatrix(camera.FieldOfView,
            camera.NearPlaneDistance, camera.FarPlaneDistance, aspectRatio);
    }
```

As is the case with the view transform, a `MatrixCamera` has a property that gives you this transform without any calculation. (Wouldn't it be nice if all cameras had these properties?)

The following version of the `GetProjectionMatrix` method returns a projection transform for all three kinds of camera: orthographic, perspective, or matrix.

```
    // Return a projection matrix for a perspective, orthographic, or matrix camera.
    public static Matrix3D GetProjectionMatrix(Camera camera, double aspectRatio)
    {
        if (camera is PerspectiveCamera)
            return GetProjectionMatrix(camera as PerspectiveCamera, aspectRatio);
        if (camera is OrthographicCamera)
            return GetProjectionMatrix(camera as OrthographicCamera, aspectRatio);
        if (camera is MatrixCamera)
            return (camera as MatrixCamera).ProjectionMatrix;
        throw new ArgumentException("Unknown camera type " +
            camera.GetType().FullName, "camera");
    }
```

The Projection3 example program demonstrates the `GetProjectionMatrix` method. It uses most of the same code used by the Projection3 example program to generate its scene. After it creates the scene's objects and applies the view transform to them, this program uses the following code to apply the projection transform to the target box.

```
// Get the projection transformation.
Matrix3D projMat = Cameras.GetPerspectiveProjectionMatrix(
    60,0.125, double.PositiveInfinity,
    mainViewport.ActualWidth / mainViewport.ActualHeight);

boxMesh.ApplyTransformation(projMat);
edgeMesh.ApplyTransformation(projMat);

// Rotate the camera so it makes sense.
RotateTransform3D rot = D3.Rotate(D3.YVector(), D3.Origin, 180);
cameraMesh.ApplyTransformation(rot);

// Move the objects a bit so they're not so close
// to the camera.
TranslateTransform3D trans =
    new TranslateTransform3D(0, 0, 1f);
boxMesh.ApplyTransformation(trans);
edgeMesh.ApplyTransformation(trans);
```

This code calls the `GetPerspectiveProjectionMatrix` method to get the projection transform. It then applies the transform to the box and its wireframe.

The code does not apply the projection transform to the fake "camera" because you don't need to transform the camera that is making the projection. (If you apply the transform in the example program, you get really weird results because the "camera" surrounds the viewing position, which is currently at the origin.)

The transformation matrix returned by `GetPerspectiveProjectionMatrix` actually moves the scene's objects to the positive side of the Z axis. The example program's code rotates the "camera" objects so they point towards the target box so the scene makes more sense.

> **NOTE:** Behind the scenes it doesn't really matter which way the camera is facing at this point. All that matters now are the objects' X and Y coordinates, so you can mostly ignore their Z coordinates.

The example finishes by moving the target box a bit farther away from the "camera" so it's easier to see. That's purely to make the final picture look better. Otherwise the objects are quite close to the "camera's" lens so they're hard to see.

Figure 31-5 shows the Projection3 example program displaying its scene. If you run the program and view the scene from different angles, you'll see that the box and its wireframe have been flattened until they are almost two-dimensional. They still have slightly different Z coordinates, however, so they look different from the front and back.

Viewport Transform

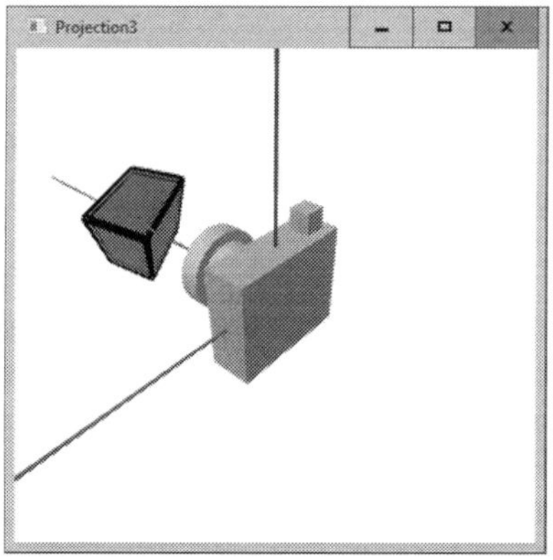

Figure 31-5: Projection scales X and Y coordinates.

After the projection transform, you can think of the objects as belonging in two-dimensional space. Their positions are given by their X and Y coordinates, and you can ignore their Z coordinates.

The viewport transform maps the objects onto the viewport. Compared to the previous transforms, this one is simple. The following `GetViewportMatrix` method returns a viewport transform.

```
public static Matrix3D GetViewportMatrix(Rect rect)
{
    double scaleX = rect.Width / 2;
    double scaleY = rect.Height / 2;
    double offsetX = rect.X + scaleX;
    double offsetY = rect.Y + scaleY;
    return new Matrix3D(
        scaleX,       0, 0, 0,
             0, -scaleY, 0, 0,
             0,       0, 1, 0,
       offsetX, offsetY, 0, 1);
}
```

This transform simply scales the bounding volume so it fills the target rectangle and centers the result.

Combined Transformations

The following `GetWorldToViewportMatrix` method builds a combined matrix representing the complete transformation from world coordinates to viewport coordinates.

```
public static Matrix3D GetWorldToViewportMatrix(Viewport3DVisual visual)
{
    Camera camera = visual.Camera;
    Rect rect = visual.Viewport;
    Matrix3D result = Matrix3D.Identity;

    // If the camera has a transform, add its inverse to the result.
    Transform3D transform = camera.Transform;
    if ((transform != null) && (!transform.Value.IsIdentity))
    {
        Matrix3D matrix = transform.Value;
        matrix.Invert();
        result.Append(matrix);
    }

    // Add the view, projection, and viewport transformations.
    result.Append(GetViewMatrix(camera));
    result.Append(GetProjectionMatrix(camera, rect.Width / rect.Height));
    result.Append(GetViewportMatrix(rect));

    return result;
```

```
}
```

This method takes as a parameter a Viewport3DVisual object. It gets that object's camera and viewport, and initializes the result matrix to the identity matrix.

If the camera has a transform associated with it, the code applies its inverse to the result. The code then gets the view, projection, and viewport transforms and adds them to the result.

When the method is finished, the result matrix is ready to transform points from world coordinates into the pixel-based coordinate system used by the viewport.

The following Convert3DPoint method converts a three-dimensional point into two dimensions just as a program's camera would.

```
public static Point Convert3DPoint(Point3D point3d, Viewport3D vp)
{
    // Get the combined transformation matrix.
    Viewport3DVisual visual =
        VisualTreeHelper.GetParent(vp.Children[0]) as Viewport3DVisual;
    Matrix3D matrix = GetWorldToViewportMatrix(visual);

    // Transform the point.
    point3d = matrix.Transform(point3d);
    return new Point(point3d.X, point3d.Y);
}
```

The method uses VisualTreeHelper.GetParent to get the Viewport3DVisual associated with the Viewport3D object. It calls GetWorldToViewportMatrix to get the combined transform matrix and then applies it to the point. The method then simply returns a new two-dimensional Point object created from the transformed point's X and Y coordinates.

This method works well, but if you want to convert many three-dimensional points into two dimensions, it would be inefficient to rebuild the transform matrix for every point. The following Convert3DPoints method converts an array of three-dimensional points without building the matrix for each separately.

```
public static Point[] Convert3DPoints(Point3D[] points3d, Viewport3D vp)
{
    // Get the combined transformation matrix.
    Viewport3DVisual visual =
        VisualTreeHelper.GetParent(vp.Children[0]) as Viewport3DVisual;
    Matrix3D matrix = GetWorldToViewportMatrix(visual);

    // Copy the points.
    int numPoints = points3d.Length;
    Point3D[] copiedPoints = new Point3D[numPoints];
    Array.Copy(points3d, copiedPoints, numPoints);

    // Transform the copied points.
    matrix.Transform(copiedPoints);

    // Convert the Point3Ds into Points.
```

```
        Point[] points2d = new Point[numPoints];
        for (int i = 0; i < numPoints; i++)
        {
            points2d[i] = new Point(copiedPoints[i].X, copiedPoints[i].Y);
        }
        return points2d;
    }
```

This method gets the `Viewport3DVisual` object and the combined transform matrix as before. It then copies the three-dimensional points into a new array so it doesn't mess up their original values.

Next, the code calls the transform matrix's `Transform` method to transform all of the copied points. It creates an array holding `Point` objects, fills it with two-dimensional versions of the transformed points, and returns the result.

Locating Points

At this point, we're finally ready to map points in three-dimensional space to positions on the screen. The CirclePoints example program shown in Figure 31-6 draws circles around a cube's corners.

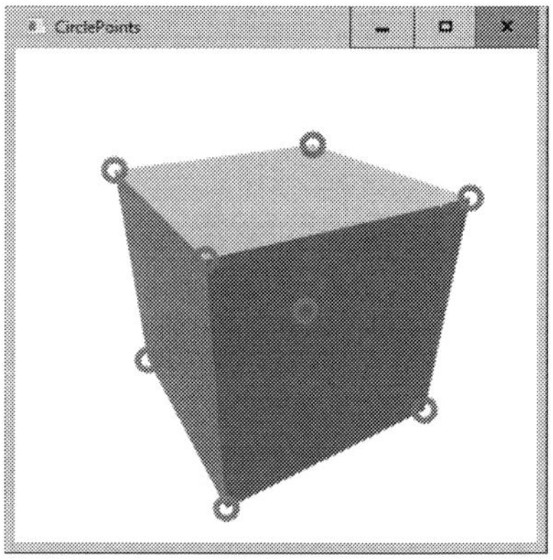

Figure 31-6: The CirclePoints example program draws circles around a cube's vertices.

In order for the program to update the circles' positions, the program needs to know when the camera's position changes. To make that possible, I modified the `SphericalCameraController` class so it raises a `CameraPositionChanged` event whenever it moves its camera. The code that defines and raises the event is straightforward so it isn't shown here.

The CirclePoints example program uses `Ellipse` controls to draw the circles. It uses the following code to define variables to position the circles.

```
    // The points' locations and circles.
    private Point3D[] PointLocations =
    {
        new Point3D(2, 2, 2),
        new Point3D(2, 2, -2),
        new Point3D(2, -2, 2),
        new Point3D(2, -2, -2),
        new Point3D(-2, 2, 2),
        new Point3D(-2, 2, -2),
        new Point3D(-2, -2, 2),
        new Point3D(-2, -2, -2),
    };
    private Ellipse[] PointCircles;
```

The `PointLocations` array holds the locations of the cube's vertices. The `PointCircles` array will hold the `Ellipse` controls that draw the circles. The program's `DefineModel` method uses the following code snippet to initialize the `PointCircles` array.

```
        PointCircles = new Ellipse[PointLocations.Length];
        for (int i = 0; i < PointLocations.Length; i++)
        {
            PointCircles[i] = new Ellipse();
            foreCanvas.Children.Add(PointCircles[i]);
            PointCircles[i].Width = 20;
            PointCircles[i].Height = 20;
            PointCircles[i].Stroke = Brushes.Red;
            PointCircles[i].StrokeThickness = 5;
        }
        PositionCircles();
```

This code allocates the `PointCircles` array and then loops through the cube's vertices. For each vertex, the code creates an `Ellipse` and adds it to the `foreCanvas` control defined in the program's XAML code. The code then makes each `Ellipse` a circle 20 pixels wide and 20 pixels tall. It makes the `Ellipse` draw itself in red with a five-pixel wide stroke.

After it creates the ellipses, the code calls the following `PositionCircles` method to position them.

```
        private void PositionCircles()
        {
            Point[] points = Cameras.Convert3DPoints(PointLocations, mainViewport);
            for (int i = 0; i < PointLocations.Length; i++)
            {
                Canvas.SetLeft(PointCircles[i], points[i].X - 10);
                Canvas.SetTop(PointCircles[i], points[i].Y - 10);
            }
        }
```

This method calls `Cameras.Convert3DPoints` to find the vertices' positions on the viewport. It then moves the `Ellipse` controls to those positions, minus an offset to center the circles over the points.

Whenever you move the camera, the program catches the camera controller's `CameraPositionChanged` event and calls `PositionCircles` to move the circles to the vertices' new locations.

> **NOTE:** The program also calls `PositionCircles` when the program's window resizes.

Labeling Points

The original goal of this chapter was to be able to display two-dimensional labels on top of a three-dimensional scene. It's taken a while, but now we can finally do that. The LabelPoints example program shown in Figure 31-7 is very similar to the CirclePoints program except it places `Label` controls beside the cube's vertices instead of circling them.

The program uses the following code snippet to initialize the `PointLabels` array that holds its `Label` controls.

```
PointLabels = new Label[LabelLocations.Length];
for (int i = 0; i < LabelLocations.Length; i++)
{
    PointLabels[i] = new Label();
    foreCanvas.Children.Add(PointLabels[i]);
    PointLabels[i].Content =
        string.Format("({0}, {1}, {2})",
            LabelLocations[i].X,
            LabelLocations[i].Y,
            LabelLocations[i].Z);
    PointLabels[i].Background =
        new SolidColorBrush(
            Color.FromArgb(64, 255, 255, 255));
    PointLabels[i].FontWeight = FontWeights.Bold;
}
PositionLabels();
```

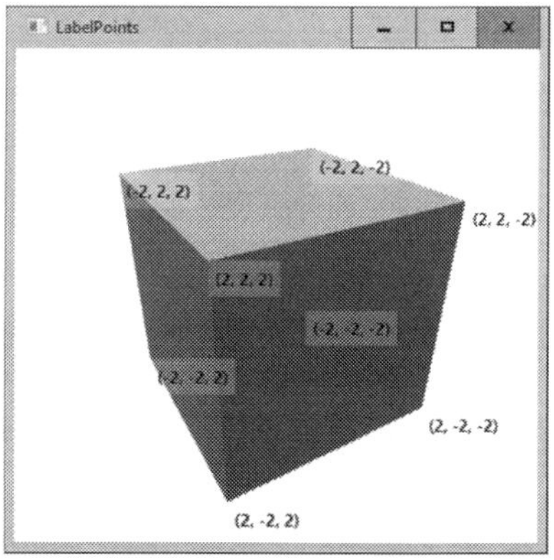

Figure 31-7: The LabelPoints example program places `Label` controls near a cube's vertices.

This code allocates the `PointLabels` array and then loops through the cube's vertices. For each vertex, the code creates a `Label` control and adds it to the `foreCanvas` control. The code then sets each control's content so it displays its vertex's coordinates.

Next, the code gives the `Label` a translucent white background to make the `Label` stand out better when it sits above the three-dimensional scene. The loop finishes by making the new `Label` use a bold font.

After it creates the labels, the code calls the following `PositionLabels` method.

```
private void PositionLabels()
{
    Point[] points = Cameras.Convert3DPoints(LabelLocations, mainViewport);
    for (int i = 0; i < LabelLocations.Length; i++)
    {
        Canvas.SetLeft(PointLabels[i], points[i].X);
        Canvas.SetTop(PointLabels[i], points[i].Y);
    }
}
```

Like the `PositionCircles` method used by the CirclePoints program, this method calls `Cameras.Convert3DPoints` to find the vertices' positions on the viewport. It then moves the `Label` controls to those positions.

Whenever you move the camera, the program catches the camera controller's `CameraPositionChanged` event and calls `PositionLabels` to move the labels to the vertices' new locations.

> **NOTE:** Also like the CirclePoints program, the LabelPoints program calls `PositionLabels` when the program's window resizes.

Summary

This chapter explained how you can display two-dimensional circles, labels, and other annotations on a three-dimensional scene. The first step is mapping positions from three to two dimensions. The next chapter does the opposite: it explains how to map points in two dimensions into a three-dimensional scene. That lets you allow the user to click on objects to select and manipulate them.

Chapter 32

Moving Objects

Chapter 31 explained how to determine where a three-dimensional point will be drawn in the program's two-dimensional viewport. This chapter does the opposite: it shows how to map a point on the viewport, such as the mouse's position, to the three-dimensional object at that position. Fortunately, Microsoft provides support for mapping from two to three dimensions, so this is much easier than mapping from three to two.

The following section explains how you can perform the basic two-to-three dimensional mapping needed to provide hit testing. The section after that explains how you can use those techniques to let the user move objects within a scene.

Hit Testing

The .NET Framework's `VisualTreeHelper` class provides methods for working with visual trees. Fortunately for us, the methods work with both two- and three-dimensional objects within a tree. For example, if a window contains a `Viewport3D` object and that viewport contains `GeometryModel3D` objects, then the `VisualTreeHelper` methods can work with both.

In particular, the `VisualTreeHelper` class's `HitTest` method takes as input a point on the viewport and returns the three-dimensional model at that point that is closest to the camera's position. That lets you provide hit testing for a three-dimensional scene fairly easily.

The SelectBox example program shown in Figure 32-1 lets you click on the cubes in its scene to select them.

Figure 32-1: The SelectBox example program lets you click on a box to select it.

Up to this point, this book's examples have mostly used the `SphericalCameraController` class to let the user move the camera's position, and that class captures mouse events. To allow the user to interact with the objects in a scene, the SelectBox example adds the following code to the `SphericalCameraController` class's `MouseControl_MouseDown` event handler.

```
// Only respond to right mouse down.
if (e.RightButton == MouseButtonState.Released) return;
```

Now the camera controller only responds to right mouse presses and the main program can handle left mouse events.

The SelectBox program uses the following class-level variables to manage the currently selected box.

```
// The currently selected model and mesh.
private GeometryModel3D SelectedModel = null;

// The materials for selected and deselected models.
private Material SelectedMaterial, DeselectedMaterial;
```

As you can probably guess from the name, the `SelectedModel` variable keeps track of the currently selected model. The `SelectedMaterial` and `DeselectedMaterial` variables hold references to the materials used to draw selected and deselected models. The program uses the following code to initialize those materials.

```
SelectedMaterial = new DiffuseMaterial(Brushes.Fuchsia);
DeselectedMaterial = new DiffuseMaterial(Brushes.LightBlue);
```

The rest if the program's startup code is similar to the code used by previous examples. In this program, the `DefineModel` method creates 125 cubes in a 5×5×5 grid. Each cube is contained in its own model, so the program can change their materials individually.

The program's XAML code defines a `Grid` that contains a `Border` with a white background. The `Border` holds the `Viewport3D` control.

> **NOTE:** Normally, if a mouse event occurs over an empty part of the viewport, the viewport does not report the event. That means if you don't capture the events higher up in the visual tree, for example in the `Border` or `Grid` that contain the viewport, then you can only interact with the mouse if it is over an object. In the SelectBox program, that would mean that you could select a cube but you could not deselect it by clicking on an empty part of the scene.
>
> All of this is the reason why the program uses a `Border` with a (nontransparent) white background. (You saw something similar in the "Click and Drag" section in Chapter 5, which explains how to use the mouse to control the camera.)

When the user presses the mouse down over the `Border` control, the following event handler executes.

```
// See if the user clicked on anything.
private void mainBorder_MouseDown(object sender, MouseButtonEventArgs e)
{
    // Only respond to left mouse down.
    if (e.LeftButton == MouseButtonState.Released) return;
```

```
        // Get the mouse's position relative to the viewport.
        Point mousePos = e.GetPosition(mainViewport);

        // Perform the hit test.
        HitTestResult result =
            VisualTreeHelper.HitTest(mainViewport, mousePos);
        RayMeshGeometry3DHitTestResult meshResult =
            result as RayMeshGeometry3DHitTestResult;
        GeometryModel3D model = null;
        if ((meshResult != null) && (meshResult.ModelHit is GeometryModel3D))
            model = meshResult.ModelHit as GeometryModel3D;

        // Select the new model.
        SelectModel(model);
    }
```

This method exits if the user didn't press the left mouse button. It then gets the mouse's position in relation to the `Viewport3D` control. That gives the two-dimensional coordinates that we need to map into the three-dimensional scene.

Next, the method uses the `VisualTreeHelper` class's `HitTest` method to see what object in the viewport lies at that position. The code then passes the object at that position to the following `SelectModel` method.

```
    private void SelectModel(GeometryModel3D model)
    {
        // Deselect any previously selected model.
        if (SelectedModel != null) SelectedModel.Material = DeselectedMaterial;

        // Select the new model.
        SelectedModel = model;
        if (model != null) model.Material = SelectedMaterial;
    }
```

If there is already a selected model, this method sets its `Material` to `DeselectedMaterial` so it looks normal. The method then saves the newly selected model in the `SelectedModel` variable and, if the new model is not `null`, it sets the new model's `Material` to `SelectedMaterial`.

> **NOTE:** The SelectBox program makes each cube in a separate model because a model can use only one material. That means you cannot use different materials to make one box selected and another deselected in the same model.
>
> An alternative strategy would be to change the texture coordinates of the selected part of a model. For example, you could make a material where texture coordinates with $0 \leq u \leq 0.5$ are one color and coordinates with $0.5 \leq u \leq 1$ are a different color.

Download the SelectBox example program to see additional details. You may also want to experiment with the program to see what else you can make it do. For example, you might make the cubes disappear when clicked, perhaps with a popping sound. You might also experiment to see how many cubes the program can handle. On my system, I can make around 10,000 cubes before I notice a performance impact.

Moving Objects

Before you can allow the user to move objects in a three-dimensional scene, you need to decide how the user will specify that movement.

One simple method would be to let the user select an object as explained in the preceding sectionand then enter X, Y, and Z coordinates for the object in text boxes.

In a less precise but more interactive method, the user could press keys to move objects in the X, Y, and Z directions. For example, the u, d, l, r, f, and b keys could represent up, down, left, right, forward and backward. Or you could use the normal and shifted X, Y, Z keys to modify the object's coordinates by fixed amounts.

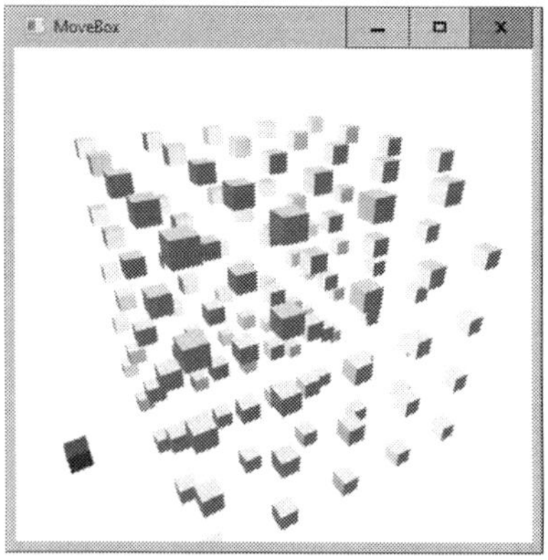

Figure 32-2: The MoveBox example lets you drag cubes into new positions.

Dragging objects with the mouse would be even more interactive, but then you need to decide exactly how mouse movement should change an object's position. After all, the mouse is moving in a two-dimensional plane but the scene's objects can move in three dimensions.

The MoveBox example program shown in Figure 32-2 lets you click and drag to move boxes. The box remains at a fixed distance from the viewing position, so the mouse moves it along the surface of an invisible sphere. The program acts as if you're sitting in front of the scene and reaching out to move the boxes while keeping your arm straight out in front of you.

This may seem complicated, but it's actually not too hard with a relatively simple trick. First, set up a hidden viewport with a camera identical to the one used in the "real" viewport. Next, make a sphere centered at the camera with radius equal to the distance between the camera and the object that you're trying to move.

> **NOTE:** The `VisualTreeHelper` class's hit testing method culls backfaces, so it won't return a hit for an object that is improperly oriented. Because the hidden viewport's camera is *inside* the sphere, you must give the sphere a `BackMaterial` so the camera can see it.

Now, as the user drags the mouse, use the techniques described in the preceding section to map the mouse position (in the "real" viewport) to the inside of the sphere (in the hidden viewport). That tells you where you should move the object that the user is dragging.

The MoveBox example program uses the following variables to manage the selected model.

```
// The currently selected model and mesh.
private GeometryModel3D SelectedModel = null;
private MeshGeometry3D SelectedMesh = null;

// The materials for selected and deselected models.
private Material SelectedMaterial, DeselectedMaterial;
```

These variables are similar to those used by the SelectBox example described in the preceding section with the addition of the `SelectedMesh` variable. Because this example will change the position of a cube, it needs to know the coordinates of the cube's vertices, and those are stored in the mesh.

When the program starts, its `Window_Loaded` event handler calls the following `MakeDragEnvironment` method to prepare the hidden viewport for later use.

```
// Variables used to drag a box.
private Viewport3D DragViewport;
private PerspectiveCamera DragCamera;
private Model3DGroup DragGroup;
private Point3D DragPoint;

// Make the drag environment.
private void MakeDragEnvironment()
{
    DragViewport = new Viewport3D();
    DragViewport.Visibility = Visibility.Hidden;
    mainGrid.Children.Add(DragViewport);

    ModelVisual3D visual3d = new ModelVisual3D();
    DragViewport.Children.Add(visual3d);

    DragGroup = new Model3DGroup();
    visual3d.Content = DragGroup;

    DragCamera = new PerspectiveCamera();
    DragViewport.Camera = DragCamera;
}
```

This code starts with some class-level variables that keep track of the hidden viewport's objects. The method creates a new `Viewport3D`, hides it, and places it in the program's main `Grid` control.

Next, the code puts a `ModelVisual3D` object inside the `Viewport3D`. It then places a `Model3DGroup` inside the `ModelVisual3D` object. Later this group will hold the sphere.

The method finishes by adding a camera to the viewport.

When the user presses the mouse down on the "real" viewport, the following `mainBorder_MouseDown` event handler executes.

```
// See if the user clicked on anything.
private void mainBorder_MouseDown(object sender, MouseButtonEventArgs e)
{
    // Only respond to left mouse down.
    if (e.LeftButton == MouseButtonState.Released) return;

    // Deselect any previously selected mesh.
    if (SelectedModel != null)
    {
        SelectedModel.Material = DeselectedMaterial;
        SelectedModel = null;
        SelectedMesh = null;
    }

    // Get the mouse's position relative to the viewport.
    Point mousePos = e.GetPosition(mainViewport);

    // Perform the hit test.
    HitTestResult result =
        VisualTreeHelper.HitTest(mainViewport, mousePos);
    RayMeshGeometry3DHitTestResult meshResult =
        result as RayMeshGeometry3DHitTestResult;
    if ((meshResult == null) || !(meshResult.ModelHit is GeometryModel3D)) return;

    // Record the model, mesh, and point that were hit.
    SelectedModel = meshResult.ModelHit as GeometryModel3D;
    SelectedModel.Material = SelectedMaterial;
    SelectedMesh = meshResult.MeshHit;
    DragPoint = meshResult.PointHit;

    // Initialize the drag environment
    // Make the drag viewport fit the visible one.
    DragViewport.Width = mainViewport.ActualWidth;
    DragViewport.Height = mainViewport.ActualHeight;

    // Make the camera match the main viewport's camera.
    DragCamera.FieldOfView = TheCamera.FieldOfView;
    DragCamera.UpDirection = TheCamera.UpDirection;
    DragCamera.LookDirection = TheCamera.LookDirection;
    DragCamera.Position = TheCamera.Position;

    // Make a sphere with surface at the distance of the hit point.
    double distance = meshResult.DistanceToRayOrigin;
    MeshGeometry3D mesh = new MeshGeometry3D();
    mesh.AddSphere(TheCamera.Position, distance, 60, 30);

    // Make a model with a material and back material.
    GeometryModel3D model = mesh.MakeModel(Brushes.Green);
    model.BackMaterial = model.Material;
    DragGroup.Children.Add(model);

    // Capture mouse events.
    mainBorder.CaptureMouse();
    mainBorder.MouseMove += mainBorder_MouseMove;
    mainBorder.MouseUp += mainBorder_MouseUp;
}
```

This code deselects the previously selected model if there is one and performs a hit test as described in the preceding section. If there is a hit, the code saves references to the model and mesh that were hit.

Next, the code prepares the hidden drag environment for use. It gives the hidden viewport the same size as the "real" one and makes the hidden camera match the "real" camera.

The code then creates a sphere centered at the camera's position and with radius equal to the distance between the camera (where the hit testing ray originates) and the object that was hit. Because the `AddSphere` method creates outwardly-oriented triangles, the code gives the sphere a `BackMaterial` so the `HitTest` method can see it from inside the sphere.

The method finishes by installing event handlers for the `Border` control's `MouseMove` and `MouseUp` events. The following code shows the `MouseMove` event handler.

```
// The user dragged the mouse. Move the selected box.
private void mainBorder_MouseMove(object sender, MouseEventArgs e)
{
    // Get the mouse's new position.
    Point newPoint = e.GetPosition(mainBorder);

    // See where the ray from the camera to the new point hits the drag sphere.
    HitTestResult result =
        VisualTreeHelper.HitTest(DragViewport, newPoint);
    if (result == null) return;
    RayMeshGeometry3DHitTestResult meshResult =
        result as RayMeshGeometry3DHitTestResult;

    // Translate the selected model.
    SelectedMesh.ApplyTransformation(
        new TranslateTransform3D(meshResult.PointHit - DragPoint));
    DragPoint = meshResult.PointHit;
}
```

This method gets the mouse's current position. It then uses the `VisualTreeHelper` class's `HitTest` method to see where that point lies on the hidden viewport's sphere. The result's `PointHit` property gives the coordinate of that point.

The code subtracts the previous mouse location stored in `DragPoint` from the new point to see how much the mouse has moved along the surface of the sphere. It translates the selected object by that amount and updates the `DragPoint` variable.

The following code shows the `mainBorder_MouseUp` event handler.

```
// The user released the mouse. Stop tracking mouse events.
private void mainBorder_MouseUp(object sender, MouseButtonEventArgs e)
{
    mainBorder.ReleaseMouseCapture();
    mainBorder.MouseMove -= mainBorder_MouseMove;
    mainBorder.MouseUp -= mainBorder_MouseUp;

    // Remove the drag sphere.
    DragGroup.Children.Clear();
```

```
}
```

This code releases the mouse capture so mouse events are no longer constrained. It then uninstalls the mouse event handlers and removes the sphere model from the hidden `Model3DGroup` so it will be ready for use the next time the user presses the mouse button.

Summary

This chapter explained how you can map two-dimensional positions on a viewport to the three-dimensional objects that it contains. You can use that ability to allow the user to manipulate the objects in a scene, for example by selecting and moving them.

This chapter explained one way you can let the user interact with objects, but there are many others. For example, instead of moving the selected object on the surface of a sphere, you could move it on a plane perpendicular to the ray between the camera and the object.

Some drawing tools, such as Unity, take a different approach. When you select an object, they display arrows pointing in the X, Y, and Z directions. You can then click and drag the arrows to move the object parallel to the corresponding coordinate axes. That makes it easier to position objects more precisely. For example, that lets you adjust an object's X position without messing up its Y and Z coordinates.

I'm sure you can provide that sort of interaction in WPF, but it would be a lot of work, and if you really need those more complicated features, you may be better off using some other tool such as Unity to build your models. Then you can load your models into your WPF program.

The next chapter explains how you can do that. It shows how you can load one kind of three-dimensional model into a WPF application.

Chapter 33

Models

The MoveBox example program described in Chapter 32 lets you move objects, but it's a far cry from a scene editor. It provides no way for you to interactively add, remove, scale, rotate, group, or align objects. It also provides no way to save and restore scenes.

In principle, you could use WPF to build a complete scene editor that does all of that, but in practice it would be a lot of work. Fortunately, you don't really need to build a scene editor because there are lots of them already available. Unity (`unity3d.com`), Blender (`blender.org`), and SketchUp (`sketchup.com`) are just a few of the many three-dimensional drawing tools that you can download from the internet.

After you use a scene editor to create a scene, you can save it in a file and then load that file into your WPF programs. This chapter explains how you can load some models into you programs so you can take advantage of the masterpieces that you or others have created using scene editors.

File Formats

Scene editors save scenes in many different file formats, and each format provides different features. For example, some may provide different methods for grouping objects or defining sophisticated materials.

This chapter shows how to load obj files. An obj file holds information about objects and may include object vertices, normals, texture coordinates, and smoothing information. An obj file may also define object groups, a feature that isn't supported directly by WPF.

> **NOTE:** The obj file format was defined in the 1980s by Wavefront Technologies, a graphics company that specialized in animation software. The format was created for their Advanced Visualizer product, which was used to create several blockbuster movies including *Terminator 2: Judgment Day* and *Jurassic Park*.

An obj file can also include references to mtl files, which hold information about the materials used by objects. An mtl file can define multiple materials, each of which can specify diffuse and specular colors, and texture maps.

Materials can also include information that isn't supported by WPF such as ambient colors (ambient colors in WPF are provided by an `AmbientLight`, not by the scene's objects), transparency, reflectivity, shadow information, and bump maps.

I decided to support obj files instead of some other file format for several reasons. First, obj files are relatively simple. Although they do include features that are beyond the ability of WPF, they don't waste space on too many extras that WPF cannot use.

They also store their information in text rather than binary, so it's much easier to figure out what's going on when your program has trouble loading a file. Because they are text files, you can edit the data by hand if necessary to modify a model or fix problems. I've had to do that many times.

The following sections describe the format of obj and mtl files. The section after those describes C# code that you can use to load obj models.

Obj Files

A key idea behind obj files is that a program should be able to write information about one object into the file without extensive knowledge about any other objects. For example, suppose you write several objects into an obj file and then want to write another object into the file. You can write that object's vertices into the file followed by its texture coordinates, normals, and face (polygon) data in blocks. There's no need to describe every vertex in the entire scene all at once.

In fact, you don't even need to know how many vertices have already been written into the file. For example, suppose you have written 100 vertices into the file for previous objects and now you want to add 10 more vertices for a new object. When you're describing the new object's faces, its first vertex would have index 101 (values are numbered starting at one in obj files).

Alternatively, you can use *relative indexing* where negative indices refer to the most recent values added to the file. The index -1 refers to the most recently added vertex, -2 refers to the second-to-last vertex, and so forth. You would write the new object's vertex information into the file and then use relative indexing to indicate which vertices make up the object's triangles. You don't need to know how many vertices (or texture coordinates or normals) came before.

This scheme allows a sort of write-and-forget strategy for building an obj file.

> **NOTE:** Most of the models I have seen use absolute indexing not relative indexing.

The following code shows the basic layout of an obj file.

```
# This is a comment.

# Read a material library.
mtllib my_model.mtl

# Use the material named brick.
usemtl brick

# Vertex list.
v -0.498530 0.712498 -0.039883
v -0.501666 0.699221 -0.063813
...
# Vertex texture coordinates.
vt  2 1.975 0
vt  2 1.9625 0
...
# Vertex normals.
vn  -0.935893 -0.305088 -0.176142
vn  -0.972374 -0.202154 -0.116713
...
# Smoothing group.
s 1

# Named object.
o alien

# Named group.
g left_arm

# Faces.
f 34//1 1243//2 593//3
f 52//4 27//5 40//6
...
```

NOTE: These are not the only items that might be in an obj file, but they are enough to get you pretty far. Many of the other possible items are unsupported by WPF. For example, the file can include information about the lighting model, ray tracing, and shadow casting, none of which are supported by WPF.

Other features are not directly supported by WPF, but you might be able to implement them on your own. For example, obj files can define curves and surfaces in addition to simple triangles.

For more information about the obj file format, see the following web pages.

- "Wavefront .obj file" at Wikipedia (tinyurl.com/mk86am8)
- "Wavefront OBJ File Format Summary" (`tinyurl.com/qzd2tll`)
- "Object Files (.obj)" at paulbourke.net (`tinyurl.com/8o236zo`)

The comments in the previous obj file code describe the pieces of the obj file. The following sections describe those pieces in greater detail.

Comments

Any text after a `#` character on a line is a comment. Many tools put version information in a comment at the beginning of the file so you know what program generated the file.

Some applications also include summary comments after sections of the obj file. For example, after a vertex list the program might include a comment saying how many vertices were in the list.

Other programs may include comments that indicate what object they are defining. For example, a comment might say "spacefish" before defining vertices, textures, and normals that will be used by the spacefish object. Later, an `o` or `g` element would define the spacefish object or group.

Material Library

The `mtllib` command tells you to load a material library (mtl) file. An mtl file defines one or more materials for use by the obj file.

Normally an obj file's main mtl file has the same name as the obj file but with the mtl extension. For example, the obj file `AlienCity.obj` would have an associated file `AlienCity.mtl`. However, an objct file can include multiple `mtllib` statements to load multiple mtl files.

The section "Mtl Files" later in this chapter explains the basic material file format.

Materials

The `usemtl` statement tells you to use the material with the given name. That material should be defined in an mtl file that was loaded by the mtllib statement.

Vertex Lists

A vertex list gives the X, Y, Z, and W coordinates for the vertices that define the current piece of the model.

The W coordinate is used to represent a point in homogeneous coordinates. The W coordinate is optional and defaults to 1. (For more on homogeneous coordinates, see the section "Homogeneous Coordinates" in Chapter 9.)

Vertex Texture Coordinates

Vertex texture coordinates include U, V, and W values. You should remember the U and V coordinates from Chapter 7.

The W coordinate is multiplied by the material's texture transformation to get the final position in the texture image. This value is optional and defaults to 0.

I'm not going to cover texture transformations so I won't use W coordinates.

Vertex Normals

Vertex normals are relatively straightforward. Each includes X, Y, and Z components. The only trick here is to be aware that these normals may not all have unit length.

Smoothing Groups

A smoothing group allows the model to indicate that a group of objects should be smoothed. In WPF that means their triangles should share vertices so the drawing engine produces a smooth result.

The file can specify the smoothing group number as in `s 3`.

The commands `s off` and `s 0` disable smoothing on the following faces.

The default smoothing group is number 1, so the command `s on` places the faces that follow in smoothing group 1.

> **NOTE:** If the file defines vertex normals for a set of points, they should supersede smoothing groups for those points.

Named Objects and Groups

Named objects and groups provide a higher-level three-dimensional structure for a model. For example, an object named Robot might include several polygon groups named Head, LeftArm, RightArm, Torso, and so forth.

WPF only keeps track of triangles so it cannot take full advantage of object and group structures. You can capture the structure if you like, although at some point you need to convert the objects with their polygonal faces into the triangles that WPF can handle.

Faces

A face list defines the vertices that make up the faces in part of the model. WPF only supports triangles, but the faces in an obj file can be any type of polygon.

Each point in face list must include a vertex number. It can also optionally include a texture coordinate index and/or a normal index.

The vertex, texture coordinate, and normal indices are separated by slash (/) characters. For example, the following code defines a face that uses vertex indices 1, 2, and 5.

```
f 1 2 5
```

That statement doesn't include any slash characters so it doesn't use texture coordinates or normals.

The following code defines a face that uses vertices 1, 2, and 5 having texture coordinates 10, 21, and 9.

```
f 1/10 2/21 5/9
```

The following face uses vertices 1, 2, and 5, texture coordinates 10, 21, and 9, and normals with indices 17, 12, 33.

```
f 1/10/17 2/21/12 5/9/33
```

Keep in mind that all of these values are indices. For example, the first point in the preceding statement uses the 1st vertex, 10th texture coordinate, and 17th normal defined in the file.

If a face doesn't use texture coordinates but does use normals, then the file omits the texture coordinates as in the following statement.

```
f 1//17 2//12 5//33
```

Mtl Files

A material template library (mtl file) describes one or more materials for use with obj files. An mtl file can define any number of materials starting with the `newmtl` command.

The following code shows the most common pieces of a material's definition.

```
newmtl left_eye_material
Ka 0.000000 0.000000 0.000000
Kd 0.640000 0.640000 0.640000
Ks 0.500000 0.500000 0.500000
Ns 96.078431
map_Kd Head Model Eyes Anime.png
d 1.000000
illum 2
```

The `newmtl` command begins a new material and gives it a name. An obj file refers to the material by this name.

The Ka, Kd, and Ks commands describe the material's ambient, diffuse, and specular colors respectively. The colors are defined by their red, green, and blue components, which have values between 0 and 1. For example, the color component values 1.0, 0.5, and 0.0 specify yellow.

> **NOTE:** To convert from mtl-style color components to WPF style values, simply multiply by 255.

The Ns command specifies the material's specular reflection exponent, which can have values between 1 and 1000. Small values such as 1 or 10 produce a dispersed specular reflection. Large values such as 80 or 100 produce a sharper reflection.

Various map commands indicate image files that define the material's features. For example, the map_Kd command indicates the image that should be used for the material's diffuse color map. Other map commands specify the specular color map, ambient color map, bump map, and opacity texture map.

The d command indicates the material's *dissolve* or opacity. The value 0.0 means the material is completely transparent and the value 1.0 means it is completely opaque.

Some modelling programs use the Tr command instead of d. The Tr command indicates the material's *transparency*. Transparency is the complement of dissolve, so Tr = 1 - d.

The illum command specifies the material's illumination model. Different illumination models indicate such features as transparency, ray tracing, highlights, refraction, reflection, and shadows. WPF doesn't support those, so I'm going to ignore this command. I'm only mentioning it because it's fairly common.

Other commands that are not discussed here specify such things as halo factors, options for other commands, shadows on invisible surfaces, horizontal and vertical texture blending, turbulence, roughness, sheen, and much more.

Reading Files

The obj and mtl file formats are intended to be extensible. You can add new features and then other programs that load the files simply ignore any features that they don't understand. This is important for us because there are many features in obj and mtl files that we can't use and therefore don't really need to understand. Because they are intended to be extensible, they make it easy to ignore unnecessary features.

The LoadObj example program shows how you can load obj and mtl files. The following three sections describe data structures used by the program to hold object and material information before it is converted into the vertices and materials required by WPF. The sections after that explain the code that parses the obj and mtl files.

Storing Objects

The LoadObj example program uses the following `ObjModel` class to hold information about an object.

```
// Hold information for an object model.
private class ObjModel
{
    public string Name = "";
    public string MaterialName = "";
    public List<ObjFace> Faces = new List<ObjFace>();
    public List<Point3D> Vertices = new List<Point3D>();
    public List<Vector3D> Normals = new List<Vector3D>();
    public List<Point> TextureCoordinates = new List<Point>();
}
```

This class stores the object's name. That name isn't used by WPF so you could omit it, but I've included it in case you want to use it. For example, you might want your program to discard objects in the model that have certain names, or you might want to change the materials used by objects with specific names.

The class also stores the object's material name. It needs that name to give the object the correct material.

Next, the class defines a list of `ObjFace` objects. Those keep track of the polygons that make up the object. The `ObjFace` class is described in the following section.

The `ObjModel` class finishes with lists to hold the object's vertices, normals, and texture coordinates.

Storing Faces

The LoadObj example program uses the following `ObjFace` class to hold information about one of an object's polygons.

```
// Hold information on a face.
private class ObjFace
{
    public List<int> Vertices = new List<int>();
    public List<int> Normals = new List<int>();
    public List<int> TextureCoords = new List<int>();
    public int SmoothingGroup = 0;

    // Initialize a face from a line of data.
    public ObjFace(List<Point3D> AllVertices, List<Vector3D> AllNormals,
        List<Point> AllTextureCoordinates, string line)
    {
        // Break into fields.
        char[] separators = { ' ' };
        string[] fields =
```

```
            line.Split(separators, StringSplitOptions.RemoveEmptyEntries);

        // Process the fields.
        for (int i = 1; i < fields.Length; i++)
        {
            // Split into sub-fields.
            string[] subfields = fields[i].Split('/');

            // Save the vertex ID.
            int index = int.Parse(subfields[0]);
            if (index < 0) index = AllVertices.Count + index + 1;
            Vertices.Add(index);

            if (subfields.Length > 1)
            {
                // Save the vertex texture coordinates.
                if (subfields[1].Length > 0)
                {
                    index = int.Parse(subfields[1]);
                    if (index < 0) index = AllTextureCoordinates.Count + index + 1;
                    TextureCoords.Add(index);
                }

                // Save the vertex normal.
                if (subfields.Length > 2)
                {
                    if (subfields[2].Length > 0)
                    {
                        index = int.Parse(subfields[2]);
                        if (index < 0) index = AllNormals.Count + index + 1;
                        Normals.Add(index);
                    }
                }
            }
        }
    }
}
```

This class defines lists to hold the face's vertices, normals, and texture coordinates. It also defines a `SmoothingGroup` field to record the face's smoothing group.

The bulk of the class is its constructor, which reads the face data from a line in the obj file. Recall that those lines contain a sequence of values that may include vertex, texture coordinate, and normal indices. For example, the following statement shows a face command that includes all three types of data.

```
f 25/39/5 24/40/5 31/41/5 30/42/5
```

The `ObjFace` constructor breaks the line into fields separated by spaces and then loops through those fields, skipping the first field because it is the `f` command.

The code breaks each field into subfields separated by the slash (/) character and saves those fields as vertex, texture coordinate, and normal indices.

The code is complicated somewhat by two factors. First, the code performs some tests to ensure that it doesn't try to parse a missing texture coordinate or normal index.

Second, the code performs some extra calculation if an index is negative. The `AllVertices`, `AllTextureCoordinates`, and `AllNormals` lists contain all of the vertices, texture coordinates, and normals defined by the obj file so far. If an index is negative, then it refers to one of the recent indices as described earlier in this chapter.

For example, suppose the `AllVertices` list contains 10 vertices numbered 1 through 10, and a new face's vertex index is -1. Then the corresponding absolute vertex index is 10-1+1=10. That's the most recent vertex index, as desired.

Storing Materials

The LoadObj example program uses the following `ObjMaterial` class to store information about a material defined in an mtl file.

```
// Hold information for a mtl file material.
public class ObjMaterial
{
    public string Name = "";
    public string Filename = null;
    public double Ns, Alpha;
    public Point3D Kd, Ks, Ka;
    public MaterialGroup MatGroup;
}
```

This class is relatively straightforward. It begins with the material's name. This is important because the obj file identifies materials by name.

The `Filename` field holds the name of the material's texture file, if it has one.

The next few fields hold the material's color properties `Ns` (specular power), `Alpha` (opacity), and diffuse, specular, and ambient color components.

> **NOTE:** This version of the program doesn't use the material's ambient color components and opacity values. It stores them in case you want to try to modify the program to use them.

The `MatGroup` field holds a material group that the material can use later if it needs to display diffuse, specular, and textured materials.

Reading Obj and Mtl Files

The LoadObj example program uses the `ObjLoader` class to read an obj file and store its data. The class begins with the following variable declarations to hold the model's data.

```
// Raw data.
private List<Point3D> AllVertices = new List<Point3D>();
public List<Point> AllTextureCoordinates = new List<Point>();
public List<Vector3D> AllNormals = new List<Vector3D>();

// Materials.
private ObjMaterial NewMaterial = null;
private List<ObjMaterial> AllMaterials = new List<ObjMaterial>();

// Object models.
private ObjModel NewObjectModel = null;
private List<ObjModel> AllObjectModels = new List<ObjModel>();
```

This code declares lists to hold all of the file's vertices, texture coordinates, and normals. It then makes variables to hold the material it is currently reading and a list of all materials. Similarly, it makes variables to hold the model it is currently reading and a list of all of the file's models.

The following constructor loads and processes an obj file.

```
// Load the obj file.
public ObjLoader(string dir, string objfile,
    bool invertTextures = false, bool zIsUp = false)
{
    // Read the obj file.
    ReadObjFile(dir, objfile);

    // Process the models.
    ProcessModels(invertTextures, zIsUp);
}
```

The `dir` and `objfile` parameters hold the name of the directory containing the obj file, and the file's name.

In WPF texture coordinates start with (0, 0) in the upper left corner and increase downward and to the right. Unfortunately many three-dimensional drawing tools place (0, 0) in the lower left corner and make coordinates increase upward and to the right. The `invertTextures` parameter tells the constructor whether that is the case and the code should invert the texture.

If you don't know whether an obj file uses inverted textures, try loading it. If the textures aren't loaded properly, they may appear upside down. More likely, however, the textures will be just plain weird. In Figure 33-1, a spaceship file was loaded correctly with textures inverted on the left and incorrectly with textures not inverted on the right.

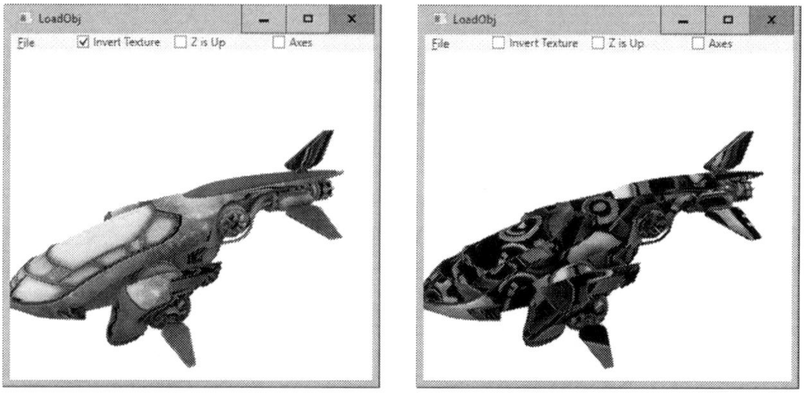

Figure 33-1: Program LoadObj can load an obj file with textures inverted (left) or not inverted (right).

The final parameter to the `ObjLoader` class's constructor is the boolean value `zIsUp`. Like WPF, many three-dimensional drawing programs use the Y axis as the "up" direction, but some use the Z axis instead. This parameter tells the class whether it should rotate the file's objects to orient them properly if the file uses Z as "up." If you load a file and everything is sideways, try changing this parameter's value.

The `ObjLoader` constructor doesn't do much work; it just calls the `ReadObjFile` method to read the file and the `ProcessModels` method to convert the model and material data into WPF formats. The following sections describe those methods and their helper methods, including `ReadMtlFile`, which actually reads the mtl file.

ReadObjFile

The following code shows the `ReadObjFile` method. It's long but relatively straightforward.

```
// Read the obj file.
private void ReadObjFile(string dir, string objfile)
{
    char[] whitespace = { ' ', '\t' };
    List<string> unknown = new List<string>();

    // The current smoothing group.
    int smoothingGroup = 0;

    // The current material name.
    string curMatName = "";

    // Read the file.
    using (StreamReader file = new System.IO.StreamReader(dir + objfile))
    {
        while (!file.EndOfStream)
        {
            // Read the next line.
            string line = CleanLine(file.ReadLine());
```

```
if (line.Length == 0) continue;

string[] fields =
    line.Split(whitespace, StringSplitOptions.RemoveEmptyEntries);
switch (fields[0])
{
    case "o":       // Object model.
    case "g":       // Group.
        // Only create a new one if the current one isn't empty.
        if ((NewObjectModel == null) || (NewObjectModel.Faces.Count > 0))
        {
            NewObjectModel = new ObjModel();
            AllObjectModels.Add(NewObjectModel);
        }
        NewObjectModel.MaterialName = curMatName;
        if (fields.Length > 1) NewObjectModel.Name = fields[1];
        smoothingGroup = 0;
        break;

    case "v":       // Vertex.
        double x = double.Parse(fields[1]);
        double y = double.Parse(fields[2]);
        double z = double.Parse(fields[3]);
        AllVertices.Add(new Point3D(x, y, z));
        break;

    case "vt":      // Texture coordinates.
        double u = double.Parse(fields[1]);
        double v = double.Parse(fields[2]);
        AllTextureCoordinates.Add(new Point(u, v));
        break;

    case "vn":      // Normal.
        double nx = double.Parse(fields[1]);
        double ny = double.Parse(fields[2]);
        double nz = double.Parse(fields[3]);
        AllNormals.Add(new Vector3D(nx, ny, nz));
        break;

    case "f":       // Face.
        ObjFace face = new ObjFace(
            AllVertices, AllNormals, AllTextureCoordinates, line);
        face.SmoothingGroup = smoothingGroup;
        NewObjectModel.Faces.Add(face);
        NewObjectModel.MaterialName = curMatName;
        break;

    case "s":       // Smoothing.
        if (fields.Length == 0) smoothingGroup = 0;
        else if (fields[1] == "off") smoothingGroup = 0;
        else if (fields[1] == "on") smoothingGroup = 1;
        else if (!int.TryParse(fields[1], out smoothingGroup))
            smoothingGroup = 0;
        break;

    case "usemtl":      // Material.
        if (fields.Length > 1) curMatName = fields[1];
        break;
```

```
                case "mtllib":      // Material file.
                    string mtlfile = line.Substring(6).Trim();
                    ReadMtlFile(dir, mtlfile);
                    break;

                default:
                    if (!unknown.Contains(fields[0]))
                        unknown.Add(fields[0]);
                    break;
            }
        }
    }

    // If the final model is empty, remove it.
    if (AllObjectModels[AllObjectModels.Count - 1].Faces.Count == 0)
        AllObjectModels.RemoveAt(AllObjectModels.Count - 1);

    // List unknown tokens.
    if (unknown.Count > 0)
    {
        Console.WriteLine("Unknown obj tokens:");
        foreach (string token in unknown)
            Console.WriteLine("    " + token);
    }
}
```

The method first defines an array holding the whitespace characters that it will ignore when it reads the file. It then creates a list of strings named `unknown`. When it parses the obj file, it will place any commands that it doesn't understand in this list. After you load a file, you can review this list to see if the file includes any commands that you want to add to the code.

The method then sets the variable `smoothingGroup` to 0 to indicate that no smoothing is in effect. It sets the current material's name to a blank string and then starts reading the file.

While it has not reached the end of the file, the code reads a line from the file and calls the following `ClearLine` method to remove any comments.

```
// Remove comments and trim the line.
private string CleanLine(string line)
{
    if (line.Contains("#")) line = line.Substring(0, line.IndexOf("#"));
    return line.Trim();
}
```

The `CleanLine` method simply removes any comment following a # character, trims whitespace, and returns the result.

After it cleans the line, the `ReadObjFile` method skips the line if it is blank.

If the line is not blank, the method splits it into fields separated by whitespace characters (space or tab). It then uses a `switch` statement to take action for different commands stored in the line's first field.

If the command is `o` or `g`, the method starts a new object. (The program treats both objects and groups as new objects. You could modify the code to preserve the groups within objects if you like.)

If the current object is empty, the code simply uses it to load the new object. If the current object isn't empty, the code creates a new object (so the old object is not overwritten) and adds the new object to the `AllObjectModels` list. It makes the new object use the current material name and sets the current smoothing group to 0 to indicate that the new object isn't initially using smoothing.

If the line has a second field, the code uses it as the new object's name. For example, the following statement creates a new object named "Head."

```
g Head
```

If a line's command is `v`, then it contains a vertex. The `ReadObjFile` method parses the vertex's X, Y, and Z coordinates, uses them to make a new `Point3D`, and adds the point to the `AllVertices` list.

The method handles the `vt` and `vn` commands similarly, creating new normal and texture coordinate entries.

If the line's command is `f`, then it contains a face. The code creates a new `ObjFace` object, using its constructor to parse the line. It sets the new face's `SmoothingGroup` and adds the face to the current object's `Faces` list.

The code then sets the current object's `MaterialName` to the current material. Some obj files select a material at the end of an object's definition so that material can be used by the next object. That means the program cannot assume that a new material applies to the current object. Instead it sets the object's material when the file defines a new face for the object.

If a line's command is `s`, it contains a smoothing command. The code parses the second field in the line to see whether it is `on`, `off`, or a number and updates the current `smoothingGroup` value accordingly.

If the command is `usemtl`, then the line contains the name of the material that the program should start using. The code saves the new material's name but does not make the current object use it (as explained two paragraphs earlier).

If a line's command is `mtllib`, then the second parameter is the name of an mtl file that defines materials. The code calls the `ReadMtlFile` method described shortly to read the mtl file.

Finally, if the line contains some other command, the method adds it to the `unknown` list if it is not already in the list.

After it finishes reading all of the obj file's lines, the code removes the final object if it is empty. It then displays any unknown commands in the Console window.

ReadMtlFile

The following code shows the `ReadMtlFile` method. Like the `ReadObjFile` method described in the preceding section, it's a bit long but reasonably straightforward.

```
// Read the mtl file.
private void ReadMtlFile(string dir, string mtlfile)
{
    char[] whitespace = { ' ', '\t' };
    List<string> unknown = new List<string>();
    using (StreamReader file = new System.IO.StreamReader(dir + mtlfile))
    {
        while (!file.EndOfStream)
        {
            // Read the next line.
            string line = CleanLine(file.ReadLine());
            if (line.Length == 0) continue;

            string[] fields =
                line.Split(whitespace, StringSplitOptions.RemoveEmptyEntries);
            switch (fields[0])
            {
                case "newmtl":  // Material.
                    NewMaterial = new ObjMaterial();
                    AllMaterials.Add(NewMaterial);
                    if (fields.Length > 1) NewMaterial.Name = fields[1];
                    break;

                case "Ns":      // Specular power.
                    NewMaterial.Ns = double.Parse(fields[1]);
                    break;

                case "Tr":      // Transparency.
                    NewMaterial.Alpha = 1 - double.Parse(fields[1]);
                    break;

                case "d":       // Dissolve.
                    NewMaterial.Alpha = double.Parse(fields[1]);
                    break;

                case "Kd":      // Diffuse color.
                    double kdx = double.Parse(fields[1]);
                    double kdy = double.Parse(fields[2]);
                    double kdz = double.Parse(fields[3]);
                    NewMaterial.Kd = new Point3D(kdx, kdy, kdz);
                    break;

                case "Ks":      // Specular color.
                    double ksx = double.Parse(fields[1]);
                    double ksy = double.Parse(fields[2]);
                    double ksz = double.Parse(fields[3]);
                    NewMaterial.Ks = new Point3D(ksx, ksy, ksz);
                    break;
```

```
                case "Ka":          // Ambient color.
                    double kax = double.Parse(fields[1]);
                    double kay = double.Parse(fields[2]);
                    double kaz = double.Parse(fields[3]);
                    NewMaterial.Ka = new Point3D(kax, kay, kaz);
                    break;

                case "map_Kd":      // texture file.
                    NewMaterial.Filename = dir + line.Substring(6).Trim();
                    break;

                default:
                    if (!unknown.Contains(fields[0]))
                        unknown.Add(fields[0]);
                    break;
            }
        }
    }

    // List unknown tokens.
    if (unknown.Count > 0)
    {
        Console.WriteLine("Unknown mtl tokens:");
        foreach (string token in unknown)
            Console.WriteLine("    " + token);
    }
}
```

Like the `ReadObjFile` method, this one starts by defining an array of whitespace characters and creating a list to hold unknown commands. Also like the `ReadObjFile` method, this one reads each line, calls `CleanLine` to remove comments, and skips any blank lines. It then splits each line into fields separated by whitespace and uses a `switch` statement to handle the different commands.

If a line's command is `newmtl`, it is defining a new material. The code creates a new `ObjMaterial` object and sets its name.

If the command is `Ns`, `Tr`, or `d`, then it defines a simple numeric value. The code parses the value and saves it appropriately in the current material.

If the command is `Kd`, `Ks`, or `Ka`, then it defines a color value. The code parses the red, green, and blue color components and saves them in the current material's appropriate fields.

If the command is `map_Kd`, then it identifies a texture file, so the code saves the texture file name in the current material's `Filename` field.

If the line contains some other command, the method adds it to the `unknown` list if it isn't already present.

After it finishes reading the mtl file, the method displays any unknown commands in the Console window.

ProcessModels

After it finishes reading the data from the obj and mtl files, the program uses the following `ProcessModels` method to convert the data into a format that works with WPF.

```
// Process the models.
private void ProcessModels(bool invertTextures, bool zIsUp)
{
    // Make the dictionary of materials.
    foreach (ObjMaterial material in AllMaterials)
    {
        // Make the material's MaterialGroup.
        material.MatGroup = new MaterialGroup();

        // Transparency. (Not used.)
        byte alpha = (byte)(material.Alpha * 255);

        // Diffuse.
        byte diffR = (byte)(material.Kd.X * 255);
        byte diffG = (byte)(material.Kd.Y * 255);
        byte diffB = (byte)(material.Kd.Z * 255);
        Color diffColor = Color.FromArgb(255, diffR, diffG, diffB);
        SolidColorBrush diffBrush = new SolidColorBrush(diffColor);
        DiffuseMaterial diffMat = new DiffuseMaterial(diffBrush);
        material.MatGroup.Children.Add(diffMat);

        // If it has a file, use it.
        if (material.Filename != null)
        {
            // Use the file.
            string filename = material.Filename;
            ImageBrush imgBrush = new ImageBrush();
            imgBrush.ViewportUnits = BrushMappingMode.Absolute;
            imgBrush.TileMode = TileMode.Tile;

            // Invert the texture if necessary.
            if (invertTextures)
            {
                TransformGroup trans = new TransformGroup();
                trans.Children.Add(new ScaleTransform(1, -1));
                trans.Children.Add(new TranslateTransform(0, 1));
                imgBrush.Transform = trans;
            }

            imgBrush.ImageSource =
                new BitmapImage(new Uri(filename, UriKind.Relative));
            DiffuseMaterial imgMat = new DiffuseMaterial(imgBrush);
            material.MatGroup.Children.Add(imgMat);
        }

        // Specular.
        byte specR = (byte)(material.Ks.X * 255);
        byte specG = (byte)(material.Ks.Y * 255);
        byte specB = (byte)(material.Ks.Z * 255);
        Color specColor = Color.FromArgb(255, specR, specG, specB);
        SolidColorBrush specBrush = new SolidColorBrush(specColor);
        SpecularMaterial specMat = new SpecularMaterial(specBrush, material.Ns);
        material.MatGroup.Children.Add(specMat);
```

```
        // We ignore Ka and Tr.

        // Add it to the materials dictionary.
        MtlMaterials.Add(material.Name, material);
    }

    // Convert the object models into meshes.
    foreach (ObjModel model in AllObjectModels)
    {
        // Make the mesh.
        MeshGeometry3D mesh = new MeshGeometry3D();
        Meshes.Add(mesh);
        MeshNames.Add(model.Name);
        MaterialNames.Add(model.MaterialName);

        // Make a new list of smoothing groups.
        Dictionary<int, Dictionary<Point3D, int>> smoothingGroups =
            new Dictionary<int, Dictionary<Point3D, int>>();

        // Engtry 0 is null (no smoothing).
        smoothingGroups.Add(0, null);

        // Make the faces.
        foreach (ObjFace face in model.Faces)
        {
            // Make the face's vertices.
            int numPoints = face.Vertices.Count;
            Point3D[] points = new Point3D[numPoints];
            for (int i = 0; i < numPoints; i++)
                points[i] = AllVertices[face.Vertices[i] - 1];

            // Get texture coordinates if present.
            Point[] textureCoords = null;
            if (face.TextureCoords.Count > 0)
            {
                textureCoords = new Point[numPoints];
                for (int i = 0; i < numPoints; i++)
                    textureCoords[i] =
                        AllTextureCoordinates[face.TextureCoords[i] - 1];
            }

            // Get normals if present.
            Vector3D[] normals = null;
            if (face.Normals.Count > 0)
            {
                normals = new Vector3D[numPoints];
                for (int i = 0; i < numPoints; i++)
                    normals[i] = AllNormals[face.Normals[i] - 1];
            }

            // Get the point dictionary for this smoothing group.
            // Add new groups if needed.
            if (!smoothingGroups.ContainsKey(face.SmoothingGroup))
            {
                smoothingGroups.Add(face.SmoothingGroup,
                    new Dictionary<Point3D, int>());
            }
```

```
                Dictionary<Point3D, int> pointDict = smoothingGroups[face.SmoothingGroup];

                // Make the polygon.
                mesh.AddPolygon(pointDict: pointDict,
                    textureCoords: textureCoords, normals: normals,
                    points: points);
            }

            // If Z is up, rotate the model.
            if (zIsUp)
            {
                mesh.ApplyTransformation(D3.Rotate(D3.XVector(), D3.Origin, -90));
            }
        }
    }
```

This method first loops through the material data and converts `ObjMaterial` objects into `MaterialGroup` objects. It uses `ObjMaterial` properties to add a diffuse material to the group.

If the material has a texture file name, the code uses it to create an `ImageBrush`. If the `invertTextures` parameter is `true`, the method uses transformations to flip the image brush vertically and translate it so it begins in the texture's upper left corner. It then adds the image material to the group.

The code then adds a specular material to the group, using its red, green, and blue color components plus the specular power `Ns`.

The code then adds the finished material to a dictionary, using its name as a key.

> **NOTE:** The code adds the diffuse, texture, and specular materials to the material group in that order so the texture (if present) covers the diffuse material, and the specular material (if defined) provides highlights on top of everything. If the specular material is undefined, its red, green, and blue color components default to 0 so that material adds no color to the result.

Having created the materials, the `ProcessModels` method loops through the file's object models. For each model, it creates a `MeshGeometry3D` object and adds it and its name to the `ObjLoader` object's `Meshes` and `MeshNames` lists.

Next, the method creates a `smoothingGroups` dictionary to hold smoothing groups, using the groups' indices as keys.

> **NOTE:** An obj file may not define smoothing groups sequentially. For example, it might define group numbers 1, 2, and 5. That's why the code stores the groups in a dictionary instead of an array.

Each entry in the smoothingGroups dictionary is itself a dictionary. That dictionary is used by the methods described in earlier chapters to smooth objects.

> **NOTE:** Recall that the AddPolygon method takes an optional pointDict parameter that gives the indices of a set of points. When it needs to find a point's index in the mesh's TextureCoordinates list, it uses that dictionary to allow the mesh's triangles to share points and produce a smooth result.

After creating the dictionary of point dictionaries, the method adds a null point dictionary to represent smoothing group 0. If an object has no smoothing, then the program will pass null into AddPolygon so its faces won't be smoothed.

The code then loops through the model's faces. It looks up each face's points by index in the AllVertices list and adds them to an array. Similarly, if the face has texture coordinates or normals, the code looks them up by index and adds them to arrays.

Next, the code looks for the face's smoothing group in the smoothingGroups dictionary. Initially that dictionary only contains an entry for group 0, which represents no smoothing. If the face's group isn't yet in the dictionary, the code adds it so future faces in the group will share vertices with this face.

Finally, the code calls AddPolygon to create the face's triangles. It passes that method a point dictionary for smoothing, texture coordinates, and normals. The dictionary, texture coordinates, and normals will be null if the face doesn't use them.

After it has processed all of the object's faces, the method checks its zIsUp parameter and uses a transformation to turn the model right side up if it must. It uses the D3 class's Rotate method described in Chapter 9 to make a transformation that rotates -90° around the X axis to rotate the model's Z axis onto WPF's Y axis.

Program LoadObj

The preceding sections describe most of the interesting code in the LoadObj example program, but the main program still has a bit more work to do. I could have put much of that work in another helper class, but I decided to leave it in the main program to give the program more flexibility.

The following code snippet shows how the program loads an obj file.

```
// Load the file.
ObjLoader loader = new ObjLoader(dir, objfile, invertTextures, zIsUp);

// Fit in the box -4 <= {x, y, z} <= 4.
loader.FitToBox(new Rect3D(-4, -4, -4, 2 * 4, 2 * 4, 2 * 4));
```

```
// Make a new list for the mesh names.
MeshNames = new Dictionary<MeshGeometry3D, string>();

// Display the meshes.
int totalPoints = 0;
int totalTriangles = 0;
for (int i = 0; i < loader.Meshes.Count; i++)
{
    totalPoints += loader.Meshes[i].Positions.Count;
    totalTriangles += loader.Meshes[i].TriangleIndices.Count;
    Console.WriteLine("Mesh " + loader.MeshNames[i] +
        ", Material: " + loader.MaterialNames[i] +
        ", Points: " + loader.Meshes[i].Positions.Count +
        ", Triangles: " + loader.Meshes[i].TriangleIndices.Count);

    // Get the mesh.
    MeshGeometry3D mesh = loader.Meshes[i];

    // Get the mesh's material.
    MaterialGroup matGroup;
    string matName = loader.MaterialNames[i];
    if (loader.MtlMaterials.ContainsKey(matName))
        matGroup = loader.MtlMaterials[matName].MatGroup;
    else
    {
        // Use a default material.
        matGroup = new MaterialGroup();
        matGroup.Children.Add(new DiffuseMaterial(Brushes.LightBlue));
    }

    // Make the model.
    GeometryModel3D model = mesh.MakeModel(matGroup);
    model.BackMaterial = model.Material;
    MainGroup.Children.Add(model);

    // Save the mesh's name.
    MeshNames.Add(mesh, loader.MeshNames[i]);
}
Console.WriteLine("Total meshes:    " + loader.Meshes.Count);
Console.WriteLine("Total points:    " + totalPoints);
Console.WriteLine("Total triangles: " + totalTriangles);
```

This code creates an `ObjLoader` object. That object's constructor loads the obj file and any associated mtl files, and performs all of the other tasks described earlier in this chapter.

Next, the code calls the loader's `FitToBox` method, which I'll describe shortly. That method uniformly scales all of the objects in the model so they fit within a box. In this example, the box is a cube with a corner at the point (-4, -4, -4) and with width 8.

The program then loops through the loader's meshes. It displays some data such as the mesh's and material's names in the Console window. It gets each mesh's material, creating a default if the mesh has no material, and uses the mesh and material to create a `GeometryModel3D` object.

The code also saves the mesh's name in the MeshNames dictionary, which is created at the main program's class level. The program uses that dictionary for hit testing as described in Chapter 32. See the section "Hit Testing" at the beginning of that chapter for more information on hit testing.

The following two sections describe the FitToBox method and the GetBoxMapping method that it uses.

FitToBox

The following code shows the ObjLoader class's FitToBox helper method.

```
// Fit the meshes to the indicated box.
public void FitToBox(Rect3D box)
{
    // Get the combined bounds of all meshes.
    Rect3D bounds = Meshes[0].Bounds;
    for (int i = 1; i < Meshes.Count; i++) bounds.Union(Meshes[i].Bounds);

    // Get the transformation.
    Transform3DGroup group = MeshExtensions.GetBoxMapping(bounds, box);

    // Apply the transformation to all meshes.
    foreach (MeshGeometry3D mesh in Meshes)
        mesh.ApplyTransformation(group);
}
```

This method loops through the ObjLoader object's meshes and calls their Bounds methods to get their bounding boxes. It uses the bounding boxes' Union methods to combine them all into a single bounding box for all of the meshes.

The code then calls the GetBoxMapping method described in the next section to get a transformation that maps the bounds into a new bounding box. It finishes by looping through the meshes, applying that transformation to each.

GetBoxMapping

The GetBoxMapping method uses the following code to make a transformation that scales and translates one box so it fits within another.

```
public static Transform3DGroup GetBoxMapping(Rect3D source, Rect3D dest)
{
    // Translate to center the source at the origin.
    Transform3DGroup group = new Transform3DGroup();
    group.Children.Add(new TranslateTransform3D(
        -(source.X + source.SizeX / 2),
        -(source.Y + source.SizeY / 2),
        -(source.Z + source.SizeZ / 2)));

    // Calculate the scale factor.
    double xscale = dest.SizeX / source.SizeX;
```

```
        double yscale = dest.SizeY / source.SizeY;
        double zscale = dest.SizeZ / source.SizeZ;
        double scale = xscale;
        if (scale > yscale) scale = yscale;
        if (scale > zscale) scale = zscale;

        // Scale.
        group.Children.Add(new ScaleTransform3D(scale, scale, scale));

        // Translate to center in the desired box.
        group.Children.Add(new TranslateTransform3D(
            dest.X + dest.SizeX / 2,
            dest.Y + dest.SizeY / 2,
            dest.Z + dest.SizeZ / 2));

        // Return the transformation.
        return group;
    }
```

The goal is to transform the `Rect3D` named `source` so it fits within `dest`.

The method first creates a `Transform3DGroup` to hold a sequence of transformations. It then adds a translation to move the source box so it is centered at the origin.

Next, the code calculates the X, Y, and Z scale factors that it would need to use to stretch the source box to fill the destination box completely. It sets the variable `scale` to the smallest of the scale factors so it can scale the source box uniformly and still have it fit within the destination box. The code uses `scale` to make a scale transformation and adds it to the transform group.

Finally, the code translates the result so it is centered in the destination box. The method finishes by returning the transform group.

Using the Program

To use the LoadObj example program, run it and use its checkboxes to indicate whether you want to invert textures, make the Z axis be "up," or display the coordinate axes. Then use the File menu's Open command to select the obj file that you want to load.

If you change the checkboxes, reload the obj file.

The program assumes that it can find any necessary mtl or texture files relative to the obj file's directory. For example, the obj file might us the following statement to specify an mtl file in the same directory.

```
mtllib ghosts.mtl
```

An obj or mtl file could also specify a file location relative to the obj file's directory. For example, the following statement in an mtl file would indicate that the texture file `Face.png` is in the `Textures` subdirectory.

```
map_Kd Textures/Face.png
```

The download for the LoadObj example program on the book's web site includes a `Models` directory that contains some models that you can load. The `NoTextures` subdirectory contains a few models that don't have textures. To save space, I've included only a few relatively small sample models.

Obtaining Models

There are several ways you can obtain models. First, you can use a three-dimensional drawing tool to create your own models. Either pick a tool that can save models in Wavefront obj format or look for a library that you can use to load models in other formats into a C# program. There are also some online converters that can load a model in one format and save it in obj format.

You can also download models from online repositories. For example, TurboSquid (`turbosquid.com`), Free3D (`free3d.com`), and CGTrader (`cgtrader.com`) have thousands of models available in various formats.

However, there are a couple of disadvantages and gotchas that you should watch out for when you download models online. The following list summarizes a few.

- Cost—Many models are free but many others cost between a few dollars and thousands of dollars. You can't blame people for charging for their models because some have obviously taken a huge amount of work to develop. Even if a model is worth the price, however, be sure that it doesn't suffer from any of the other problems listed here before you pay for it.
- Permissions—Some models may have restricted permissions that may prevent you from using them for certain purposes. Sometimes it's even hard to tell what permissions are available. For example, I found several models of celebrity faces. In some cases, the artist who created the model released it into the public domain, but the images of the celebrities may be restricted. You can use them for "editorial uses," but you cannot use them in products such as games without the celebrities' permission.
- Size—Some models are truly enormous! I found one lovely gazebo model that weighed in at over 150 MB. Sometimes these models include reflection maps, bump maps and other image files that the LoadObj example program doesn't use so you can delete them. Other models use extremely high resolution texture files and you can save space by shrinking them and using a lossy file format such as jpg instead of png. However, some models just define a lot of faces. The gazebo model I mentioned defines more than 3.3 million triangles! It's beautiful but takes a long time to load and the program can't rotate it quickly because it's so complex.

- Data errors—Some models may have data errors such as missing points or points that don't line up perfectly. For example, the seam between two edges of a solid might not quite match so there's a small gap between them.
- Incomplete data—Many model artists don't normally use obj files so when they export their models they may forget necessary pieces. I've seen models with obj files but no corresponding mtl files. I've also seen models with no texture images. If the models are small, you may be able to create your own mtl and texture files or replace textures with solid colors, but it can be a lot of work getting large models to work properly.
- Z-fighting—Some models suffer from z-fighting (described in the section "Adding Axes" in Chapter 12). Overlapping coplanar faces may flicker as you rotate the model. (I suspect that some other drawing tools may have a way to break ties that WPF doesn't use so z-fighting doesn't occur in those tools.)
- Unknown commands—The LoadObj example program handles the fewest obj and mtl file commands that let you produce a reasonably nice result. Some models may produce much better results if you handle more commands. (If you add more commands to the program, please post a comment on the book's web site so others can take advantage of your improvements!)
- Unneeded data—Some models include other data that you can't use in WPF such as rigging data used for animation. WPF doesn't support rigging so the models will be bigger than necessary for your purposes. You may be able to remove that data, but it could be a lot of work.
- Tricky formats—Some model artists don't use Windows so their models may only be available compressed in non-zip formats such as rar and tar. If necessary, you can find a tool to decompress those formats or convert them into zip files, but that adds an extra step.

The following table lists some models, mostly from TurboSquid, that you can try to load into your programs. Be sure to note the model's size before you download it. Also note that these models were free when I wrote this but their prices may change.

Model	URL
3d scan man	`tinyurl.com/y7kv8xen`
Casual man	`tinyurl.com/y8v23wk7`
European Old House	`tinyurl.com/y7rhors5`
Gazebo	`tinyurl.com/ycoys5ej`
House	`tinyurl.com/y7hmqszh`

Model	URL
Medieval castle	`tinyurl.com/y9u29adu`
Model planes	`tinyurl.com/yas559jr`
Old building	`tinyurl.com/y8g9nh5p`
Robot	`tinyurl.com/yb9krqbv`
Sci-Fi city	`tinyurl.com/ya85wvpo`
Spaceship 1	`tinyurl.com/y89unn82`
Spaceship 2	`tinyurl.com/ydxsmm4e`
Specter sports car	`tinyurl.com/y8twa8wg`
Stylized character head	`tinyurl.com/y6wkp497`
The Stanford bunny	`tinyurl.com/y7289v4a`
The Stanford dragon	`tinyurl.com/y8tf5v69`
The Utah teapot	`tinyurl.com/n92ja3g`
Tropical fish	`tinyurl.com/y7uy6nco`

The Utah teapot (1975), Stanford bunny (1994), and Stanford dragon (1996) are all classic models in three-dimensional programming. See their Wikipedia entries for information about their origins.

Summary

This chapter explained how you can load models saved in Wavefront obj format into your WPF applications. You can load multiple models and add your own objects to build a complete, full-featured scene.

> **NOTE:** Interestingly, Visual Studio 2017 can load obj files! Simply expand the File menu's Open submenu and select File. If you pick an obj file and click Open, Visual Studio displays it. Unfortunately, it's not clear how you can leverage that capability to load models into your applications. If you figure that out, please post a comment on the book's web site. (You could make this entire chapter unnecessary!)

The next chapter returns to techniques for building objects within your application. It explains how you can make some useful types of three-dimensional charts and graphs in WPF.

Chapter 34

Charts and Graphs

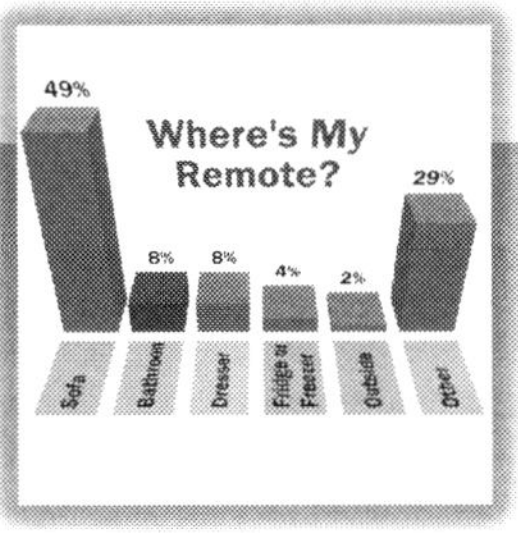

This chapter explains some ways you can make three-dimensional charts and graphs. Most of these just require you to put together methods and techniques that you've learned in earlier parts of the book. For example, you can make a three-dimensional bar chart simply by creating suitably arranged boxes.

In fact, in a sense the previous parts of this book were all leading up to this chapter. The examples in this chapter test your ability to combine previous techniques to build three-dimensional scenes including basic shapes and text.

Because these programs reuse earlier techniques to build complex scenes, they tend to be long and light on new concepts. For that reason, I'm going to skip most of their code and focus on describing their most novel techniques at relatively high level. You can always download the example programs to see all off the minutiae.

The following sections explain how you can build three-dimensional bar charts, pie charts, and graphs. Subsections describe variations of the main chart and graph types.

Bar Charts

A bar chart is basically a collection of boxes with heights corresponding to some value. Common variations of bar charts display bars in a single row, bars in rows and columns, and stacked bars that have sections of different colors. The following sections describe examples that demonstrate hose kinds of bar charts.

Basic Bar Charts

The BarChart example program shown in Figure 34-1 draws a basic bar chart showing the most common strange places where people find their remote controls. This program simply draws some boxes and labels.

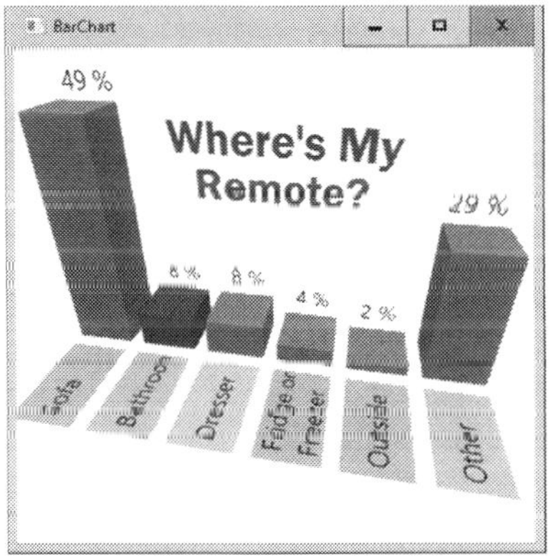

Figure 34-1: A bar chart is basically a collection of boxes.

This example draws its boxes in a row that is parallel to the X axis, but that's not the only way you could arrange the boxes. For example, you could use any of the modifications in the following list.

- Make the row parallel to the Z axis
- Make the bars horizontal instead of vertical
- Arrange the bars in a circle, spiral, or some other pattern
- Use hexagonal prisms, cylinders, cones, or other shapes instead of boxes
- Use the width and depth of the boxes to represent additional data
- Use raw values instead of percentages
- Place text showing values on the sides of the boxes
- Display horizontal lines behind the bars indicating multiples of 10%
- Use color to indicate some other piece of data such as making taller boxes redder

The possibilities are limited only by your imagination.

NOTE: In fact, there are so many possible options that you should probably sketch your design on paper before you start programming so you can decide whether you'll like the final result. If you just start writing code and then move things around, you could waste hours!

The two most interesting pieces of code in this example are the `MakeBars` and `MakeLabel` methods. As I'm sure you can guess, `MakeBars` draws the program's bars and `MakeLabel` draws a label.

The following code shows the `MakeBars` method.

```
// Make a row of bars in the X direction.
private void MakeBars(double xmin, double ymin,
    double zmin, double dx, double gap,
    double[] values, string[] frontLabels, string[] topLabels,
    Brush[] barBrushes, Brush[] bgBrushes, Brush[] fgBrushes,
    FontFamily ff, Model3DGroup group)
{
    double x = xmin;
    double fontSize = 0.4;
    for (int i = 0; i < values.Length; i++)
    {
        // Make the bar.
        MeshGeometry3D barMesh = new MeshGeometry3D();
        Point3D corner = new Point3D(x, ymin, zmin);
        barMesh.AddBox(corner,
            D3.XVector(dx),
            D3.YVector(YScale * values[i]),
            D3.ZVector(dx));
        group.Children.Add(barMesh.MakeModel(barBrushes[i]));

        // Display the front label.
        const double textWid = 1.8;
        MakeLabel(frontLabels[i],
            new Point3D(x + dx, ymin, textWid + zmin + dx + gap),
            D3.ZVector(-textWid), D3.XVector(-dx),
```

```
                bgBrushes[i], fgBrushes[i], fontSize, ff,
                HorizontalAlignment.Left, VerticalAlignment.Center, group);

            // Display the top label.
            MakeLabel(topLabels[i],
                new Point3D(x,
                    ymin + YScale * values[i],
                    zmin - 0.1),
                D3.XVector(dx), D3.YVector(dx),
                Brushes.Transparent, fgBrushes[i], fontSize, ff,
                HorizontalAlignment.Center, VerticalAlignment.Bottom, group);

            x += dx + gap;
        }
    }
```

This method takes an abundance of parameters that determine the following.

- The minimum X, Y, and Z coordinates where the boxes should start
- The width of the boxes (which is also their depth) and the space between them
- The values, which in this example are fractions such as 0.49 for 49%
- Labels to display in front of the bars
- Labels to display above the bars
- Brushes to use when drawing the bars
- Background and foreground brushes for the front labels
- The font family to use for text
- The `Model3DGroup` that should hold the scene's objects

Other values such as the font sizes are hardwired into the method. You could make them additional parameters if you like. I decided that the parameters used here gave a reasonable level of flexibility, and I didn't want to make an already lengthy parameter list even longer.

The method starts by creating a variable `x` to track the X coordinate of the boxes as it draws them. It then enters a loop where it does the interesting work.

For each value, the method uses the `AddBox` mesh extension method described earlier in the book to make the value's box. It then calls the `MakeLabel` method (described shortly) to make the labels in front of and above the box.

The code then increases variable `x` to position the next box.

The following code shows the `MakeLabel` method.

```
    // Make a label.
    private void MakeLabel(string text, Point3D ll,
        Vector3D vRight, Vector3D vUp,
        Brush bgBrush, Brush fgBrush,
        double fontSize, FontFamily fontFamily,
        HorizontalAlignment hAlign, VerticalAlignment vAlign,
        Model3DGroup group)
    {
```

```
        double wid = vRight.Length;
        double hgt = vUp.Length;
        MeshGeometry3D mesh = new MeshGeometry3D();
        group.Children.Add(
            mesh.AddSizedText(text,
                fontSize, wid, hgt,
                ll, ll + vRight, ll + vRight + vUp, ll + vUp,
                bgBrush, fgBrush, hAlign, vAlign, fontFamily));
    }
```

This method is basically a wrapper for the `AddSizedText` method described in Chapter 30. The `MakeLabel` method's first three parameters give the text to draw, the point where the text's lower left corner should be, and vectors pointing in the text's desired right and up directions.

The method uses its parameters to calculate the values that it needs to pass into `AddSizedText` and then calls that method to draw the text. It finishes by converting the text's mesh into a model and adding it to the program's `Model3DGroup`.

> **NOTE:** The other example programs described in this chapter also use this `MakeLabel` method.

The other parts of the BarChart example program are less interesting. They load the data, calculate the size of the bars, and figure out where to start drawing to center the chart properly. The main program also calls the `MakeLabel` method to make the chart's title, "Where's My Remote?"

> **NOTE:** This program and some of the others described in this chapter use actual data. When I didn't make up data, the program's `LoadData` method includes a comment that tells where I found it.

The remaining code isn't particularly interesting, so I won't show it here. Describing all of the code used by the examples in this chapter would add about 100 pages to the book without teaching you much. You can always download the examples to see all of their details.

Figure 34-2: This chart's values change over time.

Row/Column Bar Charts

As you can probably guess, a row/column bar chart displays bars in rows and columns. Typically that kind of chart displays a series of values that change over time. For example, each row might represent a different product and each column might represent sales figures for the products over time.

The RowColumnBarChart example program shown in Figure 34-2 displays this kind of bar chart. The rows represent different kinds of dinosaurs and the columns represent the months September, October, and November. The height of the bars indicate the number of dinosaurs spotted of each kind during those months. (Yes, I made up this data.)

The most interesting part of this program is the `MakeRowColumnBars` method shown in the following code.

```
// Make rows of bars in the X and Z directions.
private void MakeRowColumnBars(double xmin, double ymin,
    double zmin, double dx, double gap,
    double[,] values, string[] frontLabels, string[] sideLabels,
    Brush[,] barBrushes, Brush[] bgBrushes, Brush[] fgBrushes,
    FontFamily ff, Model3DGroup group)
{
    int numX = values.GetUpperBound(0) + 1;
    int numZ = values.GetUpperBound(1) + 1;
    double x = xmin;
    double z;
    double fontSize = 0.3;
    for (int ix = 0; ix < numX; ix++)
    {
        z = zmin;
        for (int iz = 0; iz < numZ; iz++)
        {
            // Make the bar.
            MeshGeometry3D barMesh = new MeshGeometry3D();
            Point3D corner = new Point3D(x, ymin, z);
            barMesh.AddBox(corner,
                D3.XVector(dx),
                D3.YVector(YScale * values[ix, iz]),
                D3.ZVector(dx));
            group.Children.Add(barMesh.MakeModel(barBrushes[ix, iz]));

            z += dx + gap;
        }

        // Display the front label.
        const double textWid = 2;
        MakeLabel(frontLabels[ix],
            new Point3D(x + dx, ymin, z + textWid),
            D3.ZVector(-textWid), D3.XVector(-dx),
            bgBrushes[ix], fgBrushes[ix], fontSize, ff,
            HorizontalAlignment.Left, VerticalAlignment.Center, group);

        x += dx + gap;
    }

    // Display the side labels.
    z = zmin + dx;
    double xmax = xmin + numX * dx + (numX - 1) * gap;
    for (int iz = 0; iz < numZ; iz++)
    {
        const double textWid = 2;
```

```
            MakeLabel(sideLabels[iz],
                new Point3D(xmax + gap, ymin, z),
                D3.XVector(textWid), D3.ZVector(-dx),
                Brushes.Transparent, Brushes.Black, fontSize, ff,
                HorizontalAlignment.Left, VerticalAlignment.Center, group);
            z += dx + gap;
        }
    }
```

This method first uses the values array's `GetUpperBound` method to determine the number of rows and columns that it will make. It then creates variables `x` and `z` to keep track of the locations of the rows and columns as it builds the chart's boxes.

Next, the method makes variable `ix` loop over the rows in the X direction. Inside that loop, it makes variable `iz` loop over the columns in the Z direction. Within the inner loop, the code calls the `AddBox` extension method to draw the appropriate box.

After the inner loop ends but still inside the outer loop, the code draws the label in front of the row.

For example, in Figure 34-2, the first pass through the outer `ix` loop draws the values for the velociraptor on the left of the figure. The inner `iz` loop draws each of the velociraptor boxes. Then the call to `MakeLabel` draws the label "Velociraptor."

After it finishes drawing the boxes and the front labels, the `MakeRowColumnBars` method uses another loop to draw the side labels giving the months.

Stacked Bar Charts

In a stacked bar chart, each bar has differently colored sections to provide information about subsets of its data. For example, in the StackedBarChart example program shown in Figure 34-3, a bar's height represents the total number of people in the United States military for a particular year. Each bar has colored sections showing the number of people enlisted in the Army, Navy, Air Force, and Marines. (Coast Guard data wasn't included in the source I used.)

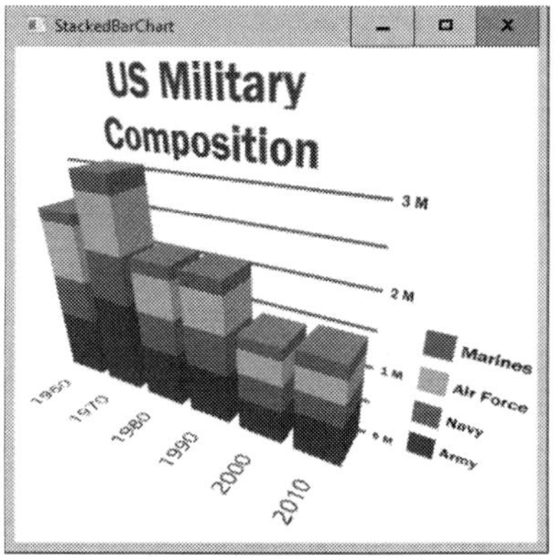

Figure 34-3: Colored boxes give information about each value's composition.

You could combine the row/column and stacked bar charts, but it might be hard to understand the data because the bars in the front might make it hard to see the lower pieces of the bars behind them.

The most interesting piece of the StackedBarChart example program is the following `MakeStackedBars` method.

```
// Make a row of stacked bars in the X direction.
private void MakeStackedBars(double xmin, double ymin,
```

```
        double zmin, double dx, double gap,
        double[,] values, string[] frontLabels,
        Brush[] barBrushes, Brush bgBrush, Brush fgBrush,
        FontFamily ff, Model3DGroup group)
    {
        double x = xmin;
        int numX = values.GetUpperBound(0) + 1;
        int numZ = values.GetUpperBound(1) + 1;
        double fontSize = 0.45;
        for (int ix = 0; ix < numX; ix++)
        {
            double y = ymin;
            for (int iz = 0; iz < numZ; iz++)
            {
                // Make this piece of the bar.
                MeshGeometry3D barMesh = new MeshGeometry3D();
                Point3D corner = new Point3D(x, y, zmin);
                barMesh.AddBox(corner,
                    D3.XVector(dx),
                    D3.YVector(YScale * values[ix, iz]),
                    D3.ZVector(dx));
                group.Children.Add(barMesh.MakeModel(barBrushes[iz]));
                y += YScale * values[ix, iz];
            }

            // Display the front label.
            const double textWid = 1.5;
            MakeLabel(frontLabels[ix],
                new Point3D(x + dx, ymin, textWid + zmin + dx + gap),
                D3.ZVector(-textWid), D3.XVector(-dx),
                bgBrush, fgBrush, fontSize, FontFamily,
                HorizontalAlignment.Left, VerticalAlignment.Center, group);

            x += dx + gap;
        }
    }
```

Like the `MakeRowColumnBars` method, this code begins by using the `values` array's `GetUpperBound` method. This time it uses the method to find the number of "main values" and the number of pieces in each.

The method then loops through the main values. For each main value, the code loops through the value's pieces and calls `AddBox` for each.

After it draws all of a value's pieces, the code draws the label in front of its boxes.

This example's main program draws a title as usual. It also draws lines behind the bars showing multiples of one million people. Finally, it draws a key to the side to match the colored bar pieces with the different armed services. (That's much easier to see in color than it is in the book.) Download the example program to see how that code works.

Pie Charts

In a pie chart, a circle is divided into pieces much as you might divide a pie. Together the pieces add up to some total value. A slice's size indicates its fraction of the total. For example, if a value is one quarter of the total, then its slice fills one quarter of the circle.

> **NOTE:** You can define a slice's fraction by its outer arc length, inner angle, or area. All of those values are multiples of each other so all work. For example, a slice that fills one third of the circle also uses one third of the total arc length and one third of the full inner angle or 360°/3=120°.

Like bar charts, there are several common variations of pie charts. The following sections describe four: basic pie charts, stacked pie charts, ragged pie charts, and circle charts.

Basic Pie Charts

The PieChart example program shown in Figure 34-4 displays the percentages of people with various blood types in the United States. (While looking up this data, I learned that those percentages vary by region and country. Who knew?)

Some pie charts display each slice's numeric or percentage value on the slice, next to the slice, or nearby with a line connecting it to the slice. The PieChart example program displays the percentages in a color-coded key (which is much easier to read in color than it is in the book).

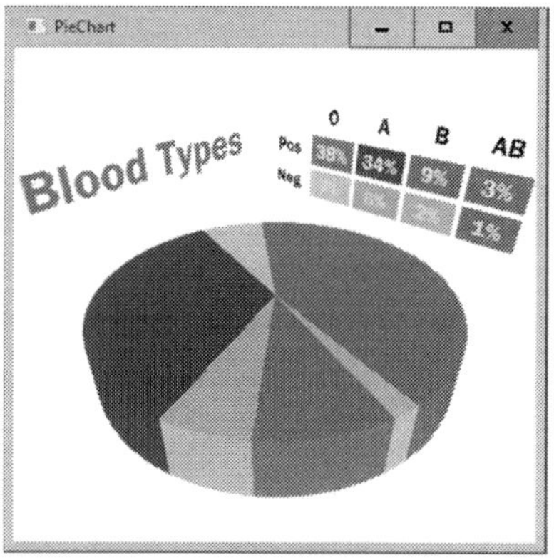

Figure 34-4: The size of a piece in a pie chart indicates its fraction of the total.

The most interesting pieces of this program are the `MakePieSlices` method shown in the following code and the `AddPieSlice` helper method that it calls.

```
// Make pie slices.
private void MakePieSlices(Point3D center, double r, double height,
    double[] values, Brush[] brushes, int numPieces, Model3DGroup group)
{
    // Calculate percentages.
    double total = values.Sum();
    int numValues = values.Length;
    double[] percents = new double[numValues];
    for (int i = 0; i < numValues; i++) percents[i] = values[i] / total;

    // Draw slices.
    double minTheta = 0;
    for (int i = 0; i < numValues; i++)
    {
```

```
            double maxTheta = minTheta + 360.0 * percents[i];
            MeshGeometry3D mesh = new MeshGeometry3D();
            int slicePieces = (int)(numPieces * percents[i]);
            if (slicePieces < 2) slicePieces = 2;
            mesh.AddPieSlice(center, height, minTheta, maxTheta,
                r, slicePieces);
            group.Children.Add(mesh.MakeModel(brushes[i]));

            minTheta = maxTheta;
        }
    }
```

The MakePieSlices method first converts each value into a percentage. To do that, it uses the LINQ extension method Sum to add up the values. It then loops through the values dividing each by the total.

Next, the method loops through the values to draw their slices. It multiplies the value's percentage by 360 to determine the angle it should span.

The code then calculates the number of pieces the program should use to draw the slice. This is similar to the number of slices used to draw a cylinder or sphere. Larger numbers produce a smoother result but use more triangles. This code also ensures that the number of pieces for a slice is at least two, so even thin slices have a bit of curve.

After it makes those preparations, the code calls the following AddPieSlice method to draw the pie slice.

```
    // Make a pie slice counter clockwise as seen from above
    // between angles minTheta and maxTheta in degrees.
    public static void AddPieSlice(this MeshGeometry3D mesh,
        Point3D center, double height, double minTheta, double maxTheta,
        double r, int numSections)
    {
        // Center of the slice.
        Point3D topCorner = center + D3.YVector(height);
        Point3D botCorner = center;

        // Unit vectors in X and Z direction for sines and cosines.
        Vector3D vx = D3.XVector(r);
        Vector3D vz = D3.ZVector(-r);

        // Convert thetas into radians.
        minTheta *= Math.PI / 180;
        maxTheta *= Math.PI / 180;

        // Point dictionaries for smoothing.
        Dictionary<Point3D, int> topDict = new Dictionary<Point3D, int>();
        Dictionary<Point3D, int> botDict = new Dictionary<Point3D, int>();
        Dictionary<Point3D, int> outDict = new Dictionary<Point3D, int>();

        double dtheta = (maxTheta - minTheta) / numSections;
        double theta = minTheta;
        // Vector in the direction of theta.
        Vector3D v = vx * Math.Cos(theta) + vz * Math.Sin(theta);
        Point3D[] topPoints =
```

```
{
    topCorner,
    topCorner,
    topCorner + v,
};
Point3D[] botPoints =
{
    botCorner,
    botCorner + v,
    botCorner,
};
Point3D[] outPoints =
{
    topCorner,
    topCorner,
    botCorner + v,
    topCorner + v,
};
for (int i = 0; i < numSections; i++)
{
    theta += dtheta;

    // Vector in the direction of theta.
    v = vx * Math.Cos(theta) + vz * Math.Sin(theta);

    // Top.
    topPoints[1] = topPoints[2];
    topPoints[2] = topCorner + v;
    mesh.AddPolygon(topDict, points: topPoints);

    // Bottom.
    botPoints[2] = botPoints[1];
    botPoints[1] = botCorner + v;
    mesh.AddPolygon(botDict, points: botPoints);

    // Outer face.
    outPoints[0] = outPoints[3];
    outPoints[1] = outPoints[2];
    outPoints[2] = botCorner + v;
    outPoints[3] = topCorner + v;
    mesh.AddPolygon(outDict, points: outPoints);
}

// Side1.
Dictionary<Point3D, int> side1Dict = new Dictionary<Point3D, int>();
v = vx * Math.Cos(minTheta) + vz * Math.Sin(minTheta);
Point3D[] side1Points =
{
    botCorner,
    botCorner + v,
    topCorner + v,
    topCorner,
};
mesh.AddPolygon(side1Dict, points: side1Points);

// Side2.
Dictionary<Point3D, int> side2Dict = new Dictionary<Point3D, int>();
v = vx * Math.Cos(maxTheta) + vz * Math.Sin(maxTheta);
Point3D[] side2Points =
```

```
        {
            topCorner,
            topCorner + v,
            botCorner + v,
            botCorner,
        };
        mesh.AddPolygon(side2Dict, points: side2Points);
    }
```

This method sets variables `topCorner` and `botCorner` to the slice's top and bottom corners at the center of the pie. It then defines two vectors, `vx` and `vz`, pointing in the X and Z directions and with lengths equal to the pie's radius. The code will later multiply these by the sines and cosines of angles to produce points on the pie's outer edge.

Next, the code converts the minimum and maximum angles from degrees (which are easy to work with) to radians (which are used by the `Math` library).

The method then creates point dictionaries for the slice's top, bottom, and outer faces so it can smooth the triangles in each of those three groups.

Next, the code creates three arrays to hold points defining polygons for the slice's top, bottom, and outer face.

After all that setup, the code finally gets down to work. It loops through the desired number of sections. For each section, it calculates the angle where the piece ends. It uses that angle to find a vector `v` that points from the piece's corner to the edge of the slice at the new angle. For example, in Figure 34-5 the vector from the corner point T0 to the point T2 gives one such vector.

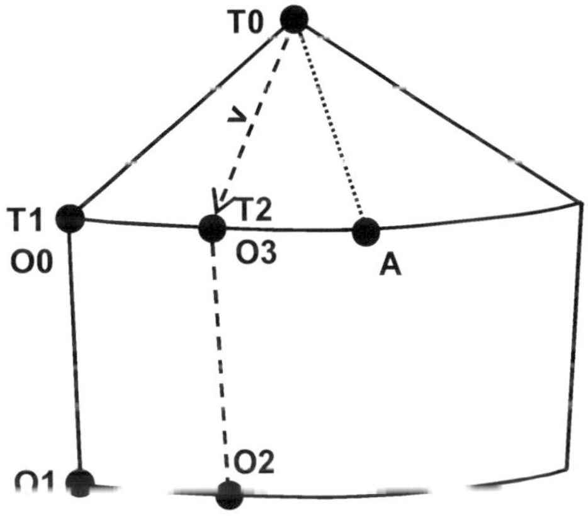

Figure 34-5: Points T0, T1, and T2 make top wedges. Points O0, O1, O2, and O3 make outer faces.

The code then uses some vector arithmetic involving the center point and the vector `v` to find the points it needs to update the arrays of top, bottom, and outer face points. The code updates the arrays so they use points from the previous piece plus some new points to define the new piece.

To see how those updates work, consider Figure 34-5 again. The points T0, T1, and T2 define a triangle on the top of the pie slice. (You can verify from the figure that those points are outwardly oriented.) To prepare for the next triangle, the code sets T1 = T2 and then sets T2 = A. Now the points T0, T1, and T2 define the next triangle on the slice's top. The code updates the bottom and outward face points similarly.

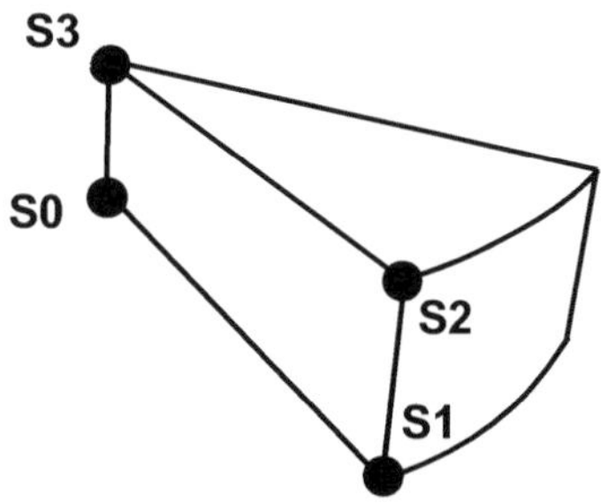

Figure 34-6: Points S0, S1, S2, and S3 define a slice's side.

As it updates each of the point arrays, the code adds the new polygons to the pie slice's mesh.

After it has created all of the top, bottom, and outward face triangles, the method still needs to make the pie slice's sides. It first makes the side with the smaller side angle held by the variable `minTheta` and then the side with the larger angle stored in variable `maxTheta`.

Figure 34-6 shows how the code uses points S0, S1, S2, and S3 to define the first side. The method defines the slice's other side similarly.

NOTE: This example doesn't really need to define a pie slice's sides because they are hidden by the sides of the adjacent pie slices.

You would need those sides, however, if you made an exploded pie chart where some of the slices were pulled out away from the center of the pie.

Stacked Pie Charts

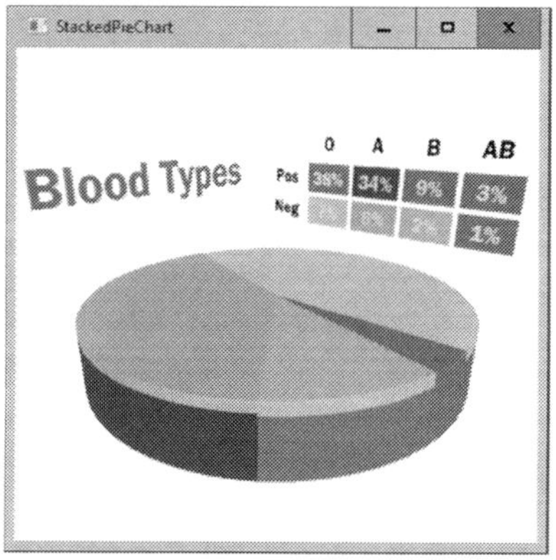

Figure 34-7: A stacked pie chart breaks values into pieces.

Just as you can divide bars in a stacked bar chart to break values into pieces, you can do the same with a pie chart. The StackedPieChart example program shown in Figure 34-7 uses that technique to break the major blood types O, A, B, and AB into their Rh positive and negative pieces. This makes it easier to compare the relative sizes of the main types. It also emphasizes the fact that the Rh negative categories are relatively small for each of the main blood types.

Although this kind of chart makes those comparisons easier, it makes it a bit harder to see all of the values simultaneously. For example, in Figure 34-7 you can barely see the division between O+ and O- on the pie's right edge. If you rotated the pie or it had other categories on its far side, you would only be able to see the topmost pieces of those slices. (Of course, this is all easier to see in color rather than in this book.)

The most interesting part of the StackedPieChart example program is the `MakeStackedBars` method shown in the following code.

```
// Make stacked pie slices.
private void MakeStackedPieSlices(Point3D center, double r, double height,
```

```
        double[,] values, Brush[,] brushes, int numPieces, Model3DGroup group)
    {
        // Calculate percentages.
        int numLevels = values.GetUpperBound(0) + 1;
        int numWedges = values.GetUpperBound(1) + 1;
        int numValues = values.Length;
        double total = 0;
        foreach (double value in values) total += value;
        double[,] percents = new double[2, numWedges];
        for (int level = 0; level < numLevels; level++)
            for (int slice = 0; slice < numWedges; slice++)
                percents[level, slice] = values[level, slice] / total;

        // Draw slices.
        double minTheta = 0;
        for (int wedge = 0; wedge < numWedges; wedge++)
        {
            // Get this wedge's total percent.
            double wedgePercent = 0;
            for (int level = 0; level < numLevels; level++)
                wedgePercent += percents[level, wedge];

            // Calculate the size of the wedge in degrees.
            double maxTheta = minTheta + 360.0 * wedgePercent;

            int wedgePieces = (int)(numPieces * wedgePercent);
            if (wedgePieces < 2) wedgePieces = 2;

            // Make the slices.
            double y = center.Y;
            for (int level = 0; level < numLevels; level++)
            {
                // Calculate the slice's height.
                double sliceHgt = height * percents[level, wedge] / wedgePercent;

                MeshGeometry3D mesh = new MeshGeometry3D();
                Point3D sliceCenter = new Point3D(center.X, y, center.Z);
                mesh.AddPieSlice(sliceCenter, sliceHgt,
                    minTheta, maxTheta, r, wedgePieces);
                group.Children.Add(mesh.MakeModel(brushes[level, wedge]));

                y += sliceHgt;
            }
            minTheta = maxTheta;
        }
    }
```

This method is basically a cross between the `MakePieSlices` method used by the PieChart example program and the `MakeStackedBars` method used by the StackedBarChart example program. It converts the values into percentages and then loops through the values much as the PieChart program did.

This method calls a stack of slices a "wedge." For each wedge, the code adds up the percentages of pieces that make up the wedge. It uses that total to determine the angle that the wedge should occupy.

The method then loops through the wedge's slices and uses the `AddPieSlice` method described earlier to draw them. The only trick here is that the method must keep track of the Y coordinates where it should draw the slices.

Ragged Pie Charts

In a ragged pie chart, the slices use their heights to provide some additional information. For example, suppose you have a manufacturing business. A slice's angle might indicate the number of units sold of a particular product. The slice's height might indicate the total revenue or profit from selling that product.

For a more concrete example, suppose a Chevrolet dealership sells 100 Spark LSs at \$13,000 and 50 Tahoes at \$47,000 for a total of 150 cars. The Spark slice would occupy 360°×100/150=240°, and the Tahoe slice would occupy 360°×50/150=120°. Vertically the Spark revenue slice would have a height of 100×\$13,000=\$1,300,000 and the Tahoe slice would have a height of 50×\$47,000=\$2,350,000, so the Tahoe slice would be much taller. (Of course you would need to scale the heights appropriately to make a reasonable chart.)

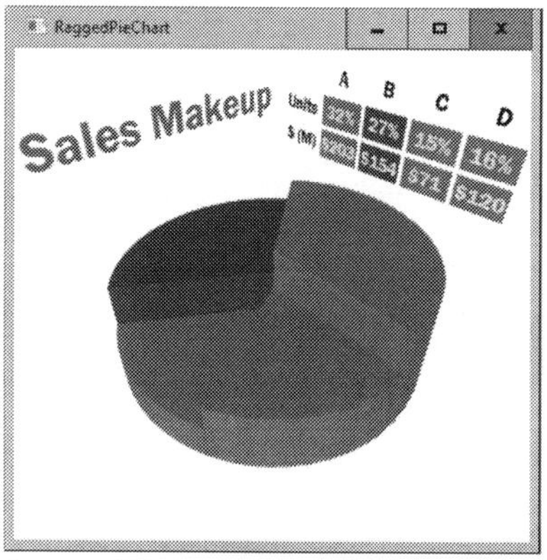

Figure 34-8: A ragged pie chart shows two values for each slice.

This kind of chart lets you examine two values for each slice, but it can be harder to understand than a normal pie chart, particularly if it contains many values. Depending on the chart's orientation, some short slices may be hidden behind taller slices.

The RaggedPieSlice example program shown in Figure 34-8 demonstrates this technique. Its most interesting piece of code is the `MakeRaggedPieSlices` method shown in the following code.

```
// Make ragged pie slices.
private void MakeRaggedPieSlices(Point3D center, double r, double[] values,
    double[] heights, Brush[] brushes, int numPieces, Model3DGroup group)
{
    // Calculate percentages.
    double total = values.Sum();
    int numValues = values.Length;
    double[] percents = new double[numValues];
    for (int i = 0; i < numValues; i++) percents[i] = values[i] / total;

    // Draw slices.
    double minTheta = 0;
    for (int i = 0; i < numValues; i++)
    {
        double maxTheta = minTheta + 360.0 * percents[i];
        MeshGeometry3D mesh = new MeshGeometry3D();
        int slicePieces = (int)(numPieces * percents[i]);
        if (slicePieces < 2) slicePieces = 2;
```

```
            mesh.AddPieSlice(center, heights[i], minTheta, maxTheta,
                r, slicePieces);
            group.Children.Add(mesh.MakeModel(brushes[i]));

            minTheta = maxTheta;
        }
    }
```

This method converts the values into percentages as usual and then loops through the values. For each value, the code calculates its slice's angle as in the preceding programs. It then calls the `AddPieSlice` method to draw the slice, passing that method the slice's desired height.

Circle Charts

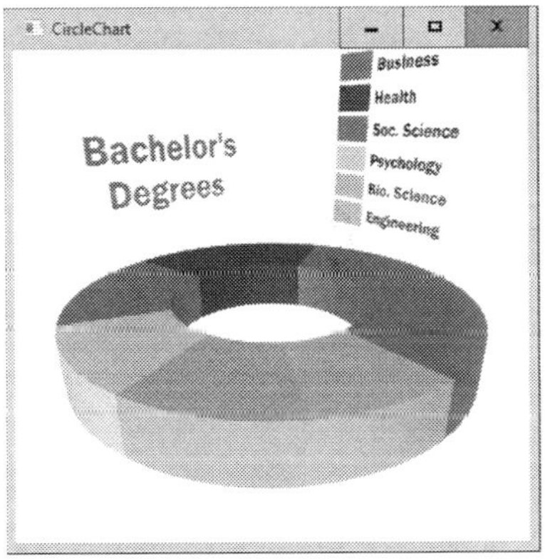

Figure 34-9: A circle chart's "slices" are pieces of a torus.

A circle chart or torus chart is similar to a pie chart except the slices are sections of a thick circle or torus with a rectangular cross section. The CircleChart example program shown in Figure 34-9 displays this kind of chart.

Some variations use a torus with a circular cross section, so the slices are basically slices of a donut.

The most interesting piece of the CircleChart example program is the `MakeCircleChart` method shown in the following code.

```
// Make circle chart pie slices.
private void MakeCircleChart(Point3D center, double r1, double r2,
    double height, double[] values, Brush[] brushes, int numPieces, Model3DGroup group)
{
    // Calculate percentages.
    double total = values.Sum();
    int numValues = values.Length;
    double[] percents = new double[numValues];
    for (int i = 0; i < numValues; i++) percents[i] = values[i] / total;

    // Draw slices.
    double minTheta = 0;
    for (int i = 0; i < numValues; i++)
    {
        double maxTheta = minTheta + 360.0 * percents[i];
        MeshGeometry3D mesh = new MeshGeometry3D();
        int slicePieces = (int)(numPieces * percents[i]);
        if (slicePieces < 2) slicePieces = 2;
        mesh.AddCircleSlice(center, height, minTheta, maxTheta,
            r1, r2, slicePieces);
        group.Children.Add(mesh.MakeModel(brushes[i]));

        minTheta = maxTheta;
    }
```

```
}
```

Like the other pie chart style methods, this one converts its values into percentages and then loops through the values. For each value, the code calls the `AddCircleSlice` method shown in the following code to draw the value's slice.

```
// Make a circle slice counter clockwise as seen from above between angles
// minTheta and maxTheta in degrees.
public static void AddCircleSlice(this MeshGeometry3D mesh,
    Point3D center, double height, double minTheta, double maxTheta,
    double r1, double r2, int numSections)
{
    // Center of the slice.
    Point3D topCorner = center + D3.YVector(height);
    Point3D botCorner = center;

    // Unit vectors in X and Z direction for sines and cosines.
    Vector3D v1x = D3.XVector(r1);
    Vector3D v1z = D3.ZVector(-r1);
    Vector3D v2x = D3.XVector(r2);
    Vector3D v2z = D3.ZVector(-r2);

    // Convert thetas into radians.
    minTheta *= Math.PI / 180;
    maxTheta *= Math.PI / 180;

    // Point dictionaries for smoothing.
    Dictionary<Point3D, int> topDict = new Dictionary<Point3D, int>();
    Dictionary<Point3D, int> botDict = new Dictionary<Point3D, int>();
    Dictionary<Point3D, int> outDict = new Dictionary<Point3D, int>();
    Dictionary<Point3D, int> inDict = new Dictionary<Point3D, int>();

    double dtheta = (maxTheta - minTheta) / numSections;
    double theta = minTheta;

    // Vector in the direction of theta.
    Vector3D v1 = v1x * Math.Cos(theta) + v1z * Math.Sin(theta);
    Vector3D v2 = v2x * Math.Cos(theta) + v2z * Math.Sin(theta);
    Point3D[] topPoints =
    {
        topCorner + v1,
        topCorner + v2,
        topCorner + v2,
        topCorner + v1,
    };
    Point3D[] botPoints =
    {
        botCorner + v2,
        botCorner + v1,
        botCorner + v1,
        botCorner + v2,
    };
    Point3D[] outPoints =
    {
        topCorner + v2,
        botCorner + v2,
        botCorner + v2,
        topCorner + v2,
```

```
        };
        Point3D[] inPoints =
        {
            botCorner + v1,
            topCorner + v1,
            topCorner + v1,
            botCorner + v1,
        };
        for (int i = 0; i < numSections; i++)
        {
            theta += dtheta;

            // Vector in the direction of theta.
            v1 = v1x * Math.Cos(theta) + v1z * Math.Sin(theta);
            v2 = v2x * Math.Cos(theta) + v2z * Math.Sin(theta);

            // Top.
            topPoints[0] = topPoints[3];
            topPoints[1] = topPoints[2];
            topPoints[3] = topCorner + v1;
            topPoints[2] = topCorner + v2;
            mesh.AddPolygon(topDict, points: topPoints);

            // Bottom.
            botPoints[0] = botPoints[3];
            botPoints[1] = botPoints[2];
            botPoints[2] = botCorner + v1;
            botPoints[3] = botCorner + v2;
            mesh.AddPolygon(botDict, points: botPoints);

            // Outer face.
            outPoints[0] = outPoints[3];
            outPoints[1] = outPoints[2];
            outPoints[2] = botCorner + v2;
            outPoints[3] = topCorner + v2;
            mesh.AddPolygon(outDict, points: outPoints);

            // Inner face.
            inPoints[0] = inPoints[3];
            inPoints[1] = inPoints[2];
            inPoints[2] = topCorner + v1;
            inPoints[3] = botCorner + v1;
            mesh.AddPolygon(inDict, points: inPoints);
        }
    }
```

This method is similar to the `AddPieSlice` method described in the section "Basic Pie Charts" earlier in this chapter. There are two main differences.

The first difference is that the slice's sides do not go all the way to the center of the pie. Instead they stop at the circle's inner edge.

The second difference is that the circle slice needs an inner surface. The code that creates it is similar to the code that creates a normal pie slice's outer face. The only tricky part is properly orienting the inner surface's points so its polygons are outwardly oriented.

NOTE: As in the basic pie chart, the circle chart program doesn't really need to define the slices' sides because they are hidden by the sides of the adjacent slices. You would need the sides if you made an exploded circle chart where some of the slices were pulled away from the center of the circle.

Because this method is so similar to the `AddPieSlice` method, I won't describe it. You should be able to walk through the code to see how it works. Refer to the description of the `AddPieSlice` method in the section "Basic Pie Charts" if necessary to refresh your memory.

Graphs

Bar charts and pie charts generally show discrete values. Graphs show how values change over some other dimension such as time. For example, a graph might show how product sales changed over the course of a year.

The following sections describe several types of three-dimensional graphs.

Line Graphs

A line graph displays data points with related points connected by lines. The LineGraph example program shown in Figure 34-10 uses this type of graph to show the sales figures for four fictitious products over five months.

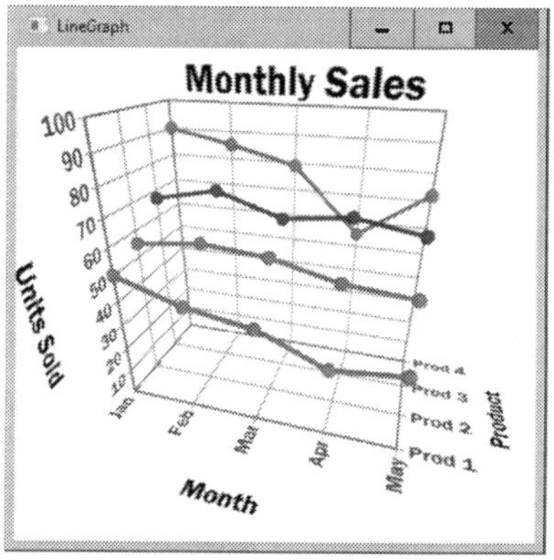

Figure 34-10: A line graph connects related points with lines.

The heart of the example is the `MakeLineGraph` method. That method is relatively straightforward, however, so I won't show its code here. It simply loops through the data, drawing a small sphere for each value and connecting adjacent values with three-dimensional segments.

The `DrawPlotBox` method that is also used by the example is much more interesting. That method draws the three-sided box shown in Figure 34-10. It draws the lines on the sides of the box and the labels along the box's front edges.

Unfortunately, that method is about four pages long, so instead of printing the code here, I'll describe it at a high level, and you can download the example program to see the details if you like.

The method first uses vector arithmetic to find the points that outline the box's three sides. It then uses the `AddSegment` method to draw segments connecting them.

Next, the method uses loops to draw the lines on the sides that have different X, Y, and Z values. For example, the lines on the bottom face pointing toward you in Figure 34-10 have different X values. The vertical lines on the back side of the box also have different X values. The code loops through the X values drawing those lines.

As it loops through the X values, the method also draws the labels that represent the different values. In this example, those labels display the months Jan, Feb, Mar, Apr, and May.

The code uses similar loops to draw the other box lines and labels that have different Y and Z values.

Next, the method uses loops to draw tick marks along the box's front edges beside the labels. The method finishes by drawing the title labels, which in this example say "Units Sold," "Month," and "Product."

Ribbon Graphs

A ribbon graph is similar to a line graph except it represents each set of related values with a ribbon instead of a line. The RibbonGraph example program shown in Figure 34-11 demonstrates this style.

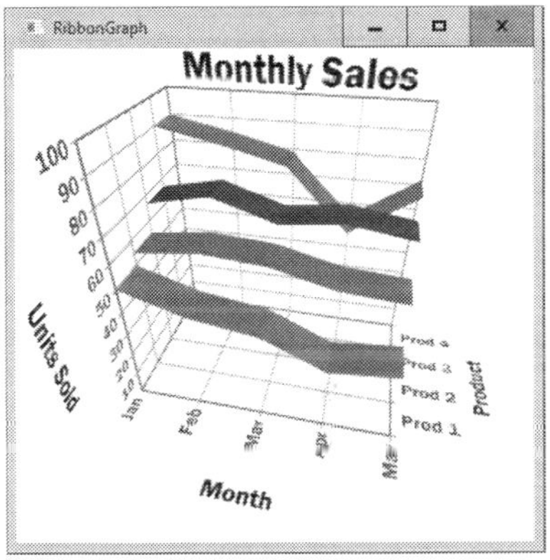

Figure 34-11: A ribbon graph connects related values with ribbons instead of lines.

The key to the RibbonGraph program is the `MakeRibbonGraph` method. It is similar to the `MakeLineGraph` method used by the LineGraph example program and is similarly straightforward. In fact, the `MakeRibbonGraph` method is even simpler because it doesn't draw spheres for each of the data points.

Because the `MakeRibbonGraph` method is so straightforward, I won't show it here. It calls the `MakePlotBox` method described earlier to make the three-sided plot box and then loops through the data drawing rectangles to connect related values.

I do want to mention one important difference between this program and the LineGraph program. When drawing a line graph, the values typically sit on the lines parallel to them. For example, in Figure 34-10 the first product's values lie at the front of the plot box and the fourth product's values sit on the box's back face.

In contrast, a ribbon graph's ribbons have horizontal thickness so they sit *between* the box's lines. In Figure 34-11, the first ribbon starts at the plot box's front edge but extends back into the box for some distance

Another way to see the difference is to note that the box in Figure 34-10 is three units deep while the box in Figure 34-11 is four units deep.

This difference means the two program must differ slightly in how they create their plot boxes. Download the examples if you want to see the details.

Area Graphs

An area graph is similar to a ribbon graph with the area under each ribbon filled in. The AreaGraph example program shown in Figure 34-12 shows this kind of graph.

This program is a fairly simple modification of the RibbonGraph example so I won't show the code here. The only difference is that the AreaGraph program draws four sides and a bottom below each ribbon. Download the example if you want to see the details.

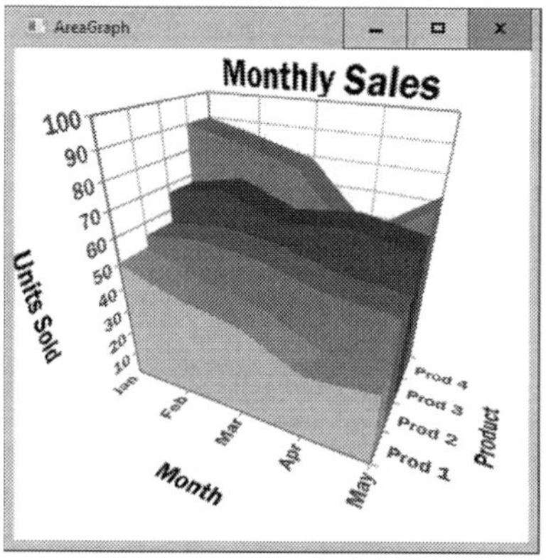

Figure 34-12: An area graph is similar to a ribbon graph with the areas under the ribbons filled in.

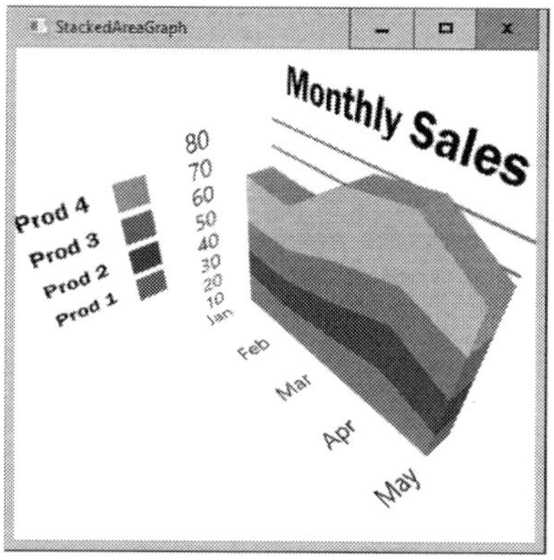

Figure 34-13: A stacked area graph is similar to a single slice of an area graph divided into strips.

Stacked Area Graphs

Drawing on your experience with stacked bar charts and stacked pie charts, you can probably figure out that a stacked area graph is similar to an area graph that's divided into colored strips. The StackedAreaGraph example program shown in Figure 34-13 draws this kind of graph.

This example is more similar to the StackedBarChart example program than it is to the AreaGraph program. In particular, it uses specialized code to draw its labels and the lines behind the data rather than using the `MakePlotBox` method.

Download the example to see how it works.

Scatter Plots

A *scatter plot* or *bubble plot* shows discrete data points in three dimensions, allowing you to compare three facets of the data. For example, the ScatterPlot example program shown in Figure 34-14 plots the price, horsepower, and mileage of 50 different models of cars.

If you turn the scene in various directions, you can compare any pair of variables. Figures 34-15 through 34-17 compare mileage with horsepower, base price with mileage, and base price with horsepower, respectively.

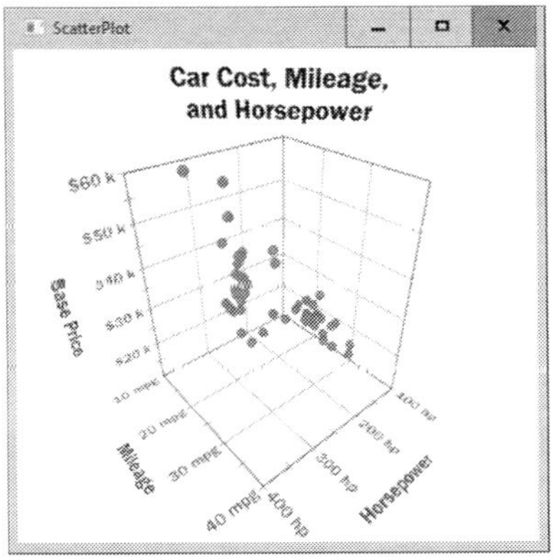

Figure 34-14: This view shows mileage, cost, and horsepower.

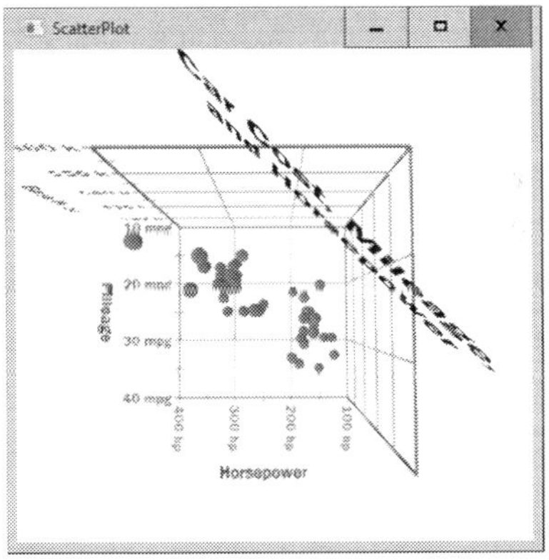

Figure 34-15: This view shows mileage versus horsepower.

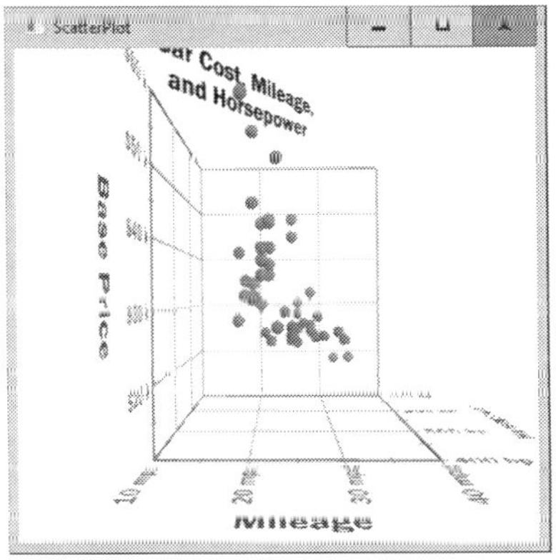

Figure 34-16: This view shows base price versus mileage.

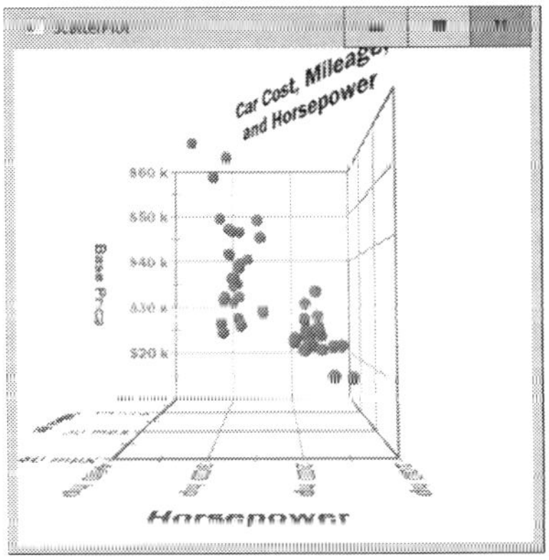

Figure 34-17: This view shows base price versus horsepower.

Some scatter plots draw circles on the plot box showing the projections of the data points onto the box's sides. That makes it a bit easier to compare pairs of dimensions. That can be particularly useful if the plot is displayed as a non-interactive picture. It's easy enough to view the scene from different positions if you are working with an interactive program, but you can't do that with a fixed picture.

Scatter plots may seem complicated, but the code that plots the data is actually relatively simple. The ScatterPlot example program uses the `MakePlotBox` method used by other examples in this chapter to draw its box and labels. To plot the data values, it simply creates a sphere using a car's mileage, base price, and horsepower (all suitably scaled) for the point's X, Y, and Z coordinates.

There are several ways you can enhance this kind of plot. For example, you could give the spheres different radii or colors to represent some other piece of information such as the car's weight or overall rating.

You could also represent the points with boxes, cylinders, or some other shape instead of spheres. Then you could use the boxes' dimensions to provide additional information about a dimension. For example, a box's height might indicate a range of prices.

Surface Graphs

A surface graph shows a representation of a value that varies as a function of two variables. For example, Figure 34-18 shows a surface defined by the following equation.

$$y = 1 + \frac{4\cos(x^2 + z^2)}{2 + x^2 + z^2}$$

The surface can also be defined by data obtained experimentally, business data such as sales over time and region, or other sources.

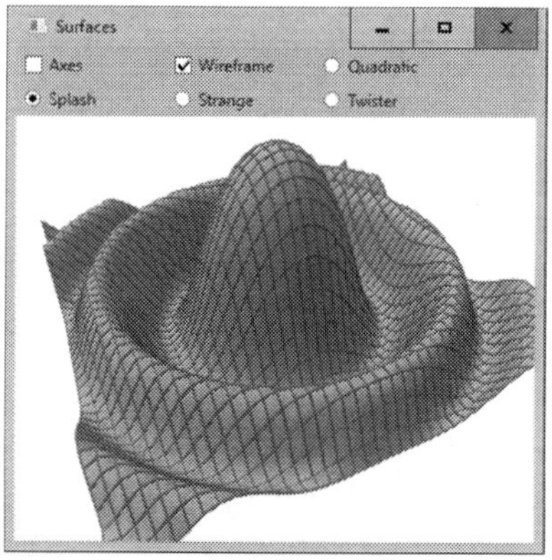

Figure 34-18: A surface graph shows a function y=F(x, z).

The Surfaces example program shown in Figure 34-18 was described in Chapter 26, "Surfaces." See that chapter for information about the program and how to build this kind of graph.

Summary

This chapter explained how to create charts and graphs. The basics are easy: you just arrange boxes, spheres, labels, and other objects that you already know how to make to create the scene.

The next chapter explains how you can build something else using techniques that you already know: skeletons. Skeletons seem complicated, but as you'll see, they are surprisingly easy to create and control.

Chapter 35 Skeletons

In this context, a skeleton isn't a spooky Halloween monster or a suicidal sport in the Winter Olympics. It's a collection of digital "joints" and "bones" arranged in a hierarchy that controls the meshes that define some sort of object. An obvious example would be a skeleton to control an animated person. The skeleton determines how a person's pieces move when the joints are manipulated. The *skin* determines the appearance of the person's skin, hair, clothing, and anything else needed to define the person's shape.

Skeletons don't always need to be used to build people, however. For example, you could use skeletons to control dogs, horses, spiders, and octopi. Basically you can use a skeleton to control any object that consists of a hierarchical arrangement of pieces. For example, you could use a skeleton to control the pieces of a tank. The tank's pieces move with its body. The treads rotate beneath the body. The turret rotates horizontally and moves the cannon with it. The cannon rotates vertically on the turret. A complicated tank model might include hatches, a machine gun, and other pieces that could also move.

> **NOTE:** The process of building a skeleton and attaching it to a model is called *rigging* and the skeleton is often called a *rig*. For a more in-depth overview of rigging, see `tinyurl.com/y95okt2e`.

This chapter explains how you can use simple skeletons to control hierarchical objects.

> **NOTE:** This discussion may seem a bit esoteric and you may have a hard time imagining how you can apply the concepts to a WPF program. Keep reading until you get to the example and hopefully it will all make more sense. Then you can reread the following sections after you see the example to see again how the pieces fit together.

Skeletons

In general, a *skeleton* consists of bones and joints that are roughly analogous to those that you find in a human or animal skeleton. The following section explains how a scene's objects and transformations relate to skeletons. The sections after that explain how you can implement a skeleton relatively easily in WPF.

Basics

A *bone* determines how far apart two joints are. For example, your forearm determines the distance between your wrist and your elbow. No matter how you move your arm, your wrist and elbow are always the same distance apart. (Barring painful accidents.)

A *joint* determines how two bones can be rotated in relation to each other. For example, your elbow determines the angle between your upper and lower arms.

Transformations

Building a skeleton may seem like a daunting problem, but it's actually fairly simple if you look at it the right way. You can use relatively simple objects to create each of the skeleton's bone and joints to rotate and translate from one bone to the next. If that seems confusing, don't worry. An example should make it fairly easy to understand.

Consider Figure 35-1. The goal is to build the skeleton shown at the end in step D. You can think of this as a simplified arm with a block for a hand. The hand is at the end of a forearm, and the elbow is turned to a particular angle.

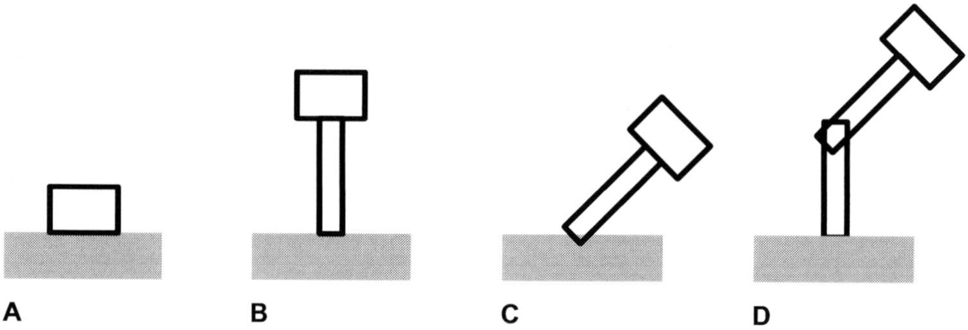

Figure 35-1: You can build a skeleton by using simple objects and transformations.

You can build this scene by following the steps shown in Figure 35-1 from left to right. First, you draw the hand. You can draw it at the origin or any other position that is convenient. Generally the place where you draw objects is the root or origin of the hierarchical skeleton. Figure 35-1 step A shows the scene at this point.

Now you add the next bone, which in this case is the forearm. To do that, you transform the objects drawn so far (which right now is just the hand) to offset them for the next bone (the forearm). In this case, that means moving the hand up by the length of the forearm. After you move the hand, you add the forearm object to the scene. The result is shown in Figure 35-1 step B.

Next, you add a transformation to represent any action on the joint at this point. In this example, the joint is the elbow. We want the elbow to be bent in the final result, so you rotate all of the objects created so far (the hand and forearm) through the desired angle. At this stage, the elbow is at the origin, so this is a relatively simple rotation around one of the coordinate axes. Figure 35-1 step C shows the result so far.

Now you just repeat the previous two steps to add bones and joints until the skeleton is complete. In this example, the next bone is the upper arm, so you translate the bones (the hand and forearm) up by the length of the upper arm and then you add the upper arm as shown in Figure 35-1 step D.

In a more complicated skeleton, you would continue adding bones and joints until you had finished the skeleton.

Groups

The process really is quite simple, although it can be hard to visualize. The most confusing part is keeping track of the bone hierarchy and which bones depend on which transformations. Fortunately the `Model3DGroup` class provides a very simple way to do that.

The `Model3DGroup` class has a `Children` property that you can use to make a single object represent any number of child objects, which for our purposes are the bones. The `Children` collection can also hold other `Model3DGroup` objects, so you can use it to model a whole hierarchy of bones.

The `Model3DGroup` class also has a `Transform` property that automatically transforms the objects that the group contains. For example, you can place objects in a `Model3DGroup` object to represent part of the skeleton, such as the hand and forearm. Then you can apply a rotation transformation to the group to represent rotation at the elbow.

In practice, each new bone comes with two transformations: one to position it relative to its parent bone and one to represent the joint between the new bone and its parent. One way to handle the two transformations is by using two `Model3DGroup` objects.

> **NOTE:** Real skeletons may have relatively complicated joints. For example, your shoulder uses a ball-and-socket joint (or spheroidal joint) that lets you rotate your upper arm in almost any direction on its side of your body. You can model that rotation as a combination of two simpler rotations, each around an axis.

Assembling the skeleton's pieces isn't hard, but you do need to follow a couple of steps to properly arrange the offset transformation for a new bone. The following `JoinBones` method wraps up those steps to make building a skeleton a bit easier.

```
// Join two bones together.
private Model3DGroup JoinBones(Model3DGroup parentGroup, Transform3D offset)
{
    Model3DGroup offsetGroup = new Model3DGroup();
    offsetGroup.Transform = offset;
    parentGroup.Children.Add(offsetGroup);

    Model3DGroup result = new Model3DGroup();
    offsetGroup.Children.Add(result);
    return result;
}
```

This method takes two inputs. The first is a parent `Model3DGroup` object. In the previous example, this might be the group holding the upper arm and hand.

The second parameter is a transformation that offsets the parent bones from the new bone that we are adding. In the previous example, this would be a vertical translation that moves the forearm and hand up by the length of the upper arm.

The method creates a new `Model3DGroup` object to represent the offset. It gives the new group the offset transformation and then adds it to the parent group's `Children` collection.

Next, the method creates another `Model3DGroup` object to represent the new joint. It adds the group to the offset group's `Children` collection and then returns the newly created group. The main program can add more bones to this group. It can also use this group's `Transform` property to manipulate the joint at this point in the skeleton. For example, it could rotate the group to bend the skeleton's elbow.

The next section describes an example so you can see how this works in practice.

Robot Arm

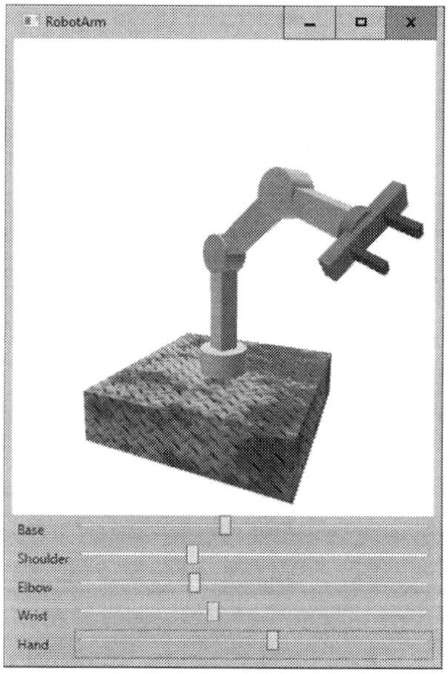

Figure 35-2: The RobotArm example program uses sliders to control a skeleton.

The RobotArm example program shown in Figure 35-2 builds a simple skeleton containing five joints. The arm begins with a joint at the base that rotates the arm around the Y axis. The arm then includes three bones separated by two joints that act as elbows. The wrist joint lets you rotate the hand around the axis of the last arm bone.

Finally, the hand lets you adjust a "joint" that moves the hand's fingers closer together or farther apart. This is actually implemented as two transformations, one for each finger.

The following code shows how the program builds its scene. I've stripped the code to the bone (pun intended) so it shows only the key pieces related to building the skeleton's bones and joints. Ignore all of the undefined constants and variables and focus on how the code creates the objects and joints.

```
// Define the model.
private void DefineModel()
{
    // Make the ground.
    ...

    // This group represents the whole robot.
    RobotGroup = new Model3DGroup();
    MainGroup.Children.Add(RobotGroup);

    // Base.
    ...
    MeshGeometry3D baseMesh = new MeshGeometry3D();
    baseMesh.AddBox(new Point3D(-baseWidth / 2, 0, -baseWidth / 2),
        D3.XVector(baseWidth), D3.YVector(baseLength), D3.ZVector(baseWidth));
    GeometryModel3D baseModel = baseMesh.MakeModel(Brushes.Pink);

    ...
    baseMesh.AddCylinder(bPgon, D3.YVector(bJointWidth), true);

    BaseGroup = JoinBones(RobotGroup, new TranslateTransform3D(0, groundY, 0));
    BaseGroup.Children.Add(baseModel);

    // Shoulder.
    ...
    MeshGeometry3D shoulderMesh = new MeshGeometry3D();
    shoulderMesh.AddBox(new Point3D(-shoulderWidth / 2, 0, -shoulderWidth / 2),
        D3.XVector(shoulderWidth), D3.YVector(shoulderLength),
        D3.ZVector(shoulderWidth));

    ...
    shoulderMesh.AddCylinder(sPgon, D3.ZVector(sJointWidth), true);
    GeometryModel3D shoulderModel = shoulderMesh.MakeModel(Brushes.LightGreen);

    ShoulderGroup = JoinBones(BaseGroup, new TranslateTransform3D(0, baseLength, 0));
    ShoulderGroup.Children.Add(shoulderModel);

    // Elbow.
    ...
    MeshGeometry3D elbowMesh = new MeshGeometry3D();
    elbowMesh.AddBox(new Point3D(-elbowWidth / 2, 0, -elbowWidth / 2),
        D3.XVector(elbowWidth), D3.YVector(elbowLength), D3.ZVector(elbowWidth));

    ...
    elbowMesh.AddCylinder(ePgon, D3.ZVector(eJointWidth), true);
    GeometryModel3D elbowModel = elbowMesh.MakeModel(Brushes.LightBlue);

    ElbowGroup = JoinBones(ShoulderGroup,
```

```
                new TranslateTransform3D(0, shoulderLength, 0));
            ElbowGroup.Children.Add(elbowModel);

            // Wrist.
            ...
            MeshGeometry3D wristMesh = new MeshGeometry3D();
            wristMesh.AddBox(new Point3D(-wDx / 2, 0, -wDz / 2),
                D3.XVector(wDx), D3.YVector(wDy), D3.ZVector(wDz));

            ...
            wristMesh.AddCylinder(wPgon, D3.YVector(wDy), true);
            GeometryModel3D wristModel = wristMesh.MakeModel(Brushes.Red);

            WristGroup = JoinBones(ElbowGroup, new TranslateTransform3D(0, elbowLength, 0));
            WristGroup.Children.Add(wristModel);

            // Finger 1.
            ...
            MeshGeometry3D finger1Mesh = new MeshGeometry3D();
            finger1Mesh.AddBox(new Point3D(-fDx / 2, 0, -fDz / 2),
                D3.XVector(fDx), D3.YVector(fDy), D3.ZVector(fDz));
            GeometryModel3D finger1Model = finger1Mesh.MakeModel(Brushes.Green);

            Finger1Group = JoinBones(WristGroup, new TranslateTransform3D(-fDx / 2, wDy, 0));
            Finger1Group.Children.Add(finger1Model);

            // Finger 2.
            MeshGeometry3D finger2Mesh = new MeshGeometry3D();
            finger2Mesh.AddBox(new Point3D(-fDx / 2, 0, -fDz / 2),
                D3.XVector(fDx), D3.YVector(fDy), D3.ZVector(fDz));
            GeometryModel3D finger2Model = finger2Mesh.MakeModel(Brushes.Green);

            Finger2Group = JoinBones(WristGroup, new TranslateTransform3D(fDx / 2, wDy, 0));
            Finger2Group.Children.Add(finger2Model);
        }
```

The code starts by creating the metal box that represents the scene's ground. It then creates a `Model3DGroup` to represent the robot arm as a whole. You can use this group to transform the entire arm. For example, if you set the group's `Transform` property to a translation up by one unit, then the entire arm moves one unit up off of the ground. This is how you would move a more complicated skeleton such as a person, robot, or tank in a scene.

After it adds the `RobotGroup` to the program's main `Model3DGroup`, the code creates the arm's base segment. It creates a mesh to represent that part of the arm and adds two objects to it. The first object is a box representing the first arm's bone. The second is a cylinder representing the joint that rotates the arm's base around the Y axis.

NOTE: Strictly speaking, the skeleton doesn't include the visible objects, in this case the first arm segment and the base joint cylinder. Those objects are *attached* to the skeleton. In fancier applications, those objects might be clothing or muscles that might deform or stretch

> when the skeleton moves. That topic is far outside the scope of this book. The examples in this chapter use simple objects that don't change shape when they move.

Next, the program calls the `JoinBones` method to join a new `Model3DGroup` object to the `RobotGroup`. It saves the new group in the class-level variable `BaseGroup`. This group contains the arm's hierarchy starting with the base objects. Eventually it will contain the entire robot arm hierarchy.

Later I'll describe the code that lets you manipulate this group. When you rotate this group around the Y axis, the entire arm rotates.

After it finishes creating the base group, the program repeats the same steps to create the next arm segment. It makes a new mesh and adds a box (for the arm bone) and a cylinder (for the elbow joint).

The code then calls `JoinBones` again. This time the parent group is `BaseGroup`, the group that contains the arm's first section. This makes the new group, `ShoulderGroup`, a child of the base group. Because the shoulder group is contained in the base group, when the base group moves, the shoulder group does, too.

The code adds the shoulder model (its bone box and joint cylinder) to the shoulder group.

The program repeats the steps again to create the next arm bone and its joint. It then repeats the same steps for the wrist. The wrist bone is the relatively thin box perpendicular to the final arm bone. Its joint is the cylinder attaching the wrist bone to the final arm bone.

The code finishes by adding the robot's fingers. The program creates two boxes to represent the fingers and calls `JoinBones` twice to add the fingers to the wrist. It adds the fingers separately so they have their own joints and can be moved independently.

> **NOTE:** The example program gives each section of the arm a different color so it's easy to see which pieces of the scene belong to which part of the arm. The base bone and joint are pink, the next arm bone and joint are green, the final arm bone and joint are blue, the wrist components are red, and the fingers are green. Download the example to see it in color.

Notice that the program uses the `JoinBones` method to join both finger bones to the `WristGroup`. That's because both of the fingers move in relation to the wrist, so they are children of the wrist. This arrangement occurs in many skeletons. For example, in a human figure both upper arms rotate in relation to the shoulders and both upper legs rotate in relation to the hips.

That's the end of the code that sets up the robot arm scene. You can download the example program to see all of the details about how the code creates the objects if you like.

When you adjust one of the program's `Slider` controls, an event handler takes action and adjusts the appropriate skeleton joint. For example, the following XAML code shows how the program defines the base joint's slider.

```
<Slider Grid.Row="1" Grid.Column="1"
    Name="baseSlider" ValueChanged="baseSlider_ValueChanged"
    Minimum="-180" Maximum="180" Value="0"/>
```

Notice that the control's `Minimum` and `Maximum` properties give bounds for the angles through which the base can rotate. Bounds on other joints determine their rotations. For example, they prevent you from rotating a knee joint forward. (A rotation that is impossible for a knee that hasn't been through a snowboarding crash or other traumatic accident.)

When you adjust the slider, the following `baseSlider_ValueChanged` event handler executes.

```
private void baseSlider_ValueChanged(object sender,
    RoutedPropertyChangedEventArgs<double> e)
{
    BaseGroup.Transform = D3.Rotate(D3.YVector(), D3.Origin, baseSlider.Value);
}
```

This code uses the `D3` class's `Rotate` method to create a transformation that rotates around the Y axis. (The `Rotate` method was described way back in Chapter 9. See the section "Transformation Classes" in that chapter is if you want to see how it works.)

The code passes the value of the slider into the `Rotate` method, so the method rotates by that number of degrees.

The event handler simply assigns the rotation transformation to the `BaseGroup` object's `Transform` property. That makes the group rotate all of the objects that it contains. Because those objects include the `ShoulderGroup`, that group also rotates. Similarly the `ShoulderGroup` contains the rest of the skeleton's hierarchy, so when you rotate the `BaseGroup`, the entire arm rotates.

For another example, consider the following definition of the shoulder slider.

```
<Slider Grid.Row="2" Grid.Column="1"
    Name="shoulderSlider" ValueChanged="shoulderSlider_ValueChanged"
    Minimum="-160" Maximum="160"/>
```

When you adjust this slider, the following event handler executes.

```
private void shoulderSlider_ValueChanged(object sender,
    RoutedPropertyChangedEventArgs<double> e)
```

```
{
    ShoulderGroup.Transform = D3.Rotate(D3.ZVector(), D3.Origin, shoulderSlider.Value);
}
```

This code rotates the `ShoulderGroup` much as the previous event handler rotated the `BaseGroup`. Notice that this time the axis of rotation is the Z axis. The axis is the one used by this group *as it was originally created* without any other transformations. In this example, the arm segment was created with its box pointed vertically. Rotating it around the Z axis makes its joint bend to the left or right, depending on whether the angle is positive or negative.

The base group transformation applies to the first shoulder, so it automatically makes the shoulder rotate in the correct direction for the arm's current orientation. This is one of the nice features of the hierarchical `Model3DGroup` structure. You rotate an object with respect to its default position and orientation as it was originally created and the hierarchy makes sure the result is appropriate for the skeleton's current configuration.

The slider and code that manages the next arm joint is similar.

The wrist slider and its code is a bit different because it rotates the wrist around the Y axis. Again that rotation is with respect to the wrist's original orientation when it was first created. At that point, rotation around the Y axis rotates the wrist around the axis of the arm bone to which it is connected. Even if you adjust the other sliders to give the wrist a new orientation, this rotation still rotates the wrist around the axis of that arm bone.

The final pieces of the arm are its fingers. The following code shows how the program defines its hand slider.

```
<Slider Grid.Row="5" Grid.Column="1"
    Name="handSlider" ValueChanged="handSlider_ValueChanged"
    Minimum="0" Maximum="0.5"/>
```

When you adjust this slider, the following event handler executes.

```
private void handSlider_ValueChanged(object sender,
    RoutedPropertyChangedEventArgs<double> e)
{
    Finger1Group.Transform = new TranslateTransform3D(-handSlider.Value, 0, 0);
    Finger2Group.Transform = new TranslateTransform3D(handSlider.Value, 0, 0);
}
```

Instead of rotating, this code translates the fingers. It moves one finger one direction and the other finger the other direction, making them move closer together or farther apart.

Robot

Despite omitting some specifics, the preceding section included a lot of detail explaining how to set up and use the robot arm skeleton. Hopefully you were bored by too much detail instead of hopelessly lost. Setting up a skeleton can be a bit confusing, but the code is actually relatively short. Once you set up the skeleton, manipulating its joints is remarkably easy.

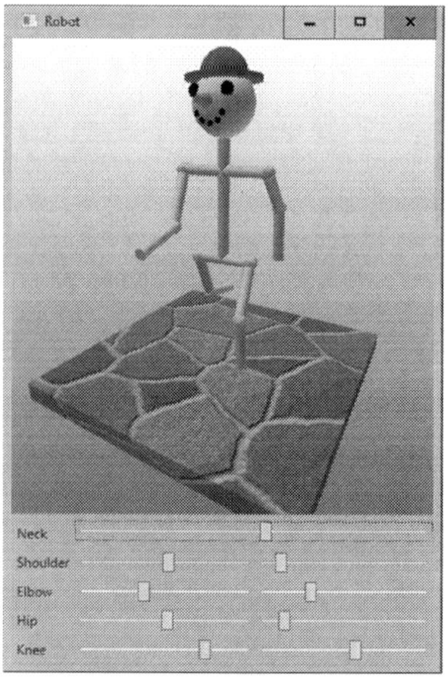

Figure 35-3: The Robot example builds a humanoid skeleton.

In this section, I'll describe the Robot example program shown in Figure 35-3 at a higher level. You can use this program's sliders to adjust the robot's neck, shoulders, elbows, hips, and knees.

All skeletons need a root group that acts as the skeleton's origin. In a sense, this is the skeleton's "position," so if you move this object, the entire skeleton moves.

The robot arm described in the preceding section uses its base as its root. This example uses the robot's head for its root. The object that you use as the root is largely up to you, but it seemed easier to me to position the robot by moving its head than by moving some other parts such as its waist or neck.

The `RobotGroup` variable is the `Model3DGroup` that represents the skeleton as a whole. It contains the `Model3DGroup` named `HeadGroup`, which contains objects representing the robot's head, nose, eyes, mouth, and hat.

The `NeckGroup` contains a cylinder representing the robot's neck. The corresponding slider applies a transform to this group to rotate the neck around the Y axis. Rotating this joint makes the rest of the body rotate.

The `ShoulderGroup` contains a horizontal cylinder representing the robot's shoulders. It is offset from the top of the neck group downward by the length of the neck. This group doesn't represent a joint so it doesn't have a slider.

The program attaches a left upper arm group to the `ShoulderGroup`. Its offset transform moves the upper arm to the left of the shoulder's center so the upper arm attaches to the left end of the shoulder bone. The upper arm's slider rotates the upper arm around the X axis, so this part of the arm rotates in and out of the screen when the robot is in its initial orientation.

Next, the program attaches a left lower arm segment to the left upper arm. Its slider rotates the left elbow around the X axis.

The program handles the robot's right upper and lower arm segments the same way it handles the left.

The next piece of the skeleton is the backbone. In this program, the `BackGroup` contains the backbone and hips, It doesn't contain a joint, so you cannot rotate the hips separately.

That means the hips and shoulders are always parallel. You could add a joint here if you want to add some extra flexibility. (For example, if the robot is a gymnast or yogi.)

The program finishes by adding upper and lower leg sections to the hips much as it adds the arm bones to the shoulders.

This skeleton includes a lot of bones and joints, but it's pieces are no more complicated than the robot arm's skeleton described in the preceding section; there are just more of them. Download the example program to see all of the details.

Summary

This chapter explained how to build skeletons to control a hierarchical object model. In a more serious animation project, such as for a game or movie, you would probably use more interesting objects than simple cylinders and boxes. For example, you might cloak the bones in clothing, armor, or muscles.

Rigging a model may involve some other steps, as well, such as modeling how the character's clothing or muscles change when the skeleton moves. Fortunately if you're rigging at that level, you're probably using higher-level and more specialized tools than Visual Studio.

Few business applications use skeletons. I've included them mostly because they're interesting, fun, and provide examples of how you can use transformations to make complex arrangements of objects relatively simple.

Afterword

The first part of this book told you how to get started. It showed how to use points, triangle indices, and texture coordinates to build objects. It explained how WPF's projections, cameras, lights, and materials work to produce a finished result that looks reasonably of realistic. No one is likely to mistake the results for photographs, but with some work, a scene can look convincing enough to help the viewer suspend disbelief and enjoy an interesting three-dimensional experience.

The second part of the book explained techniques for building and manipulating objects including vector arithmetic and transformations. It then gave more than a dozen examples showing how to build various shapes such as polygons, spheres, tori, and the Platonic solids. By using similar techniques, you can create all sorts of interesting shapes and scenes.

The final part of the book showed how to build some more advanced objects such as geodesic solids, parametric surfaces, two- and three-dimensional text, and skeletons. It even showed how you can load obj models created in other drawing packages so you can leverage more powerful drawing tools to build complicated scenes relatively easily.

I could continue writing hundreds if not thousands of pages, showing how to build more and more complex objects, but at some point I need to stop writing and you need to take over. You have the basic techniques; now you need to put them to use. Think about the scene you'd like to create, make a few sketches for reference, and then see what you can build. With some practice and imagination, you'll be able to create interesting objects, engaging environments, and fascinating creatures controlled by your programs.

When you've created something interesting, please visit the book's web site and post a picture or two. I (and I'm sure many others) would love to see what you've created.

You can also visit the book's web site to post questions, start discussions, and connect with me and other readers. Feel free to email me at RodStephens@csharphelper.com to let me know what you liked or didn't like.

Also please visit the book's page wherever you bought the book and post a brief review. Books like this one live or die based on their online reviews. Not only can you help the book, but you can also help others decide whether they should buy the book.

Now fire up Visual Studio and start creating!

Index

Also by Rod Stephens

The C# Helper Top 100

This practical guide describes the 100 most popular posts in the C# Helper (`csharphelper.com`) web site. This practical guide describes 100 complete examples demonstrating useful tips, tricks, and techniques for C# programmers. Some deal with common, everyday tasks; others with more advanced subjects that developers encounter only occasionally. Every example includes a simple, easy-to-understand explanation together with a working example program that you can download from the book's web site.

The book's 100 example programs demonstrate useful and interesting techniques in such topics as:

- 3-D Programs
- Serialization
- Graphics
- Printing
- Graphing
- DataGridView, ListView, TreeView
- Cryptography
- Algorithms
- Image Processing
- Mathematics
- Geometry
- Microsoft Office Integration

Interview Puzzles Dissected

Whether you're applying for a programming job or a position on Wall Street, interview puzzles are the norm at many high-tech companies. This book explains how to solve more than 200 of the hardest and most common interview puzzles in use. This fascinating guide:

- Shows how to solve more than 200 challenging puzzles
- Reveals underlying techniques for solving new problems
- Tells how to show interviewer that you can *think*
- Explains how to get "partial credit"
- Includes programming challenges to give you a deeper understanding of puzzles (obviously only if you're a programmer)
- Much, much more!

27956815R00234

Printed in Great Britain
by Amazon